3590

AF873074

THE MBASIC® HANDBOOK

THE MBASIC® HANDBOOK

Walter A. Ettlin
Gregory Solberg

Osborne/McGraw-Hill
Berkeley, California

Published by
Osborne/McGraw-Hill
2600 Tenth Street
Berkeley, California 94710
U.S.A.

For information on translations and book distributors outside of the U.S.A., please write to Osborne/McGraw-Hill at the above address.

THE MBASIC® HANDBOOK

234567890 DODO 89876543

ISBN 0-88134-102-9

Judy Ziajka, Acquisitions Editor
Paul Hoffman, Technical Editor
Geta Carlson, Copy Editor
Jan Benes, Text Design
Eric Ettlin, Illustrations
Yashi Okita, Cover Design

ACKNOWLEDGMENTS

We'd like to offer special thanks to the Ettlin family (Cynthia for her typing and proofing, Eric for his descriptive illustrations, and Mark for his contribution to the exercise solutions) and to Grant and Leslie Solberg.

WAE
GS

Contents

Introduction

This book explains not only the commands, functions, and operators that are usually treated in books about BASIC but also those that often get only superficial treatment. In addition, full discussions of Microsoft's powerful line editor and programming aids are presented. Throughout this book careful consideration is given to the proper form and structure of the programs. As each new command, statement, or function is presented, it is illustrated by a simple example. Tutorials that involve larger programs are presented at the end of most chapters. These tutorial programs integrate the new ideas presented in the chapter with concepts explained in previous chapters.

Microsoft BASIC, which we shall refer to throughout this book as MBASIC, is one of the most popular versions of BASIC used on microcomputers. What is more, Microsoft wrote the proprietary versions of BASIC used on some of the most popular microcomputers, including Apple, Radio Shack, and IBM, all of which are very similar to MBASIC.

This text is intended for the beginner in programming as well as the experienced programmer. It is divided into three sections entitled "Basic Tools," "Advanced Tools," and "Power Tools."

Section I, "Basic Tools," explains the basic commands of BASIC. Chapter 1 provides some background information about running MBASIC from CP/M and discusses the keyboard, focusing on the keys that play a special role in MBASIC. In Chapter 2 you will begin programming, learning the commands LET, INPUT, and PRINT, along with the arithmetic operators. Chapter 3 explains the housekeeping chores of MBASIC: that is, how to load and save your programs, how to look at what files are on a disk, and so on.

Chapter 4 examines the decision-making process in programming. You are introduced to the concept of program branching through the IF/THEN and GOTO statements.

Chapter 5 explains MBASIC's line editor through numerous examples. Chapter 6 shows you how to control output to both the printer and the screen, using the LLIST, LPRINT, PRINT USING, and LPRINT USING statements. Chapter 7 shows you how to control the precision of your output by defining the output to be integer-, single-, or double-precision. Chapter 7 also introduces the powerful loop-control pairs FOR/NEXT and WHILE/WEND.

Chapter 8 acquaints you with some of MBASIC's built-in functions. The functions emphasized include those used by all programmers, such as TAB, SPC, RND, and SGN, and also the mathematical functions, like SIN, COS, and LOG. Chapter 9 continues the discussion of functions, presenting the string functions LEFT$, RIGHT$, and MID$, along with several others.

Section II, "Advanced Tools," deals with commands and functions that separate the amateur from the serious programmer. Chapter 10 explains the command OPTION BASE and the MOD operator, both of which are important tools for the serious programmer. Chapter 11 takes up the subject of organizing your programs through subroutines. Chapter 12 presents two of MBASIC's most useful types of programs: namely, sorting and searching programs.

Chapter 13 shows you how to manage a task encountered by every programmer: that is, debugging your program. Regardless of how experienced or careful you are, program bugs will occur. A systematic approach to eliminating bugs is presented in this chapter.

Chapters 14 and 15 explain sequential and random-access files. The next two chapters, 16 and 17, are devoted to Boolean operators and user-defined functions, two topics that are generally treated superficially or neglected completely by most books on BASIC. Each topic is presented in enough detail to enable you to make full use of these powerful programming tools.

Section III, "Power Tools," addresses the professional programmer. Chapter 18 presents some commercial programming aids, such as a word processor, a cross-reference generator, a program to index files, and a compacting program. Chapter 19 explains how to write a menu driver that ties in a series of programs. Chapter 20 uses the menu driver with the final presentation of a payroll program that is first presented in Chapter 2 and is subsequently enhanced at various points throughout the book. Chapter 21 once again employs the menu driver and presents an exceptionally useful mailing list program. A program to build keyed files is also demonstrated in this chapter. Finally, Chapter 22 deals with writing user documentation, the goal of which is to help the nonprogrammer operate your program as smoothly as possible.

If you prefer not to type in longer programs, the programs from the Tutorial sections of the chapters are available on an eight-inch, IBM-formatted, single-density disk. The programs provided on the disk are the same as those presented in this book; no additions have been made. The programs are intended for tutorial purposes only.

For more information about ordering one of these disks, write to:

EAS
11 Primrose Ct.
Walnut Creek, CA 94598

I.

Basic Tools

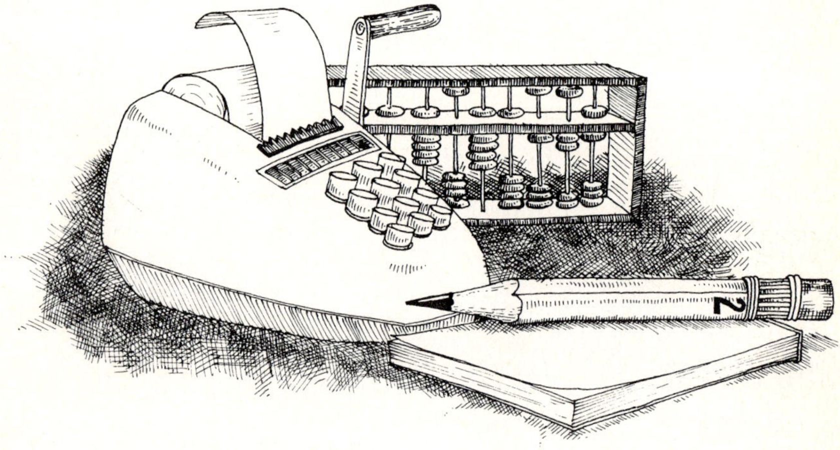
2

1

In the Beginning

You are reading this book to learn a new language, Microsoft BASIC, a language that allows you to communicate with a computer. The word BASIC is an acronym, a combination of the first letter of each of the words in the name *Beginner's All-purpose Symbolic Instruction Code.* In learning any language—whether it is a foreign language or a language to communicate with computers—a key factor is, of course, the vocabulary. In BASIC, fortunately, the vocabulary is relatively small—just over 100 words, often called *keywords.* Although the vocabulary is small, however, there is a very precise meaning for each keyword.

If you were a beginning student in Spanish, you could talk to someone using improper sentence construction. The person you were speaking to might still understand what you were saying by inferring from your remarks what you actually mean. But when you communicate with a computer, the computer will take each statement that you make literally. So it is up to you to provide the information in the precise format and use the proper syntax for each statement you write.

What Is a Program?

A program is a series of statements that the computer will execute one at a time. A program can be as short as one statement or it can be longer than this chapter. There are many languages that programs can be written in. Here, of course, we are interested only in programs written in Microsoft BASIC.

Before we go any further, let's take a look at a sample BASIC program:

```
10 PRINT "Hello"
20 PRINT "Goodbye"
30 END
```

In considering this program, we will not attempt to go into the details. Instead, we will look just at the main characteristics.

Each line begins with a line number (**10**, **20**, **30**), followed by one of MBASIC's keywords or instructions (**PRINT**, **END**). Notice also that each of the line numbers is a multiple of ten. This is a common programming practice, since if you later discover that additional instructions are needed, you can insert them by assigning them one of the missing line numbers (for example, 15 may be inserted between 10 and 20). The program is executed in line number sequence.

You will also notice that the program has both upper- and lowercase letters. In particular, **PRINT** and **END** are uppercase because these are Microsoft BASIC instructions. The "**Hello**" and "**Goodbye**" are in lowercase because they are not instructions. Historically, BASIC programs have been entirely in uppercase. In this book we encourage the use of lowercase when appropriate.

Starting Microsoft BASIC

One of the most basic components of your computer's operation is the disk operating system (DOS), which is sometimes called simply the *operating system*. The most common DOS used with MBASIC is *CP/M*. CP/M, which stands for Control Program/Microcomputers, is a program written especially for your brand of computer. CP/M provides a standard means of communicating with your computer's disk drive, screen, and keyboard. This means that any computer that has a version of CP/M written for it will run MBASIC.

Operation of your computer with CP/M requires a disk with CP/M on it, usually referred to as a *system disk*. On computers with floppy disks, a system disk must be in the computer at all times. If your computer has a built-in hard disk, the CP/M program may reside on the hard disk. In addition, starting up your microcomputer with CP/M is a little different for each brand of computer. The process usually involves inserting a system disk into one of your disk drives and then pressing the RESET switch on your computer. The computer will then try to read the CP/M program from the disk.

When you start or *boot* your computer with CP/M, the first thing that appears on the screen is a sign-on message. This message gives CP/M's version number and some other data, depending on your particular machine. CP/M is now in the computer's internal memory and will allow you to communicate with the computer. Below the sign-on message is the *prompt* **A>**. CP/M prints a prompt to let you know that it is ready for your next command. (On computers using MP/M, the prompt will be **0A>**.)

The letter *A* in the prompt tells you which disk drive you are *logged onto.* If you have two disk drives, the second one will have the prompt **B>** (or **0B>** for MP/M) when you are logged onto it.

When your prompt is **A>**, we say that you are "logged onto the A drive." This means that any information that the computer reads from the disk will come from the disk in drive A unless you specifically tell it to look on a different drive.

When CP/M first starts, it is normally logged onto the A drive. In order to change to the B drive, type **B**: and press the RETURN key. You should then receive the prompt **B>**. If you wish to return to the A drive, just type **A**: and press RETURN. Note that you must have a disk properly inserted into the B drive before you can log onto the B drive.

DISPLAYING THE DIRECTORY

When you are in CP/M and want to see what is stored on your disk, you use the CP/M directory command called DIR. When you enter the DIR command, the screen will display all of the *files* on the logged-on disk drive. All programs or other information stored on your disk are referred to as files. A sample screen display of all the files on a disk will look something like this:

```
A>DIR
A: PIP      COM : STAT     COM : SEA      WE  : GUESS    BAS
A: MBASIC   COM
A>
```

The **A**: on the left of the screen indicates the disk drive whose directory is being displayed. If you have additional drives, you may log onto any of these and display the directory for the disk they contain. However, a system disk with CP/M on it must be in the A drive at all times.

LOADING MICROSOFT BASIC

The Microsoft BASIC program (referred to as MBASIC) is generally called MBASIC.COM, MSBASIC.COM, or BASIC80.COM, but the program may have some other name. Check your disks to determine the name (use the DIR command). Now, with the disk containing Microsoft BASIC in the logged-on drive, type **MBASIC** (or the appropriate name) and press RETURN. (It is not necessary to type the letters *.COM.*) CP/M will then load the file MBASIC.COM and execute it. On the screen will appear MBASIC's sign-on message. The **Ok** below the sign-on message is MBASIC's prompt, letting you know it is ready for you to begin to write or run programs.

When you enter MBASIC, you will see a short horizontal line (or sometimes a box) under the **Ok** prompt. This is known as the *cursor*. The cursor indicates the exact place on the screen where a character will appear when you press one of your keyboard keys. You can write anything you want, of course, but regardless of how much you write, the cursor will always appear just to the right of your last entry. Try greeting MBASIC by typing **HELLO**. After you press RETURN, the message "Syntax error" appears on the screen. A *syntax error* means that MBASIC did not understand a word that you typed. Syntax errors will be discussed later in this chapter, but you will probably see a few more before then.

To return to CP/M from MBASIC, give the SYSTEM command and press RETURN. You should get the same CP/M prompt that you had before you loaded MBASIC. In fact, the CP/M program stays in memory along with the MBASIC program. Now that you are back in CP/M, you will have to load MBASIC all over again to get the **Ok** prompt.

Modes of Operation

There are three modes of operation for Microsoft BASIC. The mode that you are in determines what MBASIC will do with the instructions you give it. When you start MBASIC, you receive the prompt **Ok**. You then have two modes available to you immediately.

DIRECT MODE

In the *direct mode,* MBASIC acts very much like a calculator. No line numbers are required. Direct mode is not, of course, the main purpose of MBASIC, but it is useful at times—particularly when you are debugging programs or solving short problems in which you want to perform quick calculations. For example, if you want to add two numbers together, just type

```
PRINT 4+3
 7
Ok
```

After typing the **3**, press RETURN; the answer **7** comes up immediately. The instructions are lost as soon as the calculation is executed; that is, you must type **PRINT 4+3** again to get the same result.

Direct mode is also referred to as *command mode.*

INDIRECT MODE

The second mode is the *indirect mode.* This is what you will be using most of the time. In this mode you first put a *line number* on each statement you want MBASIC to execute. For example, the numbers that we have just added in direct mode would look like this in indirect mode:

```
10 PRINT 4+3
```

You can put virtually any number at the beginning of a statement. When it has a line number in front of it, a statement is known as a *program line,* and an accumulation of such lines is known as a *program.* Once you have a program, you can run it and get your results. The indirect mode saves your instructions in the computer along with their line numbers so that you can print them to the screen or to the printer as many times as you wish simply by typing **RUN**. Try this with the preceding example, as follows:

```
10 PRINT 3+4
RUN
 7
Ok
RUN
 7
Ok
```

EDIT MODE

The third MBASIC mode is the *edit* mode. This is a very powerful tool for correcting and editing BASIC programs. It allows you to move the cursor quickly to any position you want in a line, to insert or delete text, or to find or replace text.

For the time being, it is enough for you to know that if you make a typing mistake when you write or "enter" a line, you do not need to worry about it. In case of a mistake, you can simply press RETURN and rewrite the line. For example, let's say that you accidentally enter

```
10 PFINT "Hello"
```

There are two things you can do. First, if you discover the error before you press RETURN, you can use the BACKSPACE key (sometimes called RUBOUT), backspace to the **F**, and correct the error by retyping the rest of the line. If you have already pressed RETURN or feel it is too much work to backspace over half the line, you can simply retype the line with the same line number. If you type two lines numbered with a 10, the second will automatically replace the first. Note that typing just a line number followed with a RETURN deletes or "kills" *everything* that you entered using that line number.

As you begin to write longer programs in MBASIC, you will find the edit mode extremely useful. The details of the edit mode will be gone over thoroughly in Chapter 5. If at any time in the next few chapters you feel that you would like to know more about correcting typing errors and editing, place a bookmark wherever you are and turn to Chapter 5.

Kinds of Data

There are two general categories of data used with MBASIC: *numeric data* and *string data.* Numeric data, of course, consists of numbers. You are already familiar with some of the things that MBASIC can do with numeric data. For instance, MBASIC programs can add, subtract, multiply, and divide numeric data.

String data can consist of letters, punctuation marks, and digits. In short, string data can be any combination of characters. Strings can be any length up to 255 characters. For instance, in lines 10 and 20 of the program example presented at the beginning of the chapter, the **"Hello"** and **"Good bye"** are both string data. You will be using string data even in your first program, but the full scope of things that MBASIC can do with strings is not covered until Chapter 9.

Both numeric and string data can be input and output by MBASIC programs. For example, if you are interested in writing a payroll program to keep track of employees, you could think of an employee's name and address as string data, whereas an employee's salary and age consist of numbers and would therefore be numeric data. The discussion of variables in Chapter 2 will show how programs can store both kinds of data.

Kinds of Instructions to MBASIC

The instructions to MBASIC fall into four categories.

COMMANDS

In their most common use, commands are instructions that are given to MBASIC in direct mode and that are executed immediately when you press RETURN. Two commands that you will use quite often are RUN and LIST.

STATEMENTS

Statements are instructions to MBASIC that are preceded by a line number and that are not executed until the entire program is run. The PRINT statement in lines 10 and 20 of the sample program is a statement that you will use frequently.

It is possible that an MBASIC instruction can be used as both a command and a statement. For instance, the PRINT instruction is usually thought of as a statement, but it can also be used as a command in the direct mode. On the other hand, RUN is usually thought of as a command; but if it is preceded by a line number, then it is executed when the program reaches that line, since it is being used as a statement.

FUNCTIONS

Functions are "subprograms" that are built into the BASIC interpreter. They save you, the programmer, from having to code these frequently used operations. One of the more commonly used functions is SQR, which determines the square root of a number.

OPERATORS

Operators define what is done with numeric or string data. Some operators—for example, the plus sign (+) and minus sign (−)—are used for calculations. Others, such as the greater than sign (>) and the less than sign (<), are used for comparing data.

Getting to Know Your Computer

Your computer consists of several devices. These include a keyboard, a display screen, one or more disk drives, possibly a printer, and the computer itself with its internal memory.

THE KEYBOARD

MBASIC runs on many different computers. Some have built-in keyboards, whereas others require that a separate terminal be added. What is more, the keyboards themselves vary from one computer to another. The letters and numbers are standard, but from that point on, there are many possible variations.

RETURN — When you have finished typing a line and wish to transfer it to the computer's memory, you press the RETURN key. On many terminals the name of this key is ENTER or RET. Throughout this book we will always use the term RETURN when referring to this key. Pressing the RETURN key also moves you to the next line.

SHIFT and CAPS LOCK — The SHIFT key has the same function on a computer that it has on a typewriter. It causes either an uppercase letter to be printed or the upper symbol to be printed if there are two symbols on the key (as with the numbers and punctuation marks). The CAPS LOCK key affects only the letters, causing uppercase letters to be printed. Once pressed, the CAPS LOCK key stays in effect until it is released by a second pressing.

CONTROL — The CONTROL or CTRL key is similar to the SHIFT key. When pressed together with another character, it causes a special message to be sent to the computer instead of the character printed on the key. But in general, these control characters are not transmitted to the screen and their messages are not apparent to the operator. We will elaborate on control characters in later chapters. In this book, control characters are written as CTRL-X or ^X to indicate holding down the CTRL key and any other letter (in this case X).

If your terminal does not have the CTRL key, there will be a combination of keys to press to perform this function. You will have to consult the manual that comes with your terminal to determine what they are.

BACKSPACE and DELETE

Again, your terminal may or may not have these keys. The BACKSPACE and DELETE keys will both delete the character immediately to the left of the cursor. These keys are most commonly used for correcting typing errors before the RETURN key is pressed. If your keyboard does not have these keys, your manual will tell you the combinations of keys to press to perform these functions. Older versions of CP/M do not recognize the BACKSPACE key. If you have CP/M version 2.0 or later, you will find the BACKSPACE key much easier to use than the DELETE key.

REPEAT

Many terminals have a REPEAT key. When a particular key is pressed at the same time as the REPEAT key, the character represented by the first key repeats rapidly until the REPEAT key is released. On other terminals, simply holding down any key will cause the character it represents to repeat after a short period of time. The repetitions stop when the key is released.

ESCAPE

The ESCAPE key is used in editing MBASIC programs while in the edit mode (see Chapter 5). When you are inserting characters, the ESCAPE key tells MBASIC that you are through inserting characters and that any text you enter is to be considered as edit commands. This key may be labeled ESC or ALT on your keyboard.

TAB

The TAB key works like its counterpart on a typewriter. TAB stops are usually set at every eight columns. Pressing the TAB key will move the cursor to the right, bringing it to the next tab stop. The TAB key is used mainly for aligning program statements or output for better readability. The TAB key otherwise acts much like the space bar.

LINE FEED — Pressing LINE FEED causes the cursor to move down one line on the screen. But in contrast to the RETURN key, LINE FEED does not cause the material you are entering to be transferred to the computer's memory. LINE FEED is used when you are entering a line in an MBASIC program that is greater in length than the number of columns that your terminal supports. When you have finished entering the material, which may be on two or more lines, the RETURN key must be pressed.

If your keyboard does not have one of the keys we have just discussed, it may be possible to simulate the function with the CTRL key. For example, if your terminal does not have a LINE FEED, you can simultaneously press the CONTROL key and the J key. This combination of keys will send the same message to the computer that LINE FEED would. Other useful control keys are CTRL-I for TAB and CTRL-H for BACKSPACE.

If you are a typist and just starting to work on a computer, there are two standard keys that are different. On your computer keyboard, there are distinct keys for one (**1**) and for zero (**0**), and consequently you cannot interchange **0** with the letter **O** or **1** with the lowercase letter **l**.

THE DISPLAY SCREEN

The common display screen for computers using CP/M and MBASIC has 80 columns and 24 lines. If your screen and keyboard are in one unit, you may also have specially labeled keys that affect the screen display. For example, some terminals have a key to clear the screen, usually labeled CLEAR or RESET. When this key is pressed, the screen is cleared of characters and the cursor moves to the upper left-hand side of the screen, which is called the *home position.*

Quite often the special keys like the CLEAR key affect only the screen and not the computer's memory. If you have an MBASIC program displayed on the screen and you press CLEAR, the screen goes blank. This does not mean that your program is lost. The program remains in the computer's memory even though it is no longer displayed. Similarly, each time you type lines to the computer, the other lines scroll up the screen. The lines that are pushed up off the screen are still remembered.

THE COMPUTER'S INTERNAL MEMORY

When you write a program in MBASIC, you press RETURN when you have completed each line. This action causes the line you just typed to be entered and stored in the computer's memory. Most current microcomputers that use CP/M come with sufficient memory to store about 64 thousand characters (that is, letters, digits, and so on). Part of this memory is used by CP/M and part by MBASIC. The portion of memory remaining for your program is thus less than 64,000 characters.

DISK MEMORY

The computer's memory is only capable of holding information when it is turned on. In order for you to retain your programs from one programming session to the next, you must have a means of storing your programs when the computer is turned off. The most common device used with microcomputers is the *floppy disk.* A single floppy disk can hold anywhere from 70K bytes or characters (1K = 1 thousand) to 1.2MB (1MB = 1 Megabyte = 1 million bytes), depending on the disk's density, size, and configuration. The information is stored in the files we saw before.

USING THE PRINTER

You may also wish to use your printer to keep copies of your programs on paper. A program listing on paper is called a *hard copy.* A hard copy is an excellent way to store your programs in a format that you can read.

Syntax Error

If you make a mistake while you are programming in MBASIC, you may get a "Syntax error" message on your screen. Don't panic! *Syntax* is the exact manner in which the symbols (letters, numbers, and punctuation) in a BASIC language statement or command must be ordered. Thus, a *syntax error* simply means a wrong ordering of symbols.

When you get a "Syntax error" message, look for misspelled command words, check the number, type, and order of any parameters in the statement, and make sure you have not omitted anything. These are the most common mistakes. Then either retype or edit the offending line until the syntax is correct.

Interpreters and Compilers

The following section is essentially background information on programming languages. You do not need to read it in order to be able to write an MBASIC program, and you may simply go on to the next chapter at this point if you wish.

We have already mentioned that Microsoft BASIC (MBASIC) is a computer language, but it is also a computer program. Computers read languages in two different ways: through an *interpreter* or through a *compiler*. Both interpreters and compilers are programs that read a program as input and turn it into instructions which a computer can execute directly. Interpreters and compilers are in a sense translators that translate from a given language (like MBASIC) into *machine language*, a language that the computer can execute directly.

A compiler reads the whole program and builds a complete set of instructions for the entire program before any statements are executed. An interpreter reads each program statement and executes it before reading the next statement. While Microsoft sells both an interpreter and a compiler for the MBASIC language, this book deals exclusively with the use of the interpreter. Using the interpreter is the best way to learn any computer language. A compiler, however, can make more efficient use of your computer's time and memory. Therefore, after you become an expert MBASIC programmer, you may wish to use the compiler instead of the interpreter.

Writing and running a program using a compiler is a three-step process. First you must write the *source program*. This requires an additional program, usually called a *text editor*, which allows you to type your program into the computer's memory. Next you instruct the compiler to compile your program. The compiler generates an *object program* and lists any errors in your source program. If there are errors, you must then edit the program again to make corrections. Finally, if there are no compile errors, you may instruct the computer to execute the object program, since the object program is now in a machine-readable language.

Writing a program with an interpreter, on the other hand, is much simpler. The interpreter allows you to enter and try your program with the interpreter's editor. Errors in your source program are detected when the program runs. The MBASIC interpreter includes a simple text editor so that you can correct errors immediately and run your program again as soon as you have finished correcting it, with no intermediate compile step.

The process of detecting and correcting errors in your program is called *debugging.* Since debugging is made much easier with an interpreter, you may wish to write your programs with the MBASIC interpreter.

If you own the MBASIC compiler, you can compile programs so that they can run faster after you and the interpreter are satisfied that they are written correctly. If you choose to use the Microsoft interpreter and compiler, you must take note that there are slight differences between the two. These differences are listed in the Microsoft BASIC compiler manual.

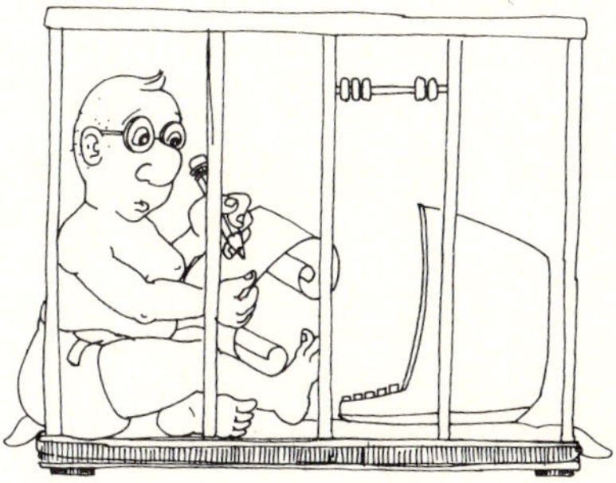

2

First Program

Commands:	RUN, LIST, NEW
Statements:	LET, PRINT, INPUT, END
Operators:	+, −, /, *, ^

Learning to write a BASIC program is like learning to ride a bicycle: the only way to learn is by doing. And once you learn it, you will remember it. As you go through this book, each chapter will introduce and explain a group of instructions or keywords. For each instruction an example or group of examples will be presented to show you how to use the keyword appropriately in a simple program.

After all the instructions have been introduced, applications will be presented. These are programs of a more practical nature. In these programs, groups of instructions (commands, statements, operators, or functions) will be combined to solve a problem.

We will return to one of these application programs, the PAYROLL program, again and again. The PAYROLL program handles the payroll records for a small company. If this application is relevant to you, the programming skills you gain in this tutorial should allow you to modify our final version, presented in Chapter 19, to your specific requirements.

Be sure you understand the examples and applications, but also do the exercises at the end of each chapter. These will give you practice in using the skill you are learning, and so your skills will improve more rapidly.

In Chapter 1, we discussed some of the vocabulary of MBASIC and the syntax for writing an instruction for MBASIC. You also saw how MBASIC operates in direct mode. Now you will write your first program.

Creating a Simple Program [PRINT, RUN]

You will use one statement and one command almost every time you write a program. The statement is PRINT and the command is RUN.

Every useful program has some type of *output.* Output refers to the words or results of calculations that your program creates. In most cases, the output is sent to the screen or the printer. Thus, in a typical program you will use some form of output statement, like PRINT, a great many times.

Enter the following line into the computer and press RETURN:

```
10 PRINT "YESTERDAY I DIDN'T KNOW WHAT A PROGRAM WAS."
```

Note that all program lines must be entered exactly as shown if the program results are to match the illustrations in this book. The computer can be very unforgiving about small discrepancies in spacing or punctuation.

Let's take a look at this simple program. First, notice that every line you enter starts with a number. A line number may be any whole number from 0 to 65529. A reasonably good plan is to start with the number 10 and number the lines consecutively in multiples of ten (10, 20, 30...). Second, notice that immediately following the line number, you write the BASIC instruction: in this case, **PRINT**. When you finish typing in the line, press RETURN. Pressing RETURN stores the line in the computer's memory, where it is ready for execution when the program is run.

RUNNING A PROGRAM WITH THE RUN COMMAND

To run this program, we need another command, RUN. Type **RUN**, press RETURN, and you will have the following output:

```
RUN
YESTERDAY I DIDN'T KNOW WHAT A PROGRAM WAS.
Ok
```

The **Ok** following the output from your program means that MBASIC is ready to receive additional statements or commands. The shaded type is what you enter. Let's add a second line to our program. Type in the following:

```
20 PRINT " TODAY I'M A PROGRAMMER."
```

Displaying Your Program [LIST]

Let's consider another command. Enter the LIST command and press the RETURN key. Your program will be reprinted on the screen with the lines in correct numerical order.

```
LIST
10 PRINT "YESTERDAY I DIDN'T KNOW WHAT A PROGRAM WAS."
20 PRINT " TODAY I'M A PROGRAMMER."
Ok
```

Lines are always stored in numerical order in the computer's memory. Therefore, LIST always shows the program with the lines in numerical order, regardless of the order in which you entered them or what you did in between.

The information enclosed in double quotation marks is called a *string constant.* In line 20 of the example above, " **TODAY I'M A PROGRAMMER**" is the string constant. A string constant will print out exactly as it appears in your program and may contain letters, numbers, or any other valid characters.

Now run the program and let's consider the output. Type **RUN** and press RETURN.

```
RUN
YESTERDAY I DIDN'T KNOW WHAT A PROGRAM WAS.
 TODAY I'M A PROGRAMMER.
Ok
```

Notice that in the program listed above, line 20 contains a space between the first quotation marks and **TODAY**. When you run the program, the output retains this space.

START AT LINE NUMBER AND BEGIN EXECUTION

You may also specify a line number with the RUN command. This is useful at times with longer programs when you are only interested in the output from a particular section of a program, but let's try it here:

```
RUN 20
 TODAY I'M A PROGRAMMER.
Ok
```

Replacing a Line

We now want to make a change in line 10. There is no way to alter anything in a line once you have pressed RETURN—unless you use edit mode, which would require considerable explanation and is covered in Chapter 5. But if you simply start a new line by entering **10**, the entire previous contents of line 10 will have disappeared. Try it now by entering **10** and then using the LIST command:

```
10
LIST
20 PRINT " TODAY I'M A PROGRAMMER."
Ok
```

But we want not only to delete line 10, but also to change it. One way to make a change in a program is to simply reenter one or more lines with changes in the text. Type in line 10 again, and this time end the line with a semicolon.

```
10 PRINT "YESTERDAY I DIDN'T KNOW WHAT A PROGRAM WAS.";
```

To see what has happened, type **LIST** and press RETURN. Notice that the old line 10 has been replaced with the new line 10.

```
LIST
10 PRINT "YESTERDAY I DIDN'T KNOW WHAT A PROGRAM WAS.";
20 PRINT " TODAY I'M A PROGRAMMER."
Ok
```

Run the program and notice the difference in the output.

```
RUN
YESTERDAY I DIDN'T KNOW WHAT A PROGRAM WAS. TODAY I'M A PROGRAMMER.
Ok
```

Placing the semicolon at the end of line 10 makes the output from lines 10 and 20 continuous. Line 20 will be on the same line as the output from line 10.

The PRINT statement is very versatile. We will expand on its uses in later chapters.

Clearing Memory
[NEW]

When you have finished working with a program and wish to begin work on another one, give the NEW command. This command erases your program from memory and clears all the variables that you may have created (variables are discussed later in this chapter). You are now ready to enter a new program. In this program, we will tell the computer to add two numbers and then to multiply two numbers.

Enter and run the following example:

```
10 PRINT "The sum of 4 + 3 is ";4+3
20 PRINT "The product of 4 x 3 is";4*3

RUN
The sum of 4 + 3 is 7
The product of 4 x 3 is 12
Ok
```

In this example we used lowercase letters in the string constants. Also notice that the arithmetic operation is printed out on the screen just as it appears within the quotation marks. But the output from the arithmetic operation at the end of each line returns the results of 4+3 and 4*3. Notice also that in order to multiply in BASIC, the symbol used is the asterisk (*), not the times sign (×).

Adding a Line

Let's add a line to this program to find the difference between 4 and 3, and then make the computer print out the result. Enter the following:

```
15 PRINT "The difference of 4 - 3 is";4-3

LIST
10 PRINT "The sum of 4 + 3 is ";4+3
15 PRINT "The difference of 4 - 3 is";4-3
20 PRINT "The product of 4 x 3 is";4*3
Ok
```

Now is a good time to LIST our program and see what the computer has done with line 15.

Line 15 was automatically inserted between lines 10 and 20. This is the reason that we often enter program line numbers in multiples of 10, so that if we wish to add lines at some later time, we can do so without retyping several lines. You can, of course, use any other multiples you like, such as 50, 100, and so on.

You can specify a line number range in the LIST command, much as you can in the RUN command. Try these examples:

```
LIST 15
15 PRINT "The difference of 4 and 3 is ";4-3
Ok
```

Here we have asked MBASIC to list just one line, line 15. Now let's ask MBASIC to list all the lines from 10 to 15 inclusive:

```
LIST 10-15
10 PRINT "The sum of 4 + 3 is ";4+3
15 PRINT "The difference of 4 - 3 is";4-3
Ok
```

There are no lines between 10 and 15, so all we get is these two. Finally, let's list all the lines from line 15 to the end of the program:

```
LIST 15-
15 PRINT "The difference of 4 and 3 is ";4-3
20 PRINT "The product of 4 times 3 is ";4*3
Ok
```

Ending Your Program
[END]

Although a program will end when there are no more statements to process, it is a good idea to use the END statement. It not only returns you to the direct mode, but also closes any files that you might have used in the program. You will be working with files in later chapters. Add an END statement at line 30 as follows:

```
30 END
```

It is a good idea to LIST and check your program after making changes and before running it. Your program listing should look like this:

```
LIST
10 PRINT "The sum of 4 and 3 is";4+3
15 PRINT "The difference of 4 and 3 is";4-3
20 PRINT "The product of 4 times 3 is";4*3
30 END
Ok
```

The END statement is *not* always on the last line of the program. If an END statement is encountered in the middle of the program, the program stops executing right then.

Storing Data in a Variable

Before we begin entering data into the computer, you must first know how to store the input data in a *variable*. A variable is a place to store information in the computer's memory. Variables can be used to store numeric data or string data, which we described in Chapter 1. In Microsoft BASIC, a variable name may be of any length, but only the first 40 characters are significant. The restrictions in choosing your variable name are that the first character must be a letter; after that, any letter or number may follow. Also the period (.) may be used to make your variable names read more clearly. The period is the only punctuation mark that may be used in a variable name.

A variable name may not be identical to a keyword, although keywords may form a part of a variable name. Keywords include all those words that are used as commands, statements, functions, and operators. In addition, a variable may not start with the letters FN, which indicate that something is a function. The use of FN will be discussed in Chapter 16.

Note that these naming conventions apply to both numeric and string variables. One additional feature of string variable names, however, is that they must be followed by a dollar sign ($). When used at the end of a variable name, the dollar sign is sometimes called a *type declarator* because it tells MBASIC that the variable holds a string.

Figure 2-1 shows some examples of legal and illegal variable names, both numeric and string.

Interacting with the Computer
[INPUT]

The INPUT statement allows you to enter data into a program during execution. Let's try it with this example, but do not forget to clear the computer's memory with the NEW command first:

```
10 PRINT "Hi!  What's your name";
20 INPUT USERNAME$
30 PRINT "Glad to know you, ";USERNAME$
40 END
```

Now run the program.

```
RUN
Hi!  What's your name?
```

The **USERNAME$** at the end of line 20 is a string variable. When a program encounters an INPUT statement, it stops and waits for you to supply some input. We might respond by typing **WALT** and pressing RETURN. Our input is then stored in the variable, **USERNAME$**. After entering **WALT** and pressing RETURN the program

Legal names:	
A	A$
A1	PEOPLE.WITH.1.CAR
LAST.NAME$	THE.LIST
XYZ	A3210
Illegal names:	**Reason:**
LIST	Keyword
LIST$	Keyword
FNXY	Begins with "FN"
1A	Begins with a number

Figure 2-1.
Legal and illegal variable names

continues to line 30. This is what the whole dialogue looks like:

```
RUN
Hi! What's your name? WALT
Glad to know you, WALT
Ok
```

Note that there is no question mark at the end of the prompt string in line 10. The **INPUT** statement in line 20 provides the question mark automatically, so it is unnecessary for you to type it.

Now replace line 20 and add lines 30, 40, and 50, as they appear in the following program sample. List your program to see that it matches exactly the listing shown.

```
10 INPUT "Hi! What's your name";USERNAME$
20 PRINT "Glad to know you ";USERNAME$;", how old are you";
30 INPUT AGE
40 PRINT AGE;"! I wouldn't have taken you for a day over";AGE-1
50 END
```

Before you run the program, let's look at it more closely. In line 10 the **INPUT** statement has a string and a semicolon preceding the variable **USERNAME$**. This is an abbreviated way of getting BASIC to print a prompt and a question mark before waiting for your input. Line 10 here does the same thing that lines 10 and 20 do in the previous version of this program, combining the old lines 10 and 20 into one line. Also, pay particular attention to the expression at the end of line 40 (**AGE−1**). Now run the program:

```
RUN
Hi! What's your name?
```

Again you enter your name or a fictitious name and press RETURN. Here is what happens:

```
RUN
Hi! What's your name? WALT
Glad to know you WALT, how old are you?
```

Once again the cursor prompts you to enter data. You can, of course, enter any kind of data, but we'll assume you want to be polite to the computer and enter your true age. After you press RETURN, the following appears:

```
RUN
Hi! What's your name? WALT
Glad to know you WALT, how old are you? 40
 40 ! I wouldn't have taken you for a day over 39
Ok
```

Run the program again and this time, in response to the question on age, type in the word for your age instead of the number.

```
RUN
Hi!  What's your name? WALT
Glad to know you WALT, how old are you? Forty
?Redo from start
?
```

This message indicates that you have entered the wrong variable type. Because the variable AGE does not end with a $, the program expects a numeric response to the prompt, whereas you entered a string. The program has ignored the **Forty** and is still waiting for a response of the correct type, which is in this case a number. Now enter your age as a number. The program will proceed as before.

```
RUN
Hi!  What's your name? WALT
Glad to know you WALT, how old are you? Forty
?Redo from start
? 40
 40 ! I wouldn't have taken you for a day over 39
Ok
```

Try one other change with this program. See if you can change line 40 so that when the program runs, the output will show a period at the end of the line. (See line 20 for a clue.)

Now let's try INPUT with more than one variable. Clear the memory with the NEW command and enter the following:

```
10 INPUT "Enter your first name, last name, and age ";FIRST$,LAST$,AGE
20 PRINT FIRST$,LAST$,AGE
```

In this case we have three variables in the INPUT statement. When the program pauses for you to enter data, you must enter the same number of data items as there are variables. Data items may be either numeric or string and, of course, must agree with the variable type. All data items must be separated by commas when entered. If too many data items are entered, or too few, or the wrong type, you will again receive the message "**?Redo from start**".

Run the program.

```
RUN
Enter your first name, last name, and age ? FRED,SLUGG,77
FRED      SLUGG     77
```

Retype line 10 and add a colon after **age**. Now change the semicolon after the second quote to a comma.

```
10 INPUT "Enter your first name, last name, and age: ",FIRST$,LAST$,AGE
20 PRINT FIRST$,LAST$,AGE
```

Now run the program and notice the difference:

```
RUN
Enter your first name, last name, and age: FRED,SLUGG,77
FRED      SLUGG     77
```

Using a comma instead of a semicolon after the prompt string suppresses the question mark. If you use the comma in this way, you will usually want to include some kind of punctuation inside the prompt string. This is why we inserted the colon.

Alternatively, you can place a semicolon after the word INPUT. If you do this, the cursor will stay on the same line after you finish entering data and will continue to print on that line.

To see how this works, give the NEW command and enter the following program. Notice the comma instead of a semicolon after the prompt string in lines 20 and 30.

```
10 PRINT "Enter two numbers each followed by RETURN"
20 INPUT ;"First number: ",A
30 INPUT ;" + ",B
40 PRINT " =";A+B
```

Enter the boldface information below, and be sure to press RETURN after each entry.

```
RUN
Enter two numbers each followed by RETURN
First number: 34
```

After you enter RETURN, the program now prompts you to enter the second value:

```
First number: 34 + 12
```

The program then prints out the sum:

```
First number: 34 + 12 = 46
Ok
```

Assigning Values to a Variable [LET]

LET is the *assignment* statement of MBASIC. Using LET, you can "assign" the value of an expression to a variable. The expression may be something as simple as the number 5, or it may be a complicated algebraic expression.

After clearing the memory with the NEW command, enter and run the following:

```
10 LET A=3
20 LET B=6
30 PRINT A;B;A+B

RUN
 3  6  9
Ok
```

We will now add a few more lines to the preceding program:

```
40 LET A=A*B
50 PRINT A
```

When we now enter the RUN command, we obtain the results of the entire program:

```
RUN
 3  6  9
 18
Ok
```

Now let's go over the entire program. In lines 10 and 20 the simple expressions 3 and 6 are assigned to the variables **A** and **B** respectively. Notice that in line 40, the variable **A** is assigned a new value. The new value of A is the product of the value previously assigned to A and the variable B. There is no limit to the number of times you can change the value in a variable.

You might think that variable B was somehow "lost" when we multiplied A times B, but this is not the case. In fact, B is still very much intact. We can see this by writing still another line and once again running the program:

```
60 PRINT B
```

```
RUN
 3  6  9
 18
 6
Ok
```

At this point we can list the whole program:

```
LIST
10 LET A=3
20 LET B=6
30 PRINT A;B;A+B
40 LET A=A*B
50 PRINT A
60 PRINT B
Ok
```

Clear the previous program and variables with the NEW command, and enter and run the following program:

```
10 BASE=4
20 HEIGHT=6
30 PRINT "AREA=";1/2*BASE*HEIGHT;"sq. in."
```

```
RUN
AREA= 12 sq. in.
Ok
```

In this example we use the words **BASE** and **HEIGHT** to name the variables instead of using simple letters as in the last example. Note also that the word LET has been omitted. LET is optional. If you leave it out, MBASIC will simply assume it is there.

If you use the value **.5** in line 30 instead of **1/2**, BASIC would process the program just the same. Try it by rewriting line 30.

For the next example, let's try something a little more practical. Suppose you buy a car and obtain a loan for $8500, with a simple interest rate of 17%. How much of your first month's payment will be interest? The formula for simple interest is

Interest = Principal × Rate × Time (in years)

Note that in line 30, we use **T=1/12** to represent one month. Enter and run the following program:

```
10 P=8500
20 R=.17
30 T=1/12
40 INTEREST=P*R*T
50 PRINT "Interest for first month will be";INTEREST;"dollars."


RUN
Interest for first month will be 120.417 dollars.
Ok
```

ASSIGNING STRINGS WITH LET

The LET statement may be used with both numeric and string variables. As an example of assigning strings to a variable, enter and run the following:

```
10 A$=" HOW"
20 B$=" NOW"
30 C$=" BROWN"
40 D$=" COW"
50 PRINT A$;B$;C$;D$
60 PRINT C$;D$;B$;A$
70 PRINT A$,C$,D$,A$


RUN
 HOW NOW BROWN COW
 BROWN COW NOW HOW
 HOW           BROWN          COW            HOW
Ok
```

Notice that the printed values of the variables in line 70 are spaced farther apart than the other lines. This is because commas were used as separators instead of semicolons. Using the comma with the PRINT statement automatically starts the second variable in column 15 on the display. The third variable starts in column 30 and the fourth in column 45. Spacing is done automatically by MBASIC.

The order in which you have the string variables printed makes no difference. You may use them any number of times and, just as with numeric variables, you may reassign them within the same program.

Working With Arithmetic Operators [+, −, /, *, ^)

Up to this point, you have used four of the five arithmetic operators: addition, subtraction, multiplication, and division. The last arithmetic operator that you will be using is exponentiation (raising to a power). Consider the following problem. A baseball diamond is a square. The distance between each of the successive bases is 90 feet. What is the area of a baseball diamond? The formula to find the area of a square is $A=S^2$. (This means A equals S squared; S is a side and A is the area.)

The equation $A=S^2$ raises S to the second power. But MBASIC does not allow you to use superscripts. Therefore, to raise a number to a power in MBASIC, you must use the caret symbol (^). Placing a ^ between S and the exponent 2 (A=S^2) in MBASIC raises the variable S to the power of 2. Look for this symbol on your keyboard. It is often placed above the 6 key. If it is, in order to use it you must first hold down the SHIFT key and then press the 6 key at the same time. On other keyboards, the caret symbol may be above the N key or somewhere else. After you find it, try using it by entering this program:

```
10 SIDE=90
20 A=SIDE^2
30 PRINT "The area of the baseball diamond is";A;" sq. ft."

RUN
The area of the baseball diamond is 8100 sq. ft.
Ok
```

ORDER OF OPERATIONS

Before you can use the arithmetic operators in any type of complicated mathematical expression, you need to know their *order of precedence*. Order of precedence means the order in which the arithmetic operations take place. Table 2-1 shows this order.

If you use more than one operator in an expression, MBASIC will evaluate the one highest in the list first. If two operators have the same order, they are evaluated from left to right. Multiplication and division are of the same order; they are processed as they are encountered from left to right. The same rule applies to addition and subtraction. Consider the following examples:

```
NEW
10 A=3+8/2
20 PRINT A
RUN
 7
Ok
```

The computer first evaluates 8/2 because division (/) is a higher order than addition (+). Of course, 8 divided by 2 is 4. The computer then adds 3 to the 4 to obtain the final result, 7.

```
10 A=8/4*3
20 PRINT A
RUN
 6
Ok
```

Division and multiplication occur in order from left to right.

```
10 A=9/3+2^2
20 PRINT A
RUN
 7
Ok
```

The 2 is squared first, then the division takes place, and finally the addition.

```
10 A=2+3-4
20 PRINT A
RUN
 1
Ok
```

Addition and subtraction occur in order from left to right.

Table 2-1.
Order of Precedence

Operator	Operation	Order
^	Exponentiation	Highest
*, /	Multiplication, division	Middle
+, −	Addition, subtraction	Lowest

CHANGING THE ORDER OF OPERATION WITH PARENTHESES ( )

Parentheses override the order of precedence. Whatever operation occurs in parentheses is performed first.

```
10 A=3*(4+2)
20 PRINT A
RUN
 18
Ok
```

Here addition comes first, then multiplication. There is implied multiplication as in algebra (that is, 3(4+2)=18). In MBASIC, however, the multiplication symbol (*) must always be present (that is, 3*(4+2)=18).

```
10 A=(6+3)/(1+2)
20 PRINT A
RUN
 3
Ok
```

First **6+3** is added, then **1+2**, and finally the division takes place. When there is more than one set of parentheses, they are evaluated from left to right.

```
10 A=(4-3)*7
20 PRINT A
RUN
 7
Ok
```

Subtraction comes first and then multiplication.

```
10 A=2*(1+6/2)^(2+1)
20 PRINT A
RUN
 128
Ok
```

First **6/2** is evaluated, then added to 1. The result is 4. Next **2+1** is added, and the 4 is raised to the power of 3, giving 64. Finally, this is multiplied by 2 to give the result, **128**.

Now let's apply some of these ideas to a problem. This problem determines your age in days. Clear memory with the NEW command and enter the following program:

```
10 PRINT "Enter your birthday in the form MONTH,DAY,YEAR:";
20 INPUT "",M1,D1,Y1
30 INPUT "What is the date today";M2,D2,Y2
40 AGE.DAYS=(Y2-Y1)*365 +(M2-M1)*30 +D2-D1
50 PRINT "Your age in days is approximately ";AGE.DAYS
```

Notice that the variable **M2** for the month is a numeric variable, not a string variable. Therefore, if you enter "October" instead of 10 when you are prompted to supply the date, MBASIC will flash a message on the screen that reads "?Redo from start". You can enter a word only for a string variable. Of course, if the programmer had been more alert, you would have been told that the month needs to be entered numerically.

Once you have entered the preceding program, list it and make sure everything is exactly as it should be. Then run it:

```
RUN
Enter your birthday in the form MONTH,DAY,YEAR:10,9,32
What is the date today?10,16,82
Your age in days is appproximately  18257
Ok
```

The purpose of the two quotation marks after **INPUT** in line 20 is to suppress the question mark normally associated with the INPUT statement. The double quotation marks allow a comma to be added before the first variable to suppress the question mark. In line 40 notice that the difference of years is enclosed in parentheses. This makes the subtraction, **Y2−Y1**, take place before multiplication by 365.

This program, of course, only gives an approximation of your age in days, since not all months are exactly thirty days. In later chapters you will find out how you can easily change this program to calculate accurate results when working with calendar dates. You may wish to return to the problem at that time to make these additions.

TUTORIALS

Tutorial 2-1: Sum and Average

Find the sum and average of the following numbers: 7, 13, 4, and 9.

In deciding how to set up a problem to be solved, we have to consider how the data is going to be entered, what to do with the data once it is in the computer, and finally how we are going to format the output. In this example we will use the assignment (LET) statement to enter the data.

To find the sum, we just add the four numbers. To find the average, we use the formula: the average equals the sum of a set of numbers divided by the number of numbers in the set.

You always have to pay particular attention to the output. Remember that, in many cases, you will be writing the program not only for yourself but for someone else as well. This is why you should indicate with a comment what the numbers mean rather than just having them appear on the screen. In this case, we can use the PRINT statement with a string constant and a variable to label and print the results.

Enter and run the following:

```
10 LET A=7
20 LET B=13
30 LET C=4
40 LET D=9
50 SUM=A+B+C+D
60 AVERAGE=SUM/4
70 PRINT "THE SUM OF";A;B;C;D;"IS";SUM
80 PRINT "AVERAGE=";AVERAGE
90 END


RUN
THE SUM OF 7 13 4 9 IS 33
AVERAGE= 8.25
Ok
```

Lines 10 through 60 are all assignment statements. In the first four statements the optional word LET has been used. In lines 50 and 60 LET has been omitted. The output lines, 70 and 80, print a string constant describing the output of the results that were calculated in lines 50 and 60.

MULTIPLE STATEMENTS PER LINE (USING THE COLON)

Now try this variation. All of your data could be entered on a single line. Instead of entering each data item on a separate line as was done in lines 10 through 40, you may enter the following as line 10:

```
10 A=7:B=13:C=4:D=9
```

This illustrates your option of entering multiple statements on the same line as long as they are separated by colons. Enter line 10 as shown above. Our program now looks like this:

```
LIST
10 A=7:B=13:C=4:D=9
20 LET B=13
30 LET C=4
40 LET D=9
50 SUM=A+B+C+D
60 AVERAGE=SUM/4
70 PRINT "SUM= ";SUM
80 PRINT "AVERAGE=";AVERAGE
90 END
```

If you run the program, BASIC will process the program correctly but lines 20, 30, and 40 will no longer be necessary. Let's eliminate them from the program.

ELIMINATING A LINE FROM A PROGRAM

To eliminate a line, just type the line number and press RETURN. For the example above, type **20** RETURN, **30** RETURN, and **40** RETURN. List the program and you will have the following:

```
LIST
10 A=7:B=13:C=4:D=9
50 SUM=A+B+C+D
60 AVERAGE=SUM/4
70 PRINT "SUM=";SUM
80 PRINT "AVERAGE=";AVERAGE
90 END
```

Run the program and note that the output is the same as for the previous problem.

Now let's try another variation. Eliminate lines 10 and 60 by typing **10** RETURN, **60** RETURN. Now re-enter lines 50 and 80 as follows:

```
50 SUM=7+13+4+9
80 PRINT "AVERAGE =";SUM/4
```

List the program and you will have the following:

```
LIST
50 SUM=7+13+4+9
70 PRINT "SUM=";SUM
80 PRINT "AVERAGE=";SUM/4
90 END
```

Run the program and you will get the same result again. Food for thought: How many ways can you write this program?

Tutorial 2-2: Payroll

The Martinez Widget Co. produces 300 widgets per day. The company has 3 employees: Fred, Susan, and Ted. Fred makes $4.78 an hour, Susan makes $5.01 an hour, and Ted makes $7.43 an hour. Each employee works eight hours per day. What is the labor cost for each widget?

To solve this problem on the computer, you will need the instructions to MBASIC introduced in this chapter. But first read the problem carefully to be sure you understand exactly what is wanted.

The objective of the problem is to find out the labor cost for each widget. To determine this, we first need to know the total labor cost, which is the sum of the daily wages of the three employees. Fred earns $4.78 an hour; therefore, during an eight-hour day he earns ($4.78 × 8) dollars. Susan's and Ted's daily wages can be figured in the same way. The total wages for the day are the sum of Fred, Susan, and Ted's daily wages. Now to get the labor cost per widget, we divide the total labor cost per day by the total number of widgets produced in one day. Enter the following:

```
10 FW=4.78
20 SW=5.01
30 TW=7.43
40 NUM.WIDGETS=300
50 TOTAL.WAGES=8*(FW+SW+TW)
```

(***Tutorial** 2-2: Continued*)

```
60 UNIT.COST=TOTAL.WAGES/NUM.WIDGETS
70 PRINT "Total daily wages =";TOTAL.WAGES
80 PRINT "Unit labor cost per widget=";UNIT.COST;"dollars."
90 END
```

```
RUN
Total daily wages = 137.76
Unit labor cost per widget= .4592 dollars.
Ok
```

Now let's take a look at the program and see what has been done and why. Line 70 prints the results that were calculated in line 50 along with the string constant describing what the numbers stand for. Line 80 prints the results that were calculated in line 60. It is worthwhile to get in the habit of performing your calculations in an assignment statement as we did in line 60. The alternative is to do this in the PRINT statement. For example:

```
70 PRINT "Total daily wages=";8*(FW+SW+TW)
```

At first glance this may appear to save time. But in most programs you will want the output in more than one line. By using an assignment statement, the result may be printed any number of times without your having to retype the expression.

We have only begun to explain the instructions and procedures presented in this chapter. They will be expanded on as you proceed through this book.

EXERCISES

1. Indicate which of the following are valid names for numeric variables.

   a. A　　*c.* NUMBER　　*e.* X213　　*g.* X6B
   b. 1B%　　*d.* X　　*f.* ABC　　*h.* YES$

2. Indicate which type of constant each of the following variables represents.

   a. PHONE.NUM$　　*c.* XYZ
   b. MILES　　*d.* AGE

3. Solve each of the following, using the direct mode.

   a. 5×6−4
   b. 5×6−3
   c. 5×(6−3)
   d. 12−4×2
   e. (42−7)−(2+1)
   f. (96−2×30)−9

4. Write a program to determine the value of each of the following expressions. Use the LET statement to assign the values for A, B, and C, where A=2, B=3, and C=5.

   a. X=A+2B−C
   b. X=(A−B)C
   c. X=BC/A(A+B)
   d. X=(A+B)/(C−A)

5. Rewrite Tutorial 2-1 using INPUT to enter variables A, B, C, and D instead of LET.

6. Write a program to convert the following Fahrenheit temperatures to Celsius. Use INPUT to enter the following data: 32, 68, 212, 98.6. (Hint: C=(5/9)×(F−32))

7. Write a program to find the areas of the indicated figures. Use the LET statement to assign the given values to the variables. In your output statements, use string constants to identify the results.

   a. triangle (A=1/2bh)
   b=8, h=11

   b. (A=S^2)
   s=6

   c. circle(A=3.1416r^2)
   r=3

   d. trapezoid
   (A=1/2(b1+b2)h)
   b1=8, b2=6, h=4
   Assign all variables on the same line.

8. Write a program that will print your name and address onto the screen. First display your name and address on a single line and then in address label format.

3

Organizing Your Programs

Commands:	SAVE, FILES, LOAD, NAME, KILL, SYSTEM
Statements:	REM

Not only does the computer read programs, but people also need to read them. To make the program more readable, it helps to include *comments.*

Adding Comments to a Program [REM]

A comment is a piece of text contained in your program that is ignored by MBASIC. Comments are put in programs solely for the benefit of people reading the program. If you save a program, you probably intend to work with it at some later time, and if you have not included comments, you may no longer remember what the program was designed to do or how a particular part of the program works.

The statement used to enter a comment is REM, which is short for "remark." Everything on a line following a REM statement is considered a comment and is ignored by the computer during execution of the program. Its only purpose is to give the person reading the program some information. REM may be the only MBASIC statement on a line, or it can be appended to a line containing other statements. Enter the following program:

```
50 LET  FW = 4.78
60 LET  SW = 5.01
70 LET  TW = 7.43
80 TOTAL.WAGES = 8*(FW+SW+TW)
90 UNIT.COST = TOTAL.WAGES/300
100 PRINT "Unit cost of widgets:";UNIT.COST
110 END
```

This is similar to Tutorial 2-2, the payroll problem that you entered in Chapter 2. We will use it to illustrate the use of REM statements. Enter the following lines:

```
10 REM -            -=*PAYROLL*=-
20 REM -            Determine labor cost per widget
30 REM -            08/23/82
40 REM
```

Now give the LIST command to see your program:

```
LIST
10 REM -            -=*PAYROLL*=-
20 REM -            Determine labor cost per widget
30 REM -            08/23/82
40 REM
50 LET  FW = 4.78
60 LET  SW = 5.01
70 LET  TW = 7.43
80 TOTAL.WAGES = 8*(FW+SW+TW)
90 UNIT.COST = TOTAL.WAGES/300
100 PRINT "Unit cost of widgets:";UNIT.COST
110 END
```

It is a common practice to place a heading at the beginning of your programs using REM statements. The heading we have used here consists of the name of the program, a brief description of the program, and the date it was written, but, of course, you can put whatever information you wish into REM statements. Other heading information might consist of the programmer's initials or dates for each time the program was modified, along with a description of what was changed. Notice that line 40 is blank. A blank comment line is probably the most commonly used comment line. It is used to improve readability by separating portions of the program, like the heading and the main body.

The REM statement may also be abbreviated with a single quotation mark ('). This abbreviation is most useful when remark statements are appended to the end of a line.

Reenter lines 50 through 70 as shown in the following program segment. If you append remarks to a statement as shown here, you may not enter multiple statements on the line after the single quotation mark. Everything after a REM statement or single quotation mark is ignored when the program is executed.

```
50 LET  FW = 4.78            '  FW = Fred's pay rate
60 LET  SW = 5.01            '  SW = Susan's pay rate
70 LET  TW = 7.43            '  TW = Ted's pay rate
```

Enter lines 75 and 85 as shown below and LIST the program:

```
75 REM - Determine total wages
85 REM - Determine unit cost of widgets
```

```
LIST
10 REM -              -=*PAYROLL*=-
20 REM -              Determine labor cost per widget
30 REM -              08/23/82
40 REM
50 LET FW = 4.78          'FW = Fred's pay rate
60 LET SW = 5.01          'SW = Susan's pay rate
70 LET TW = 7.43          'TW = Ted's pay rate
75 REM - Determine total wages
80 TOTAL.WAGES = 8*(FW+SW+TW)
85 REM - Determine unit cost of widgets
90 UNIT.COST = TOTAL.WAGES/300
100 PRINT "Unit cost of widgets:";UNIT.COST
110 END
```

Lines 75 and 85 show another common use of the REM statement. Each of these lines indicates what is happening on the following line.

The listing above illustrates a fully annotated program with appropriate REM statements. The remark statements are always optional; after all if the computer could read your comments, you would not have to write the program! Keep in mind that programs continuously change with their environment. You will generally be writing a program for yourself or someone else to use and modify. A program with plenty of appropriate remark statements is much easier for you to read at a later date and also makes it easier for anyone else looking at your program to understand the logic involved.

Setting Up a Data Disk

In this and future chapters, you will be saving many of the programs that you write. If you have a single-drive system, you will need to save your programs on the same disk with MBASIC and CP/M. If you have two or more drives, you may wish to save these programs on one of the other drives. Before storing programs on a disk, you must prepare the disk so that the operating system can read and write on it. This is called *formatting*. Formatting procedures vary from one computer system to another. Refer to your system manual in order to prepare the disk.

Naming a Program

Before you can save a program, you must decide on a name. Files under CP/M have a *file name* and *extension*. As many as eight characters may be used for the name. These eight characters may consist of any letter or number and many other symbols on your keyboard. However, you cannot use the symbols *, ?, or :. Following the name, a period and three characters for the optional extension may be added. If you do not supply an extension, MBASIC will assume the extension .BAS.

The following are examples of acceptable program names: PAYROLL, CHAPTER1.WAE, SAMPLE.PRP. Be especially careful always to use capital letters when specifying a filename, since MBASIC uses the exact characters. If you save a file from MBASIC with a lowercase name, you will not be able to access it from CP/M because CP/M reads everything you type as uppercase. For example, if you save a program with the name **lower.bas**, you will not be able to use CP/M commands like ERA and TYPE on that file.

Displaying the Disk Directory
[FILES]

Any material that is saved on the disk is referred to as a *file*. A file can be something as complicated as the Microsoft BASIC interpreter or something as simple as the first program you save.

In order to display files on your disk, use the FILES command. The FILES command is analogous to the **DIR** command of CP/M. FILES displays all the files that are on your logged-on drive. As mentioned in Chapter 1, the logged-on drive is given in the CP/M prompt just before loading MBASIC. For example, if your CP/M prompt is **A>**, your logged-on drive is A.

Try listing the disk directory by typing the FILES command:

```
FILES
MBASIC  .COM  STAT    .COM  PIP     .COM  PAYROLL .BAS
PROB1   .BAS  PROB2   .BAS  PROB3   .BAS  PROB12  .BAS
Ok
```

This display illustrates what is on our disk. Yours will be different, of course. Note that the program you just saved, PAYROLL, has the extension .BAS, which was supplied by MBASIC. Notice that unlike the DIR command of CP/M, the FILES command does not show which drive the files are on.

USING WILD CARDS WITH FILES

With the FILES command, MBASIC uses the wild card characters * and ? to display a group of files with similar names or prefixes. A ? will match *any individual* character in a file name, and the asterisk (*) will match any string of characters, regardless of length in either the file name or the extension. For example, you can list all the ".COM" files with the following command:

```
FILES "*.COM"
```

This will result in

```
MBASIC  .COM  STAT    .COM  PIP     .COM
Ok
```

The asterisk (*) matched a file name of any length while the .COM restricted the list to only those files with the extension .COM. The information inside the double quotation marks is often called a *template*. Only those files which match the template are listed.

Let's say you want to list all of the MBASIC programs that begin with the letters PROB and end with just one other letter. We can do this with the question mark wild card as follows:

```
FILES "PROB?.BAS"
PROB1   .BAS  PROB2   .BAS  PROB3   .BAS
Ok
```

In this case the question mark acts as a wild card for any character in the fifth position of the file name. Note that the program named PROB12.BAS is not displayed. Why not?

DISPLAYING FILES ON OTHER DRIVES

As you might have guessed, the FILES command without a file name specified is the same as FILES "*.*". In fact, the *.* is assumed by MBASIC if no file name is given. To display the files on drives other than the logged drive, you must indicate the disk. To do this, precede the file name with the name of the disk drive, that is, A or B and a colon. For example, to list all the files on the B drive, type

```
FILES "B:*.*"
```

Note that the meaning of the wild card characters ? and * is not quite consistent with CP/M commands.

Saving a Program
[SAVE]

After choosing an appropriate name, use the SAVE command, with the file name enclosed in quotation marks to save your program. To save the current program with the name "PAYROLL", type the following:

```
SAVE "PAYROLL"
```

When you save a program, a copy of the program is saved on the disk, but the program also remains in memory. You can verify that the program is still in memory with the LIST command.

Saving a program in the manner just demonstrated saves the program on the drive you are logged onto. You may also save your program on any of your other drives. In order to save the program on the B drive, use SAVE "B:PAYROLL". The B: designates the B drive and must be included within the quotation marks. You may use any letter that corresponds to one of your drives. If no letter is used, then the SAVE command defaults to your logged-on drive. Be sure to use all uppercase letters in the file name.

Loading a Program
[LOAD]

To transfer a program from the disk to memory, you use the LOAD command. When you use the LOAD command, the file name must be enclosed in double quotation marks. First type **NEW** to clear the computer's memory. Now type

```
LOAD "PAYROLL"
```

Now type **LIST** and your program will be displayed. Notice that you do not have to use the .BAS extension since it is supplied by MBASIC. However, if the program has any other extension, you must supply it in the file name.

The RUN command may also be used to load a program. If you key in **RUN "PAYROLL"**, then the RUN consists of two steps: load and execute. When you load the program with the command RUN, the program is transferred from the disk to the computer and execution begins immediately. Try this out by clearing memory with the NEW command and using RUN to load and execute the PAYROLL program:

```
RUN "PAYROLL"
Unit cost of widgets: 4.82
Ok
```

Be sure to use all uppercase letters in the file name.

Changing a File Name
[NAME]

In order to change the name of a file on the disk, use the NAME command. Try this with the program PAYROLL.BAS. Let's change the name PAYROLL to WIDGETS. To do this, enter the following:

```
NAME "PAYROLL.BAS" AS "WIDGET.BAS"
```

Now display the disk directory with the command FILES and note that the name of the file has been changed, while the data in the file has not:

```
FILES
MBASIC  .COM STAT   .COM PIP    .COM WIDGET .BAS
PROB1   .BAS PROB2  .BAS PROB3  .BAS PROB12 .BAS
Ok
```

Note that with this command you must always supply the extension (that is, .BAS). The NAME command does not have a default file name extension.

Erasing a Disk File
[KILL]

You can erase a file from the disk by using the KILL command. To use this, type KILL and the full file name enclosed in quotation marks. As with the NAME command, MBASIC will not supply the extension .BAS with this command.

To erase the WIDGET program, type

```
KILL "WIDGET.BAS"
```

Now when you list the disk directory, the file WIDGET.BAS will have disappeared.

```
FILES
MBASIC  .COM STAT   .COM PIP    .COM PROB1  .BAS
PROB2   .BAS PROB3  .BAS PROB12 .BAS
Ok
```

Notice that the WIDGET program was erased only from the disk and still remains in the computer's memory. List your program to be sure.

As a safety precaution, the KILL command only works when the full file name is supplied. You cannot use the wild cards * and ? as you can with the FILE command. If you use the KILL command without a file name, you will receive the message "Missing operand".

Returning to CP/M
[SYSTEM]

In order to return to CP/M from MBASIC, use the SYSTEM command.

```
SYSTEM
```

The SYSTEM command exits from MBASIC and any program stored in the computer's memory. The **A>** or **B>** prompt appears to indicate that you are now back in CP/M.

While you are programming, you will often find it necessary to transfer between MBASIC and CP/M. When you do move between MBASIC and CP/M, be sure to save your program *before* you use the SYSTEM command. Otherwise, when you return to MBASIC from CP/M, MBASIC will not be aware of any program you previously had in memory.

EXERCISES

1. Rewrite your program from question 7 in Chapter 2 (areas of geometric figures) to include comments. Use both full-line comments and comments at the ends of statements.

2. Which of the following program names are illegal? Why?

   a. FRIZ8000   *c.* QUEST?

   b. 1LINEPROG   *d.* LOW_BAR

3. What command would you use to display

   a. All the files with ".DAT" as an extension?

   b. Only files whose file names are two characters long?

   c. Only files whose file names have "A" as the third letter?

4. Identify the commands that would be used in the following sequence. "After I finished my program, I stored it to disk with the filename HAPPY. I cleared memory, but then decided I wanted to run the program again, so I retrieved the program. After running the program, I didn't like the name HAPPY, so I changed it to STUPID, then realized that I didn't like the program at all, so I erased it from disk and exited to CP/M."

4

Making Decisions

> Commands: READ, DATA, GOTO,
> IF/THEN, RESTORE,
> IF/THEN/ELSE
>
> Operators: >, <, <>, >=, <=, AND, OR

This chapter describes the methods you use to make choices in your MBASIC programs. First, however, we will show how you can use commands other than INPUT to get data.

Reading in Data
[READ, DATA]

An alternative to the INPUT statement for entering data into a computer progam is the READ and DATA statements. When MBASIC gets to a READ statement, it immediately looks for the first DATA statement in the program. The values in the DATA statement are then assigned to the variables in the order encountered.

Enter and run the following:

```
10 READ A,B,C,D
20 ANS = A+B+C+D
30 PRINT "A+B+C+D = ";ANS
40 DATA 17,13,3,27
```

```
RUN
A+B+C+D = 60
Ok
```

When MBASIC encounters the **READ** statement in line 10, it immediately looks through the program to find the first **DATA** statement. Since there are four variables in the **READ** statement in line 10, it reads the four data items in line 40. If there were more than four data items, it would read only the first four.

In line 20 the sum of the four numbers is determined and stored in the variable **ANS**. The **PRINT** statement in line 30 prints the string constant "A+B+C+D = " and the value stored in the variable **ANS**. It makes no difference where the data statement is located in the program, but it is usually appropriate to put it near the beginning or the end of the program for easy reference.

Another way of writing the previous program is to place the data on separate lines, as shown here:

```
10 READ A,B,C,D
20 ANS = A+B+C+D
30 PRINT "A+B+C+D=";ANS
40 DATA 17
50 DATA 13
60 DATA 3
70 DATA 27
```

This program runs exactly like the last example. How you group data in DATA statements is up to you; it should simply be in a format you will understand when you read the program.

If there are fewer data items than the number of variables in the READ statement, you will get the error message on the screen: "Out of DATA in 10". Try running the previous example with one data item removed:

```
10 READ A,B,C,D
20 ANS = A+B+C+D
30 PRINT "A+B+C+D =";ANS
40 DATA 17,13,3
```

```
RUN
Out of DATA in 10
```

The READ and DATA statements can also be used with strings. Enter and run the following:

```
10 READ A$,B$,C$,D$
20 PRINT "Meet the Flintstones"
30 PRINT A$,B$,C$,D$
40 END
50 DATA "Fred","Wilma","Barny","Betty"
```

```
RUN
Meet the Flintstones
Fred          Wilma          Barny          Betty
Ok
```

It was mentioned earlier that data may be separated into several DATA statements or combined into one statement. This is also true for the READ statements, as illustrated here:

```
10 READ A$,B$
20 READ C$,D$
30 PRINT "Meet the Flintstones"
40 PRINT A$,B$,C$,D$
50 END
60 DATA "Fred","Wilma","Barny","Betty"
```

Running this program will produce the same output as the previous example. It makes no difference how many READ statements you have as long as there is sufficient data for each variable. The main consideration is the logical association of variables and data.

Branching
[GOTO]

Normally MBASIC proceeds through a program's lines in numerical order. But there are times when you want to change this normal flow. This is called *branching*. There are two types of branching: *conditional* and *unconditional*.

MBASIC has several statements that allow you to change the flow of a program. GOTO is an unconditional branching statement. When MBASIC reaches the line number with a GOTO statement, it transfers directly to the line number GOTO indicates. Conditional branching, on the other hand, causes program flow to change only when a specific condition is met. Examples of this type of branching will be given a little later in this chapter.

A simple example of unconditional branching is

```
10 PRINT "One"
20 GOTO 40
30 PRINT "Two"
40 PRINT "Three"

RUN
One
Three
Ok
```

Notice how the **GOTO** in line 20 prevented MBASIC from running the **PRINT** statement in line 30.

STOPPING AN ENDLESS LOOP

One of the errors that every programmer faces sooner or later when working with the GOTO statement is writing a program that repeats itself continuously. This is referred to as an *endless loop*. Let's consider an example of this now so that if it happens to you accidentally, you will know how to break the loop. Enter the following:

```
10 PRINT "Hiccup!"
20 GOTO 10
```

First, line 10 prints "Hiccup!", then MBASIC advances to line 20. Line 20 has a GOTO statement which sends it back to line 10. MBASIC executes line 10 again, and the process is repeated continuously. This program is an endless loop. To stop the loop, you need to press the CTRL and C keys simultaneously. MBASIC provides this as a way to interrupt a program. Typing CTRL-C stops the program execution and returns you to MBASIC command mode.

Now try this by running the program, and as soon as you have seen the message a sufficient number of times, pressing CTRL-C. The program will stop and you will see the message on the screen "Break in line 10", or "Break in line 20", depending on when you type the CTRL-C. Some versions of MBASIC simply say "Break in 10" instead of "Break in line 10".

```
RUN
Hiccup!
Hiccup!
Hiccup!
Hiccup!
Hiccup!
^C
Break in line 20
Ok
```

As a second example of this type, enter the following:

```
10 A=1
20 GOTO 10
30 PRINT "The value of A is";A
40 END
```

In this example nothing is printed on the screen because the endless loop involves a section of the program without a PRINT statement. When this happens, the first thought of the new programmer might be that something is wrong with the computer because the PRINT statement is not executed. The solution, of course, is the same as in the previous example: type CTRL-C and you will be returned to direct mode. If your program ever "locks up" in this way, remember to try typing CTRL-C before reaching for the power switch on your computer. This way your program will remain unchanged in memory.

Conditional Branching [IF/THEN]

Almost any time you want to solve a problem, there is a decision to be made. With MBASIC you can have the program make decisions. You can do this in several ways, but the most frequently used is the IF/THEN statement. The syntax of the IF/THEN statement is

IF *relation* THEN *action*

where *relation* is a true-false relationship, and *action* is any valid MBASIC statement. Every IF statement must have a THEN clause on the same line, and you cannot use the THEN clause by itself.

IF/THEN uses the relational operators to make comparisons, so we will consider the relational operators first.

RELATIONAL OPERATORS [>, <, <>, <=, >=]

The relational operators supported by MBASIC are shown in Table 4-1. They can be used to compare either numeric or string expressions.

MBASIC always acts on the relational operators as it encounters them from left to right in a statement. Therefore, we do not have to consider order of precedence as we did with the arithmetic operators.

Now let's try conditional branching with a program. Enter and run the following:

```
10 INPUT "How old are you? ";AGE
20 IF AGE>20 THEN GOTO 50
30 PRINT "Have a Coke."
40 END
50 PRINT "Have a martini."
60 END
```

```
RUN
How old are you? 17
Have a Coke.
Ok
RUN
How old are you? 34
Have a martini.
Ok
```

What will happen if you enter 20 for the age?

Table 4-1.
Relational Operators

MBASIC Symbol	Description
=	Equal to
<>	Not equal to
>	Greater than
<	Less than
>=	Greater than or equal to
<=	Less than or equal to

DUMMY DATA

Enter and run this next example:

```
10 READ A
20 IF A>0 THEN PRINT A;
30 GOTO 10
40 END
50 DATA 17,13,3,27

RUN
 17 13 3 27
Out of DATA in 10
Ok
```

The "Out of DATA" message comes because line 10 tried to read a fifth data item which is not present. Now let's consider the solution to this little difficulty.

One method of telling the computer when it has reached the end of your data is to add a special number that marks the end of the DATA statement. This special number is referred to as *dummy data.* Although it does not make any difference what the number is, the number should be outside the range of realistic values for the data you are working with.

The next program reads in the following numbers: 47, 10, 83, 61, 98, 7, 18, 36, 88, 41, and 50. It then prints out only those numbers that are greater than or equal to 50. At the end of the data statement, we add the number −1, which is our dummy data. Its only purpose is to tell the program that there is no more data. The program will transfer execution to line 50 when **A** equals −1. Enter and run the program to verify the output:

```
10 READ A
20 IF A = -1 THEN GOTO 50
30 IF A >= 50 THEN PRINT A;
40 GOTO 10
50 END
60 DATA 47,10,83,61,98,7,18,36,88,41,50,-1

RUN
 83 61 98 88 50
Ok
```

What do you think would happen if line 40 were accidentally typed as GOTO 20?

REUSING THE SAME DATA

[RESTORE]

Now let's consider a variation on this problem. Enter the following:

```
10 INPUT "Print numbers above what value? ";MIN
20 READ A
30 IF A=-1 THEN GOTO 10
40 IF A>MIN THEN PRINT A;
50 GOTO 20
60 DATA 47,10,83,61,98,7,18,36,88,41,50,-1

RUN
Print numbers above what value? 75
83 98 88
Print numbers above what value? 29
Out of data in 20
```

In this program you are asked to indicate the minimum value for the numbers to be printed. When the program has read all the data and gets to the dummy data, line 30 sends you back to line 10 and asks you for a new minimum value. But unfortunately, all of the data has been read and is therefore unavailable to another READ statement. When you enter a new value, you will get the message "Out of DATA in line 10". One way to prevent this is to enter a new line, numbered 15, with the statement RESTORE. This resets the data pointer to the first item of data. By using the RESTORE statement, you can run the program as many times as you wish. You now have the following:

```
15 RESTORE
Ok
LIST
10 INPUT "Print numbers above what value? ";MIN
15 RESTORE
20 READ A
30 IF A=-1 THEN GOTO 10
40 IF A>MIN THEN PRINT A;
50 GOTO 20
60 DATA 47,10,83,61,98,7,18,36,88,41,50,-1
Ok
```

EXITING FROM A PROGRAM

The preceding program has one additional difficulty. There is no way to stop the program except by pressing CTRL-C. To fix this, add the following line (line 12) to the program: IF MIN=0 THEN END. Of course, we must also inform the user of the program of this option. Thus, at the end of your prompt for the INPUT statement, add the words "Type 0 to end." If you list the program, you now have the following:

```
LIST
10 INPUT "Print numbers above what value? (Type 0 to end) ";MIN
12 IF MIN=0 THEN END
15 RESTORE
20 READ A
30 IF A=-1 THEN GOTO 10
40 IF A>MIN THEN PRINT A;
50 GOTO 20
60 DATA 47,10,83,61,98,7,18,36,88,41,50,-1
Ok
```

Now you can run the program and exit in a normal fashion.

COUNTING LOOP

A second method of ending a loop is to use a *counter*. The program below is similar to the last one, except in this case we will test a variable called COUNT to terminate the program.

```
10 READ COUNT
20 IF COUNT = 0 THEN GOTO 70
30 READ A
40 IF A <= 50 THEN PRINT A;
50 COUNT = COUNT - 1
60 GOTO 20
70 END
80 DATA 8,47,83,61,98,7,18,41,50

RUN
 47 10 7 18 41 50
Ok
```

In line 10 the value for **COUNT** is read as the first item in the DATA statement, so **COUNT** is equal to 8. Line 20 checks this value; when it becomes 0, the program will end. Line 30 begins to read the data and prints out those values that are less than or equal to 50. In line 50 **COUNT** is decremented by 1, and the program returns to line 20. As soon as it has read eight values, **COUNT** will be equal to 0 and the program will end.

More Branching
[IF/THEN/ELSE]

A variation of the IF/THEN statement is the IF/THEN/ELSE statement. The ELSE gives you a second choice for branching. If the condition following IF is true, the program performs the statements following THEN. If it is false, it performs the statements following ELSE. Enter and run the following:

```
10 INPUT "How old are you? ";AGE
20 IF AGE>20 THEN PRINT "Have a martini." ELSE PRINT "Have a Coke."
30 END

RUN
How old are you? 13
Have a Coke.
Ok
RUN
How old are you? 21
Have a martini.
Ok
```

This is the same example we used earlier, but it has been reduced from six lines to three.

Using Logical Operators [AND, OR]

Now we will deal with the two most commonly used logical operators, AND and OR. These two operators are commonly used to control program flow or to make compound comparisons. Later in the book, we will go into other applications of the logical operators.

First let's use both AND and OR to make a double comparison. Enter and run the following:

```
10 READ A
20 IF A<0 THEN END
30 IF A>10 AND A<20 THEN PRINT A
40 DATA 7,16,4,25,-1
50 GOTO 10

RUN
 16
Ok
```

This program prints only those numbers that are greater than 10 and less than 20. Now change line 30 as shown below:

```
30 IF A<10 OR A>20 THEN PRINT A

RUN
 7
 4
 25
Ok
```

The program now prints only those numbers that are less than 10 or greater than 20.

Notice that the variable A in line 30 must be explicitly stated on each side of the logical operator. The statement "IF A>10 AND <20 PRINT A" would give you a syntax error.

Now try the following example:

```
10 INPUT "How old are you? ";AGE
20 IF AGE<7 THEN PRINT "Have a glass of milk."
30 IF AGE>=7 AND AGE<=20 THEN PRINT "Have a Coke."
40 IF AGE>20 THEN PRINT "Have a martini."
50 END

RUN
How old are you? 13
Have a Coke.
Ok
RUN
How old are you? 5
Have a glass of milk.
Ok
RUN
How old are you? 21
Have a martini.
Ok
```

As another example, enter the following:

```
10 READ NAM$,AGE,SEX$
20 IF NAM$ = "" THEN GOTO 50
30 IF AGE >= 18 AND SEX$="F" THEN PRINT NAM$,AGE
40 GOTO 10
50 END
60 REM - NAME DATA
70 DATA GEORGE,19,M
80 DATA WILMA,15,F
90 DATA LISA,20,F
100 DATA MIKE,13,M
110 DATA RITA,18,F
120 DATA SAM,18,M
130 DATA JODY,19,F
140 DATA "",0,""

RUN
LISA          20
RITA          18
JODY          19
Ok
```

Notice the data items in lines 70 through 140. When data is associated in groups like this, each group is referred to as a *record*. Note also that line 140 contains the dummy data to terminate this program. Only the variable NAM$ checks for this dummy data, but there must be data items for the variables AGE and SEX$ as well, or you will get the error message "Out of DATA in line 10".

Now try one more example by making a change in line 30 so that we can use the OR operator. Type in the following for line 30:

```
30 IF AGE >= 18 OR SEX$="F" THEN PRINT NAM$,AGE
```

Can you predict the output before you run the program?

```
RUN
GEORGE        19
WILMA         15
LISA          20
RITA          18
SAM           18
JODY          19
Ok
```

TUTORIALS

Tutorial 4-1: Finding the Largest Value

Write a program to find and print out the largest number in the following set of data. Use the READ and DATA statements for data entry.

DATA: 4,34,29,43,8,2,11,83,15,9,−1

USING A FLOWCHART

We will approach the solution to this problem a little differently than we did earlier. We will use what is called a *flowchart.* Figure 4-1 shows the shapes of the boxes in our flowchart.

With the flowchart drawn, it is easier to write and debug the program. By looking at the flowchart in Figure 4-2, you can trace the execution of the program and can see exactly what the program is meant to do. This can be especially helpful if your program goes into an endless loop, since the flowchart will show you all the possible places that an endless loop might occur.

Shape	Purpose
	Starts and ends a flowchart diagram
	Assigns values to a variable
	Indicates when data is entered into or output from a program
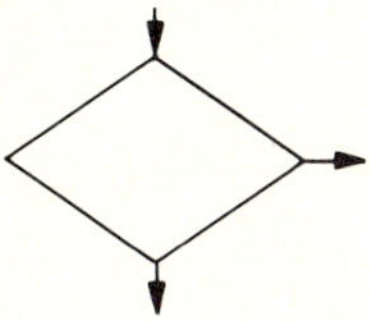	Indicates a decision statement; always has one arrow pointing in and two pointing out
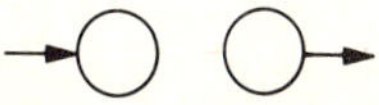	Indicates a connection from one part of the program to another; always occurs in pairs

Figure 4-1.
Flowchart symbols

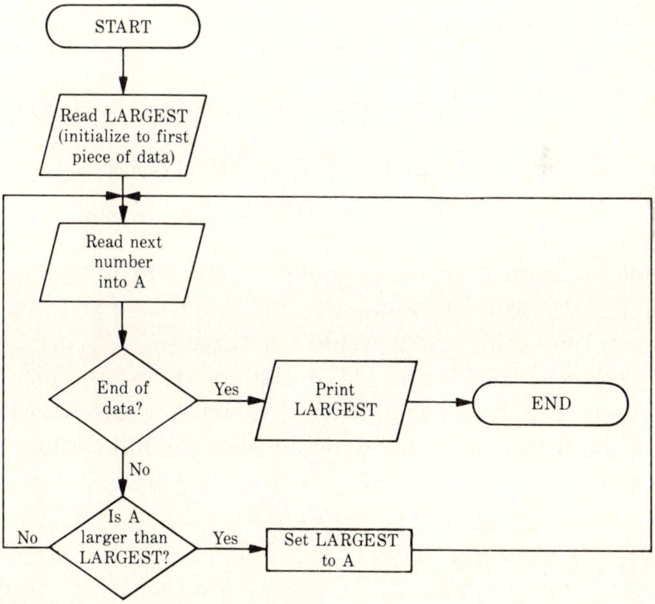

Figure 4-2.
Flowchart for finding largest number

Again, we will use dummy data to signify when we have read the last data item. In addition, we need a holder to keep the largest value. Each time we read a new value from the DATA statement, we will let the variable **A** hold that value. A substitution of **A** for **LARGEST** will be made if **A** is greater than **LARGEST**.

```
10 REM -        -=*LARGEST*=-
20 REM -        10/24/82
30 REM -
40 READ LARGEST                    'Initialize
50 READ A
60 IF A=-1 THEN 90
70 IF A > LARGEST THEN LARGEST = A
80 GOTO 50
90 PRINT "The largest number is";LARGEST
100 END
110 DATA 4,3,29,43,8,2,11,83,15,9,-1

RUN
The largest number is 83
Ok
```

In line 40, we initialize the variable **LARGEST**. The program loops through lines 50 to 80, each time replacing the value held in **LARGEST** with the value held in **A**, if it is greater. As soon as the value −1 (the dummy data) is read, the program proceeds to line 90 and prints the value held in **LARGEST**.

Tutorial 4-2: Translating Numerals To Words

Write a program to input an integer from 1 to 10 and print out the word that stands for that integer. For example, if your answer to INPUT is 3, then your output would be "three."

We will use the READ and DATA statements to assign the words "one" through "ten" to a variable. Our variable in the READ statement must be terminated with a dollar sign ($), indicating a string variable.

```
10 REM -              -=*NBR10*=-
20 REM -              10/24/82
30 REM -
40 INPUT "Enter an integer from 0 to 10: ",X
50 I=0
60 READ NUMBER$
70 IF I=X THEN 100
```

(Tutorial 4-2: Continued)

```
80 I=I+1
90 GOTO 60
100 PRINT "The number is ";NUMBER$
110 END
120 DATA zero,one,two,three,four,five,six,seven,eight,nine,ten

RUN
Enter an integer number from 0 to 10: 2
The number is two
Ok
RUN
Enter an integer number from 0 to 10: 10
The number is ten
Ok
```

In line 50, the counter **I** is initialized to 0. In the loop section of this program, lines 60 through 80, the computer reads and compares the numbers. If the word does not match the number, the computer returns to 60 to process the loop once more. As soon as the match is found, it proceeds to line 100 and prints the word stored in the variable **NUMBER$**.

In this problem, instead of using dummy data to terminate our READ statement, we use a counting loop. The counting loop is appropriate to use when you have a fixed number of items in the DATA statement. Dummy data, on the other hand, should be used when you might change the number of data items in the list. In this case we input the count from the user in line 40. What will happen if the user inputs a number greater than 10? How might you resolve this problem?

Tutorial 4-3: Payroll Problem

Let's return to our payroll program and replace some of the statements with instructions that have been introduced in this chapter.

```
10 REM -                 -=*PAYROLL.C4*=-
20 REM -                 08/16/82
30 REM -
40 INPUT "Number of widgets produced per day? ",WIDGETS
50 TOTAL.WAGES=0
60 READ EMP.RATE
70 IF EMP.RATE=0 THEN 110               'Zero rate signals end of data
80 EMP.EARN=EMP.RATE*8                  'Compute employee earnings
90 TOTAL.WAGES=TOTAL.WAGES+EMP.EARN     'Total employee wages
100 GOTO 60
```

(Tutorial 4-3: Continued)

```
110 UNIT.COST=TOTAL.WAGES/WIDGETS       'Compute unit cost
120 PRINT "Unit cost = ";UNIT.COST
130 END
140 DATA 4.78,5.01,7.43,0
```

In this program, we have made full use of the REM statements. Both forms of the comment statement (REM and the single quotation mark) have been used to add comments to an existing line. In line 40, the INPUT statement is used along with its prompt to input the number of widgets produced per day. The third change that has been introduced is the use of READ and DATA statements to enter the wages, rather than the LET statement that was used in Chapter 2. Here 0 is used as a dummy data value rather than −1. As we progress through this book, we will continue to add new instructions to make the program and its applications more practical.

EXERCISES

1. Write a program to read in ten numbers and print out only those numbers whose values are >= 10 and <= 20. Use the following data: 17, 4, 37, 41, 26, 11, 1, 40, 32, 16.

2. Use a READ and DATA statement to enter in the following numbers: 16, 28, 83, 47, 32, 7, 19, 81, 57, 93. Have your program determine the sum and average of the numbers.

3. Write a program to read in ten first names. Print the names out in a column. Use dummy data to terminate the READ loop. Use the following data: TOM, FRED, GREG, WALT, MARK, SAM, SALLY, MARY, ANN, SUE.

4. Change problem 3 so the names are printed out in a single line, and use a counter to terminate reading the names. (Hint: You will need to insert a blank, " ", to separate the names.)

5. Rewrite the payroll program so that it will "loop" to ask the user for additional values for EMP.RATE.

5

Editing a Program

Statements:	EDIT, AUTO, DELETE, RENUM, CONT
Control Characters:	^R, ^H, ^U, ^A, ^I, ^C, ^S, ^Q, ^O

The commands presented in this chapter deal with the housekeeping chores of writing a BASIC program. As you begin writing longer programs, you will need to learn to correct program statements. The sooner you become proficient with the editor, the easier it will be for you to write and correct errors in MBASIC programs.

Editing Your Program
[EDIT]

Enter and run the following:

```
10 IF X = 3 THEN END
20 PRINT "THE GIANTS WILL WIN THE PENNANT THIS YEAR."
30 X = X + 1
40 GOTO 10

RUN
THE GIANTS WILL WIN THE PENNANT THIS YEAR.
THE GIANTS WILL WIN THE PENNANT THIS YEAR.
THE GIANTS WILL WIN THE PENNANT THIS YEAR.
Ok
```

Now let's use the editor to make some changes. To edit an MBASIC program statement, you use the command EDIT followed by the number of the line you wish to edit. This is also called entering edit mode, which we described in Chapter 1.

```
EDIT 20
```

LOOKING AT THE LINE (L)

You are now in edit mode. On the screen the following appears:

```
20 ▒
```

In this section, the position of the cursor is marked by a shaded box. In the preceding illustration, the cursor is two spaces to the right of the 20.

In order to see the line you are going to edit, press **L**. Line 20 appears on the screen with the cursor again on the left.

```
20 PRINT "THE GIANTS WILL WIN THE PENNANT THIS YEAR."
20 ▒
```

A good habit to get into when you first enter the edit mode is to type **L** so that the line you are about to edit appears on the screen immediately above the cursor.

Now press SPACE three or four times. Notice that the cursor moves one space to the right each time, exposing a new character in line 20 as it moves. You could, of course, repeat this process until the entire line was on the screen.

Press **L** again so that the cursor is again on the left-hand side of the screen.

Now let's try a couple of quicker ways to move the cursor to a desired position on the line. Type the number **14** (nothing appears to happen on the screen) and then press SPACE. The cursor moves 14 columns, to the **N** in the word **GIANT**:

```
20 PRINT "THE GIA▒
```

Now press **8** and then SPACE. The cursor moves eight more spaces to the right:

```
20 PRINT "THE GIANTS WILL▒
```

With this combination of keys, you can quickly move to any position in the line you are editing.

Now press **L** again and try another way to move the cursor.

SEARCHING FOR CHARACTERS (S)

With the cursor on the left-hand side of the screen, type **S** for *S*earch. When you use the S command, nothing happens, but you are telling the editor to move the cursor to the first occurrence of the next key you press. Now press the letter **A**. The cursor moves immediately over the first **A** in that line (the **A** in **GIANTS**):

```
20 PRINT "THE GI▒
```

Now press the number **3**, then the **S**, and then the **N**. The cursor passes over the **N** in **GIANTS**. Because you pressed the 3 before the S, you were telling the editor to search for the third occurrence (after the cursor) of the letter **N**. That is why it passed over the **N** in **GIANTS** and the **N** in **WIN** and then stopped on the first **N** in **PENNANT**.

Of course, moving the cursor is not the only thing you are interested in doing with the editor. You may have an extra letter in a word, or possibly a word that you want to change or eliminate.

DELETING CHARACTERS (D)

Type **L** again so that the cursor is on the left. Move the cursor over the **N** in **GIANTS**. As you may have guessed, the code to tell the editor to *D*elete is the letter D. Type **D**, and you will see the letter **N** bracketed by backslashes (\N\) as shown here:

```
20 PRINT "THE GIA\N\░
```

These marks are used to give you visual proof of what has been deleted from the line you are editing. Press **L** once and then again so that you can see how the line appears without the letter **N**:

```
20 PRINT "THE GIA\N\TS WILL WIN THE PENNANT THIS YEAR."
20 PRINT "THE GIATS WILL WIN THE PENNANT THIS YEAR."
20 ░
```

Now move the cursor over the **G** of **GIATS** and press **5D** and **L**. The remaining letters are bracketed by backslashes.

```
20 PRINT "THE \GIATS\ WILL WIN THE PENNANT THIS YEAR."
20 ░
```

You can use this procedure to delete any number of characters you wish.

In some situations, you may wish to change characters instead of deleting them.

CHANGE CHARACTERS (C)

Move the cursor over the **T** in **THIS**. Type **C** for *C*hange and the letter **N**. The cursor is now over the **H** in **NHIS**, since the **T** changed to **N**. Type **3C** and the letters **EXT**, which will change the word **THIS** to **NEXT**. Just as with the D for delete, the number you type before the C tells the editor how many letters you are going to change.

Press **L** twice and line 20 appears like this:

```
20 PRINT "THE  WILL WIN THE PENNANT NEXT YEAR."
20 ░
```

We eliminated the word **GIANTS** with the result that we no longer have a proper sentence.

INSERTING CHARACTERS (I)

Move the cursor to the space before the **W** in **WILL**.

```
20 PRINT "THE ░WILL WIN THE PENNANT NEXT YEAR."
```

In the position where the word **GIANTS** used to be, let's enter **ROYALS**. To do this, type **I** for *I*nsert and then type **ROYALS**. Now press ESCAPE and then **L** and you have

```
20 PRINT "THE ROYALS WILL WIN THE PENNANT NEXT YEAR."
20 ░
```

This procedure is important and causes a lot of problems for most programmers when they start to use the editor. You must press ESCAPE in order to leave insert mode. If you are still in insert mode, any edit command, such as pressing the SPACE bar to move the cursor, will not be interpreted as an instruction to the editor. The keys you press will simply continue to be inserted until you press ESCAPE.

Use **D** and **I** to change line 20 from

```
20 PRINT "THE ROYALS WILL WIN THE PENNANT NEXT YEAR."
```

to

```
20 PRINT "THE GIANTS WILL WIN THE PENNANT THIS YEAR."
```

Did you remember to press ESCAPE to leave insert mode?

FINISHING THE EDIT (RETURN)

When you are satisfied with the line you are editing, press RETURN and you will return to the MBASIC direct mode. The functions just described are the most commonly used editing functions, but here are some additional editing commands that you will find useful as you write more programs.

EXTENDING THE LINE (X)

Typing X for e*X*tend moves the cursor immediately to the end of the line and places you in insert mode. To try this, enter edit mode again by giving the command EDIT 20. Now type **X**. The cursor moves to the end of the line.

```
20 PRINT "THE GIANTS WILL WIN THE PENNANT THIS YEAR."░
```

Press BACKSPACE twice to move the cursor over the period and type **OR MAYBE NEXT.**" and ESCAPE. Line 20 now reads

```
20 PRINT "THE GIANTS WILL WIN THE PENNANT THIS YEAR OR MAYBE NEXT." ░
```

GETTING THE OLD LINE AGAIN (A)

If you do not like this addition to line 20, first press ESCAPE to get out of insert mode. Then type **A** for *A*gain and **L** to see the line. Now you have

```
20 PRINT "THE GIANTS WILL WIN THE PENNANT THIS YEAR."
20 ▒
```

The A command cancels any changes you make while in edit mode. You are still in edit mode and may begin editing again if you wish.

ENDING EDIT (E)

Typing **E** for *E*nd has the same effect as pressing RETURN. Like RETURN, E places you back in direct mode. However, when you press E, the portion of the line after the cursor is not printed, although it is still in the computer's memory.

QUITTING WITHOUT CHANGING (Q)

Pressing **Q** for *Q*uit does the same thing as A, except that you exit edit mode and return to direct mode.

HACKING THE END OF THE LINE (H)

Pressing **H** eliminates everything to the right of the cursor and causes you to enter insert mode automatically. In order to change

```
20 PRINT "THE GIANTS WILL WIN THE PENNANT ▒HIS YEAR."
```

to read

```
20 PRINT "THE GIANTS WILL WIN THE PENNANT SOME DAY."
```

move the cursor over the **T** in **THIS** and type **H**; then type **SOME DAY."** and press ESCAPE.

KILLING UP TO A CHARACTER (K)

Pressing **K** *K*ills everything in the line you are editing from the position of the cursor to the letter you indicate. Thus K is really a search and delete command.

```
20 PRINT "THE GIANTS WILL WIN THE PENNANT SOME DAY."
20 ▒
```

Move the cursor over the **T** in **THE**, and type **K** and **W**. This gets rid of everything in line 20 up to **W** in **WILL**. The screen shows this:

```
20 PRINT "\THE GIANTS \▒
```

Press **L** once and you have

```
20 PRINT "\THE GIANTS \WILL WIN THE PENNANT SOME DAY."
20 ▒
```

To see the line as it will appear in your program, press **L** again:

```
20 PRINT "WILL WIN THE PENNANT SOME DAY."
20 ▒
```

Sometimes it is more convenient to use the K command to delete a portion of a line than it is to use the D command. We will leave it to you to complete the line with the team of your choice.

If you intend to do a lot of programming or even just a little, it is well worth the effort to spend an hour or so practicing with the editor now. You will find that if you become proficient with it now, it will save you a great many hours in the long run.

Automatically Entering Line Numbers [AUTO]

The AUTO command instructs MBASIC to enter line numbers for you. To use this command efficiently, you should have a carefully planned program with a flowchart and a good idea of the program's final form. If you give the AUTO command without indicating a line number, the value 10 for both the first line number and increment will be used.

After you give the AUTO command, MBASIC displays your first line number, 10. Enter your first program line, and then press RETURN. MBASIC prompts you with **20**. Enter your next line, and so on. To get out of automatic line numbering, press CTRL-C. For example:

```
AUTO
10 PRINT "This is a short  program."
20 END
30 ^C
Ok
```

Now give the NEW command to clear memory, and enter the program again with the following AUTO command:

```
110 PRINT "This is a short  program."
105 END
110 ^C
Ok
```

The first number after AUTO indicates the beginning number of your program, and the second is the number of lines to increment each time.

If you tell AUTO to overwrite lines in your current program, it will put an asterisk after each line number that exists to tell you that you are losing your old lines. If you do not want to overwrite these lines, type CTRL-C to exit from AUTO.

Deleting Line Numbers
[DELETE]

You have already learned how to delete a single line by typing the line number and pressing RETURN. The DELETE command allows you to delete any section of a program you wish.

Enter the following program:

```
100 READ A
105 IF A = -1 THEN GOTO 120
110 IF A >= 50 THEN PRINT A
115 GOTO 100
120 END
125 DATA 47,10,83,61,98,7,18,36,88,41,50,-1

DELETE 110-115
LIST
100 READ A
105 IF A = -1 THEN GOTO 120
120 END
125 DATA 47,10,83,61,98,7,18,36,88,41,50,-1
Ok
```

Entering a dash and a line number deletes all lines from the beginning of the program to the number you type.

```
DELETE -105
LIST
120 END
125 DATA 47,10,83,61,98,7,18,36,88,41,50,-1
Ok
```

There is no way to delete from a line number to the end of the program unless you know the last line number.

```
DELETE 120-
Illegal function call
Ok
```

Renumbering a Program [RENUM]

As you write longer programs, you will find that you frequently add new lines or delete existing ones. Before long, the numbering of the program lines will be very haphazard. The command to renumber a program is RENUM. By using RENUM appropriately, you can immediately renumber the program, starting at any line number and using any increment.

Enter the following:

```
5 READ A
10 IF A = -1 THEN GOTO 25
15 IF A >= 50 THEN PRINT A
20 GOTO 5
25 END
30 DATA 47,10,83,61,98,7,18,36,88,41,50,-1
```

```
RENUM
LIST
10 READ A
20 IF A = -1 THEN GOTO 50
30 IF A >= 50 THEN PRINT A
40 GOTO 10
50 END
60 DATA 47,10,83,61,98,7,18,36,88,41,50,-1
Ok
```

The default values for RENUM are to start the program at line 10 and increment the numbers by 10. Notice that the **25** in line 10 has changed to **50**, corresponding to the new location of line 25.

```
RENUM 100,30,5,
LIST
10 READ A
20 IF A = -1 THEN GOTO 110
100 IF A >= 50 THEN PRINT A
105 GOTO 10
110 END
115 DATA 47,10,83,61,98,7,18,36,88,41,50,-1
Ok
```

The number **100** tells MBASIC the first line number to use: **30** indicates the old line number at which to start renumbering and **5** is the new increment.

Using Control Characters [^R,^H,^U,^A,^I,^C,^S,^Q,^O]

MBASIC supports the use of several control characters for entering programs. Some of these control characters are useful when entering or running a program, while the usefulness of others depends largely on the characteristics of your terminal. We will describe each control function, but you will have to decide on their value with respect to your terminal. For instance, CTRL-I is interpreted by MBASIC as the TAB key. If your terminal has a TAB key, then you would use that key instead.

^R Pressing CTRL-R causes the line you are currently working on to be retyped. For instance, if you have made corrections in a line and your terminal shows deleted characters within brackets or by some other means, typing ^R will redisplay the line in its correct form, showing exactly what will be entered into memory when you press RETURN.

DELETE Pressing DELETE causes the \ symbol and the letters being deleted to be printed. If you have just typed in

```
10 PINT▒
```

and the cursor is just after the T, press DELETE three times. The screen now displays

```
10 PINT\TNI▒
```

Now enter the letters **RINT**. The screen shows

```
10 PINT\TNI\RINT▒
```

To see the corrected version, press ^R.

^H Pressing ^H has the same effect as BACKSPACE: it deletes the last character typed in by moving the cursor one space to the left. Most terminals have a BACK-

SPACE key that you would use instead of pressing the two keys to make ^H. Either BACKSPACE or ^H is more convenient to use than the DELETE key since the deleted characters do not remain on the screen.

^U Pressing ^U causes MBASIC to ignore whatever you are currently entering. If you have entered a line and there are several mistakes, it may be easier to start over with a new line. Type ^U and begin entering the line again.

^A This key sequence allows you to change from direct mode to edit mode. If you are entering a line and you notice you have made an error early in the line, type ^A to enter edit mode. Or if you have typed in a line followed by RETURN and you then notice an error, press ^A before typing anything else and you will be in edit mode.

Type L after entering edit mode to see the line you are editing. If you have entered edit mode with ^A, you can also edit the line numbers. Suppose you are entering a line and forgot the word PRINT, as in this example:

```
10 "NOW IS THE TIME FOR ALL GOOD ░
```

Press ^A and you have

```
!░
```

Entering edit mode in this manner causes an ! to be printed on the left side of the screen without a line number. You may now use all the features of the editor to make your corrections.

^I Pressing ^I works like the tab function. Tabs are set every eight columns. Pressing ^I moves the cursor to the next tab stop. Most terminals have a TAB key.

^C As you already know, ^C can be used to interrupt a program in an endless loop. It can also be used to interrupt any program at any time.

^S Typing this sequence suspends program execution. If there is output on the screen that you would like to review before it moves up, type ^S. The material will stay on the screen, allowing you to examine it. This sequence differs from ^C in that it does not return you to command mode.

```
10 A=5
20 PRINT A;"        ";A+5;"        ";A+10
30 A=A+15
40 GOTO 20
```

```
RUN
 5          10          15
 20         25          30
 35         40          45
 50         55          60
^S
```

^Q This sequence resumes execution of a program that you have stopped by pressing ^S. On some computers, pressing any key will resume execution of the program. However, the standard for most computers that employ ^S to cause a pause during output is to accept only ^Q in order to continue.

```
^Q
 65         70          75
 80         85          90
etc.
```

^O This sequence is used to stop the output of a program. The program continues to run, but no output is displayed at the terminal. Typing ^O a second time resumes the output to the terminal.

```
RUN
 5          10          15
 20         25          30
 35         40          45
 50         55          60
^O

^O
 1005          1010          1015
etc.
```

Of course, the numbers that are displayed when output resumes depend on the time interval to the second ^O.

Continuing a Program [CONT]

After stopping a program with ^C, you can continue its execution from where it left off with the CONT command as long as you have not edited the program or added or deleted lines.

Try this now. Run the previous example.

```
RUN
 5        10        15
 20       25        30
 35       ^C
Stop in Line 20
Ok
```

Your line number may be different. Now give the CONT command and the program will continue execution.

```
40       45
50       55        60
etc.
```

CHANGING A LINE NUMBER

At times you may need to change a line number to move the line to a different position in the program. There are two reasons why you may wish to do this. First, because of an error in programming, you may have placed the line in the wrong spot to begin with, and second, because you want the same or a similar line in another place in the program. You cannot use the RENUM command to change the order. That is, the RENUM command will allow you to change line numbers, but it will not let you copy a line from one place to another. However, you can copy a line by using ^A.

As an example, enter the following program:

```
10 IF A=1000 THEN END
20 A=1
30 PRINT A;"    ";A+1;"    ";A+2
40 A=A+3
50 GOTO 30
```

Either from examining or running the program, you will find there is an error: **IF A = 1000 THEN END** should be placed after line 30. So let's go ahead and change the line number of 10 to 35. To do this, first give the command **EDIT 10** and press RETURN to immediately exit the edit mode. The following will appear on the screen:

```
EDIT 10
10 IF A=1000 THEN END
```

Now before you press any other key, press ^A; you are now in edit mode. Since the last line you were editing was line 10, ^A will put you in edit mode, so that you can edit line 10, including the line number. Press **L** twice to see the line without the line number. Now press **I** and type in 35. Press RETURN, then enter the **LIST** command:

```
LIST
10 IF A=1000 THEN END
20 A=1
30 PRINT A;"    ";A+1;"    ";A+2
35 IF A=1000 THEN END
40 A=A+3
50 GOTO 30
```

Line 10 has been copied to line 35, but it also remains as line 10. You know how to get rid of an unwanted line: type **10** and RETURN. List the program, and you have the desired result:

```
LIST
20 A=1
30 PRINT A;"    ";A+1;"    ";A+2
35 IF A=1000 THEN END
40 A=A+3
50 GOTO 30
```

Practice this a few times. You will find it very useful.

EXERCISES

1. Describe in words the results of the following commands:

   a. RENUM 5,10,15
   b. AUTO 1000,100
   c. DELETE −70
   d. DELETE 70−100
   e. AUTO 3
   f. RENUM 100,90

2. Given the program line

```
120 PRINT "The some is ";A+B+C
```

   with the cursor over the **P**, describe two ways to

   a. Remove the **A+B+C** from the end of the line.
   b. Correct the spelling of **some** to **sum**.
   c. Change the expression to **A+B+C+D**.
   d. Change the expression to **C+A+B**.

6

Formatting Output

Statements:	LLIST, LPRINT, NULL, WIDTH, WIDTH LPRINT, PRINT USING, LPRINT USING
Functions:	TAB, SPC

Up to this point all of our output, whether from a program or the listing of a program, has been to the screen. It is as easy to get a listing of your program on the printer as it is on the screen.

Using the Printer
[LLIST, LPRINT, NULL]

Let's try the printer with the following program:

```
10 A = 5
20 PRINT "  A              1/A          A SQUARED        SQUARE ROOT A"
30 PRINT "-------------------------------------------------------------------"
40 IF A > 130 THEN END
50 PRINT A,1/A,A*A,A^(1/2)
60 A = A + 25
70 GOTO 40
```

Enter the program, give the LIST command, and, of course, the listing will appear on the screen. Now, with your printer turned on and set up properly, give the LLIST command to make the output go to the printer. You will find that you use LLIST more and more as your programs become longer. Locating program errors is more convenient if you have a hard copy, since a hard copy allows you to see the whole program rather than just the portion of the program that appears on the screen. (*Hard copy* means a copy of your program printed on paper, as opposed to a listing on the screen.)

If you now run the program, the output will appear on the screen. Using the editor, change all of the PRINT statements in the program to LPRINT in lines 20, 30, and 50. Chapter 5 explains how to use the EDIT command and all of its options.

For this example, you need to use the insert command (**I**) to place the letter **L** in front of the word PRINT. To do this on line 50, first enter

```
EDIT 50
```

Press **I** for insert. Press the letter **L**:

```
50 L
```

Now press RETURN. The line now looks like this:

```
50 LPRINT A, 1/A, A*A, A^(1/2)
```

Now repeat this on lines 20 and 30, as follows. Run the new program. All the output will go to the printer.

```
RUN
 A              1/A         A SQUARED      SQUARE ROOT A
-----------------------------------------------------------

5               .2             25              2.23607
30              .0333333       900             5.47723
55              .0181818       3025            7.4162
80              .0125          6400            8.94427
105             9.52381E-03    11025           10.247
130             7.69231E-03    16900           11.4018
Ok
```

Even if you intend at the outset to send the output to the printer, it is generally wiser to first write your program using PRINT statements. When the output on the screen is correct, use the editor to change the PRINT statements to LPRINT in order to send the output to the printer.

A statement that may be necessary when working with your particular printer is the NULL command. If the printer does not print some of the characters or lines when you list a program, try giving the command NULL 10. This puts 10 null characters at the end of each line. A *null character* is a character that does not print out. Using null characters is generally only necessary with older model printers, since the purpose of printing them is to slow the stream of characters sent to the printer.

Note that 10 in this command is an arbitrary number. Experiment with smaller or larger numbers to determine the least number of nulls necessary for your printer to work properly.

Setting Line Length [WIDTH, WIDTH LPRINT]

The WIDTH statement is used to set the number of columns (line length) printed on the terminal. If you are using the printer, use WIDTH LPRINT to set the width at the printer. The range of columns that can be used with either the WIDTH or WIDTH LPRINT statements is 15 to 255. If 255 is used, MBASIC will not insert any carriage return character at all, so the width is really infinite. The default value for WIDTH is 80.

Change the WIDTH to 64 columns if you have a 64-column terminal. When you are working with special terminal functions, it is common to set the terminal width to 255 so that your program has complete control over where the output to the terminal or printer is to be printed.

When sending output to the printer on 13-inch-wide paper, set WIDTH LPRINT to 132. This is a common width for many printers. If your printer supports fewer columns, then, of course, you will set it to the maximum width for your printer. WIDTH and WIDTH LPRINT may both be used directly as commands or they may be used as statements in a program.

To get an idea of how the WIDTH statement works, enter and run the following program:

```
10 WIDTH 80
20 I = 1
30 PRINT I,
40 IF I = 20 THEN END
50 I = I + 1
60 GOTO 30

RUN
 1              2              3              4              5
 6              7              8              9              10
 11             12             13             14             15
 16             17             18             19             20
Ok
```

The comma at the end of line 30 causes the numbers to be spread out at 15-column intervals. Since line 10 sets the screen width to 80, MBASIC automatically inserts a carriage return so that each line does not exceed 80 columns.

Now change line 10 to read "10 WIDTH 50", and run the program:

```
RUN
 1              2              3
 4              5              6
 7              8              9
 10             11             12
 13             14             15
 16             17             18
 19             20
Ok
```

Now MBASIC inserts a carriage return in your output to keep lines within 50 columns. Once you give the WIDTH or the WIDTH LPRINT commands, the setting stays in effect until you set it again or until you reload MBASIC. In order to set the width from 50 back to 80 columns, give the WIDTH 80 command.

Positioning the Output
[TAB, SPC]

This is your first encounter with MBASIC functions. *Functions* are small programs built into BASIC to save you the trouble of writing the code in your program. Many of the functions are used frequently by all programmers; others are very seldom used. The use that you make of a particular function depends largely on the type of programming you do. Here we will use two functions, TAB and SPC. Others will be introduced throughout this text as the programs bring them into play.

The TAB function is similar to the TAB key on a typewriter. It moves the cursor to the position specified in the *argument,* which is enclosed in parentheses. If the cursor is already beyond that column, it moves to that column on the next line.

Enter and run the following:

```
10 PRINT "TENANT";TAB(30);"RENT"
20 PRINT "SMITH, JOHN";TAB(30);"$425.00"
```

```
RUN
TENANT                        RENT
SMITH, JOHN                   $425.00
Ok
```

The TAB function has a range of 0 to 255 positions. Of course, you will not use large values like 255 unless your printer or screen can handle a very wide margin. The TAB function may be used with either the PRINT or LPRINT statements, but you cannot use it in any other statements.

Run the following example in which the TAB argument is a variable:

```
10 L = 5
20 PRINT TAB(L);"BOO";
30 IF L = 25 THEN END
40 L = L + 5
50 GOTO 20
```

```
RUN
     BOO  BOO  BOO  BOO  BOO
Ok
```

SPACING IN YOUR OUTPUT

The SPC function is also used to position the output from your program. The output is placed the number of spaces to the right of the current cursor position that is indicated in the SPC function argument. Try this by replacing TAB with SPC in the two previous examples. Note the change in output:

```
10 PRINT "TENANT";SPC(30);"RENT"
20 PRINT "SMITH, JOHN";SPC(30)"$425.00"


RUN
TENANT                              RENT
SMITH, JOHN                              $425.00
Ok


10 L = 5
20 PRINT SPC(L); "BOO";
30 IF L=25 THEN END
40 L = L + 5
50 GOTO 20


RUN
     BOO          BOO               BOO                    BOO
       BOO
Ok
```

Formatting Numeric Output
[PRINT USING, LPRINT USING]

All the programs you will write will produce output in one form or another, whether to the screen, to the printer, or to a disk file. The PRINT USING statement is a versatile tool for formatting this output.

SCREEN OUTPUT

With PRINT USING you can right-justify, align decimal points, or insert commas and dollar signs. The syntax of the PRINT USING command is

PRINT USING formatstring; output

The *formatstring* is a list of special characters that specify how the *output* is to be printed. Here is an example of a PRINT USING command:

```
10 PRINT USING "##.#-";CASH
```

Any characters in the format string that are not specific formatting codes are printed out exactly.

The various characters that are used in the format string are illustrated in the following discussion. Examples will be given for each individual case. Combinations of these format strings will be shown at the end of this section.

\#	The number sign (#) is used within the format string to represent numeric positions. If fewer numbers are printed than are called for by the number of positions in the string, then the numbers will be right-justified. Right-justified refers to the numbers against the right-hand side of the field (for example, right-justified: | 23|; left-justified: |23 |).

```
10 A = 8263:B = 17
20 PRINT USING "¦######¦";A
30 PRINT USING "¦######¦";B

RUN
¦  8263¦
¦    17¦
Ok
```

A decimal point may be placed at any position in the format string between the number signs. If there are more positions to the right of the decimal point in the number than the format string calls for, the number will be rounded off. If there are fewer, zeros will be added.

```
10 A=1432.676:B=12.3
20 PRINT USING "#####.##";A
30 PRINT USING "#####.##";B

RUN
 1432.68
   12.30
Ok
```

\+ A plus sign may be placed at the beginning or end of the format string. This causes the sign of the number, either a plus or a minus, to be placed before or after the number, depending on where in the format string you place the plus sign.

```
10 A=96.341:B=-31.67
20 PRINT USING "+###.##";A
30 PRINT USING "+###.##";B
40 PRINT USING "###.##+";A


RUN
 +96.34
 -31.67
 96.34+
Ok
```

– The negative or minus sign at the end of the format string causes a minus sign to be printed *after* negative numbers.

```
10 A=-48.44:B=123
20 PRINT USING "####.##-";A
30 PRINT USING "####.##-";B


RUN
  48.44-
 123.00
Ok
```

Notice that the variable **B** is not printed with a trailing minus sign (–), since it is a positive number.

** Two asterisks placed at the beginning of the format string cause the leading spaces to be filled with asterisks. The two asterisks also indicate two print positions.

```
10 A=167.341
20 PRINT USING "**######.##";A


RUN
*****167.34
Ok
```

$$ Two dollar signs at the beginning of the format string cause a dollar sign to be printed immediately to the left of

the output. The two dollar signs also indicate two print positions, one of which is the dollar sign.

```
10 A=97.128
20 PRINT USING "$$###.##";A
```

```
RUN
  $97.13
Ok
```

**$ Two asterisks and a dollar sign placed at the beginning of the format string combine the effects of two asterisks and two dollar signs, causing asterisks to fill in blank spaces if spaces should occur and also causing a dollar sign to be placed immediately to the left of the number. This indicates three print positions.

```
10 A=73.04
20 PRINT USING "**$######.##";A
```

```
RUN
******$73.04
Ok
```

A comma preceding the decimal causes a comma to occur to the left of every third digit to the left of the decimal, which is useful for representing numbers in multiples of 1000.

```
10 A=1723841
20 PRINT USING "#########,.##";A
```

```
RUN
 1,723,840.00
Ok
```

A comma at the right of the format string causes the numbers printed to be separated by a comma.

```
10 A=17:B=88:C=142
20 PRINT USING "###.##,";A;B;C
```

```
RUN
 17.00, 88.00,142.00,
Ok
```

^^^^ Four carets (^^^^) placed after the last number sign (#) will cause the number to be printed in exponential notation.

```
10 A=.00043
20 PRINT USING "##.##^^^^";A

RUN
 4.30E-04
Ok
```

_ An underscore (_) placed in a format string causes the next character to be taken as literal.

```
10 A=421
20 PRINT USING "_####_#";A

RUN
#421#
Ok
```

If the percent sign (%) is printed to the left of a number in your output, this indicates that the number you are trying to place in the field is larger than the format string. The limit on the size of a number substituted in the format string of a PRINT USING statement is 24 digits.

```
10 A=1631
20 PRINT USING "###";A

RUN
%1631
Ok
```

If additional variables are added to the end of your PRINT USING statement, they will continue to reuse the fields on an alternate basis until all variables have been printed. For instance, more than one variable may be assigned to the same format field.

```
10 A=9347.102 :B=16.786 :C=298432.1
20 PRINT USING "########,.##";A;B;C

RUN
    9,347.10       16.79  298,432.00
Ok
```

USING A FORMAT VARIABLE

A useful way to vary the PRINT USING statement is to set a string variable equal to the format string at the beginning of your program. Then you may use the string variable at any point. This is a particularly useful technique in programs dealing with dollars and cents, since the same format string may be used in these programs at several points.

```
10 FORMAT$ ="$$######,.##"
20 A=6784.5
30 PRINT USING FORMAT$;A

RUN
   $6,784.50
Ok
```

Further examples of the PRINT USING statement, with various combinations of the symbols just discussed, are presented in the following discussion.

Note that more than one format field may be included in the same format string as follows:

```
10 A=12362 : B=95.786
20 PRINT USING "**#########,.##      $$#####.##";A;B
30 REM              FIELD 1           FIELD 2

RUN
*****12,362.00         $95.79
Ok
```

The format string is everything between the double quotation marks. In this example the format string contains two fields. The number of spaces you have between your fields, whatever it is, will be retained in the output. The number of fields contained in a format string is, in fact, restricted only by the length of the line.

Now let's go back and take a look at the example we introduced at the beginning of this chapter. Clear the memory of your computer and load the first example of Chapter 6. Using the editor, change lines 20 and 50 so that the program appears as follows:

```
10 A = 5
20 PRINT TAB(2);"A";TAB(11);"1/A";TAB(21);"A SQUARED";TAB(32);"SQUARE ROOT A"
30 PRINT "-------------------------------------------"
40 IF A>130 THEN END
50 PRINT USING "###     #.####     #######.###      ##.###";A,1/A,A*A,A^(1/2)
60 A=A+25
70 GOTO 40
```

Run the program and you have the following output:

```
RUN
 A        1/A       A SQUARED  SQUARE ROOT A
----------------------------------------------
  5     0.2000        25.000        2.236
 30     0.0333       900.000        5.477
 55     0.0182      3025.000        7.416
 80     0.0125      6400.000        8.944
105     0.0095     11025.000       10.247
130     0.0077     16900.000       11.402
Ok
```

Two major changes have been made in this program. In line 20 we have used the TAB function in order to better control the table heading. In line 50 the PRINT USING statement with four fields in the format string is used to control the output from our variables. In line 30 a small change was made, shortening the line that underlines the heading. Run the program and note the output is presented in a much neater fashion than at the beginning of the chapter, before we had access to the PRINT USING statement. You will use the PRINT USING statement in almost all of the programs that you write from this point on. Work with it until you can use it quickly and with confidence.

PRINTER OUTPUT

When you wished to send output to the printer, you changed PRINT to LPRINT. Now use the editor to change PRINT USING to LPRINT USING. The output will be sent to the printer instead of to the screen.

Formatting String Output

Now let's take a look at the three format characters used with PRINT USING for string output.

\n spaces\ The backslashes tell MBASIC to leave the same number of characters for the string as there are spaces between the quotation marks, that is, two more than the number of spaces between the back-slashes. Enter and run the following:

```
10 A$="ABCDEFG"
20 PRINT USING "\    \";A$     ' 4 spaces between "\"
30 PRINT USING "\  \";A$       ' 2 spaces between "\"
40 PRINT USING "\\";A$         ' 0 spaces between "\"

RUN
ABCDEF
ABCD
AB
Ok
```

! The exclamation mark (!) indicates that only the first character of the string is to be printed. Add the following line to your program:

```
50 PRINT USING "!"; A$
RUN
ABCDEF
ABCD
AB
A
Ok
```

& The ampersand tells MBASIC to allow space for the complete string to be printed.

```
10 LAST$ = "SMITH":FIRST$ = "MIKE":ADD$ = "123 OAK ST."
20 CITY$ = "MARTINEZ":STATE$="CA":ZIP$="94553"
30 PRINT USING "&, & :& :& :& :&";LAST$;FIRST$;ADD$;CITY$;STATE$;ZIP$

RUN
SMITH, MIKE :123 OAK ST. :MARTINEZ :CA :94553
Ok
```

Combining Strings

Two strings may be joined (concatenated) with the plus (+) operator to create a third string. Try this with the following example:

```
10 A$="GOOF"
20 B$="BALL"
30 C$=A$+B$
40 PRINT C$;" ";"SURPRISED?"

RUN
GOOFBALL SURPRISED?
Ok
```

It makes no difference whether the strings are assigned to variables with an assignment statement or an INPUT statement. Try the following:

```
10 INPUT "Enter first number (A$) ";A$
20 INPUT "Enter second number (B$) ";B$
30 C$=A$+B$
40 PRINT "A$ + B$ = ";C$

RUN
Enter first number (A$) ? 246
Enter second number (B$) ? 135
A$ + B$ = 246135
Ok
```

In the following example, you may use a space between strings as is done in line 30; or you can directly print out strings that are added together without assigning them to a variable, as is done in line 50.

```
10 LAST$="NEUMAN"
20 FIRST$="ALFRED"
30 A$=FIRST$+" "+LAST$
40 PRINT A$
50 PRINT LAST$+", "+FIRST$

RUN
Alfred Neuman
Neuman, Alfred
Ok
```

Now let's use some of these new ideas in our applications.

TUTORIALS

Tutorial 6-1: Interest

Here is a simple program for compound interest. The program determines how much interest you would receive on a savings account that is compounded monthly. It also tells you what your principal will be at the end of each month and what your current balance is.

```
10 REM -                -=*INTEREST.C6*=-
20 REM -                Simple Interest Table
30 REM -                11/25/82
40 REM -
100 INPUT "Enter yearly interest rate in percent %",RATE
110 RATE = RATE/100                     'Convert RATE to a decimal
120 INPUT "Enter starting balance $",BALANCE
130 INPUT "Enter number of years to calculate: ",YEAR
140 PRINT
150 PRINT "Month    principal   interest     balance"
160 PRINT "-----  -----------  ---------  -----------"
170 FRMT$=" ###   $$######,.##  $$###.###  $$######,.##"
180 MONTH = 1                           'Start at month 1
190 IF MONTH > 12*YEAR THEN 260         'Are we done yet?
200 PRINCIPAL = BALANCE                 'Principal is last month's balance
210 INTEREST = PRINCIPAL*RATE*(1/12)    'Compute interest on princpal
220 BALANCE = PRINCIPAL + INTEREST      'Compute new balance
230 PRINT USING FRMT$;MONTH;PRINCIPAL;INTEREST;BALANCE
240 MONTH = MONTH + 1
250 GOTO 190
260 PRINT
270 PRINT USING "Ending balance:                **$####,.##";BALANCE
280 END
```

In line 110 the interest rate is converted to a decimal by dividing the percentage by 100. Lines 190 through 220 contain the main part of the program in which all the calculations are done.

Pay particular attention to line 230. Here, our PRINT USING statement is included with the format variable **FRMT$**, which controls all of the output. Notice that in line 170, the variable **FRMT$** is exactly the same length as the heading in the PRINT statement in lines 150 and 160. Using a variable for a format string allows you to place your format string directly under the headings, as it is here, so that you can see immediately that everything will line up properly and so that you do not have to return to make continual adjustments to get the spacing in your format string correct.

Keep in mind that we are using the default precision for variables, which means that we have only six places in our output. So this program will work accurately for figures up to $9,999.99. If you enter a starting balance over this amount, you will only have accuracy to six places. Here are the results of running the program with a starting balance of $1,000:

```
RUN
Enter yearly interest rate in percent %12
Enter starting balance $1000
Enter number of years to calculate: 1

Month    principal    interest      balance
-----  -----------  ----------  -----------
  1     $1,000.00     $10.000    $1,010.00
  2     $1,010.00     $10.100    $1,020.10
  3     $1,020.10     $10.201    $1,030.30
  4     $1,030.30     $10.303    $1,040.60
  5     $1,040.60     $10.406    $1,051.01
  6     $1,051.01     $10.510    $1,061.52
  7     $1,061.52     $10.615    $1,072.14
  8     $1,072.14     $10.721    $1,082.86
  9     $1,082.86     $10.829    $1,093.69
 10     $1,093.69     $10.937    $1,104.62
 11     $1,104.62     $11.046    $1,115.67
 12     $1,115.67     $11.157    $1,126.83

Ending balance:                  **$1,126.83
Ok
```

Enter this program and save it, using the name INTEREST.C6. We will return to this program in the next chapter when we introduce double-precision variables, which will enable you to change the program to work with larger values.

Tutorial 6-2: Addresses

This second application will print out, in mailing label format, the information that is contained in the data statements.

```
10 REM -                   -=*LABEL.C6*=-
20 REM -                   Print mailing labels
30 REM -                   12/07/82
40 REM -
100 COL = 4                  'First column for labels
110 READ COUNT               'Get number of names
120 IF COUNT = 0 THEN 200   'Done when count = 0
```

(*Tutorial 6-2: Continued*)

```
130 READ NAM$,STREET$,CITY$,STATE$,ZIP$ 'Read in one record
140 LPRINT:LPRINT                       'Skip down onto label
150 LPRINT TAB(COL);NAM$                'Print one label
160 LPRINT TAB(COL);STREET$
170 LPRINT TAB(COL) USING "&, &. &";CITY$;STATE$;ZIP$
180 COUNT = COUNT - 1
190 GOTO 120
200 END
210 '
220 'Mailing list data.  First data is the number of names.
230 '
240 DATA 2
250 DATA "MIKE RAMSEY","1275 ELSWORTH ST. APT 8","BERKELEY","CA","94704"
260 DATA "JERRY SMITH","938 WALNUT AVE.","MARTINEZ","CA","94553"
```

In line 100 the column number in which each label is to begin is assigned to the variable **COL**. This variable is used in lines 150 through 170 as an argument to the TAB function. It is easier to change the column number in this one line than to have to make the correction in the three lines where TAB is used. Line 240 contains the number of records that are contained in your data statements and is read into the variable **COUNT**.

This program is set up for the printer. If you wish to run it on the screen, change your LPRINT statements to PRINT statements. The program uses the TAB function in conjunction with the LPRINT USING statement. Notice how you specify these together on lines 150 through 170. The TAB function must be included between LPRINT and USING. Using the TAB function after the USING will cause an error. Of course, if output were going to the screen, the TAB would be used between the PRINT and USING statements.

When you run this program, it will print out the names and addresses in the mailing label format shown below.

```
MIKE RAMSEY
1275 ELSWORTH ST. APT 8
BERKELEY, CA. 94704

JERRY SMITH
938 WALNUT AVE.
MARTINEZ, CA. 94553
Ok
```

Tutorial 6-3: Payroll

Load the payroll program from Tutorial 4-3. This time we are going to make only one minor change.

```
10 REM -                    -=*PAYROLL.C6*=-
20 REM -                    Payroll with PRINT USING
30 REM -                    12/07/82
40 REM -
100 INPUT "Number of widgets produced per day? ",WIDGETS
110 TOTAL.WAGES = 0
120 READ EMP.RATE
130    IF EMP.RATE = 0 THEN 170          'Zero rate signals end of data
140    EMP.EARN = EMP.RATE*8             'Compute employee earnings
150    TOTAL.WAGES = TOTAL.WAGES + EMP.EARN     'Total employee wages
160 GOTO 120
170 UNIT.COST = TOTAL.WAGES/WIDGETS      'Compute unit cost
180 PRINT USING "Unit cost = $$####.##";UNIT.COST
190 END
200 DATA 4.78,5.01,7.43,0
```

Notice that in line 180, the PRINT USING statement is used to control the output. In this example of the PRINT USING statement, an additional feature has been added: namely, the fact that a string may be incorporated in the format string (in this case, "Unit cost =").

```
RUN
Number of widgets produced per day? 42
Unit cost =     $3.28
Ok
```

EXERCISES

1. With the PRINT USING format string, print the following numbers with dollar signs and appropriate commas to separate thousands. Round off each number to the nearest penny. Use the following data: 7.3845, 6752.7, and 433.789.

2. Write a program to convert from the Fahrenheit temperature scale to the Celsius temperature scale for a range of Fahrenheit temperatures from 30 degrees to

215 degrees. Print your results out on both the screen and the printer, showing the results for each five degrees of change in the Fahrenheit scale. Use the formula C=5×(F−32)/9.

3. Write a program to read in the following data and print it out in table format, as shown below, with an appropriate heading. Use the following data:

Name	Age	Sex	Phone #
Mike	24	M	413-2807
Laura	23	F	214-5712
Alice	28	F	671-4242
Sam	26	M	683-9896

4. Given the following data, write a program to determine each student's grade. Find the average score for each student, and print out the names and average scores of only those students with an average score of less than 70%.

Name	Score (in %)
Mary	63, 51, 78, 71
Don	83, 62, 91, 51
Frank	72, 77, 61, 52
Betty	44, 83, 71, 68

5. Write a program to determine the amount of interest you will pay each month on a loan of $6000, where the interest is 14 1/2% per year. Use $250 as your monthly payment. Show the results in table form, indicating the interest paid each month and the remaining balance. Use the formula I=P×R×T (where P is the principal, R is the rate of interest, and T is the time in years).

7

Working With Variables And Loops

Statements: DEFINT, DEFSNG, DEFDBL, DEFSTR, FOR/NEXT, WHILE/WEND

Declaration Characters: %, !, #

Operators: \, MOD

Up to this point, the only *declaration character* we have used is the dollar sign ($) to indicate our string variables. For numeric variables we have been using *single precision*, but that is because it is the default variable type for MBASIC, not because we set the values that way. Now let's take a look at each of these numeric declaration characters in turn.

Variable Types
[%, !, #]

In Chapter 2, we introduced string variables and numeric variables. There are actually three types of numeric variables: integer, single precision, and double precision.

INTEGER VARIABLES

A percent sign (%) at the end of a variable name indicates that the variable is an *integer variable* (for example, NUMBER%). The range for integers in MBASIC is −32768 to +32767. This range is determined by the architecture of the computer, and just happens to be plus or minus 2 raised to the fifteenth power (2^{15}).

Enter and run the following:

```
10 A% = 4:B% = 7.3:C% = 7.7
20 PRINT A%,B%,C%,A
```

```
RUN
 4             7             8             0
Ok
```

Each of our variables, regardless of what we set it equal to in the program, is stored in MBASIC as an integer rounded off to the nearest whole number; that is, the 7.3 rounds to 7, and 7.7 rounds to 8. Note also that the final value in the output is 0. Since **A** has not been assigned, it takes on the default value set by MBASIC, 0. **A** and **A%** are two distinct variables, just as much so as if we had used completely different letters in their names.

SINGLE-PRECISION VARIABLES

If a variable name terminates with an exclamation mark (!), it is a *single-precision* variable. Single-precision numbers are numbers with six places (for example, 4.31467 or 431467). It makes no difference whether or not there is a decimal point. Single precision is the default value set by MBASIC if we do not set the precision. All of the numeric variables you have used so far were single precision. Enter and run the following:

```
10 A!=3.714
20 PRINT A!,A
```

```
RUN
 3.714          3.714
Ok
```

Please note that **A!** and **A** are the same variable, since they are both variable names with the same precision. This would also be true of any other variable; **B** is the same as **B!**, **GIRAFF** is the same as **GIRAFF!**, and so on.

DOUBLE-PRECISION VARIABLES

Terminating the variable with a number sign (#) indicates that it is *double precision* (for example, NUMBER#). Double-precision numeric variables are variables that hold 16 places (for example, 4,312,896,345,214,791). Notice that double precision is actually almost three times as precise as single precision. Again it makes no difference whether or not the number contains a decimal. Enter and run the following:

```
10 A# = 9
20 B# = 1
30 C# = B#/A#
40 PRINT C#

RUN
 .1111111111111111
Ok
```

This program prints out the result with accuracy to 16 places.

Now consider the following program. The output variable **C#** is declared double precision, and indeed the output has 16 places. But only the first six are necessarily accurate, since the variables **A** and **B** are by default single precision. To ensure double-precision accuracy, the output variable and at least one of the variables involved in the calculation must be double precision.

```
10 A = 9
20 B = 1
30 C# = B/A
40 PRINT C#

RUN
 .1111111119389534
Ok
```

Since we want the answer to be .1111111111111111, the numerator must also be double precision. Enter and run the following:

```
10 A# = 1/9
20 B# = 1#/9
30 PRINT A#,B#

RUN
 .1111111119389534           .1111111111111111
Ok
```

In this example we show how a type declaration may be used with constants. In line 10, the division was carried out with single-precision accuracy before it was assigned to the double-precision variable A#. To overcome this problem, declare one of the constants double precision if any mathematical operation is to be performed. Then when the result is assigned to a double-precision variable, the output will be accurate to 16 places.

The last declaration character is the dollar sign ($). You have already used this a great many times to declare your string variables, so we will not give further examples here.

Defining Variable Types [DEFINT, DEFSNG, DEFDBL, DEFSTR]

In addition to declaring variable types with the declaration characters (%, !, #, $) discussed in the previous section, you may also use MBASIC's DEF statements for this purpose. *DEF* stands for define.

There are four of these DEF statements:

DEFINT	Define variables as integers
DEFSNG	Define variables as single precision
DEFDBL	Define variables as double precision
DEFSTR	Define variables as string variables.

These statements are followed by one or more ranges of letters. The range of letters indicates that all the variables that *start* with these letters will be of the declared type. Enter and run the following:

```
10 DEFINT A-C
20 DEFSNG D-F
30 DEFDBL G-I
40 A = 5#/7# : D = 5#/7# : G = 5#/7#
50 PRINT A,D,G
```

```
RUN
 1             .714286       .7142857142857143
Ok
```

All variables in your program beginning with the letters **A** through **C** will be integers. Those variables beginning with the letters **D** through **F** will be single precision, and those beginning with the letters **G** through **I** will be double precision.

Add the following to the last example:

```
60 H=G:H!=G:H%=G
70 PRINT H,H!,H%
```

Run the program and you have the following:

```
RUN
 1             .714286       .7142857142857143
.7142857142857143            .714286       1
Ok
```

In the second line of output generated by line 70, you have the values held by **H, H!**, and **H%**. **H** is declared double precision in line 30; therefore, it prints out 16 places. **H!** and **H%** print out six and one places respectively, since the declaration characters ! and % override the precision set by the DEF statement.

You may also show a single letter, range of letters, or combination to define the starting letters. For example, DEFINT A-L, N, P-Q defines all variables starting with the letters A through L, N, and P through Q as integer.

STRING TYPE

Use the DEF statement to define strings for any given letter combination that you choose. We point it out here because MBASIC supports this statement, but we strongly recommend that you stay in the habit of using the declaration character $ when assigning strings to variables. This makes it considerably easier to read your program later, since you can quickly see which variables are strings and which are numeric.

```
10 DEFSTR A-B
20 A = "NAME":B = "PHONE NUMBER":C = "AGE"
30 PRINT A,,B,C

RUN
Type mismatch in 20
Ok
```

You may already have run across this little error message in your programming. In this case it comes from the fact that in line 10 only the variables starting with the letters A and B are defined as string variables. Notice that in line 20, **C** is set equal to the string **AGE.** Consequently, you get the "Type mismatch" error message. To fix this, you could edit line 10 so that your program appears as follows, and run the program. However, to be safe use the $.

```
10 DEFSTR A-C
20 A = "NAME":B = "PHONE NUMBER":C = "AGE"
30 PRINT A,,B,C

RUN
NAME                          PHONE NUMBER  AGE
Ok
```

One point of interest in the output from this program is the large separation between **NAME** and **PHONE NUMBER.** This is caused by the extra comma between the variables **A** and **B**, which means that the string constant represented by **B** will begin in column 30.

Integer Division
[\]

It is appropriate to use the lowest numeric precision that is suitable for your program (to save memory space). It is also appropriate to use integer division when you are sure that the result is an integer. This operator may not noticeably increase the speed of your program for a single line of code, but when used many times in a long program, it can significantly decrease the time of execution for the entire program. Keep in mind that the symbol for integer division is the backslash (\), as opposed to the division symbol (/).

Here is an example of integer division:

```
10 FOR I = TO 5
20     PRINT (I + 5)/I, (I + 5)\I, INT((I + 5)/I)
30 NEXT
```

Running this program shows that the result of using the INT function and integer division (\) will always be the same.

Modulus Arithmetic
[MOD]

The MOD operator gives the integer value that is the remainder when integer division is performed. Although this operator is not commonly used, it does come in handy for some applications.

For example, suppose you had $100 and wanted to buy as many widgets as possible at $17 each. Integer division would tell you how many you could buy with this amount of money, but the MOD operator would tell you how much money you would have left over. MOD is an operator rather than a function. The distinction between the two terms operator and function has to do with the syntax of how they are written in MBASIC.

The syntax for using the MOD operator is A MOD B, where A and B are numbers.

```
10 PRINT 7 MOD 4
20 PRINT 14 MOD 3


RUN
 3
 2
Ok
```

Working with Loops
[FOR/NEXT]

This section introduces one of MBASIC's more powerful programming tools, the FOR/NEXT loop. So far you have used two methods of ending a loop: dummy data and a counter. Now let's take a look at a third method: the FOR/NEXT loop.

The FOR/NEXT loop allows you to automatically perform a given task a specified number of times. Enter and run the following:

```
10 FOR A=1 TO 10
20    PRINT A;
30 NEXT A
40 END

RUN
 1  2  3  4  5  6  7  8  9  10
Ok
```

The FOR and NEXT statements provide a very convenient way of setting up a loop. The variable of the FOR statement, in this case **A**, is referred to as the *counter.* The counter of the FOR statement is incremented from an initial value until it reaches a final value. In this case, its initial value is set at 1 and its final value at 10 in line 10. Line 20 prints the current value of the counter **A**. Line 30 increments **A** by 1 and then jumps back to line 20 and repeats this looping process until **A** becomes 11, at which point line 40 is executed.

Notice the indentation of the previous example in line 20. This is common practice and a good habit for you to get into now. In all of your FOR/NEXT loops, indent the lines that occur between the FOR and the NEXT, regardless of how many lines there are. We will use this procedure throughout the text.

Here is how MBASIC actually executes our sample FOR/NEXT loop:

```
10 A = 1
11 IF A > 10 THEN 40
20    PRINT A
30 A = A+1: GOTO 11
40 END
```

Now let's look at a second example, which shows that you are not restricted to printing out the counter within the loop. Your program may perform any function that you wish.

```
10 FOR A = 1 TO 10
20   PRINT B;
30   B = B + 3
40 NEXT A

RUN
 0  3  6  9  12  15  18  21  24  27
Ok
```

You are not restricted to incrementing your counter by 1. If you wish your increment to be something other than 1, you must add a STEP statement to the line containing the FOR statement. If you do not declare your step value, it is always assumed to be +1.

```
10 FOR B = -15 TO 25 STEP 5
20    PRINT B;
30 NEXT B
```

```
RUN
-15 -10 -5  0  5  10  15  20  25
Ok
```

All values in the FOR/NEXT loop (counter, upper and lower bounds, and the step size) must be integer or single precision. In this example, the **STEP** equals 5. Notice also that the counter starts at −15. The counter may start at any positive or negative value that can be written with a single-precision number. You may also increment your counter in a negative direction. Any time that you use a negative STEP, the term STEP must be present, even if you want it to be −1.

```
10 PRINT
20 FOR C = 10 TO 5 STEP -.5
30    PRINT C;
40 NEXT C
```

```
RUN

 10  9.5  9  8.5  8  7.5  7  6.5  6  5.5  5
Ok
```

Of course, you can use FOR/NEXT loops with any operation including string operations. Notice that in this first example, the counter is used as the argument for the TAB function to create a set of descending **HELLO** stairs.

```
10 FOR X = 1 TO 5
20   PRINT TAB(X);"HELLO"
30 NEXT X
```

```
RUN
HELLO
 HELLO
  HELLO
   HELLO
    HELLO
Ok
```

One of the more natural uses of the FOR/NEXT loop is to control the reading of data using the counter method. The FOR/NEXT loop has the termination of the loop built in. Enter and run the following example:

```
10 READ COUNT
20 FOR X = 1 TO COUNT
30   READ A$
40   PRINT A$;" ";
50 NEXT X
60 DATA 5
70 DATA "PEG","SAM","LARRY","BRENDA","MIKE"

RUN
PEG SAM LARRY BRENDA MIKE
Ok
```

PATTERNS

Although this next example is not very useful in application programming, it is very helpful in aiding you to better understand FOR/NEXT loops. You will be using FOR/NEXT loops in many programs you write in the future. Follow the steps through carefully so that you understand why the output is in the position it is in, and why the second FOR/NEXT loop is necessary.

```
10 FOR X = 1 TO 5
20    PRINT TAB(X);"**";TAB(12 - X);"**"
30 NEXT X
40 PRINT TAB(6);"**"
50 FOR X = 5 TO 1 STEP -1
60    PRINT TAB(X);"**";TAB(12 - X);"**"
70 NEXT X

RUN
**        **
 **      **
  **    **
   **  **
    ****
     **
    ****
   **  **
  **    **
 **      **
**        **
Ok
```

You see that if we try to complete this pattern with only one FOR/NEXT loop, when the cursor gets to the lower half of the X pattern, it would print the right leg of the X and then attempt to print the left leg on the same line. Since the left leg has smaller column values than the right leg, this would not be possible. Consequently, we need the second FOR/NEXT loop (lines 50 through 70) in order to print the lower-left leg of the X before the lower-right leg.

The key point is that in line 20 the argument for the first TAB function, **(X)**, cannot be greater than the argument, **(12−X)**, of the second TAB function. This would also hold true if the TAB functions were in different lines and there were no carriage return printed between the functions.

An interesting way to get around this problem is to combine the FOR/NEXT loop with an IF/THEN/ELSE statement, as follows:

```
10 FOR X = 1 TO 11
20    IF X<=5 THEN PRINT TAB(X);"**";TAB(12-X);"**"
            ELSE IF X=6 THEN PRINT TAB(6) "**"
            ELSE PRINT TAB(12-X);"**";TAB(X);"**"
30 NEXT X

RUN
**         **
 **       **
  **     **
   **   **
    ****
     **
    ****
   **   **
  **     **
 **       **
**         **
Ok
```

Notice that line 20 takes up *three* lines and is typed in by pressing LINEFEED at the end of the first two lines.

NESTED FOR/NEXT LOOPS

FOR/NEXT loops may also be nested one inside the other. Enter and run the following problem:

```
10 PRINT "-=* COUNT DOWN *=-"
20 FOR X = 10 TO 1 STEP -1
30   PRINT X
40 NEXT X
50 PRINT "-=* BLAST OFF *=-"

RUN
-=* COUNT DOWN *=-
 10
 9
```

```
8
7
6
5
4
3
2
1
-=* BLAST OFF *=-
Ok
```

The program ran extremely fast—too fast even for NASA. Let's slow it down by using a nested loop. Add line 35:

```
35    FOR Y = 1 TO 500:NEXT Y
```

Run the program again and notice how much slower the countdown goes. The reason is that the line you added causes the computer to count from 1 to 500 without any printout between each of the successive numbers that are printed. You can experiment with this and use the editor to change the value 500 to some other value in order to make the countdown proceed at a pace that is satisfactory.

The difficulty that some programmers have when starting with nested FOR/NEXT loops is illustrated in the following figures. Figure 7-1 illustrates a correct nesting of FOR/NEXT loops. Notice that

```
10   FOR X = 1 TO A
      |          .
      |          .
      |          .
      |          .
50    |  FOR Y = 1 TO B
      |  |       .
      |  |       .
      |  |       .
      |  |       .
80    |  NEXT Y
      |          .
      |          .
      |          .
      |          .
100  NEXT X
```

Figure 7-1.
Correctly nested loop

the lines connecting the **FOR X** to the **NEXT X** and the **FOR Y** to the **NEXT Y** do not cross. Figure 7-2 shows the wrong way. It shows that the lines connecting the **FOR X** to the **NEXT X** and the **FOR Y** to the **NEXT Y** cross incorrectly. You must be careful when you nest the loops to be sure that one is completely inside the other. Regardless of the depth to which you nest the loops, be sure the lines connecting the FOR/NEXT do not cross. If you create crossing loops, you will get a "NEXT without FOR" error message.

PATTERNS WITH NESTED LOOPS

Let's return for a moment to our patterns, this time with nested loops. In the next two examples, notice not only the general shape of the output, but also the numbers that are printed:

```
10 FOR A=1 TO 5
20   FOR B=1 TO A
30      PRINT B;
40   NEXT B
50   PRINT
60 NEXT A
```

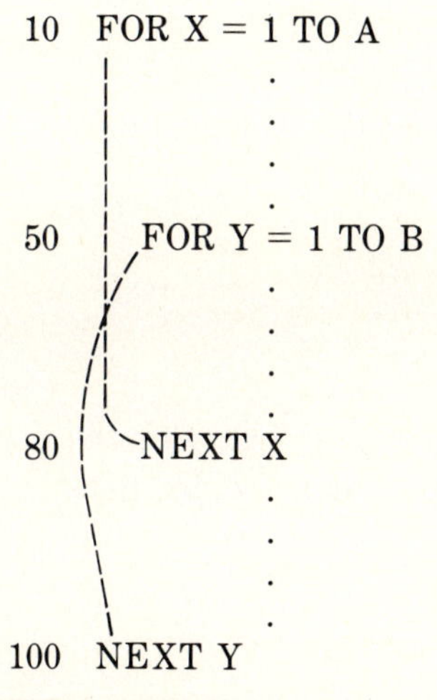

Figure 7-2.
Incorrectly nested loop

```
RUN
 1
 1  2
 1  2  3
 1  2  3  4
 1  2  3  4  5
Ok
```

When you come across a new idea like this in a program, a good procedure is to trace this program through with pencil and paper. *Trace* here means that you are to simulate the computer and determine the value for each variable of each line in the program. Usually, it only takes two or three passes through the program to see what is happening.

In the preceding example, on the first pass **A** = 1, so the inner loop is

```
20 FOR B = 1 TO 1
30     PRINT B;                Output:     1
40 NEXT B
50 PRINT
```

On the second pass **A** = 2, and the inner loop is

```
20 FOR B = 1 TO 2
30     PRINT B;                Output:     1 2
40 NEXT B
50 PRINT
```

On the third pass **A** = 3, so that the inner loop is

```
20 FOR B = 1 TO 3
30     PRINT B;                Output:     1 2 3
40 NEXT B
50 PRINT
```

Continue the trace until you are satisfied with the pattern.

Let's use the same technique, the trace, to check the output of this program, as follows:

```
10 FOR A = 1 TO 5
20     FOR B = 1 TO A
30         PRINT A;
40     NEXT B
50     PRINT
60 NEXT A
```

```
RUN
 1
 2  2
 3  3  3
 4  4  4  4
 5  5  5  5  5
Ok
```

On the first pass **A** = 1, so that the inner loop is

```
20 FOR B = 1 TO 1
30    PRINT A;              Output:        1
40 NEXT B
50 PRINT
```

On the second pass **A** = 2, so that the inner loop is

```
20 FOR B = 1 TO 2
30    PRINT A;              Output:        2 2
40 NEXT B
50 PRINT
```

On the third pass **A** = 3, so that the inner loop is

```
20 FOR B = 1 TO 3
30    PRINT A;              Output:        3 3 3
40 NEXT B
50 PRINT
```

This procedure of tracing a program can be very useful with short programs or with sections of longer programs, either to help you understand the program better or to find errors.

Now let's try another type of loop.

WHILE/WEND Loops

[WHILE/WEND]

The WHILE/WEND loop is similar to the FOR/NEXT loop except that instead of repeating the loop a fixed number of times, it repeats the loop as long as a specified condition is true. (WEND stands for "While END".) You will find the WHILE/WEND loop very useful for controlling the reading of data using the dummy data method. Note that there is no variable after WEND. If you forget to terminate your WHILE loop with WEND, you will receive the error message, "WHILE without WEND".

In a WHILE/WEND loop, you must set an initial condition before the loop is entered. This is usually done through either an assignment statement or a READ statement, as shown in the following:

```
10 A = 1 : B = 1
20 WHILE A<200
30    PRINT A;
40    B = B + 1
50    A = B ^ 2
60 WEND

RUN
 1  4  9  16  25  36  49  64  81  100  121  144  169  196
Ok
```

In this example, each time the loop returns to line 20, **A** is tested to see that it is still less than 200. Line 40 increases **B** by 1 and line 50 recalculates **A**, using the new value of **B**. Since **B** continues to increase, **A** will eventually be greater than 200, and the loop will terminate. If the WHILE condition is never exceeded **(A>200** in this case), you will be in an endless loop.

Notice that we have used the same indentation style as with the FOR/NEXT loops.

The following program illustrates the steps that MBASIC is actually performing while executing the WHILE/WEND loop of the previous example:

```
10 A = 1 : B = 1
20 IF A> = 200 THEN 70
30    PRINT A
40    B = B + 1
50    A = B ^ 2
60 GOTO 20
70 END
```

In the following example, notice that the first data item is read before the WHILE loop is entered. The loop will continue to read data and print it until the string **DONE** is encountered, and then the loop will be terminated.

```
10 READ A$
20 WHILE A$<>"DONE"
30    PRINT A$;" ";
40    READ A$
50 WEND
60 DATA "SAM","FRANK","MARY","SUSAN","DONE"
```

```
RUN
SAM FRANK MARY SUSAN
Ok
```

NESTED WHILE/WEND LOOPS

Just as you can nest FOR/NEXT loops, you may also nest WHILE/WEND loops:

```
10 A = 1
20 WHILE A< = 5
25    B = 1
30    WHILE B< = A
40         PRINT "*";
45         B = B + 1
50    WEND
55    A = A + 1
60    PRINT
70 WEND
```

```
RUN
*
**
***
****
*****
Ok
```

As a final example of loop nesting, enter and run the following, which has a FOR/NEXT loop nested within a WHILE/WEND loop:

```
10 READ B
15 PRINT "BAR GRAPH"
20 WHILE B<>-1
25      PRINT "¦";
35              FOR X=1 TO B
40                      PRINT "*";
45              NEXT
50      PRINT USING "(##)";B
55      READ B
60 WEND
65 PRINT "¦----!----!----!----!"
70 DATA 13,9,18,11,15,-1
```

```
RUN
BAR GRAPH
|*************(13)
|*********( 9)
|******************(18)
|***********(11)
|***************(15)
|----!----!----!----!
Ok
```

Now that we have gone through some simple examples of the statements and functions introduced in this chapter, let's move on to some more practical applications.

TUTORIALS

Tutorial 7-1: Expense Account

Our first application determines the expenses for a business trip of any given number of days:

```
10 REM -        -=*EXPENSE.C7*=-
20 REM -        Expense account totals
30 REM -        11/21/82
40 REM -
100 TRAVEL = 0: MEALS = 0: LODGING = 0  'Zero totals for each area
110 INPUT "Enter number of days for expense account: ";NODAYS
120 FOR DAY = 1 TO NODAYS                'Loop through each day
130    PRINT
140    PRINT "Enter expenses for day";DAY
150    INPUT "   Travel costs: ";COST
160    TRAVEL = TRAVEL + COST            'Add up travel costs
170    INPUT "   Meals: ";COST
180    MEALS = MEALS + COST              'Add up meal costs
190    INPUT "   Lodging: ";COST
200    LODGING = LODGING + COST          'Add up lodging costs
210 NEXT DAY
220 PRINT                                'Print totals for each area
230 PRINT "    -=*< T O T A L S >*=-"
240 PRINT " Travel      Meals   Lodging"
250 PRINT "--------  --------  --------"
260 PRINT USING "$$###.##  ";TRAVEL,MEALS,LODGING
270 PRINT                                'Print grand total
280 PRINT USING "Total expenses: **$#####,.##";TRAVEL + MEALS + LODGING
290 END
```

In line 100 the three expense categories covered in this program (travel, meals, and lodging) are initialized to 0. In line 110, the number of days covered by the trip is entered using the INPUT statement. The FOR/NEXT loop, lines 120-210, counts from 1 to the number of days (**NODAYS**) entered in line 110. The loop then asks you to enter the totals for each day for each of the three categories. Each category is totaled and the results printed out in line 260. In line 280 the total expenses, which are the sum of the three categories, are then printed.

```
RUN
Enter number of days for expense account: ? 3

Enter expenses for day 1
   Travel costs: ? 55.25
   Meals: ? 17.39
   Lodging: ? 0

Enter expenses for day 2
   Travel costs: ? 29.10
   Meals: ? 20.00
   Lodging: ? 71.85

Enter expenses for day 3
   Travel costs: ? 38.88
   Meals: ? 27.57
   Lodging: ? 71.85

    -=*< T O T A L S >*=-
  Travel     Meals   Lodging
 --------- --------- ---------
  123.23     64.96    143.70

Total expenses: *****$331.88
Ok
```

Tutorial 7-2: Payroll with WHILE/WEND

We return to our payroll problem, with only a couple of additional changes made to Tutorial 6-3:

```
10 REM -                -=*PAYWW.C7*=-
20 REM -                08/16/82
30 REM -
100 DEFINT A-Z
110 FORMAT$="\                         \ $$####.##" 'Set print line format
120 DASH$ = "--------------------------------" 'Separates total line
```

(*Tutorial 7-2: Continued*)

```
130 TOTAL.WAGES=0                                'Initialize total wages
140 READ EMP.NAME$,EMP.RATE!                     'Get first data record
150 WHILE EMP.NAME$<>"END"                       'Check for end of data
160    EMP.EARN!=EMP.RATE!*8                     'Compute employee earnings
170    LPRINT USING FORMAT$;EMP.NAME$;EMP.EARN!
180    TOTAL.WAGES!=TOTAL.WAGES!+EMP.EARN!       'Total employee wages
190    READ EMP.NAME$,EMP.RATE!           'Get next data record
200 WEND
210 LPRINT DASH$
220 LPRINT USING FORMAT$;"Total wages";TOTAL.WAGES!
230 END
240 REM -             **** EMPLOYEE DATA ****
250 DATA "Fred Slug",4.78
260 DATA "Hilbert Clam",5.01
270 DATA "Sam Snail",7.43
280 DATA "END",0
```

First notice that the outputs are all LPRINT statements, with the result that output will go to the printer instead of to the screen. The major change, of course, is the use of the WHILE/WEND loop to read in the employee information. In line 140 the WHILE loop is initialized with the first employee's name and rate. The WHILE loop continues to read until the string **END** is encountered, which makes it convenient for you to add in additional employees without changing any of the other information in the program. To do this, add additional employee names in the slots between the existing data statements.

```
Fred Slug                  $38.24
Hilbert Clam               $40.08
Sam Snail                  $59.44
---------------------------------
Total wages               $137.76
```

Tutorial 7-3: Payroll with FOR/NEXT

This is the same as the previous application, except that we have changed from a WHILE/WEND loop to a FOR/NEXT loop:

```
10 REM -              -=*PAYFN.C7*=-
20 REM -              08/16/82
30 REM -
100 DEFINT A-Z
110 FORMAT$="\                           \ $$#####.##" 'Set print line format
120 DASH$ = "-----------------------------------" 'Separates total line
130 TOTAL.WAGES=0                                'Initialize total wages
```

(*Tutorial 7-3: Continued*)

```
140 READ EMP.COUNT                                  'Get number of employees
150 FOR I=1 TO EMP.COUNT                            'Loop through all employees
160     READ EMP.NAME$,EMP.RATE!            'Get data record
170     EMP.EARN!=EMP.RATE!*8                       'Compute employee earnings
180     LPRINT USING FORMAT$;EMP.NAME$;EMP.EARN!
190     TOTAL.WAGES!=TOTAL.WAGES!+EMP.EARN!         'Total employee wages
200 NEXT I
210 LPRINT DASH$
220 LPRINT USING FORMAT$;"Total wages";TOTAL.WAGES!
230 END
240 REM -               **** EMPLOYEE DATA ****
250 DATA 3
260 DATA "Fred Slug",4.78
270 DATA "Hilbert Clam",5.01
280 DATA "Sam Snail",7.43
```

Notice that in line 140, the employee count is read. If you wish to add additional employees, the only item to change (besides employee names and rates) in this program would be the data in line 250 to reflect the total number of employees.

EXERCISES

1. Write programs to generate the following patterns using FOR/NEXT loops:

a.

```
#
##
###
####
#####
```

b.

```
    *
   ***
  *****
 *******
*********
```

c.

```
**    **
 **  **
  ****
   **
    **
     **
      **
```

d.

```
**   **
 **   **
  **   **
   **
**   **
 **   **
  **   **
```

e.

```
    *
   <>
  <<>>
 <<<>>>
<<<<>>>>
   ###
   ###
```

2. Write a program to generate the multiplication table up to 12×12. The output should look like this:

	1	2	3	4	5	....
1	1	2	3	4	5	....
2	2	4	6	8	10	....
3	3	6	9	12	15	....
⋮	⋮	⋮	⋮	⋮	⋮	

3. Write two FOR/NEXT timing loops, much like those in the "Blast-Off" example. Each loop is to count from 1 to 10,000, except that you should let one loop use an integer counter and the other loop use a single-precision counter.

   a. Use a stop watch or a watch with a second hand and determine the running time for each loop.

   b. What must the final value of each loop be if you want to time 5 seconds?

4. Using double precision, rewrite Tutorial 6-1 so that you may enter a starting balance of $10,000 or greater. Notice the difference in time it takes to run the program using double-precision numbers.

5. Enter and run the following program:

```
10 DEFINT X
20 PRINT "START"
30 FOR X = 1 TO 100 STEP .4
40 NEXT X
50 PRINT "END"
```

Explain what happens (or what does not happen).

8

Introduction to Functions

Statements:	RANDOMIZE
Functions:	FIX, SQR, ATN, INT, SIN, LOG, ABS, COS, EXP, RND, TAN, SGN

In Chapter 6 we introduced two functions, TAB and SPC. In this chapter, we will introduce several more. Many of these you will only use if you do programming with mathematics. But you will frequently use two of the functions, INT and RND, regardless of the type of programming you do.

Functions are short programs built into MBASIC. Each is designed to do a specific task. They save you the trouble of having to write the code to perform this task.

Let's start off with the INT function.

Changing Fractions to Integers [INT]

The function INT is used to change a decimal fraction to an integer. To see how INT works, enter and run the following:

```
10 PRINT "INT(1.67)=";INT(1.67)
20 PRINT "INT(-2.67)=";INT(-2.67)

RUN
INT(1.67)= 1
INT(-2.67)=-3
Ok
```

The INT function always rounds off a decimal fraction to the next smallest whole number. The easiest way to see this is to look at the number line shown in Figure 8-1.

As you go from left to right on the number line, the values increase. In the example, INT returned −3 because −3 is the next smallest integer value (that is, the next whole number to the left of −2.67). For the value 1.67 INT will return 1 because 1 is the next lowest integer.

The INT function can be used to round numbers to the nearest whole number, but in order to do this you have to modify the function's argument. The modification is simple: just add .5 to the number. The following program illustrates this idea:

```
10 FOR X = 1 TO 5
20    READ NUMBER
30    PRINT INT(NUMBER+.5);
40 NEXT X
50 DATA 3.71, 14.3, 6.55, -3.01, -8.68

RUN
 4  14  7 -3 -9
Ok
```

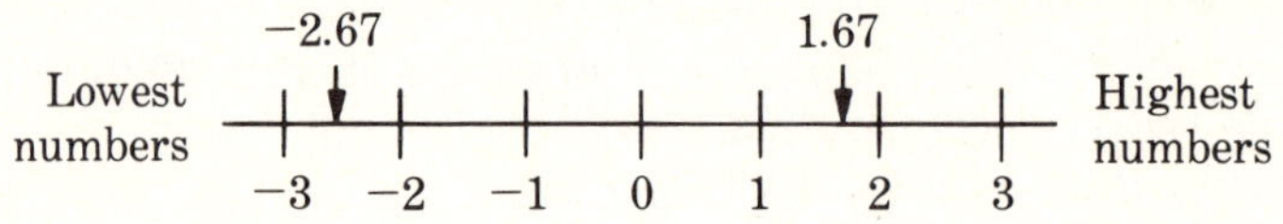

Figure 8-1.
Number line

Generating Random Numbers
[RND, RANDOMIZE]

The random number generator is useful in many applications. Besides the more obvious use of generating numbers for games of chance, it is also useful in generating large quantities of data to test business or simulation programs. It can also be used to generate test data for string applications. We will demonstrate these uses of RND shortly.

The RND function may be used to generate random numbers in any range that you choose. Used in its standard format, it produces a six-place decimal between 0 and 1, but by properly applying the mathematical operators, you can produce random numbers in any range you choose.

The RANDOMIZE statement is used to "seed" the random number generator. The random number seed determines where in the random number table your first random number will be found. Each time a program comes to the RANDOMIZE statement, it will stop and present you with the message **Random number seed (−32768 to 32767).** If you do not give the random number generator a different seed, each time the program is run, the same set of numbers will be produced. RANDOMIZE is used only in conjunction with the RND function and usually does not appear more than once in a program.

Enter and run the following:

```
10 RANDOMIZE
20 FOR X=1 TO 5
30   PRINT RND;
40 NEXT X

RUN
Random number seed (-32768 to 32767)? 23
 .557366  .0265407  .463432  .439325  .268642
Ok
```

If you ran this problem again, using the same seed, 23, you would get the same set of random numbers. If you used another seed, you would get another set of random numbers.

```
RUN
Random number seed (-32768 to 32767)? 9876
 .637145  .326897  .0591093  .173715  .398278
Ok
```

In the following example notice that in line 40 we can control the position of a decimal point by multiplying our random number **A** by a multiple of 10:

```
10 RANDOMIZE
20 FOR X=1 TO 5
30   A=RND
40   PRINT USING"##.######    ";A;10*A;100*A;
50   PRINT INT(10*A)
60 NEXT X

RUN
Random number seed (-32768 to 32767)? -3400
 0.365646    3.656460    36.564600    3
 0.758424    7.584240    75.842400    7
 0.145781    1.457810    14.578100    1
 0.068569    0.685688     6.856880    0
 0.772322    7.723220    77.232200    7
Ok
```

In line 50 we find the next smallest integer value of 10 times our random number. The highest value possible for this is 9, since the largest random number that is produced by the RND function is +.999999, and multiplying this by 10 merely moves the decimal. When you use the INT function with positive numbers, it gets rid of everything to the right of the decimal point.

Now suppose you wish to produce a set of random numbers in a specific range. The first thing to decide is how many numbers there are in that range. In the next example, let's produce 20 numbers whose range can be 0 to 100. Because we want 20 numbers produced, we will set the counter of our FOR/NEXT loop to range from 1 to 20:

```
10 RANDOMIZE
20 FOR X=1 TO 20
30   A=INT(101*RND)
40   PRINT A;
50 NEXT X

RUN
Random number seed (-32768 to 32767)? 841
 68  75  18  35  38  50  3  35  33  4  50  55  27  3  58  79  59  4  15  58
Ok
```

Notice that in line 30 we multiply our number by 101 and then take the integer of this expression. This is because the *range* of 0 to 100 is 101 numbers. Line 40 prints out the results.

Let's try this again and produce a set of 20 numbers in the range from 15 to 40. Our range covers 26 possible numbers:

```
10 RANDOMIZE
20 FOR X = 1 TO 20
30    A = INT(26*RND)+15
40    PRINT A;
50 NEXT X

RUN
Random number seed (-32768 to 32767)? 9100
 18  34  34  40  28  36  27  17  26  24  21  40  16  20  18  19  27  24  33  33Ok
```

In line 30 we multiply the random number function by 26, but we want the output to start at 15, not 0. In order to correct for this, we add 15 to the value produced by the INT function.

As a final example, let's choose our range of numbers from −20 to +20. There are 41 numbers in the range. To correct for this range, we subtract 20 from the result of the INT functions, as follows:

```
10 RANDOMIZE
20 FOR X = 1 TO 20
30    A =  INT(41*RND) - 20
40    PRINT A;
50 NEXT X

RUN
Random number seed (-32768 to 32767)?  -21325
-20  12 -14  15  12 -8 -1  15 -10  7 -17  15 -4 -7 -11  17  17 -17  20  9
Ok
```

To choose a set of random numbers in a specified range, use the following formula:

```
INT((B-A+1)*RND)+A
```

A is the lower value of the range and **B** the upper value [A<= result<=B]. It works with any combination of positive or negative integers. If your range does not need to be integers, you can leave the INT function out.

Suppose X were to be an integer greater than or equal to −5 and less than or equal to 25. B−A+1 is 31, so the resulting equation is INT(31*RND)−5.

RANDOMIZE WITH AN ARGUMENT

You can also use the RANDOMIZE statement with an argument to prevent MBASIC from asking the seed question. For example, the command RANDOMIZE 10112 is the same as the RANDOMIZE command if the user inputs the number 10112 to the seed question.

Using the Math Functions

The following section offers some direct examples of the more specialized mathematical functions. You may skip these sections without losing any programming skills you will need for general applications.

FINDING ABSOLUTE VALUE
[ABS]

The ABS function returns the absolute value (positive value) of the expression enclosed in the parentheses.

```
10 PRINT ABS (-8)
20 PRINT ABS (8*(-3))

RUN
 8
 24
Ok
```

USING THE FIX FUNCTION
[FIX]

The function FIX is similar to the INT function discussed earlier, except that it simply truncates the fractional part of either a positive or negative number.

```
10 PRINT "INT(1.67)=";INT(1.67)
20 PRINT "FIX(1.67)=";FIX(1.67)
30 PRINT "INT(-2.67)=";INT(-2.67)
40 PRINT "FIX(-2.67)=";FIX(-2.67)

RUN
INT(1.67)= 1
FIX(1.67)= 1
INT(-2.67)=-3
FIX(-2.67)=-2
Ok
```

The output from lines 10 and 20 is exactly the same; the functions INT and FIX always return the same value for the same positive number. The distinction between the two becomes apparent if you look at the output from lines 30 and 40, in which the INT function returns a −3 and the FIX function returns a −2. The only distinction between INT and FIX is in the way that they deal with negative numbers.

FINDING THE SQUARE ROOT [SQR]

The SQR function returns the square root of a number. It is easier to use the SQR function than to raise a number to the power of .5 (for example, x^.5), and the SQR function takes the same amount of time to run as raising a number to the power of .5.

Enter and run the following example:

```
10 FOR X = 1 TO 5
20     PRINT X, SQR(X)
30 NEXT

RUN
 1             1
 2             1.41421
 3             1.73205
 4             2
 5             2.23607
Ok
```

USING THE TRIGONOMETRIC FUNCTIONS [SIN, COS, TAN]

The trigonometric functions in MBASIC use angles in *radians*. The formula to convert degrees to radians is RAD=πDEG/180.

The following example shows how to find the sine, cosine, and tangent of an angle:

```
10 PI = 3.14159
20 PRINT "RADIANS       DEGREES       SIN(X)       COS(X)       TAN(X)"
30 PRINT "-------------------------------------------------------------"
40 FOR X = 0 TO PI/2 STEP .2
50     PRINT X,X*180/PI,SIN(X),COS(X),TAN(X)
60 NEXT X

RUN
RADIANS       DEGREES       SIN(X)       COS(X)       TAN(X)
-------------------------------------------------------------
 0             0             0            1            0
 .2            11.4592       .198669      .980067      .20271
 .4            22.9183       .389418      .921061      .422793
 .6            34.3775       .564643      .825336      .684137
 .8            45.8367       .717356      .696707      1.02964
 1             57.2958       .841471      .540302      1.55741
 1.2           68.755        .932039      .362358      2.57215
 1.4           80.2142       .98545       .169967      5.79789
Ok
```

Notice that the angle is in radians. The step size and range to chart may be varied in line 40 to extend your table to any number that you wish. In the MBASIC interpreter, the precision for the sine, cosine, and tangent, as well as other functions, is limited to single precision.

THE LOG AND EXP FUNCTIONS
[LOG, EXP]

The LOG function in MBASIC finds the natural log (base *e*) of a number. The function EXP gives *e* raised to the power specified. In order to get an idea of the values produced by these two functions, enter and run the following programs:

```
10 FOR X = 10 TO 100 STEP 10
20    PRINT X;LOG(X)
30 NEXT X

RUN
 10  2.30259
 20  2.99573
 30  3.4012
 40  3.68888
 50  3.91202
 60  4.09435
 70  4.2485
 80  4.38203
 90  4.49981
 100  4.60517
Ok
```

```
10 FOR X = 0 TO 5
20    PRINT X;EXP(X)
30 NEXT X

RUN
 0  1
 1  2.71828
 2  7.38906
 3  20.0855
 4  54.5982
 5  148.413
Ok
```

THE SGN Function
[SGN]

The SGN function lets you determine the sign of a number. It always returns either −1, 0, or 1, depending on whether the argument is negative, 0, or positive. For example:

```
10 FOR I = 1 TO 5
20 READ N
30 PRINT SGN(N)
40 NEXT I
50 DATA 12, -3, -3000, 0, .132

RUN
 1
-1
-1
 0
 1
OK
```

Now that we have tried each of these functions in some simple examples, let's move on to the applications.

TUTORIALS

Tutorial 8-1: Change from a Purchase

Our first application program determines the change you would receive from a purchase. It first determines the total change you are due and then lists the number of bills and coins you would receive. The maximum amount of change allowed from this program is $99.99.

```
10 REM -              -=*CHANGE.C8*=-
20 REM -              Compute change for given purchase
30 REM -              11/21/82
40 REM -
100 INPUT "Enter purchase price $",PRICE
110 INPUT "Enter cash payment $",PAYMENT
120  IF PRICE <= PAYMENT THEN 150              Check if they paid enough
130    PRINT:PRINT "Cash payment must be greater or equal to price."
```

(Tutorial 8-1: Continued)

```
140    PRINT:GOTO 100
150 CHANGE = INT(100*(PAYMENT - PRICE) + .5)     'Compute change * 100
160 PRINT:PRINT "Change is $";CHANGE/100
170 IF CHANGE <= 9999 THEN 200                   'Can't change more than $99.99
180    PRINT "Sorry, can't change that much money."
190    PRINT:GOTO 100
200 FOR I = 1 TO 10
210    READ COIN$,VALUE                          'Read coin name and value
220    N = INT(CHANGE/VALUE)                     'Compute number for this coin
230    IF N > 0 THEN PRINT N;COIN$;"(s)"         'Don't print if N = 0
240    CHANGE = CHANGE - N*VALUE                 'Compute remaining change
250 NEXT I
260 REM -
270 REM - Coin (or bill) name and value data
280 REM -
290 DATA Fifty dollar bill,5000
300 DATA Twenty dollar bill,2000
310 DATA Ten dollar bill,1000
320 DATA Five dollar bill,500
330 DATA One dollar bill,100
340 DATA Half dollar,50
350 DATA Quarter,25
360 DATA Dime,10
370 DATA Nickel,5
380 DATA Penny,1
```

Now let's take a look at some of the specifics in this program. Lines 120 through 140 check your cash payment to see that it is greater than the price of the item. If it is not greater or equal, a message is printed and the program returns to line 100 for you to enter new amounts. In line 150 the INT function is used. Remember that this truncates the value to the next smallest whole number; in other words, .5 is added to round correctly to the nearest penny. The loop in lines 200 through 250 reads the data, which includes the bill or coin and its value. The number of each that you are to receive in change is determined, and then the loop goes on to read the next value until all values are read down through the last data item, which is pennies.

```
RUN
Enter purchase price $ 47.45
Enter cash payment $ 60.00

Change is $ 12.55
 1 Ten dollar bill(s)
 2 One dollar bill(s)
```

(Tutorial 8-1: Continued)

```
 1 Half dollar(s)
 1 Nickel(s)
Ok
RUN
Enter purchase price $ 122.66
Enter cash payment $ 200.00

Change is $ 77.34
 1 Fifty dollar bill(s)
 1 Twenty dollar bill(s)
 1 Five dollar bill(s)
 2 One dollar bill(s)
 1 Quarter(s)
 1 Nickel(s)
 4 Penny(s)
Ok
```

Tutorial 8-2: Craps

Our next application simulates a crap game. It uses a variety of the MBASIC instructions developed up to this point. You need to know the rules of craps to play the game.

```
10 REM -                  -=*CRAPS.C8*=-
20 REM -                  Simulated Craps Game
30 REM -                  11/25/82
40 REM -
100 DEFINT A-Z            'Use all integers
110 RANDOMIZE             'Set random seed
120 PRINT:INPUT "How much cash do you have (Whole bills only)? ",CASH
130 PLAY$ = "Y"           'Game ends when PLAY$ = "N"
140 WHILE PLAY$ = "Y"
150    PRINT:INPUT "What would you like to bet? ",BET
160    IF BET <= CASH THEN 190                    'Check BET
170       PRINT "Look, you only have $";CASH
180       GOTO 150
190    DIE1 = INT(6*RND) + 1 : DIE2 = INT(6*RND) + 1    'Compute 1'st roll
200    POINT = DIE1 + DIE2
210    PRINT "Your first roll is";DIE1;"+";DIE2;"=";POINT
220    IF POINT = 7 OR POINT = 11 THEN 380            'Won on 1'st roll
230    IF POINT = 2 OR POINT = 3 OR POINT = 12 THEN 440 'Lost on 1'st roll
240 '
250 '  The first roll did not win or lose, roll for the POINT
260 '
270    PRINT POINT;"is your point"
280    ROLL = 0                  'Initialize ROLL for loop
```

(Tutorial 8-2: Continued)

```
290    WHILE ROLL <> POINT AND ROLL <> 7
300       DIE1 = INT(6*RND) + 1 : DIE2 = INT(6*RND) + 1 'Compute next roll
310       ROLL = DIE1 + DIE2
320       PRINT "Your roll is";DIE1;"+";DIE2;"=";ROLL
330    WEND
340    IF ROLL = 7 THEN 440      'ROLL = 7 for lose, else fall into win
350 '
360 '  Game won, print results
370 '
380    PRINT "You won!";
390    CASH = CASH + BET          'Add bet
400    GOTO 490
410 '
420 '  Game lost, print results
430 '
440    PRINT "Too bad, you lose.";
450    CASH = CASH - BET          'Subtract bet
460 '
470 '  Ask to play again
480 '
490    PRINT "  You now have $";CASH;"in cash."
500    IF CASH > 0 THEN 540
510       PRINT "Sorry pal, you ran out of money."
520       PLAY$ = "N"
530    GOTO 550
540       INPUT "Would you like to play again (Y/N)";PLAY$
550 WEND
560 PRINT:PRINT "Game ends, you have $";CASH
```

In line 100 we defined all the variables, A through Z, to be integers. This is a useful habit to get into, particularly if you are writing long programs or if your computer has memory limitations. It takes fewer bytes of memory to store an integer than it does to store a single- or double-precision number. If you use this procedure, however, keep in mind that to use single precision or double precision in the program, the variable will have to be declared with the appropriate variable (such as ! or #) type character.

Notice that lines 140 through 550 form one large WHILE/WEND loop. This loop is initialized in line 130 with **PLAYS** set equal to **Y**. Lines 160 through 180 verify that your bet is less than or equal to the cash that you have available. Lines 190 through 200 determine your point for the first roll of the dice.

Notice that the INT function is used in this program, even though all the variables have been defined in line 100 to be integers.

The reason is that we want these random numbers to be truncated rather than rounded off.

Lines 220 and 230 determine whether the first roll of the dice was a winner (7 or 11) or a loser (2, 3, or 12). If neither of these situations occurs, the program proceeds, and you roll the dice again to determine whether or not you made your point. Line 290 checks to see if either your point was made or you rolled a 7. In either case, the program jumps to line 340, where it checks to see if a 7 was rolled; if so, you lose and it jumps to line 440 and subtracts your bet from your cash on hand. If you have not lost, the program determines your new cash balance. In line 490 your balance is printed, and at line 500, if you still have cash remaining, the program proceeds to 540, where you are asked if you would like to continue the game.

```
RUN
Random number seed (-32768 to 32767)? 4321

How much cash do you have (Whole bills only)? 5

What would you like to bet? 2
Your first roll is 1 + 4 = 5
 5 is your point
Your roll is 3 + 3 = 6
Your roll is 4 + 4 = 8
Your roll is 4 + 6 = 10
Your roll is 4 + 6 = 10
Your roll is 1 + 3 = 4
Your roll is 3 + 6 = 9
Your roll is 3 + 3 = 6
Your roll is 1 + 2 = 3
Your roll is 4 + 5 = 9
Your roll is 5 + 4 = 9
Your roll is 6 + 1 = 7
Too bad, you lose.  You now have $ 3 in cash.
Would you like to play again (Y/N)? Y

What would you like to bet? 2
Your first roll is 5 + 6 = 11
You won!  You now have $ 5 in cash.
Would you like to play again (Y/N)? Y

What would you like to bet? 5
Your first roll is 6 + 2 = 8
 8 is your point
Your roll is 2 + 2 = 4
Your roll is 5 + 2 = 7
```

(Tutorial 8-2: Continued)

```
Too bad, you lose.  You now have $ 0 in cash.
Sorry pal, you ran out of money.

Game ends, you have $ 0
Ok
```

Tutorial 8-3: Prime Factors

This program determines whether or not a number is prime. A prime number is one that is divisible only by itself and 1. For example, 1, 2, 3, 5, and 7 are the first five prime numbers.

```
10 REM -                -=*PRIME.C8*=-
20 REM -                Print prime factors of a number
30 REM -                11/21/82
40 REM -
100 INPUT "Enter an integer: ",N
110 PRINT:PRINT "Prime factors of";N;"are:"
120 A = N: FACTOR = 2                   'Initialize
130 WHILE FACTOR <= SQR(A)              'Only one factor can be > SQR(A)
140    WHILE A/FACTOR = INT(A/FACTOR)   'Check for factor
150       PRINT FACTOR                  'Found a factor, print it
160       A = A/FACTOR                  'Factor it out
170    WEND
180    FACTOR = FACTOR + 1              'Try another number
190 WEND
200 IF A <> 1 AND A <> N THEN PRINT A   'Print last factor if any
210 IF A = N THEN PRINT "None,";N;"is prime."
```

Let's take a look at some of the features of this program. In line 120 we set the variable **A** equal to the number entered. The first number we divide by is our variable, **FACTOR**, which is set equal to 2. **FACTOR** also initializes our WHILE loop, which starts in line 130.

The rule we use to determine whether or not the number is prime is stated in line 130. We will try to divide N by every number from 2 to the square root of **N**. For instance, if we were testing the number 25, we would divide by 2, 3, 4, and 5. If none of these divides in evenly, we know the number is prime. In line 140 we determine whether or not **FACTOR** divides evenly into **N** by checking to see if

N divided by **FACTOR** is equal to the INT of **N** divided by **FACTOR**. If they are equal, we have found a factor, and it is printed in line 150.

If the first number we try does not divide in evenly, the factor to be checked is incremented by 1 and the program returns to line 140 to try the next **FACTOR**. In line 210 we check to see if **A** is equal to **N**. If it is, no factor has been found and you are told that **N** is prime.

```
RUN
Enter an integer:  109

Prime factors of 109 are:
None. 109 is prime.
Ok
RUN
Enter an integer:  110

Prime factors of 110 are:
 2
 5
 11
Ok
RUN
Enter an integer:  111

Prime factors of 111 are:
 3
 37
Ok
```

Tutorial 8-4: Sine Wave

This program prints a sine curve.

```
10 REM -                  -=*SINE.C8*=-
20 REM -                  Print a sine wave curve
30 REM -                  11/21/82
40 REM -
100 A=20                             'Wave amplitude
110 E=.4                             'Step size
120 FOR X = 1 TO 2*A + 1
130    PRINT "-";                    'Print Y axis
140 NEXT X
150 PRINT " Y axis"
160 YO = A + 1                       'Tab location of X axis
170 FOR X = 0 TO 4*3.14 STEP E
```

(Tutorial 8-4: Continued)

```
180     Y = Y0 + FIX(A*SIN(X) + .5)          'Compute tab location of point
190     IF Y > Y0 THEN PRINT TAB(Y0);"¦";TAB(Y);"*"       'Y is right of X axis
200     IF Y < Y0 THEN PRINT TAB(Y);"*";TAB(Y0);"¦"       'Y is left of X axis
210     IF Y = Y0 THEN PRINT TAB(Y);"*"                   'Y is on X axis
220 NEXT X
230 PRINT TAB(Y0 - 3);"X axis"
```

In lines 100 and 110, the variables for the amplitude of the wave and the step size have been set. It is convenient to set variables of this type at the beginning of your program so that if you wish to change them for successive runs of the program, they are easy to find and you only have to change them in one place.

Keep in mind that when using the TAB function, the leftmost character must be printed first. Lines 190 through 210 make the decision about whether or not to print the asterisk for the sine curve or the vertical bar for the x-axis depending on which has the smaller column value.

```
RUN
```

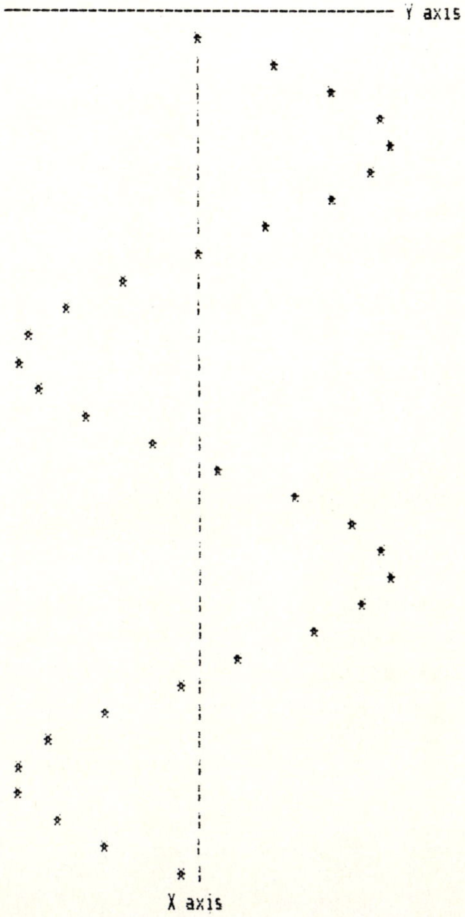


```
Ok
```

EXERCISES

1. Use the random number generator to generate ten numbers in the following ranges:

   a. 0 to 20 *b.* 10 to 45 *c.* −10 to +10
   d. −50 to 0 *e.* .34 to 1.83

2. Modify the sine wave program to print a cosine wave. Experiment with different values for the amplitude **A** and step size **E**.

3. Write a program to add two fractions, determine the lowest common denominator, and print the sum both as a decimal and in fractional form reduced to lowest terms.

4. In the crap game application the roll value is computed by adding two random numbers, each in the range 1 to 6. Lines 190-200 and 300-310 could have been written with **ROLL = INT(6*RND)+INT(6*RND)+2**, which produces a random number between 2 and 12. Why couldn't we use a statement like **ROLL = INT(11*RND)+2** to produce random numbers between 2 and 12 instead of the method mentioned above?

9

Working With String Functions

Statements:	MID$, LINE INPUT
Functions:	LEN, LEFT$, RIGHT$, MID$, INSTR, STR$, VAL, CHR$, ASC, STRING$, SPACE$, INPUT$, INKEY$
Control Characters:	^G

In the last chapter we introduced several functions. Some of those functions were of interest to the general programmer, but many were of interest only to those involved with math or engineering programming. In this chapter we introduce some of the string functions. These will be of interest to all programmers, regardless of specialty.

Finding the Length of a String
[LEN]

The LEN function is used to find the length of a string. For example:

```
10 A$="ABC"
20 PRINT LEN(A$),LEN("WXYZ")

RUN
 3             4
Ok
```

The string may be a variable or a literal, as shown in line 20.

The LEN function counts every character in the string, including spaces and special characters. A string with zero length is called an empty string or a *null string.*

```
10 A$="ABC" : B$="    "
20 C$="STUMP, SAM" : D$=""
30 PRINT LEN(A$), LEN(B$)
40 PRINT LEN(C$), LEN(D$)

RUN
 3             4
 10            0
Ok
```

In this example, line 40 prints out the length of **C$**, which is 10. This length includes not only the letters that form the names, but also the punctuation mark and the space between the last and first names. As you can see, the four spaces between the quotation marks for **B$** are all counted by the LEN function. The string **D$** was assigned no characters between the quotation marks and has a length of zero.

The LEN function is commonly used to verify the length of data entered into a program. For example, ZIP codes, phone numbers, or other fixed-length strings can be checked for proper length.

Choosing a Portion of a String
[LEFT$, RIGHT$, MID$]

The three functions LEFT$, RIGHT$, and MID$ are used to select a portion of a string. Strings have a maximum length of 255.

LEFT$ returns the leftmost characters of a string. The format for the function is LEFT$(A$,X), where *A$* represents the string you are extracting from and *X* is the number of characters for the resulting string. When *X* is greater than the length of *A$*, the function returns the entire string. If *X* is 0, a null string (a string with zero length) is returned.

```
10 A$="ABCDEFGH"
20 FOR X = 2 TO 10 STEP 2
30   PRINT LEFT$(A$,X)
40 NEXT X
```

```
RUN
AB
ABCD
ABCDEF
ABCDEFGH
ABCDEFGH
Ok
```

RIGHT$ is similar to LEFT$, except it returns the rightmost characters of the string. Again, if the number specified is greater than or equal to the length of the string, the whole string is returned.

```
10 A$="ABCDEF"
20 PRINT RIGHT$(A$,4)
```

```
RUN
CDEF
Ok
```

Adding RIGHT$ to line 30 of our first example, we have

```
10 A$="ABCDEFGH"
20 FOR X = 2 TO 10 STEP 2
30   PRINT LEFT$(A$,X),RIGHT$(A$,X)
40 NEXT X
```

```
RUN
AB            GH
ABCD          EFGH
ABCDEF        CDEFGH
ABCDEFGH      ABCDEFGH
ABCDEFGH      ABCDEFGH
Ok
```

The MID$ function is used to return characters from the middle of a string. The format is MID$(A$,X,Y). Here *A$* represents the string you want the middle of, *X* represents the position of the character you wish to start with, and *Y* tells how many characters to take.

```
10 A$="ABCDEF"
20 PRINT MID$(A$,2,3)

RUN
BCD
Ok
```

In this example, we start with the letter **B**. The third argument is 3, so we take three characters; therefore, the output is **BCD**.

If the third argument is omitted, MID$ returns all the characters to the right of the character in the position specified. To see how these three functions work together, type in the following:

```
10 A$="ABCDEFGHIJKLM"
20 FOR X = 2 TO 10 STEP 2
30   PRINT LEFT$(A$,X),MID$(A$,X,X),RIGHT$(A$,X)
40 NEXT X
```

Running the program produces the following:

```
RUN
AB            BC             LM
ABCD          DEFG           JKLM
ABCDEF        FGHIJK         HIJKLM
ABCDEFGH      HIJKLM         FGHIJKLM
ABCDEFGHIJ    JKLM           DEFGHIJKLM
Ok
```

Experiment with the numeric variables in line 3 to change the starting position in the string. Run the program to verify your predictions for the output.

Replacing a Portion of a String
[MID$]

When MID$ appears on the left side of an assignment statement, it becomes a statement or command. The MID$ statement can be used to replace a portion of a string with another string. The format of the MID$ statement is similar to the MID$ function: MID$(A$, X,

Y) = B$. The characters in *A$* beginning at position *X* are replaced by the first *Y* characters in *B$*. If *Y* is omitted, all of *B$* is used. However, regardless of whether *Y* is omitted or included, the replacement of characters cannot exceed the original length of *A$*. This means that the MID$ *statement* can never change the length of a string.

```
10 A$ = "1234567890"
20 MID$(A$,3,5) = "ABCDEFG"
30 PRINT A$

RUN
12ABCDE890
Ok
```

In the preceding example, the third through seventh characters of A$ are replaced by the characters **ABCDE**. In the following example, the third argument or length argument is omitted:

```
10 A$ = "1234567890"
20 MID$(A$,5) = "ABC"
30 PRINT A$

RUN
1234ABC890
Ok
```

The complete string **ABC** replaces characters in string **A$** beginning at the fifth position (that is, replacing the characters **567**).

Searching for Strings Within Strings [INSTR]

The INSTR function is used to search one string for the presence of a matching second string. It indicates the starting position in the first string where the match was found.

```
10 PRINT INSTR("123456789","567")

RUN
 5
Ok
```

This tells us that the string "567" is contained in the string "123456789" and that it begins in position 5. The format for INSTR may also contain a third argument. This form of the INSTR function has the format INSTR(I, X$, Y$), where *I* indicates the initial position to begin the search for *Y$* in *X$:*

```
10 A$="12345678901234567890" : B$="567"
20 PRINT INSTR(10, A$, B$)

RUN
 15
Ok
```

The preceding search starts at the tenth position in **A$**. The output shows that **B$** begins at the fifteenth character of **A$**.

If the length argument has a value greater than the length of **A$** or if **A$** is null, INSTR returns the value 0. The value 0 is also returned if **B$** is not found in **A$**.

Our next example shows how the MID$ function can be combined with the INSTR function:

```
10 A$="1234ABC89012ABC67890"
20 PRINT INSTR(A$, "ABC")
30 PRINT INSTR(11, A$, "ABC")
40 PRINT INSTR(MID$(A$,11), "ABC")

RUN
 5
 13
 3
Ok
```

Notice the difference in the output from lines 30 and 40. In both cases the search starts from the eleventh position in **A$** and locates the second occurrence of "ABC" in **A$**. The difference is that line 30 printed the absolute position of "ABC" in **A$**, whereas line 40 printed the relative position (starting at position 11) of "ABC" in **A$**. Also notice that we have used the string constant "ABC" instead of **B$**.

If the string you are searching for is a null string, the INSTR function will return an answer of 1. If the initial search position argument is used, the function will return this argument. For instance, in this example we are searching for a null string:

```
10 A$="ABCDEFGHI"
20 B$=""
30 PRINT INSTR(A$, B$)
40 PRINT INSTR(5, A$, "")
```

```
RUN
 1
 5
Ok
```

Experiment using different values for these arguments until you feel confident with this function.

Converting Between Numbers and Strings [STR$, VAL]

The STR$ and VAL functions are used to convert numbers to strings (STR$) or strings to numbers (VAL). Consider the output from the following program:

```
10 A = 123 : B = 56
20 A$ = STR$(A) : B$ = STR$(B)
30 PRINT A$,B$
40 PRINT A + B
50 PRINT A$ + B$
60 PRINT LEN(A$), LEN(B$)
```

```
RUN
 123          56
 179
 123 56
 4            3
Ok
```

Line 30 prints the strings **A$** and **B$**. The output from line 40 is 179, which is the sum of the numbers represented by the variables **A** and **B**. Line 50 shows the concatenation of the two string variables, **A$** and **B$**.

In line 60 the output from **LEN(A$)** is 4, even though **A$** is the string representation of the three-digit number 123. The STR$ function always holds a place for the sign of a number along with the number. When the number 123 was converted to a string with the STR$ function, the position for the sign was assigned to **A$** along with the number. In this case, the number is positive so it is not printed. A space was inserted in place of the plus sign; therefore, the length is 4. Again, the length of STR$(X) is always one longer than the number of digits in the number.

The argument for STR$ must be numeric but does not have to be an integer. For example:

```
10 A$ = STR$(253.15)
20 PRINT A$, LEN(A$)


RUN
 253.15        7
Ok
```

The VAL function is the opposite of STR$. It converts a string into a number. Enter and run the following:

```
10 A$ = "94598"
20 A = VAL(A$)
30 PRINT A + 2


RUN
 94600
Ok
```

Line 20 converts the string **A$** into its numeric value. The output from line 30 prints the sum of that value and 2. If you tried to add **A$** and 2, you would get the message "Type mismatch in line 30".

If the first nonblank character of the string being converted by the VAL function is not a plus sign, a minus sign, or a digit, the VAL function returns a 0. For example, VAL("SAM") would be 0 but would not give an error.

This property of the VAL function can be very convenient. If you wanted to write a program that will keep track of employees with employee numbers, you might have a statement like

```
100 INPUT "Enter employee name or number: ",EMP$
```

You could then determine if the user typed a name or number simply by using VAL(EMP$). If we know that no employee will have number 0, then VAL(EMP$) = 0 means EMP$ is a name; otherwise, VAL(EMP$) is the employee number.

Using the ASCII Character Set [ASC, CHR$]

The acronym ASCII is the name of the numeric code used by most computers to internally represent characters. The ASC function is used to return the numeric value that represents the ASCII character. If the length of a string is greater than 1, the ASC function returns the code only for the first character of the string.

For example:

```
10 X$ = "A" : Y$ = "abc"
20 PRINT ASC(X$),ASC(Y$)

RUN
 65            97
Ok
```

In the output from this example, 65 is the ASCII code for the capital letter "A", the first character of the string X$; and 97 is the ASCII code for "a", the first character of the string Y$. Attempting to take ASC of a null string will generate an "Illegal function call".

The function CHR$ returns the string that is denoted by an ASCII code number. As you can see from the following example, the numbers 65 through 90 of the code represent the capital letters A through Z:

```
10 FOR X = 65 TO 90
20    PRINT CHR$(X);
30 NEXT X

RUN
ABCDEFGHIJKLMNOPQRSTUVWXYZ
Ok
```

The ASCII code ranges from 0 to 127. The codes 0 through 31 are the control characters we have used in previous chapters. Control characters are usually used by programs to send special commands. The interpretation of control characters varies greatly from one terminal or printer to another.

The ASCII codes 65 to 90 and 97 to 122 are upper- and lowercase characters, respectively. Notice that any given lowercase letter always has a value that is greater by 32 than its corresponding uppercase letter. The codes 48 to 57 represent the characters 0 through 9 in order. The remaining codes between 32 and 127 represent the punctuation marks, and 32 is the code for a space. In spite of this standard for the ASCII set, the codes for some of the punctuation marks may vary from one printer or terminal to another.

Although only codes 0 through 127 are defined, many terminals and printers use codes 128 through 255 for special purposes, such as graphics.

Let's try one more example with the ASC function: namely, that of finding the ASCII code for the letters in a name. This program could, of course, be used to find the ASCII code of any character.

```
10 INPUT "Type in your name: ",NAM$
20 FOR I = 1 TO LEN(NAM$)
30    C$ = MID$(NAM$,I,1)
40    PRINT USING "'!' is ###";C$:ASC(C$)
50 NEXT I


RUN
Type in your name: EGBERT SNEED
'E' is  69
'G' is  71
'B' is  66
'E' is  69
'R' is  82
'T' is  84
' ' is  32
'S' is  83
'N' is  78
'E' is  69
'E' is  69
'D' is  68
Ok
RUN
Type in your name: egbert
'e' is 101
'g' is 103
'b' is  98
'e' is 101
'r' is 114
't' is 116
Ok
```

Notice in line 30 that the MID$ function (not the LEFT$ function) must be used to select the character at position **I** of **NAM$**. On the first time through the loop **I** is **1**, so that **C$** is assigned the first character of **NAM$**. On the second time through the loop **I** is **2**, so that **C$** is assigned the second character of **NAM$**. On the last time through the loop **I** is **LEN(NAM$)**, so that **C$** is assigned the last character of **NAM$**. Also recall from our discussion of formatting with the PRINT USING command (in Chapter 6) that the (!) mark in line 40 is used to print a string length of 1.

Note that the variable **NAM$** is used instead of the more descriptive variable **NAME$** because NAME is an MBASIC keyword. The NAME statement will be discussed in Chapter 14.

RINGING THE BELL
[^G]

One of the more useful control characters is ASCII character 7, which is CTRL-G. Often called ^G or BELL, this character rings the bell on your terminal. You can check to see if your terminal supports this function by giving the command PRINT CHR$(7) and listening for a sound. This control character can be used by an MBASIC program to get the operator's attention to perform a task or to warn that an error has occurred.

Creating a String of the Same Characters
[STRING$, SPACE$]

The function STRING$ is used to create a string composed of repeated identical characters. The format is STRING$(X, Y$), where *X* represents the length of the string and *Y$* is the character to be used. If *Y$* contains more than one character, only the first character is used. Run the following example:

```
10 A$ = STRING$(5,"*")
20 PRINT A$

RUN
*****
Ok
```

This function is useful to print headings for reports or tables. Enter and run the following:

```
10 A$ = STRING$(5,"*")
20 B$ = " DECEMBER REPORT "
30 PRINT A$;B$;A$

RUN
***** DECEMBER REPORT *****
Ok
```

In this next example, we add one line to the previous program, to underline the heading:

```
10 A$ = STRING$(5,"*")
20 B$ = " DECEMBER REPORT "
30 PRINT A$;B$;A$
40 PRINT STRING$(LEN(A$)*2 + LEN(B$),"=")

RUN
***** DECEMBER REPORT *****
===========================
Ok
```

By using the expression **LEN(A$)*2 + LEN(B$)**, we automatically change the length of the underline string if we change either **A$** or **B$**.

A second format for the STRING$ function is STRING$(X, Y), where *X* represents the length of the new string (as before) and *Y* represents the ASCII code of the character to be repeated. This format of the function is normally used with control codes. For example:

```
10 A$ = STRING$(5,"*")
20 PRINT A$;STRING$(5,10);A$

RUN
*****





     *****
Ok
```

In the preceding example, line 20 first prints out **A$**, the five asterisks. After this it calls the STRING$ function with a second argument of 10, which represents the ASCII code for LINE FEED. LINE FEED is a control character which, when printed to the screen, causes the cursor to move down to the same column on the next line. The first argument (5) of STRING$ causes five line feeds to be printed so that the output drops down five lines before printing **A$**, the second five asterisks.

The function SPACE$(X) prints out the number of spaces represented by the argument *X*. SPACE$(X) is identical to STRING$(X," ").

```
10 FOR X = 1 TO 5
20   PRINT X;"SPACE ";CHR$(34);SPACE$(X);CHR$(34)
30 NEXT X

RUN
 1 SPACE " "
 2 SPACE "  "
 3 SPACE "   "
 4 SPACE "    "
 5 SPACE "     "
Ok
```

Notice that in line 20 of the preceding example, we use the CHR$ function to print out the ASCII code for double quotation marks (34 is the ASCII code for double quotation marks). We need to do this because double quotation marks have a special significance in MBASIC: namely, that of enclosing strings. Therefore, the only way to print out the double quotation marks is to use the CHR$ function.

A general rule to keep in mind when working with strings is that MBASIC does not work with strings longer than 255 characters. This means that all arguments referring to a position or length of a string must evaluate to an integer between 0 and 255. However, if an argument evaluates to a decimal number, MBASIC will automatically round the number to the nearest integer before using it. For example, if *X* is 1.25, STRING$(X,"+") will be a string with one character. If *X* is 1.75, STRING$(X,"+") will be a string with two characters. For example:

```
10 FOR X = 1 TO 3 STEP .25
20    PRINT X,STRING$(X,"+")
30 NEXT X

RUN
 1            +
 1.25         +
 1.5          ++
 1.75         ++
 2            ++
 2.25         ++
 2.5          +++
 2.75         +++
 3            +++
Ok
```

Controlling Input
[INPUT$]

The INPUT$ function is used to get a string of characters from the terminal. The format is INPUT$(X), where *X* specifies how many characters to accept. Unlike the INPUT statement introduced in Chapter 4, the INPUT$ function does not *echo* (that is, reprint) the input on the screen. Sometimes it is desirable not to have the input echo on the screen as the user is typing.

```
10 PRINT "Press any key to continue. ";
20 DUMMY$ = INPUT$(1)


RUN
Press any key to continue.
Ok
```

Program execution waits at line 20 until any key is pressed at the terminal. These two statements might be useful in a program that prints instructions and waits for the user to read the instructions before continuing. Since INPUT$ is a function, its returned value must go somewhere; therefore, a dummy variable (**DUMMY$**) is used to collect the "any key" that the user typed. The name **DUMMY$** is just a convention we have chosen to mean that we are not particularly interested in which key the user typed to continue the program.

```
10 PRINT "Type in 5 characters:"
20 C$ = INPUT$(5)
30 PRINT LEN(C$),ASC(C$),C$


RUN
Type in 5 characters: [Enter 12345]
 5             49            12345
Ok
RUN
Type in 5 characters: [Enter GREG preceded by a space]
 5             32             GREG
Ok
```

In this example, notice that the argument for INPUT$ is 5, so five characters must be input from the keyboard before the program can continue. In the first run of the program, the 49 represents the ASCII code of the first character input, the 1. In the second run of the program, notice that only *four* characters are visibly printed. This is because the first character input was a space (32 is the ASCII code for the space character).

Note that INPUT$ will accept all characters except ^C as input. Recall from Chapter 4 that ^C is used to interrupt the program. Run the program and press ^C. When you stop a program in an INPUT$ statement with ^C, MBASIC does not print the usual "Break in 20" message.

The next example translates all uppercase letters, A through Z, to lowercase letters:

```
10 PRINT "Now entering lowercase mode."
20 C$ = INPUT$(1)
30 C = ASC(C$)
40 IF C >= ASC("A") AND C <= ASC("Z") THEN C = C + 32
50 PRINT CHR$(C);
60 IF C <> 13 THEN GOTO 20
70 PRINT


RUN
Now entering lowercase mode.
this is typed in as uppercase
Ok
```

The translation is performed in line 40, where if any uppercase letter is typed at the keyboard, it has 32 added to its ASCII code. Line 40 translates the letter to the corresponding lowercase letter. All other characters, such as numbers or punctuation marks, are printed on the screen just as entered. Line 60 ends the program when the RETURN key is pressed. The ASCII code for RETURN is 13.

USING THE INKEY$ FUNCTION
[INKEY$]

The INKEY$ function is similar to the INPUT$ function. INKEY$ will return the last character typed at the terminal or a null string if no characters have been typed. The difference between INKEY$ and INPUT$(1) is that INKEY$ does not wait for the user. If no key has been pressed since the last INPUT or INPUT$, program execution continues at the next statement or line number. Keep in mind that the INKEY$ function has no arguments and therefore looks a lot like a string variable.

In the next example we use the INKEY$ function to get a random number seed that depends on how long it takes the user to respond after reading some instructions. Since every user's response time will be slightly different, we can then use this "time" in the RANDOMIZE statement. If the RANDOMIZE statement is followed by an expression, as it is in line 130, that expression is used as the seed for the random number generator.

```
10 PRINT "Instructions:"
20 PRINT
30 PRINT
40 PRINT "Press any key to continue. ";
50 TIME  = -32768
60 WHILE LEN(INKEY$) = 0
70    TIME  = TIME  + 1
80 WEND
90 WHILE TIME  > 32767
100   TIME  = TIME  - 65535
110 WEND
120 PRINT:PRINT "Your lucky number is ";TIME
130 RANDOMIZE TIME
140 FOR I = 1 TO 10
150    PRINT INT(RND*10) + 1,
160 NEXT I


RUN
Instructions:


Press any key to continue.
Your lucky number is -31971
 6             5             2             8             8
 3             4             4             7             1
Ok
RUN
Instructions:


Press any key to continue.
Your lucky number is -26139
 6             3             3             1             1
 7             5             6             6             10
Ok
```

This technique is very useful for games that print instructions on the screen, since it provides a good way of getting the random seed without asking the user for it. Since INKEY$ returns a null string until a key is pressed, the WHILE loop from lines 60 through 80 counts with the variable **TIME%** until a key is pressed. When a key is pressed, **INKEY$** will become equal to the corresponding character and will no longer have length 0. Lines 90-110 prevent **TIME** from overflowing the range for the RANDOMIZE statement (−32768 to 32767). This is also the range for integer variables. If we did not check for bounds, we would get an overflow error in line 130. The FOR/NEXT loop prints ten random numbers so that you may convince yourself by running the program that it is very difficult to repeat the same set of random numbers twice.

Using Line Input
[LINE INPUT]

The LINE INPUT statement is similar to INPUT except that it allows you to enter a string containing commas and quotation marks. For example, if you want to enter a name with the last name first and a comma separating the names, INPUT would consider the comma to mean you entered input for two strings. The next example illustrates, with LINE INPUT, how you can enter names last name first using a single variable and without entering quotation marks around the input:

```
10 LINE INPUT "Enter name last name first: ",NAM$
20 PRINT NAM$


RUN
Enter name last name first: SLUG, FRED
SLUG, FRED
Ok
```

If we had used an INPUT statement in line 10 instead of using LINE INPUT, the input **SLUG, FRED** would have been considered as two separate inputs: **SLUG** and **FRED**. Using an INPUT statement would have required using two variables or entering the input enclosed in quotation marks.

The prompt for LINE INPUT does not automatically print the question mark as the INPUT statement does. If you want a question mark, you must place it in the prompt string. Also notice that since LINE INPUT accepts everything you type as one string, you cannot use LINE INPUT to input more than one string or to input numeric variables.

LINE INPUT will stop accepting characters after 255 characters have been typed. If a semicolon is used immediately after LINE

INPUT but before the string variable, no carriage return is sent to the terminal when you press RETURN.

Now let's move on to some applications that use the functions introduced in this chapter.

TUTORIALS

Tutorial 9-1: Password

Our first application program requires that the operator enter an eight-character password before the program can continue. Because the password does not appear on the screen, using the password makes the program quite secure.

```
10 REM -                    -=*PASSWORD.C9*=-
20 REM -                    Password entry for a program
30 REM -                    1/2/83
40 REM -
50 DATA "ZYXWVUTS","SAMSMITH","GREG1234",""
100 REM -                   *** START ***
110 PRINT "Please enter your 8 - character password  ";
120 PASSWORD$ = INPUT$(8)
130 PRINT
140 RESTORE                 'Set to read first password
150 READ ENTRY$             'Read first password
160 WHILE ENTRY$ <> PASSWORD$ AND ENTRY$ <> ""
170    READ ENTRY$
180 WEND
190 IF ENTRY$ = "" THEN PRINT "Invalid password.":GOTO 110
200 PRINT "Password accepted."
210 REM -
220 REM - *** MAIN PROGRAM ***
230 REM -
```

In this example, we program an eight-character password. If in line 120 the argument for INPUT$ is set to another value, however, the length of your password will, of course, change. Remember that INPUT$ does not echo any characters to the screen, with the result that you will not see the characters as you type them in. In addition, note that the carriage return is automatic after the eighth character has been entered.

When this program is run, it looks like this:

```
RUN
Please enter your 8-character password  [Enter 12345678]
Invalid password.
Please enter your 8-character password  [Enter SAMSMITH]
Password accepted.
Ok
```

The null string at the end of line 50 is used to terminate the WHILE/WEND loop in lines 160 through 180. Line 150 reads the first entry of the DATA statement and initializes the WHILE/ WEND loop. In this loop, each of the entries in the DATA statement is compared with the password you enter. If a match is found, you can proceed with the rest of the program. If no match is found, the null string terminates the loop and line 190 then prints the message "**Invalid password**". Then the program returns to line 110 for you to make another password entry. The RESTORE statement at line 140 is necessary for the case in which a user must type in the password more than once. In this case, the data must be restored so that the READ statement at line 150 will read the first password in the DATA statement.

Tutorial 9-2: Replace

Our second application allows you to replace any word or group of words in a message with whatever string you wish. If the section that is to be replaced occurs more than once in the message, all occurrences of it are replaced.

```
10 REM -                -=*REPLACE.C9*=-
20 REM -                String replacement example
20 REM -                1/2/83
100 READ MSG$
110 PRINT:PRINT MSG$
120 LINE INPUT "Replace: ",A$
130 IF LEN(A$) = 0 THEN END
140 LINE INPUT "With: ",B$
150 I = INSTR(MSG$,A$)
160 WHILE I <> 0
165 REM           (1)              (2)            (3)
170     MSG$ = LEFT$(MSG$,I-1) + B$ + MID$(MSG$,I+LEN(A$))
180     I = INSTR(I+LEN(A$),MSG$,A$)
190 WEND
200 GOTO 110
210 DATA "LIONS AND TIGERS AND BEARS, OH MY!"
```

When this program is run, it looks like this:

```
RUN

LIONS AND TIGERS AND BEARS, OH MY!
Replace: TIGERS
With: COUGARS

LIONS AND COUGARS AND BEARS, OH MY!
Replace: LIONS AND
With: ELEPHANTS OR

ELEPHANTS OR COUGARS AND BEARS, OH MY!
Replace: E
With: e

eLePHANTS OR COUGARS AND BeARS, OH MY!
Replace:
Ok
```

In lines 120 and 140, LINE INPUT is used rather than INPUT so that either the string you are replacing or the replacement string may contain commas. Pressing just the RETURN key in response to the LINE INPUT statement at line 120 will end the program at line 130. In line 150 the variable **I** is set to the position of the first occurrence of **A$** in **MSG$**. If **I** is 0, this means that the string to replace was not found, and the WHILE loop is not executed. The actual replacement happens in line 170.

```
165 REM            (1)              (2)             (3)
170    MSG$ = LEFT$(MSG$,I-1) + B$ + MID$(MSG$,I+LEN(A$))
```

The three parts of the equation on line 170 represent 1) the beginning of the message string up to the position where replacement will start; 2) the replacement **B$**; and 3) the last part of the message, which is not affected by the replacement. These three sections are concatenated to give the new message.

In the first example run, the three parts of line 170 would be

```
1) "LIONS AND "
2) "COUGARS"
3) " AND BEARS, OH MY!"
```

The WHILE loop at line 160 continues searching for **A$** in **MSG$** until **A$** is no longer found. The argument **I + LEN(A$)** of the

INSTR function in line 180 ensures that the search will start after the last replacement.

Tutorial 9-3: Cryptogram

A cryptogram is a message written in code. Our next example allows you to enter a message in uppercase letters. These letters are then exchanged with their corresponding letters in the code string. All spaces, punctuation marks, or lowercase letters are passed through unchanged.

```
10 REM -                    -=*CRYPTO.C9*=-
20 REM -                    Message encrypter
30 REM -                    1/2/83
40 REM -
100 ALPHA$ ="ABCDEFGHIJKLMNOPQRSTUVWXYZ"   'Uppercase alphabet
110 CODE$ = "KIEVNHUPOQRAXLTYSZBGWJFCMD"   'One-to-one replacements for ALPHA$
120 PRINT:LINE INPUT "Enter a message to encode: ";MESSG$
130 IF LEN(MESSG$) = 0 THEN END
140 ENCODE$ = MESSG$                       'Initialize encoded message
150 FOR I=1 TO LEN(MESSG$)
160     INDEX = INSTR(ALPHA$,MID$(MESSG$,I,1))
170     IF INDEX > 0 THEN MID$(ENCODE$,I,1) = MID$(CODE$,INDEX,1)
180 NEXT I
190 PRINT "The encoded message is    : ";ENCODE$
200 GOTO 120
```

When the program is run, it looks like this:

```
RUN

Enter a message to encode: HELLO BASIC
The encoded message is    : PNAAT IKBOE

Enter a message to encode: GOODBYE
The encoded message is    : UTTVIMN

Enter a message to encode:
Ok
```

The key part of this program is lines 140 through 180. Line 140 initially sets the encoded message **ENCODE$** equal to the original message **MESSG$**. The FOR/NEXT loop in lines 150 through 180 replaces each character in **ENCODE$** that is found in the string **ALPHA$** with the corresponding character in the string **CODE$**.

Characters in **ENCODE$** that are not found in **ALPHA$**, such as punctuation and lowercase, are left alone.

Notice that the position in **ALPHA$** of each character in **ENCODE$** is stored in the variable **INDEX. INDEX** is set to zero if the character is not found in **ALPHA$**. Also notice that in line 170 one character is replaced with the MID$ statement and MID$ function. Variable **I** is the position of the character in the **ENCODE$** string that is replaced with the character in **CODE$** at position **INDEX**. The MID$ function on the left side of the equation in line 170 tells where in **ENCODE$** the assignment is to go, and the MID$ function on the right side of the equation tells which character to assign. The string **ENCODE$** is changed "in place"; that is, its length never changes throughout the FOR/NEXT loop.

When the loop is completed, the encoded message is then printed by line 190.

EXERCISES

1. Use the random number generator to generate ten words. Have each word randomly contain from five to eight characters. Print each word.

2. Use READ and DATA statements to read in five names, last name first, with the last name and first name separated by a comma and one space. Have your program print the names last name first (as they were read in) and then first name first. Here is an example of output for one name:

```
Smith, Alfred   Alfred Smith
```

Use the following data:

```
DATA "Smith, Alfred","Jones, Tom","Surges, Mary"
DATA "Able, Susan","Waters, Larry"
```

3. Modify the program in Tutorial 9-1 to accept passwords of any length. Use INPUT$ so that the input is not echoed to the screen. Assume that the user will press RETURN following the password entry. (Hint: Input the password one character at a time until you read a RETURN character.)

4. Write a program to decode messages encoded by the program in Tutorial 9-3. (Hint: This can be done by one change to lines 160 and 170.)

10

Using Arrays

Statements:	DIM, OPTION BASE, ERASE
Functions:	FRE

Until now, all of our programs have used different letters or groups of letters to represent variables. These variables hold the data entered into the programs.

```
10 A = 1:B = 2:C = 3:D = 4
20 PRINT A,B,C,D

RUN
 1             2             3             4
Ok
```

Another and more versatile method of holding program data is to use *subscripted* variables. In this case we use a letter and a number enclosed in parentheses. The following program is the same as the previous program. This time, however, we are using a single letter, *A*, and subscripts to name our variables:

```
10 A(1)=1:A(2)=2:A(3)=3:A(4)=4
20 PRINT A(1),A(2),A(3),A(4)

RUN
 1             2             3             4
Ok
```

The numbers in parentheses are the subscripts; the variable A(1) is read aloud "A sub 1." Data assigned to subscripted variables in this manner is collectively called an *array.* In this example we used the single letter A to name the array. The rules for naming array variables are the same as those for naming the variables you have been using. The array subscripts can be any expression, from a simple constant or variable to a complicated mathematical expression.

Forming an Array

The major advantage of working with an array is that all of the data you assign to the array is stored in the computer and you can manipulate arrays as many times as you like. As an example, consider the next two programs. They have the same structure and perform the same simple task.

```
10 FOR X = 0 TO 4
20    A = X * 2
30    PRINT A;
40 NEXT X

RUN
 0  2  4  6  8
Ok
```

Now if we enter direct mode and give the command **PRINT A**, we get **8**, but the previous values of **A** (2, 4, and 6) are lost. If we want to preserve those values, we can change the program so that it uses subscripted variables in an array, as follows:

```
10 FOR X = 0 TO 4
20    A(X)=X * 2
30    PRINT A(X);
40 NEXT X
```

```
RUN
 0  2  4  6  8
Ok
```

Now print out all the variables from the direct mode. You will see that this time all the values are retained in the computer's memory:

```
PRINT A(0);A(1);A(2);A(3);A(4)
 0  2  4  6  8
Ok
```

In the first example we could, of course, have used a different letter for each variable to accomplish the same thing. But if you have a large amount of data—say, 20 names and phone numbers—using subscripted variables is by far the easier way to enter and store data.

Let's make one change in this program. In line 10 we will change our counter to go from 0 to 20. This will give our array, **A**, 21 values: **A(0)** through **A(20)**. Now when we run the program, notice that we get an error message, "Subscript out of range in 20."

```
10 FOR X = 0 TO 20
20   A(X)=X * 2
30   PRINT A(X)
40 NEXT X

RUN
 0  2  4  6  8  10  12  14  16  18  20
Subscript out of range in 20
Ok
```

We can solve this problem by using a DIM statement.

Dimensioning an Array
[DIM]

The DIM statement is required whenever you wish to use arrays that have more than 11 elements. The error in the preceding program occurred when the FOR/NEXT loop tried to print **A(11)**. If the DIM statement is not used, a maximum value for the subscript of 10 is assumed. If you attempt to enter an array value beyond that used in the DIM statement or beyond 10 if you have not used a DIM statement, you will receive the "Subscript out of range" error message.

A second function of the DIM statement is to initialize the value of all elements of the array to 0. For example:

```
5 DIM A(20)
10 FOR X = 0 TO 20
20   A(X)=X * 2
30   PRINT A(X);
40 NEXT X

RUN
 0  2  4  6  8  10  12  14  16  18  20  22  24  26  28  30  32  34  36  38  40
Ok
```

If an array is going to contain more than 11 variables, it must be dimensioned before the array is first accessed. Once the array has been accessed, it may not be redimensioned.

String Arrays

In the next example, we use several of the functions introduced in the previous chapter to produce random words. We will use subscripted variables to work with strings. An array can contain either strings or numbers.

```
10 INPUT "How many words do you want ";WORDS
20 DIM A$(WORDS)
30 RANDOMIZE
40 FOR Y = 1 TO WORDS
50    FOR X = 1 TO 5
60       A$(X) = CHR$(INT(26*RND)+65)
70       PRINT A$(X);
80    NEXT X
90 IF Y/5 = INT(Y/5) THEN PRINT ELSE PRINT " ";
100 NEXT Y

RUN
How many words do you want ? 5
Random number seed (-32768 to 32767)? 10101
VYJQB WPYLN IDBIO OBHQI MJJMI
Ok
```

First we use an INPUT statement to set the size of our array. Our variable **WORDS** is then used with a DIM statement and also in our FOR/NEXT loop. Line 60 uses three of the MBASIC functions to produce random capital letters. Integer random numbers are produced in the range 65 to 91; then the CHR$ function is used to convert these numbers to letters. The FOR/NEXT loop in lines 50-80 prints the letters in groups of five to form a "word." Notice in line 90 how the INT function is used to cause a carriage return after each set of five words is printed.

Changing the Array Base
[OPTION BASE]

You have the choice of setting the first subscript of an array to a value of 1 or leaving it at the default value of 0. No values other than 0 or 1 are permitted for the minimum subscript. One purpose in setting the minimum value of the subscript to 1 is to make programs compatible when you change from one manufacturer's version of BASIC to MBASIC.

The function OPTION BASE is used to assign a minimum value of 1 to array subscripts. It must be placed in the program before the DIM statement. There are the two possibilities for OPTION BASE. The second possibility, although legal, is unnecessary since 0 is the default value.

```
10 OPTION BASE 1     'The first array element is 1 instead of 0
20 DIM A(15)         'This will reserve 15 data elements (1-15).
```

PRINT A(1) will give the first array element, while PRINT A(0) will give a "Subscript out of range" error.

```
10 OPTION BASE 0     'This is the default mode for arrays.
20 DIM A(15)         'This will reserve 16 data elements (0-15).
```

PRINT A(0) will give the first array element.

Forming Two-Dimensional Arrays

Our array examples up to this point have shown only one-dimensional arrays. But many times it is convenient to associate data in rows and columns. For example, the newspaper often shows the major league standings, as in Table 10-1; this is one example of a two-dimensional array. Each of the rows shows the information for a team, and each of the columns shows the same type of information for all the teams.

The notation for two-dimensional arrays consists of the array name and two subscripts inside the parentheses—for example, A(2,4). The first subscript represents the row and the second subscript represents the column. In Table 10-1, the data in position (2,4) is .556.

Table 10-2 is a 3×4 array; that is, it has three rows and four columns. In order to identify any element in the array, you would use a variable name to identify the array, a number to identify the row, and a number to identify the column, such as EASTDIV(BALT, PCT). As Table 10-2 describes array **A**, **A(1,1)=4** and **A(2,3)=**9.

Table 10-1.
Example of a Two-Dimensional Array

AMERICAN LEAGUE EAST DIVISION				
	W	L	PCT	GB
BALTIMORE	11	8	.579	—
MILWAUKEE	10	8	.556	1/2
BOSTON	10	8	.556	1/2
NEW YORK	9	10	.474	2
DETROIT	8	9	.471	2
TORONTO	8	10	.444	2 1/2
CLEVELAND	8	11	.421	3

Table 10-2.
Example of a 3×4 Array

	COLUMN 1	COLUMN 2	COLUMN 3	COLUMN 4
ROW 1	4	10	5	12
ROW 2	2	3	9	6
ROW 3	11	7	1	8

Now consider the following program. First we use a nested loop to read in an array from **DATA** statements, and then we use a second nested loop to print the array.

```
120 DATA 3,6,1
130 DATA 5,2,8
140 DATA 7,4,9
145 REM                          Read in the array
150 FOR R = 1 TO 3
160   FOR C = 1 TO 3
170      READ G(R,C)
180   NEXT C
190 NEXT R
200 REM                            Print the array
210 FOR A = 1 TO 3
220   FOR B = 1 TO 3
230      PRINT USING "##";G(A,B);
240   NEXT B
250   PRINT
260 NEXT A

RUN
 3 6 1
 5 2 8
 7 4 9
Ok
```

Notice that in lines 150 through 190 where the array is read, the subscript variables **R** and **C** are used to represent row and column. In the FOR/NEXT loop for printing (lines 210 through 260) we use **A** and **B**. It makes no difference what letters are used for the subscript variables or whether they change. Just keep in mind that the first variable is the row and the second is the column.

You will often want to perform mathematical operations on an array. The following shows replacement lines for the previous program. In order to find the sum of each row in array **G**, we insert lines 225, 245, and 246. Run the program and trace through the output section to verify the output indicated.

```
210 FOR A = 1 TO 3
220   FOR B = 1 TO 3
225      SUM.ROW=SUM.ROW + G(A,B)
230      PRINT USING "## ";G(A,B);
240   NEXT B
245   PRINT "=";SUM.ROW
246   SUM.ROW = 0
260 NEXT A
```

```
RUN
 3  6  1 = 10
 5  2  8 = 15
 7  4  9 = 20
Ok
```

In the following example, we again change the output of the above 3×3 array. This time we want to find the sum of the columns for array **G**.

```
210 FOR A = 1 TO 3
220   FOR B = 1 TO 3
225      SUM.COL(A)=SUM.COL(A) +G(B,A)
230      PRINT USING "## ";G(A,B);
240   NEXT B
250   PRINT
260 NEXT A
270 PRINT " -    -    -"
280 FOR X = 1 TO 3
290   PRINT SUM.COL(X);
300 NEXT X
```

```
RUN
 3  6  1
 5  2  8
 7  4  9
 -  -  -
 15  12  18
Ok
```

In order to find the sum, we change the subscripts of our array from **A,B** to **B,A** (line 225). Notice that because we cannot print the sums of the columns until the entire array has been printed, we need a second FOR/NEXT loop to print out the sums (lines 280 through 300). Since we wait until the nested loop is completed (lines 210 through 260), we must calculate and store the sums with the subscripted array, **SUM.COL(A)**. Trace through the program by hand and then run the program to verify the output.

Our final program dealing with the array G will find the sum of the diagonals. This is shown in Figure 10-1.

Note that the row and column subscripts for diagonal 1 (DIAG1) are equal: (1,1), (2,2), and (3,3). For diagonal 2 (DIAG2), note that the row subscript decreases by 1 each time and the column subscript increases by 1. We can take advantage of these characteristics of a

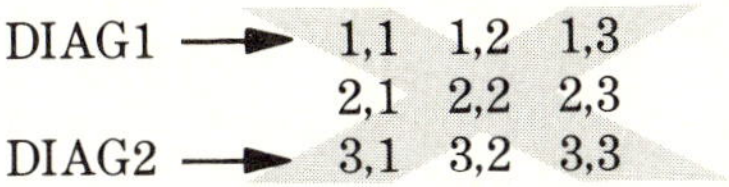

Figure 10-1.
Diagonals of a 3×3 array

square array and find the sum of the diagonals using only one FOR/NEXT loop. Again, trace the problem through to obtain your result and verify the result by running the problem.

```
210 FOR A = 1 TO 3
225      DIAG1=DIAG1 + G(A,A)
226      DIAG2=DIAG2 + G(4-A,A)
230      PRINT USING "## ";G(A,B);
250      PRINT
260 NEXT A
270 PRINT "Sum of elements for diagonal #1:";DIAG1
280 PRINT "Sum of elements for diagonal #2:";DIAG2

RUN
 3  6  1
 5  2  8
 7  4  9
Sum of elements for diagonal #1:  14
Sum of elements for diagonal #2:  10
Ok
```

MBASIC allows you to have arrays with as many as 255 dimensions, although such arrays are usually unwieldy. Some programs, especially for engineering or design, use three-dimensional arrays, but we will only use one- and two-dimensional arrays in this book.

Computing Memory Requirements For Arrays

Can we fill a two-dimensional array of 100×100 with random numbers from 0 to 1? Let's try it:

```
10 DIM R(100,100)
20 FOR I = 1 TO 100
30    FOR J = 1 TO 100
40        R(I,J) = RND
50    NEXT J
60 NEXT I
```

```
RUN
Out of memory in 10
Ok
```

In this program MBASIC tried to set aside enough memory for a 100×100 square array and failed. Why? Because the array was too big for memory. How big an array can we dimension?

Let's look at this question of array size. For example:

```
10 OPTION BASE 1
20 DIM A(500)
```

Here we are using the variables **A(1)**, **A(2)**, ..., **A(500)**, which is a total of 500 variables. Now consider the following two-dimensional array:

```
10 OPTION BASE 1
20 DIM A(200,100)
```

This creates an array of 200 rows by 100 columns, or a total of 20,000 variables, shown in Figure 10-2.

The relevant question then is whether our computer has enough memory units (bytes) to handle 20,000 variables.

As you might have guessed, different types of variables will require different amounts of memory. That is to say, a double-precision array with 100 variables will take more memory than an integer array with 100 variables. Computer memory is measured in bytes. Table 10-3 gives the amount of memory taken up by each type of variable. The single-precision, two-dimensional array A(200,100) would have required at least 80,000 bytes!

$$200\left\{\overbrace{\begin{array}{llll} A(1,1), & A(1,2), & ..., & A(1,100) \\ A(2,1), & A(2,2), & ..., & A(2,100) \\ \cdot & \cdot & \cdot & \cdot \\ \cdot & \cdot & \cdot & \cdot \\ \cdot & \cdot & \cdot & \cdot \\ A(200,1), & A(200,2), & ..., & A(200,100) \end{array}}^{100}\right.$$

Figure 10-2.
A 200×100 array

Table 10-3.
Storage Size for Numeric Variables

Type	Number of Bytes
Integer (A%)	2
Single precision (A!)	4
Double precision (A#)	8

The important thing to remember is that each variable in your program will require memory for storage. To find the total number of bytes available for your program, look at the sign-on message from MBASIC:

```
BASIC-80 Rev. 5.21
[CP/M Version]
Copyright 1977-1981 (C) by Microsoft
Created: 28-Jul-81
24286 Bytes free
Ok
```

Finding Memory Available
[FRE]

In addition to the MBASIC sign-on message, which indicates the number of bytes free in your computer, you may also use the FRE function. This is useful whenever you want to determine the amount of available memory. Note that the FRE function needs an argument but that the argument is a dummy argument. Any argument, numeric or string, used in conjunction with the FRE function will return the number of bytes not being used by MBASIC. The value returned from FRE will, of course, vary depending on the capacity of your computer and your program. We will talk more about storage in Chapter 14.

Recapturing Memory
[ERASE]

The ERASE statement is used to cancel a previous DIM statement. After you have used ERASE, you may redimension an array to a larger value if needed. You can also redimension to a smaller value in order to free captured memory space and make it available to the computer for other uses. You can erase as many arrays at one time as you can specify on a single line.

```
10 ERASE A
20 ERASE B,OLD$
```

TUTORIALS

Tutorial 10-1: Numbers

This application changes numerals that you enter at the keyboard into numbers (words) that are printed on the screen. It is an extension of Tutorial 4-2 but uses some of the instructions introduced in this chapter.

```
10 REM -                   -=*NBR999.C10*=-
20 REM -                   Longhand numbers
30 REM -                   1/2/83
40 REM -
100 DEFINT A-Z
110 DIM NUMBER$(27)
120 FOR I = 1 TO 27
130    READ NUMBER$(I)
140 NEXT I
150 PRINT: INPUT "Enter a number between 1 and 999 or enter 0 to end: ",X
160 IF X = 0 THEN END
170 IF X >= 1 AND X <= 999 THEN 200
180    PRINT "Sorry, the number must be between 1 and 999."
190    GOTO 150
200 PRINT "The number is ":
210 IF X >= 100 THEN PRINT NUMBER$(X\100);" hundred";: X = X MOD 100
220 IF X > 20 THEN PRINT " ";NUMBER$(X\10 + 18);: X = X MOD 10
230 IF X >= 1 AND X <= 20 THEN PRINT " ";NUMBER$(X);
240 PRINT "."
250 GOTO 150
260
270 DATA one,two,three,four,five,six,seven,eight,nine,ten,eleven,twelve
280 DATA thirteen,fourteen,fifteen,sixteen,seventeen,eighteen,nineteen
290 DATA twenty,thirty,forty,fifty,sixty,seventy,eighty,ninety
```

First, the numbers in the program below are read from DATA into a one-dimensional string array. Since the array has more than 11 elements, we use the DIM statement in line 110. Lines 160 through 190 check the numeral you enter to see that it is within the range for this program. Notice that in lines 210 and 220, integer division and the MOD operator are used. The integer division is faster than regular division. The key part of this program is lines 210 through 230. Let's trace through this section of the program, using the number 743 as our example.

```
Line 210  NUMBER$(X\100) = NUMBER$(7) = "seven"
          X = X MOD 100 = 43

Line 220  NUMBER$(X\10+18) = NUMBER$(22) = "forty"
          X = X MOD 10 = 3

Line 230  NUMBER$(X) = NUMBER$(3) = "three"
```

When this program is run, it looks like this:

```
RUN

Enter a number between 1 and 999 or enter 0 to end: 743
The number is seven hundred forty three.

Enter a number between 1 and 999 or enter 0 to end: 212
The number is two hundred twelve.

Enter a number between 1 and 999 or enter 0 to end: 5
The number is  five.

Enter a number between 1 and 999 or enter 0 to end: 0
Ok
```

Tutorial 10-2: Dealing Poker

Our second application uses the random number generator to deal poker hands. The important point here is to avoid the possibility of the same card showing up twice within the same round.

```
10 REM -                -=*DEAL.C10*=-
20 REM -                Deal poker hands
30 REM -                12/28/82
40 REM -
100 DEFINT A-Z
110 RANDOMIZE
```

(Tutorial 10-1: Continued)

```
120 NO.CARDS = 52
130 HAND.LEN = 5
140 NO.HANDS = 5
150 DIM CARD$(NO.CARDS)
160 INDEX$=""
170 FOR I = 1 TO NO.CARDS
180    READ CARD$(I)
190    INDEX$ = INDEX$+CHR$(I)
200 NEXT I
210 FOR HAND = 1 TO NO.HANDS
220    PRINT USING "Hand #:  ";HAND;
230    FOR I = 1 TO HAND.LEN
240       CARD = INT(RND*LEN(INDEX$)) + 1
250       PRINT USING "\ \  ";CARD$(ASC(MID$(INDEX$,CARD,1)));
260       INDEX$ = LEFT$(INDEX$,CARD - 1) + MID$(INDEX$,CARD + 1)
270    NEXT I
280    PRINT
290 NEXT HAND
300 END
310 '
320 'Card data.  *, #, ^, and @ are suits
330 '
340 DATA 2*,3*,4*,5*,6*,7*,8*,9*,10*,J*,Q*,K*,A*
350 DATA 2#,3#,4#,5#,6#,7#,8#,9#,10#,J#,Q#,K#,A#
360 DATA 2^,3^,4^,5^,6^,7^,8^,9^,10^,J^,Q^,K^,A^
370 DATA 2@,3@,4@,5@,6@,7@,8@,9@,10@,J@,Q@,K@,A@
```

To see how this is done, first consider the FOR/NEXT loop, lines 170 through 200. In line 190 the CHR$ function is used to assign a number to each card as it is read from DATA. The numbers are in sequence from 1 through 52 and are stored as characters in a string instead of as integers in an array. The nested FOR/NEXT loop in lines 210 through 290 controls the number of hands that are dealt and the number of cards dealt to each hand. Lines 240 through 260 choose the card and avoid the possibility of the same card being chosen twice. In the first pass through, line 240 chooses a random number in the range 1 to 52. This number points to a specific card. Line 250 prints out the card and line 260 removes that card's index from the list so that the card cannot be chosen a second time.

Suppose that the random number determined in line 240 was the number 29 (see Figure 10-3). The card that represents the twenty-ninth position in the list would be printed. Then in line 260, the number 29 would be removed from the list, and the **INDEX$** numbers would range from 1 through 28 and from 30 through 52, as in Figure 10-4. In a second pass, even if the number 29 were chosen

1,2,3,...,28,29,30,...,52

↑

Card to be
removed

Figure 10-3.
Deck of cards before removing a card

1,2,3,...,28,30,...,52

Figure 10-4.
Deck of cards after removing a card

again, it would go to the twenty-ninth position in **INDEX$**, which would be a character with the ASCII value of 30, and the thirtieth card would be printed.

This procedure is repeated until all five hands have been dealt. Each time the program returns to line 240, the length of **INDEX$** has been decreased by 1, and therefore the range of the random numbers has been decreased by 1.

When this program is run, it looks like this:

```
RUN
Random number seed (-32768 to 32767)? 344
Hand 1:  Q^   4^   A@   5#   K@
Hand 2:  6#   6*   J@   K#   8*
Hand 3:  10#  9#   6^   A^   3#
Hand 4:  6@   J*   Q*   A#   Q@
Hand 5:  2#   3^   10*  2@   2*
Ok
RUN
Random number seed (-32768 to 32767)? 343
Hand 1:  5^   8*   9@   9*   10@
Hand 2:  8^   6*   2^   2#   2*
Hand 3:  10^  6^   9#   K@   A#
Hand 4:  6@   3#   J@   8@   10*
Hand 5:  Q*   2@   7#   A@   5*
Ok
```

Tutorial 10-3: Payroll

We again return to our payroll program, which last appeared in Chapter 7. This time we add some of the instructions introduced in this chapter and in the previous chapter.

```
10 REM -                  -=*PAYROLL.C10*=-
20 REM -                  Employee payroll
30 REM -                  1/2/83
40 REM -
1000 DEFINT A-Z
1010 OPTION BASE 1
1020 MAX.EMP = 20                                 'Maximum number of employees
1030 FORMAT$ = "\" + SPACE$(23) + "\ $$#####.##" 'Set print line format
1040 DIM EMP.NAME$(MAX.EMP),EMP.RATE!(MAX.EMP)
1050 NO.EMP = 0                                   'Initialize no. of employees
1060 PRINT:LINE INPUT "Enter employee name: ";EMP.NAME$
1070    IF EMP.NAME$ = "" THEN 1130               'Null string signals end
1080    NO.EMP = NO.EMP + 1                       'Increment employee count
1090    PRINT USING "Enter pay rate for &: ";EMP.NAME$;
1100    INPUT EMP.RATE!(NO.EMP)
1110    EMP.NAME$(NO.EMP) = EMP.NAME$
1120    IF NO.EMP <= MAX.EMP THEN 1060            'Must check for array bounds
1130 PRINT:PRINT
1140 TOTAL.WAGES = 0                              'Initialize total wages
1150 FOR I = 1 TO NO.EMP
1160    EMP.EARN! = EMP.RATE!(I)*8                'Compute employee earnings
1170    PRINT USING FORMAT$;EMP.NAME$(I);EMP.EARN!
1180    TOTAL.WAGES! = TOTAL.WAGES! + EMP.EARN! 'Total employee wages
1190 NEXT I
1200 PRINT STRING$(LEN(FORMAT$),"-")
1210 PRINT USING FORMAT$;"Total wages";TOTAL.WAGES!
1220 END
```

In line 1010 we use OPTION BASE to set our first subscript to 1. In line 1030, **FORMAT$** holds the output for our format statement. Notice the use of the SPACE$ function. This is more convenient (and usually more accurate) than pressing the space bar exactly 23 times. It is also more convenient to change the length of this string by changing the SPACE$ argument.

In 1060, LINE INPUT is used instead of the INPUT statement so that employee names may be entered last name first and separated by a comma. Finally, in line 1200 the STRING$ function is used to set the number of hyphens needed to form the line that separates all of the employees' individual wages from the total wages. This is a more convenient method of printing than having to enter 37 dashes in a string literal.

When this program is run it looks like this:

```
RUN

Enter employee name: Ann Walters
Enter pay rate for Ann Walters: ? 7.50

Enter employee name: Barry Kulp
Enter pay rate for Barry Kulp: ? 5.50

Enter employee name: Bill Walker
Enter pay rate for Bill Walker: ? 5.50

Enter employee name:


Ann Walters                   $60.00
Barry Kulp                    $44.00
Bill Walker                   $44.00
-------------------------------------
Total wages                  $148.00
Ok
```

EXERCISES

1. Use a random number generator to generate a list with ten elements. Print out this list, and then print out the largest number in the list and the smallest number in the list.

2. Use the list from the previous problem and print out the same results, along with the position in the list of the largest and smallest values.

3. Given two sorted lists of ten numbers each, combine them into one sorted list. Use A(X) for the first list and B(Y) for the second list. Let the combined list be C(Z). Use the following data for the lists:

```
DATA 7,14,15,19,24,31,38,41,43,49
DATA 1,8,13,14,27,29,35,37,40,44
```

4. Using the random number generator, fill a 4×5 array with integers in the range 10 to 99. Find and print out the largest value and the smallest value in the array.

5. Using the array from the preceding exercise, add the elements from column 1 to the elements in column 5, and put these in column 5. Print the array before and after the addition of the columns.

6. Use the random number generator to fill a 6×8 array with numbers in the range −50 to 50. Print the array and the largest number from each column.

II.

Advanced Tools

11

Working With Subroutines

> Statements: ON/GOTO, GOSUB, RETURN, ON/GOSUB

Up to this point we have made frequent use of the GOTO statement. The GOTO statement is used for simple branching and directs the computer to a specific line of the program.

Multiple Branching [ON/GOTO]

A variation of GOTO is ON/GOTO. This involves multiple or *non-direct* branching. Multiple branching allows your program to branch to any one of several line numbers based on a condition. The expression following the ON must be reducible to an integer. The integer then tells the program which line of the optional list of line numbers to branch to.

The syntax of the ON/GOTO command is: ON expression GOTO line1, line2, line3, ... The *expression* is evaluated and rounded to an integer and must evaluate to between 0 and 255. The result of the expression specifies which line number in the list is chosen for the GOTO. For instance, if A is 2, then ON A GOTO 100, 150, 500 would cause MBASIC to go to line 150.

In the following example, if **ANS** is 1, the program branches to the first line number in the list (100); if **ANS** is 2, the program branches to the second number (200), and so on. The line numbers do not have to be in numerical order. The only thing that is crucial is their relative position after GOTO.

```
10  INPUT "Enter a number in the range(1-4): ":ANS
20  ON ANS GOTO 100,200,250,400
100 PRINT "Welcome to line 100.":END
200 PRINT "Welcome to line 200.":END
250 PRINT "Welcome to line 250.":END
400 PRINT "Welcome to line 400.":END
```

```
RUN
Enter a number in the range(1-4): ? 3
Welcome to line 250.
Ok
```

The maximum number of optional line numbers that can be specified following GOTO is 255. You could easily enter as many as ten different line options on one line. What would happen if you answered the preceding INPUT question with a number greater than the number of line numbers? Try this with the previous example by entering an answer of 7:

```
RUN
Enter a number in the range(1-4): ? 7
Welcome to line 100.
Ok
```

If the expression following ON is greater than the number of lines you have specified as options, then the program will proceed to the *next* line after the ON/GOTO. It will also go to the next line if the expression is 0.

In the next example, what follows ON is a slightly complex expression instead of a variable.

```
10 RANDOMIZE
20 ON INT(5*RND)+1 GOTO 100,200,300,400
100 PRINT "Welcome to line 100.":END
200 PRINT "Welcome to line 200.":END
300 PRINT "Welcome to line 300.":END
400 PRINT "Welcome to line 400.":END
500 PRINT "Welcome to line 500.":END


RUN
Random number seed (-32768 to 32767)? 56
Welcome to line 100.
Ok
```

The expression **INT(5*RND)+1** reduces to an integer in the range 1 through 5. In this case, with a seed of 56, the expression is reduced to 1.

Using Subroutines
[GOSUB, RETURN]

When you are writing programs in MBASIC, you will find that you frequently wish to perform the same operation more than once. If these operations are more than a couple of lines in length, it is worthwhile to write them once and "call" them each time they are needed. These calls are made with the GOSUB statement. Note also that the operations called up by the GOSUB statement are referred to as *subroutines*. Subroutines can be called from any point in your program.

Before we get into applications that use subroutines, let's be sure that you understand the sequence in which lines are executed. Note that a GOSUB statement is always used in conjunction with a RETURN statement. When the program reaches the GOSUB statement, it immediately branches to the line indicated. When the program reaches the RETURN statement, it has completed the subroutine and transfers execution of the program back to the line following the GOSUB statement.

Enter and run the following example:

```
10 PRINT "On line 10"
20 GOSUB 100
30 PRINT "On line 30"
40 GOSUB 100
50 PRINT "All done"
```

```
90 END
100 REM     This is the subroutine
110 PRINT "In the subroutine"
120 RETURN
```

```
RUN
On line 10
In the subroutine
On line 30
In the subroutine
All done
Ok
```

Figure 11-1 shows the order of execution for this example.

You may have several GOSUB commands in a program; in fact, you may have a GOSUB command within a subroutine. This is called a *nested subroutine.* In nested subroutines, the RETURN statement returns you to the line following the most recent GOSUB statement.

```
10 PRINT "On line 10"
20 GOSUB 100
30 PRINT "On line 30"
40 GOSUB 100
50 PRINT "All done"
90 END
100 REM     This is the subroutine
110 PRINT "In the subroutine"
115 GOSUB 150
120 RETURN
150 REM     Second subroutine
160 PRINT "In the second subroutine"
170 RETURN
```

```
RUN
On line 10
In the subroutine
In the second subroutine
On line 30
In the subroutine
In the second subroutine
All done
Ok
```

The sequence of line execution in the preceding program is shown in Figure 11-2. Subroutines are normally preceded by an END, STOP, or GOTO statement to prevent your program from entering these subroutines accidentally.

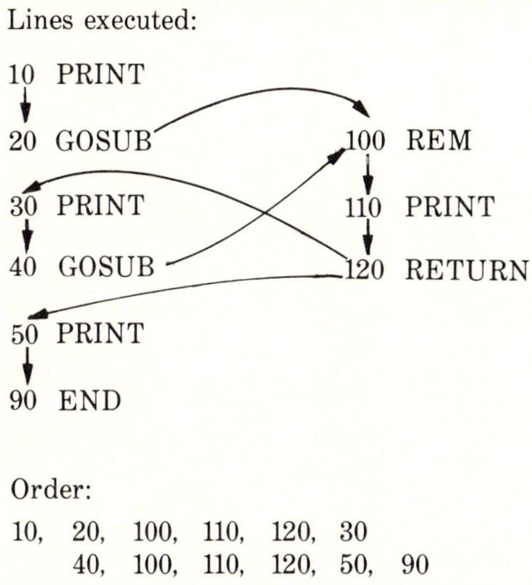

Figure 11-1.
Execution of a subroutine

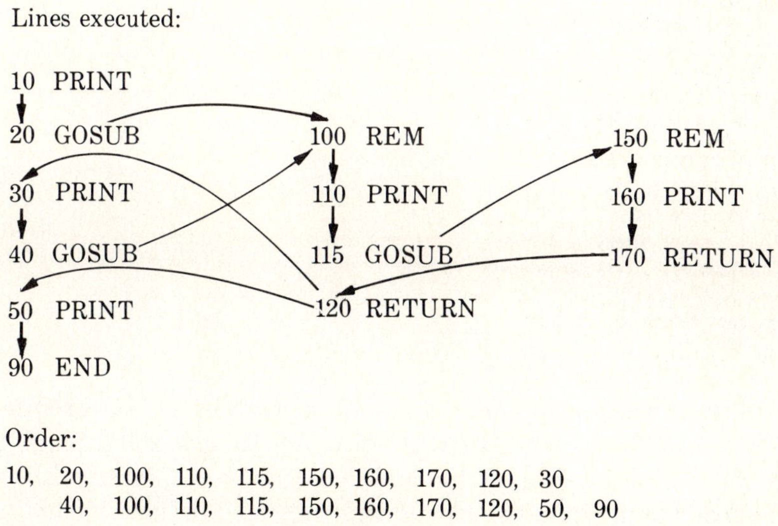

Figure 11-2.
Subroutine within a subroutine

Multiple Subroutines [ON/GOSUB]

The ON/GOSUB statement is similar to ON/GOTO in that the expression following ON reduces to an integer, which then tells the program which subroutine to transfer to from the list of line numbers presented. Enter and run the following program to be sure you understand the branching that occurs:

```
10 PRINT "Would you like to:"
20 PRINT "     1) Convert meters to feet?"
30 PRINT "     2) Convert liters to gallons?"
40 PRINT "     3) End?"
50 INPUT "Enter your choice (1-3): ";CHOICE
60 ON CHOICE GOSUB 100,200,90
70 GOTO 10
90 END
100 PRINT:PRINT  "Subroutine: meters to feet"
105 PRINT
110 RETURN
200 PRINT:PRINT "Subroutine: liters to gallons"
205 PRINT
210 RETURN
```

```
RUN
Would you like to:
     1) Convert meters to feet?
     2) Convert liters to gallons?
     3) End?
Enter your choice (1-3): ? 1

Subroutine: meters to feet

Would you like to:
     1) Convert meters to feet?
     2) Convert liters to gallons?
     3) End?
Enter your choice (1-3): ? 3
Ok
```

In the preceding example, lines 10 through 90 are referred to as the *main program*, while lines 100 through 110 and 200 through 210 are the subroutines. Lines 105 and 205 could be replaced with program code to perform the conversions indicated in lines 100 and 200 and to print the results.

Because variables in MBASIC are *global* (that is, they retain their value wherever encountered in a program), you must be careful that variables assigned in the main program do not conflict with the purpose of the subroutine.

To illustrate this, let's rewrite the blast-off example of Chapter 7, using a subroutine:

```
10 PRINT "-=* COUNT DOWN *=-"
20 FOR X = 10 TO 1 STEP -1
30    PRINT X
40    GOSUB 80  'Timing loop
50 NEXT X
60 PRINT "-=* BLAST OFF *=-"
70 END
80 FOR X = 1 TO 500:NEXT X
90 RETURN
```

```
RUN
-=* COUNT DOWN *=-
 10
 500
 500
 500
 500
 500
 500
^C
Break in 80
Ok
```

If you run this program, you will notice that it goes into an endless loop. Can you tell why? The problem is that we have used the same variable **X** in the main program and in the subroutine. This is one of the most common programming bugs that arise when you use subroutines in MBASIC. When you write a subroutine, it is very easy and, in fact, very natural to ignore the rest of the program and to concentrate just on the local purpose of the subroutine.

As you write longer programs, you will find that using subroutines becomes more and more a standard part of your programming habits. You will also find that many of the subroutines you write for one program are very useful in other programs that you develop later. For this reason, it is worthwhile to document each subroutine thoroughly with REM statements at the beginning of the subroutine. These statements should include a list of variables the subroutine uses. Since all the variables in MBASIC are global, it is important that the variables do not conflict when you copy a subroutine from one program to another program.

TUTORIALS

Tutorial 11-1: Math Quiz

Our first application is a math quiz. This is a simple quiz in the four areas of addition, subtraction, multiplication, and division.

```
10 REM -                -=*MQUIZ.C11*=-
20 REM -                Simple math quiz
30 REM -                12/20/82
40 REM -
100 RANDOMIZE
110 PLAY$="Y"
120 WHILE PLAY$="Y"
130    PRINT
140    PROB=INT(RND*4)+1                'Compute type of problem
150    ON PROB GOSUB 240,310,370,440    'Print problem and get answer
160    INPUT "= ? ",RESP                'Get user response
170    IF RESP=ANS THEN GOSUB 500 ELSE GOSUB 580 'Check against answer
180    PRINT:INPUT "Try another (Y/N)? ",PLAY$
190 WEND
200 END
210 '
220 'Addition problem subroutine
230 '
240 A = INT(RND*100) + 1 : B = INT(RND*100) + 1
250 PRINT A;"+";B;
260 ANS = A + B
270 RETURN
280 '
290 'Subtraction problem subroutine
300 '
310 ANS = INT(RND*100) + 1 : B = INT(RND*100) + 1
320 PRINT ANS+B;"-";B;
330 RETURN
340 '
350 'Multiplication problem subroutine
360 '
370 A = INT(RND*12) + 1 : B = INT(RND*12) + 1
380 PRINT A;"*";B;
390 ANS = A*B
400 RETURN
410 '
420 'Division problem subroutine
430 '
440 ANS = INT(RND*12) + 1 : B = INT(RND*12) + 1
450 PRINT ANS*B;"/";B;
460 RETURN
```

(Tutorial 11-1: Continued)

```
470 '
480 'Correct answer subroutine
490 '
500 ON INT(RND*3)+1 GOTO 510,520,530
510 PRINT "That's right!":GOTO 540
520 PRINT "Wow, you got it!":GOTO 540
530 PRINT "Far out man, you're pretty smart!"
540 RETURN
550 '
560 'Wrong answer subroutine
570 '
580 ON INT(RND*3)+1 GOTO 590,600,610
590 PRINT "Even I know that one,";:GOTO 620
600 PRINT "You can do better than that.";:GOTO 620
610 PRINT "Well, o.k. so it was kind of hard,";
620 PRINT " the correct answer is";ANS
630 RETURN
```

In line 110 the WHILE loop is initialized by setting **PLAY$** to "Y". In line 140, a type of problem is chosen with a random number; the program then transfers from line 150 to one of the four subroutines. Each of these four subroutines will print a math problem and return with the correct answer in the variable **ANS**.

Notice that in the subtraction and division subroutines, the answers are determined first, and then the problems are presented. This is to avoid the possibility of negative results in the subtraction problems and the possibility of decimal fractions in the division problems. After the problems have been generated and printed on the screen, the program returns to line 160, where the user's response is recorded.

In line 170, the response is checked against the correct answer, and again the program transfers to a subroutine to give an appropriate response. On returning to the main program, the user is asked about trying another problem.

```
RUN
Random number seed (-32768 to 32767)? 222

 94 + 36 = ? 130
Far out man, you're pretty smart!

Try another (Y/N)? Y

 101 - 34 = ? 67
Far out man, you're pretty smart!
```

(Tutorial 11-1: Continued)

```
Try another (Y/N)? Y

 110 - 13 = ? 97
That's right!

Try another (Y/N)? Y

 41 + 10 = ? 50
Even I know that one, the correct answer is 51

Try another (Y/N)? N
Ok
```

Tutorial 11-2: Payroll

We return again to the payroll problem. This time the program has been broken up into a main program with subroutines. In addition, a menu has been added.

```
10 REM -                -=*PAYROLL.C11*=-
20 REM -                Customer payroll program
30 REM -                12/27/82
40 REM -
1000 DEFINT A-Z
1010 MAX.EMP = 20                                 'Maximum number of employees
1020 FORMAT$ = "\" + SPACE$(23) + "\ $$####.##" 'Set print line format
1030 DIM EMP.NM$(MAX.EMP),EMP.RATE!(MAX.EMP)
1040 NO.EMP = 0                                   'Initialize no. of employees
1050 '
1060 'Main program
1070 '
1080 PRINT:PRINT "-=< M E N U >=-"
1090 PRINT "1) Enter names and pay rates"
1100 PRINT "2) Compute wages"
1110 PRINT "3) End"
1120 PRINT:INPUT "Select? ",SELECT
1130 IF SELECT < 1 OR SELECT > 3 THEN PRINT "Invalid selection.":GOTO 1120
1140 IF SELECT = 3 THEN END
1150 ON SELECT GOSUB 1200,1320
1160 GOTO 1080
1170 '
1180 'Enter employee names
1190 '
1200 IF NO.EMP = MAX.EMP THEN PRINT "No more room to add names.":RETURN
1210 PRINT:LINE INPUT "Enter employee name <RETURN> for done: ";EMP.NM$
1220 IF EMP.NM$ = "" THEN RETURN                 'Null string signals end
```

(Tutorial 11-2: Continued)

```
1230 NO.EMP = NO.EMP + 1                        'Increment employee count
1240 PRINT USING "Enter pay rate for &: ";EMP.NM$;
1250 INPUT EMP.RATE!(NO.EMP)
1260 EMP.NM$(NO.EMP) = EMP.NM$
1270 GOTO 1200
1290
1300 'Compute wages
1310 '
1320 PRINT:PRINT "Wages for 40 hour week":PRINT
1330 TOTAL.WAGES = 0                            'Initialize total wages
1340 FOR I = 1 TO NO.EMP
1350    EMP.EARN! = EMP.RATE!(I)*8              'Compute employee earnings
1360    PRINT USING FORMAT$;EMP.NM$(I);EMP.EARN!
1370    TOTAL.WAGES! = TOTAL.WAGES! + EMP.EARN! 'Total employee wages
1380 NEXT I
1390 PRINT STRING$(LEN(FORMAT$),"-")
1400 PRINT USING FORMAT$:"Total wages":TOTAL.WAGES!
1410 RETURN
```

In line 1130, a check is made to see whether the selection is within the appropriate range for the menu. If it is, the program transfers to one of the subroutines either to enter names and pay rates or to compute wages. On completion, the subroutines always return to the main menu.

```
RUN
-=< M E N U >=-
1) Enter names and pay rates
2) Compute wages
3) End

Select? 1
Enter employee name <RETURN> for done: Carolyn Atwood
Enter pay rate for Carolyn Atwood: ? 8.25

Enter employee name <RETURN> for done: Eric Brown
Enter pay rate for Eric Brown: ? 8.00

Enter employee name <RETURN> for done: Holly Reese
Enter pay rate for Holly Reese: ? 8.25

Enter employee name <RETURN> for done:

-=< M E N U >=-
1) Enter names and pay rates
2) Compute wages
3) End
```

(Tutorial 11-2: Continued)

```
Select? 2

Wages for 40 hour week

Carolyn Atwood              $66.00
Eric Brown                  $64.00
Holly Reese                 $66.00
----------------------------------
Total wages                $196.00

-=< M E N U >=-
1) Enter names and pay rates
2) Compute wages
3) End

Select? 3
Ok
```

EXERCISES

1. Complete the ON/GOSUB example in this chapter by writing the conversion subroutines. Also add an additional subroutine to convert Celsius to Fahrenheit.

2. Generate a list of 50 random numbers in the range 1 through 100. Give the user of the program the choice of requesting the largest or smallest number in the list. Use only one loop to find the requested number. (Hint: Use ON/GOSUB to do the comparison for largest or smallest number.)

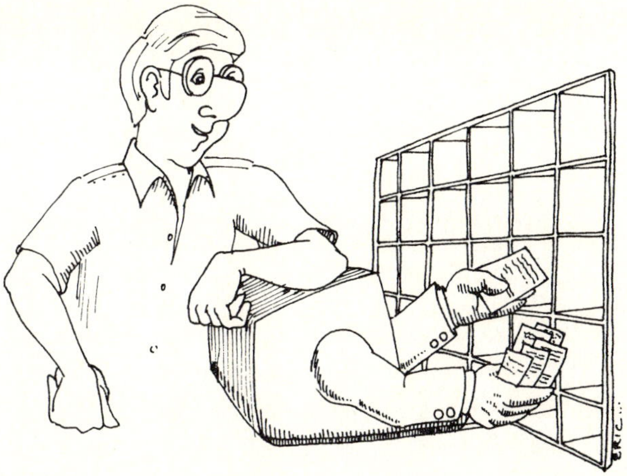

12

Sorting Numbers and Strings

Statements: SWAP

In order to sort numbers and strings, we must first consider the simple problem of exchanging the values of two variables. This is very useful when we want to rearrange the order of a list.

Exchanging Variables [SWAP]

For example, if we have a list consisting of the numbers 9, 4, and 13, we can swap the first and second numbers to obtain the sorted list 4, 9, and 13. If **A**=9 and **B**=4, what would we have to do to switch the values of **A** and **B**? Our first thought might be

```
10 A = 9:B = 4
20 A = B:B = A
30 PRINT A;B

RUN
 4  4
Ok
```

This obviously does not work. As soon as we let **A**=**B**, the first value of **A** was lost from the computer's memory. What we need is a *temporary holder*. Here we will call the temporary holder **T**.

```
10 A = 9:B = 4
20 T = A                    'T = 9  and A = 9
30 A = B                    'A = 4  and B = 4
40 B = T                    'B = 9
50 PRINT A;B

RUN
 4  9
Ok
```

The net result of these three steps is to switch the values held in **A** and **B**. The variable **T** is useful in the same way that an empty bowl is useful when you want to mix some ingredients; or you can think of **T** as a kind of valet who holds your clothes while you are changing from one outfit to another. Also note that these three statements can be written on a single line in the following manner:

```
20 T = A: A = B: B = T
```

This is the old method of exchanging the values of variables. It is shown here because it is necessary with older versions of MBASIC, as well as with many versions of BASIC from other manufacturers. With newer versions of MBASIC, you can perform this exchange of variables quickly and easily with the SWAP statement.

The SWAP statement is used to exchange the values for two variables. Either string or numeric variables may be used as long as they are of the same type. For example, a double-precision variable must be exchanged with another double-precision variable. Otherwise, you will get the error message "Type mismatch". By using the SWAP statement, the previous program becomes

```
10 A = 4:B = 9
20 SWAP A,B
30 PRINT A;B

RUN
 9  4
Ok
```

The SWAP statement makes it easy to exchange two numbers. But what if we want to exchange three or more? Let's take as an example a program that places three numbers in order. The program will generate three random numbers—A(1), A(2), and A(3)—in the range 0 to 9.

Print the numbers in the order generated. Then make whatever exchanges are necessary to print the numbers in numerical order going from the smallest to the largest. But before we do this, let's first construct a flowchart, shown in Figure 12-1. If you need a refresher on the flowchart symbols, see Tutorial 4-1.

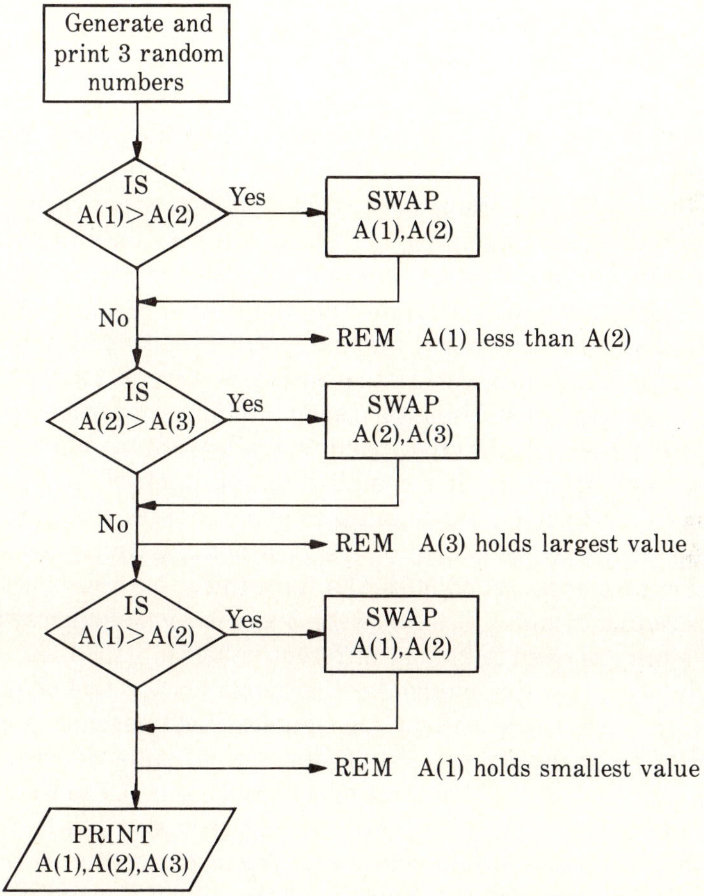

Figure 12-1.
Sorting three random numbers

From our flowchart, we obtain the following program:

```
10 RANDOMIZE
20 FOR X=1 TO 3
30   A(X)=INT(10*RND)
40   PRINT A(X),
50 NEXT X
60 PRINT
70 IF A(1)>A(2) THEN SWAP A(1),A(2)
80 IF A(2)>A(3) THEN SWAP A(2),A(3)
90 IF A(1)>A(2) THEN SWAP A(1),A(2)
100 PRINT A(1),A(2),A(3)

RUN
Random number seed (-32768 to 32767)? 23
 5             0             4
 0             4             5
Ok
```

Run this program enough times to obtain all possible orders of the randomly chosen numbers. Notice that it is important that you use the random number generator to produce your list rather than pick three numbers to test your program, since it is very easy to have a program work for a particular situation and not work for a similar one. For example, you might choose the numbers 3, 6, and 4 to test your program and find it works perfectly. But if the largest number was placed first, or two numbers the same size were in the list, the program might not work. Using the random number generator along with different seeds, on the other hand, will allow you to quickly test your program with all possible combinations of numbers.

As you can see, putting three numbers in order takes considerably more code than putting two numbers in order. At first glance, it might seem that lines 70 and 90 do the same thing, but this is not so. In the preceding example, line 70 swaps 5 and 0. Line 90 then swaps 5 and 4, since A(1) and A(2) hold different values in each line.

Clearly, if we use this method to rearrange four or five or more numbers, the code would become too complex. Let's consider a general method for rearranging a list of numbers. Assume we have the following list: 5, 3, 6, 4, 1. We want to rearrange this list so that the order will be from smallest to largest. Our procedure will be to move one number at a time from left to right whenever necessary. To do this, we will compare adjacent pairs and swap only if the number on the right is smaller than the number on the left.

Examine Table 12-1 closely. It shows our original list and the swaps that are necessary to arrive at a rearranged list.

Table 12-1.
Rearranging a List

A(1)	A(2)	A(3)	A(4)	A(5)		
5	3	6	4	1	Action Performed	
3	5				SWAP A(1),A(2)	
3	5	6			No SWAP	
3	5	4	6		SWAP A(3),A(4)	
3	5	4	1	6	SWAP A(4),A(5)	**1st Pass Complete**
3	5				No SWAP	
3	4	5			SWAP A(2),A(3)	
3	4	1	5		SWAP A(3),A(4)	
3	4	1	5	6	No SWAP	**2nd Pass Complete**
3	4				No SWAP	
3	1	4			SWAP A(2),A(3)	
3	1	4	5		No SWAP	
3	1	4	5	6	No SWAP	**3rd Pass Complete**
1	3				SWAP A(1),A(2)	
1	3	4			No SWAP	
1	3	4	5		No SWAP	
1	3	4	5	6	No SWAP	**4th Pass Complete**

The following program performs this procedure:

```
100 RANDOMIZE
110 DEFINT A-Z
120 FOR X=1 TO 5
130    A(X)=INT(RND*100)+1
140 NEXT X
150 GOSUB 270
160 PRINT
170 DONE=0
180 WHILE DONE=0
190    DONE=1
200    FOR X=1 TO 4
210       IF A(X) > A(X+1) THEN SWAP A(X),A(X+1):DONE=0
220    NEXT X
230    GOSUB 270
240 WEND
250 END
260 '
270 FOR X=1 TO 5
280    PRINT A(X);
290 NEXT X
300 PRINT
310 RETURN
```

```
RUN
Random number seed (-32768 to 32767)? 2929
 66  16  72  55  44

 16  66  55  44  72
 16  55  44  66  72
 16  44  55  66  72
 16  44  55  66  72
Ok
```

Lines 120 through 140 form a random list of five numbers. In line 170 the flag DONE is set equal to 0, which initializes our WHILE/WEND loop. In line 190 this flag is reset to 1. If a swap is made, line 210 resets the flag to 0. If no swaps are made, the flag stays set equal to 1. The list is now in order and will be printed out in lines 270 through 290.

Bubble Sort

Now let's consider a modification of the preceding program. It is called a *bubble sort* and is a very common and useful sorting routine for short lists.

```
100 DEFINT A-Z
110 SIZE=100
120 DIM A(SIZE)
130 RANDOMIZE
140 FOR I=1 TO SIZE
150    A(I)=INT(RND*200)+1
160 NEXT I
170 PRINT "The unsorted array is:"
180 GOSUB 270              'Print unsorted array
190 GOSUB 370              'Sort array with Bubble Sort
200 PRINT "The bubble sort array is:"
210 GOSUB 270              'Print sorted array
220 PRINT "Array sorted in";COMP;"comparisons and";SWITCH;"swaps."
230 END
240 '
250 'Print an array
260 '
270 FOR I=0 TO SIZE-1 STEP 10
280    FOR J=1 TO 10
290       PRINT USING "###  ";A(I+J);
300    NEXT J
310    PRINT
320 NEXT I
```

```
330 RETURN
340 '
350 'Bubble Sort
360 '
370 PRINT "Sorting array: ";
380 COMP=0:SWITCH=0
390 FOR I = 1 TO SIZE - 1
400    PRINT "*";
410    FOR J=1 TO SIZE - I
420       COMP=COMP+1
430       IF A(J)>A(J+1) THEN SWAP A(J),A(J+1):SWITCH=SWITCH+1
440    NEXT J
450 NEXT I
460 PRINT
470 RETURN
```

First note a couple of minor changes. In line 110 the size of our list is set equal to **SIZE**. Then in line 400 we insert a "heartbeat message" into the program. This can be thought of as a message that the program prints on the screen to inform the operator that the computer is still "alive." In other words, a heartbeat reminds the operator that something invisible is happening inside the computer. Otherwise, if the screen stayed the same while the computer was performing some function, the operator might think that the program was in an endless loop or that it had malfunctioned.

The major change from the previous program occurs in line 430. On each pass through the array, the largest number is located and moved to the right. Another way of thinking about this is to imagine that the largest number bubbles up to the end of the list. On each successive pass or scan through the array, therefore, the working size of the array is decreased by 1. The largest number is moved to the right end of the list, so that the size of the list that remains to be sorted is reduced. That is also the reason the heartbeat gets faster as the program progresses. The major advantage of thus reducing the workload is an increase in speed for the sort.

An interesting addition to the program is the inclusion of the variables **COMP** and **SWITCH**. Though not an essential part of the sorting and rearranging process, these variables keep a count of the exact number of comparisons and swaps that were performed in the execution of the program. They are printed out after the final list is sorted and tell the total number of comparisons and the number of switches or swaps that took place during the program's execution.

```
RUN
Random number seed (-32768 to 32767)? 1212
The unsorted array is:
163  21 126 189  59  36   1 130 158  71
130  23 101  51 107  39 196 181 120 177
 91 161  82  78   2  54 102  77  99 127
144 130 133 156 191  91 114 187 177  97
146 171  64 152 180 200 157  55 137 186
121  47  37  77 192  62 122  96 119 117
161 115  54  53  33  17  71  72 179 156
 45 111 118 130  26  57 151 169  45 133
128 189  63 194  48  82  82  25  33 137
 99 122 129  61  52 155 119 111 189  95
Sorting array: ****************************************************************
************************************
The bubble sort array is:
  1   2  17  21  23  25  26  33  33  36
 37  39  45  45  47  48  51  52  53  54
 54  55  57  59  61  62  63  64  71  71
 72  77  77  78  82  82  82  91  91  95
 96  97  99  99 101 102 107 111 111 114
115 117 118 119 119 120 121 122 122 126
127 128 129 130 130 130 130 133 133 137
137 144 146 151 152 155 156 156 157 158
161 161 163 169 171 177 177 179 180 181
186 187 189 189 189 191 192 194 196 200
Array sorted in 4950 comparisons and 2515 swaps.
Ok
```

Searching an Array

Sometimes it is useful to be able to scan a list rapidly to determine if a certain number or word is present in a given list or text. Let's suppose we have an array of numbers and we want to know if a number is in the array. In the first example, we will use a *linear search.* This method is much like looking through a deck of cards one at a time to find, say, the ace of spades. With linear search, we simply proceed through the array, one place at a time, until we find the number or until we come to the end of the array.

```
110 DEFINT A-Z
120 OPTION BASE 1
130 SIZE = 100            'This is the array size
140 DIM A(SIZE)
150 RANDOMIZE
160 GOSUB 1000            'Make list
170 GOSUB 1100            'Print list
180 INPUT "Number to search for? ",N
190 IF N=0 THEN END
```

```
200 GOSUB 1200          'Search list
210 IF INDEX=0 THEN PRINT "Not found" ELSE PRINT "Found at";INDEX
220 GOTO 180
1000 '
1010 'Make an array of random numbers
1020 '
1030 FOR I = 1 TO SIZE
1040    A(I) = INT(RND*100)+1
1050 NEXT I
1060 RETURN
1070 '
1080 'Print an array of numbers
1090 '
1100 FOR I = 1 TO SIZE
1110    PRINT USING " ###";A(I);
1120    IF I MOD 15 = 0 THEN PRINT
1130 NEXT I
1140 PRINT
1150 RETURN
1160 '
1170 'Linear search for a number N
1180 'INDEX will be zero if N is not found
1190 '
1200 I = 1
1210 WHILE I < SIZE AND A(I) <> N
1220    I = I + 1
1230 WEND
1240 IF A(I) = N THEN INDEX = I ELSE INDEX = 0
1250 RETURN
```

For this program we will first create and print out an array of 100 random numbers from 1 to 100. The number to search for, **N**, is input at line 180. Inputting a 0 here will stop the program. Line 200 calls the search routine. The search routine will return with the variable **INDEX** = **0** if **N** is not found. Otherwise, **INDEX** will be set equal to the subscript of the array where **N** was found.

```
RUN
Random number seed (-32768 to 32767)? 1800
  17  63  26  97  21 100  71  65  10  30  10  41  71  84  86
  68  35  50   3  91  47  13  40  25  75  29  99  94  29   3
  39  81   8  15  63  13  62  98  12  70  45  58 100  38   1
   3  56  14  93  48  60  59  42  59  71  35  91  87  62  53
  26  93   3  48 100  40  67  46  91  91  54  90  35  90  25
  68  33  47  25  88  23   6  96  87  78  45  58  66  76  85
 100  43  55  48  97  17  60  75 100  22
Number to search for? 91
Found at 20
Number to search for? 3
Found at 19
```

```
Number to search for? 5
Not found
Number to search for? 0
Ok
```

The key part of this rather long example is the linear search subroutine, lines 1200 through 1250. In particular, look at line 1210. It may not be obvious why we check for **I < SIZE** instead of **I <= SIZE** to see if we have looked through the entire array. To see what will happen, change the **I < SIZE** to **I <= SIZE** in line 1210. Run the program and enter a number to search for which is not in the array.

```
1210 WHILE I <= SIZE AND A(I) <> N
```

The program generates an error when **N** is not in the array. If we print **I** in the direct mode, we find that **I** is 101. The error message "Subscript out of range" is given when MBASIC tries the comparison **A(101) <> N**. The last time through the loop when line 1210 is executed, **I** is greater than **SIZE**. MBASIC is not smart enough to know that since **I <= SIZE** is false, the comparison **A(I) <> N** is not necessary; therefore, it executes the whole line anyway.

When you process arrays, you should always carefully consider the boundary conditions. Go through the loop step-by-step to see that the loop starts and ends properly.

Binary Search

Now let's look at another method of searching. Let's suppose that we already have a numerically sorted list and that we want to search for a given number within this list. We could, of course, use the linear search method described earlier, but there are better methods of searching.

Suppose, for example, that you want to look up the word "program" in a dictionary. You could start at the first page and scan through the entire dictionary, one page at a time. This would constitute a linear search and would take a long time.

A faster method, which can be used only with a sorted list, is called a *binary search.* Imagine that you have a dictionary that does not have its words in alphabetical order. You would then have no choice but to scan the dictionary, using a linear search method to find the word.

Let's suppose that we have an array of numbers that is sorted from smallest to largest. We now want to know if a number N is in the array. Using binary search, we first compare the middle number in the array with N. If they are equal, we have found the number and can stop searching.

But chances are that the search will not be quite so easy and that we will have to do more work. If N is greater than the middle number in the array, N is obviously somewhere in the higher half of the array. We can ignore the lower half. Likewise, if N is less than the middle number in the array, we know that N is in the lower half. We can therefore ignore the upper half of the array.

Once we have eliminated half of the array from our scrutiny, we go on to compare N with the middle of the remaining portion of the array. Then we repeat the steps just outlined. In this way, we can eventually determine that N is not in the array when the remaining portion of the array can no longer be divided in half because it is only one number.

Here is an example with 15 sorted numbers. The number (N) that we are searching for is 72. Initially, we set the low and high bounds of the array at 11 and 96, respectively. Then we compare N with the middle of the array.

low							Does N = 55?							high
⇩							⇩							⇩
11	12	18	22	38	42	47	55	68	72	73	84	89	95	96

Now remember that N is 72. Since N is greater than 55, we know that N must be in the upper half of the array. We therefore readjust the low point or bound. Since we know our number is greater than 55, we reset the low point to the number at the right of the number we just looked at—that is, 68:

								low			Does N = 84?			high
								⇩			⇩			⇩
11	12	18	22	38	42	47	55	68	72	73	84	89	95	96

Our working array now ranges from 68 to 96. Each time we search the array, we compare N with the subvariable halfway between the low and high boundaries. In fact, the name "binary search" comes from this idea of cutting in half or continuously dividing the list by 2.

Since N is less than 84, we move the high boundary to 73, making our new range 68 to 73. The next step looks like this:

```
                                        Does N = 72?
                                        low       high

11  12  18  22  38  42  47  55  68  72  73  84  89  95  96
```

We have found N, and we have done it in three comparisons. It would have taken ten comparisons to find N with a linear search.

Now let's see what would happen if we search for a number that is not in the array. Let's assume N is 40. Here is the first step:

```
low                       Does N = 55?                  high

11  12  18  22  38  42  47  55  68  72  73  84  89  95  96
```

We know that N is not 55 and that it is less than 55, so we set the new high point at 47 and check N against 22:

```
low     Does N = 22?     high

11  12  18  22  38  42  47  55  68  72  73  84  89  95  96
```

Since N is greater than 22, we move the low boundary to point to 38.

```
                Does N = 42?
                low       high

11  12  18  22  38  42  47  55  68  72  73  84  89  95  96
```

After comparing N with 42, we know that we must look to the left of 42, so we set the high boundary to point to 38.

Now both the low and high boundaries point to the same location.

```
             Does N = 38?
                high
                low

11  12  18  22  38  42  47  55  68  72  73  84  89  95  96
```

At this point we might conclude that the number N is not in the array, since both low and high boundaries point to 38. However, it turns out that the program requires one more step. Since N is greater than 38, we set the low boundary to point to 42.

```
                    high low
                     ⇩    ⇩
11  12  18  22  38  42  47  55  68  72  73  84  89  95  96
```

The low and high boundaries cross, which tells us that the number N is not in the array.

Using the binary search method, we have determined, with four comparisons, that 40 is not in the array. It could have taken 15 comparisons to come to this conclusion with the linear search method. Binary search is obviously much faster than linear search. If the number of elements in a list is small, of course, you probably would not notice the time difference between a linear and a binary search. The longer the list, the more time you save by using binary search. Keep in mind, however, that the list must be sorted before you can do a binary search.

Here is a note for mathematics buffs. If you wish to search through a list of M elements using a linear search, the average number of comparisons needed is M/2 if the element is in the list, and M comparisons if the element is not in the list. The number of comparisons required for a binary search is at most $\log_2 (M)$ whether or not the element is present. This means that for a list of 1000 items, only ten or less than ten comparisons are necessary. The actual time for a search is proportional to the number of comparisons.

We still need to replace the linear search subroutine of the previous search program with a binary search subroutine. Here is what the new program looks like:

```
100 DEFINT A-Z
110 OPTION BASE 1
120 SIZE = 100          'This is the array size
130 DIM A(SIZE)
140 RANDOMIZE
150 GOSUB 1000          'Make list
160 GOSUB 1300          'Bubble sort array
170 GOSUB 1100          'Print list
180 INPUT "Number to search for? ",N
190 IF N=0 THEN END
200 GOSUB 1200          'Search list
210 IF INDEX=0 THEN PRINT "Not found" ELSE PRINT "Found at";INDEX
220 GOTO 180
1000 '
1010 'Make an array of random numbers
```

```
1020 '
1030 FOR I = 1 TO SIZE
1040    A(I) = INT(RND*100)+1
1050 NEXT I
1060 RETURN
1070 '
1080 'Print an array of numbers
1090 '
1100 FOR I = 1 TO SIZE
1110    PRINT USING " ###";A(I);
1120    IF I MOD 15 = 0 THEN PRINT
1130 NEXT I
1140 PRINT
1150 RETURN
1160 '
1170 'Binary search for a number N
1180 'INDEX will be zero if N is not found
1190 '
1200 LOW = 1: HIGH = SIZE: INDEX = 0
1210 WHILE LOW <= HIGH AND INDEX = 0
1220    I = (LOW + HIGH)\2
1230    IF N = A(I) THEN INDEX = I
1240    IF N < A(I) THEN HIGH = I - 1 ELSE LOW = I + 1
1250 WEND
1260 RETURN
1270 '
1280 'Bubble Sort
1290 '
1300 PRINT "Bubble sorting array: ";
1310 FOR I = 1 TO SIZE - 1
1320    PRINT "*";
1330    FOR J=1 TO SIZE - I
1340       IF A(J) > A(J+1) THEN SWAP A(J),A(J+1)
1350    NEXT J
1360 NEXT I
1370 PRINT
1380 RETURN
```

```
RUN
Random number seed (-32768 to 32767)? 1919
Bubble sorting array: *****************************************************
*****************************************
   1   3   3   4   5   6   7   7   9   9  10  10  10  10  11
  11  11  12  14  15  15  16  19  19  19  20  21  21  22  23
  23  24  25  25  26  31  31  32  32  34  34  34  35  36  36
  36  36  38  42  43  44  45  47  52  55  56  57  58  59  60
  61  61  61  61  62  62  62  65  67  67  69  69  70  71  72
  73  76  78  80  80  80  81  83  83  83  84  86  88  89  89
  91  91  94  95  95  95  96  96  96  99
Number to search for? 67
Found at 69
```

```
Number to search for? 11
Found at 15
Number to search for? 8
Not found
Number to search for? 0
Ok
```

Line 1200 initializes the **LOW** and **HIGH** variables. It also sets **INDEX** to zero. Notice that the variable **INDEX** becomes nonzero when the number **N** is found in the array. Line 1210 controls the loop until the **LOW** and **HIGH** bounds cross or **N** is found in the array (signaled when line 1230 has set **INDEX = I**). Line 1220 sets **I** equal to the array subscript halfway between **LOW** and **HIGH**. In other words, **I** is the average of **LOW** and **HIGH**.

Notice the integer division in the formula in line 1220. When **LOW + HIGH** equals an odd number, the integer division (by 2) will round down the result to an integer. The middle number or average of 5 and 10 is 7.5, but since we are using integer division, the result is 7. Actually, it does not matter which way you round the number when **LOW + HIGH** is odd. The integer division was chosen because it is faster than single-precision division.

A Faster Way to Sort

We have seen that a binary search is much faster than a linear search. What about sorting? Is there a faster sorting algorithm than bubble sort?

There are, in fact, many algorithms that are faster than bubble sort. Although bubble sort is actually one of the slowest sort methods, it is presented here because it is the easiest sorting algorithm to follow and because it is very useful for relatively short lists (that is, lists with fewer than 20 items).

Our next example is one of the fastest sorting methods. This method is commonly referred to as *quicksort*. The quicksort method is based on two ideas. First, if the list to be sorted is cut in half, it takes only one-fourth as long to sort the list, not one-half as long, as might be expected. And second, although this may seem trivial, the key to most of the faster sorting algorithms is that a list that has only one or zero elements is already sorted. In fact, this is precisely what quicksort does: it takes a list of any length and breaks it into progressively smaller lists until each list has one or zero elements.

The first step is to pick a special number from the list that we will call the *pivot number*. The pivot number may be any number from the list. For simplicity, we select the first number in the list to be the pivot.

The second step is to move the pivot number to the final position that it will occupy in the sorted list. To accomplish this, we must move all the other numbers, positioning them in relation to the pivot number. All numbers less than the pivot will be rearranged to the left of the pivot, and all numbers greater than the pivot will be rearranged to the right of the pivot. Since the pivot number will now be greater than every number on its left and less than every number on its right, the pivot number is in the correct position and does not need to be considered again. Thus the list has, in effect, been partitioned in such a way that the original sorting problem is reduced to two smaller and simpler problems. The numbers to the left and right of the pivot number can now be thought of as two separate lists.

The third step is to sort each of these two smaller lists of numbers. We sort the smaller list in the same way that we sorted the original list. In other words, we have to select a pivot number in each of the two lists and rearrange the remaining lower and higher numbers around it exactly as we did the first time.

This procedure is said to be *recursive* because the procedure invokes itself in order to run. The dictionary defines recursive as "a procedure that can repeat itself indefinitely or until a specified condition is met." The idea behind the recursion in quicksort is to divide and conquer. At first we start with one large list to sort, and then we break it down into smaller and smaller lists, until each list contains not more than one item. When a sublist has been reduced to one element or no elements at all, the program stops working on that list and concentrates on the remaining sublists.

```
100 DEFINT A-Z
110 SIZE = 100
120 DIM A(SIZE),STK(INT(LOG(SIZE)/LOG(2))+1,2)
130 RANDOMIZE
140 FOR I = 1 TO SIZE
150    A(I) = INT(RND*100) + 1
160 NEXT I
170 PRINT "The unsorted array is:"
180 GOSUB 270              'Print unsorted array
190 GOSUB 350              'Sort array with Quicksort
200 PRINT "The Quicksort array is:"
210 GOSUB 270              'Print sorted array
```

```
220 PRINT "Array sorted in";COMP;"comparisons and";SWITCH;"swaps."
230 END
240 '
250 'Print an array
260 '
270 FOR I = 1 TO SIZE
280    PRINT USING "###  ";A(I);
290    IF I MOD 10 = 0 THEN PRINT
300 NEXT I
310 RETURN
320 '
330 'Quick Sort
340 '
350 PRINT "Quicksorting array: ";
360 SP=1:COMP=0:SWITCH=0
370 STK(SP,1)=1:STK(SP,2)=SIZE
380 WHILE SP>0
390    PRINT "*";
400    L=STK(SP,1):R=STK(SP,2):SP=SP-1
410    WHILE L<R
420       I=L:J=R:S=1
430       WHILE I<J
440          COMP=COMP+1
450          IF A(I)>A(J) THEN SWAP A(I),A(J):S=-S:SWITCH=SWITCH+1
460          IF S=1 THEN I=I+1 ELSE J=J-1
470       WEND
480       IF R-I>J-L THEN 520
490          IF J-1>L THEN SP=SP+1:STK(SP,1)=L:STK(SP,2)=J-1
500          L=I+1
510       GOTO 540
520          IF I+1<R THEN SP=SP+1:STK(SP,1)=I+1:STK(SP,2)=R
530          R=J-1
540    WEND
550 WEND
560 PRINT
570 RETURN
```

```
RUN
Random number seed (-32768 to 32767)? 5511
The unsorted array is:
 16   32   72   69    3   78   39   75   45   88
 94   86   64   72   40   24    4   35   18   98
 89   30    8   10   70    8  100    2   32   67
 61   23   72   14   32    3   64   42   56   38
 46   15   86   89   57   84   46   37   14   13
 86   31   56   99   60   35   76   38   10   72
100   61   55   51   60   52   66   47   55   83
 86   59   29   17   32   97   50   93   68   37
 25    5   75   37   72   28   34   21   94   29
 85   87   13    8   77   52   55   79   60   34
Quicksorting array: ***********************************************************
```

```
The Quicksort array is:
  2   3   3   4   5   8   8   8  10  10
 13  13  14  14  15  16  17  18  21  23
 24  25  28  29  29  30  31  32  32  32
 32  34  34  35  35  37  37  37  38  38
 39  40  42  45  46  46  47  50  51  52
 52  55  55  55  56  56  57  59  60  60
 60  61  61  64  64  66  67  68  69  70
 72  72  72  72  72  75  75  76  77  78
 79  83  84  85  86  86  86  86  87  88
 89  89  93  94  94  97  98  99 100 100
Array sorted in 670 comparisons and 201 swaps.
Ok
```

You will see that quicksort is much faster than bubble sort if you compare the relative number of comparisons and swaps necessary for quicksort and bubble sort. If you have some time, you can try working with a bigger array. Set **SIZE = 1000** instead of 100 and run both of the sort programs to compare times. Quicksort's performance (measured in number of sort items per time) actually increases for larger arrays, whereas bubble sort's performance decreases very quickly.

Mathematics buffs may be interested to note that the running time to bubble sort M elements is proportional to M^2. In contrast, the running time for quicksort is proportional to $\log_2(M)$. For a small number of elements these running times are about the same, but as M gets bigger, the difference in running times increases rapidly.

Because MBASIC does not support recursion, the quicksort program is rather complicated, with the extra code necessary to simulate recursion. For instance, you may have noticed the peculiar DIM statement for the two-dimensional **STK** array. The formula **INT(LOG(SIZE)/LOG(2))+1** is $\log_2$(SIZE) rounded up to the nearest integer. This variable is a *stack* and is used to simulate the recursion necessary for quicksort.

While there are many advantages to quicksort, the bubble sort approach has one property that most faster sorting algorithms like quicksort do not have, which is that bubble sort is so much easier to program and debug. In fact, the bubble sort method is so simple that it can be even faster than quicksort for arrays smaller than about 20 elements.

The main point is this: first use an easy sorting method like bubble sort to solve your problem, and then replace it with something more complicated like quicksort if the original performance must be improved. For most purposes, easy is best.

TUTORIALS

Tutorial 12-1: Test Scores

This program is used to sort a list of names and test scores. This needs to be done both alphabetically and by rank. We will use the quicksort routine for both sorts. The quicksort program that we used earlier in this chapter requires one important addition so that when the list is sorted alphabetically, the scores will be transferred along with the names. The addition is that when the list is sorted by rank, the names also have to be transferred with the appropriate scores.

```
10 REM -               -=*SCORES.C12*=-
20 REM -               Quicksort names and scores
30 REM -               12/27/82
100 DEFINT A-Z
110 READ SIZE
120 DIM NM$(SIZE),SCORE(SIZE),STK(INT(LOG(SIZE)/LOG(2))+1,2)
130 FOR I = 1 TO SIZE
140    READ NM$(I),SCORE(I)
150 NEXT I
160 PRINT:PRINT "The unsorted array is:"
170 GOSUB 300          'Print unsorted array
180 SORT = 1           'Set to sort by name
190 GOSUB 380          'Sort array with Quicksort
200 PRINT:PRINT "Alphabetical list:"
210 GOSUB 300          'Print sorted array
220 SORT = 2           'Set to sort by score
230 GOSUB 380          'Sort array with Quicksort
240 PRINT:PRINT "List by scores:"
250 GOSUB 300          'Print sorted array
260 END
270 '
280 'Print an array
290 '
300 PRINT:PRINT "Name                Score"
310 FOR I = 1 TO SIZE
320    PRINT USING "\                    \ ###";NM$(I);SCORE(I)
330 NEXT I
335 PRINT : PRINT "Press RETURN"; : A$=INPUT$(1)
340 RETURN
350 '
360 'Quick Sort
370 '
380 SP=1:STK(SP,1)=1:STK(SP,2)=SIZE
390 WHILE SP>0
400    L=STK(SP,1):R=STK(SP,2):SP=SP-1
```

(Tutorial 12-1: Continued)

```
410    WHILE L<R
420       I=L:J=R:S=1
430       WHILE I<J
440          ON SORT GOSUB 600,650
450          IF COMP = 1 THEN SWAP NM$(I),NM$(J):SWAP SCORE(I),SCORE(J):S=-S
460          IF S=1 THEN I=I+1 ELSE J=J-1
470       WEND
480       IF R-I>J-L THEN 520
490          IF J-1>L THEN SP=SP+1:STK(SP,1)=L:STK(SP,2)=J-1
500          L=I+1
510       GOTO 540
520          IF I+1<R THEN SP=SP+1:STK(SP,1)=I+1:STK(SP,2)=R
530          R=J-1
540    WEND
550 WEND
560 RETURN
570 '
580 'Compare names NM$(I) and NM$(J) with result in COMP
590 '
600 IF NM$(I) > NM$(J) THEN COMP = 1 ELSE COMP = 0
610 RETURN
620 '
630 'Compare scores SCORE(I) and SCORE(J) with result in COMP
640 '
650 IF SCORE(I) < SCORE(J) THEN COMP = 1 ELSE COMP = 0
660 RETURN
670 '
680 'Name and score data
690 '
700 DATA 10
710 DATA "SIMPLSON, GEORGE",83
720 DATA "FRIBURGER, RITA",73
730 DATA "SHIFFON, CLOVER",93
740 DATA "ARMADILLO, ABIGAIL",45
750 DATA "FAIRCHILD, FRED",55
760 DATA "BUMPLY, CECIL",67
770 DATA "ROGERS, RALPH",89
780 DATA "ZAT, MICHAEL",100
790 DATA "TYLER, JOHNY",66
800 DATA "STAFFOR, LIMPER",78
```

In lines 180 and 220, the flag **SORT** is set to either 1 or 2, depending on whether the sorting is by rank or is alphabetical. Within the main body of the quicksort routine, line 440 sends the program to the subroutine at 600 or 650, again depending on whether the list is to be sorted alphabetically or by rank. When it returns to line 450, if the variable **COMP** (for comparison) is equal to 1, the swap of both names and scores is made. When the alphabetical sort is completed, the program returns to line 210 and is then sent to the print routine at line 300.

When the printing is completed for the alphabetical list, the program performs a quicksort on the scores. On completion of this operation, the program returns to line 240 and is then sent back to the print routine for the final printing of the list by rank.

```
RUN

The unsorted array is:

Name                 Score
SIMPLSON, GEORGE       83
FRIBURGER, RITA        73
SHIFFON, CLOVER        93
ARMADILLO, ABIGAIL     45
FAIRCHILD, FRED        55
BUMPLY, CECIL          67
ROGERS, RALPH          89
ZAT, MICHAEL          100
TYLER, JOHNY           66
STAFFOR, LIMPER        78

Press RETURN
Alphabetical list:

Name                 Score
ARMADILLO, ABIGAIL     45
BUMPLY, CECIL          67
FAIRCHILD, FRED        55
FRIBURGER, RITA        73
ROGERS, RALPH          89
SHIFFON, CLOVER        93
SIMPLSON, GEORGE       83
STAFFOR, LIMPER        78
TYLER, JOHNY           66
ZAT, MICHAEL          100

Press RETURN
List by scores:

Name                 Score
ZAT, MICHAEL          100
SHIFFON, CLOVER        93
ROGERS, RALPH          89
SIMPLSON, GEORGE       83
```

(Tutorial 12-1: Continued)

```
STAFFOR, LIMPER        78
FRIBURGER, RITA        73
BUMPLY, CECIL          67
TYLER, JOHNY           66
FAIRCHILD, FRED        55
ARMADILLO, ABIGAIL     45

Press RETURN
Ok
```

Tutorial 12-2: Payroll

We will now include a binary search routine in our payroll program. When new names are added, the program first checks to see whether the name is already on the list. If the name is on the list, the program prints the name on the screen and allows you to change the pay rate.

```
10 REM -                -=*PAYROLL.C12*=-
20 REM -                Customer payroll program
30 REM -                12/27/82
40 REM -
1000 DEFINT A-Z
1010 MAX.EMP = 20                                  'Maximum number of employees
1020 FORMAT$ = "\" + SPACE$(23) + "\ $$#####.##" 'Set print line format
1030 DIM EMP.NM$(MAX.EMP),EMP.RATE!(MAX.EMP)
1040 NO.EMP = 0                                    'Initialize no. of employees
1050 TRUE = 1: FALSE = 0
1060 '
1070 'Main program
1080 '
1090 PRINT:PRINT "-=< M E N U >=-"
1100 PRINT "1) Enter names and pay rates"
1110 PRINT "2) Compute wages"
1120 PRINT "3) End"
1130 PRINT:INPUT "Select? ",SELECT
1140 IF SELECT < 1 OR SELECT > 3 THEN PRINT "Invalid selection.":GOTO 1130
1150 IF SELECT = 3 THEN END
1160 ON SELECT GOSUB 1210,1350
1170 GOTO 1090
1180 '
1190 'Enter employee names
1200 '
1210 IF NO.EMP = MAX.EMP THEN PRINT "No more room to add names.":RETURN
1220 PRINT:LINE INPUT "Enter employee name or <RETURN> for done: ";EMP.NM$
```

(Tutorial 12-2: Continued)

```
1230 IF EMP.NM$ = "" THEN RETURN             'Null string signals end
1240 GOSUB 1610                              'Search for name
1250 IF FOUND = TRUE THEN 1280
1260    GOSUB 1490                           'Insert name at INDEX
1270 GOTO 1290
1280    PRINT USING "Name found, pay rate is $$#.## /hour.";EMP.RATE!(INDEX)
1290 PRINT USING "Enter pay rate for &: ";EMP.NM$;
1300 INPUT EMP.RATE!(INDEX)
1310 GOTO 1210
1320 '
1330 'Compute wages
1340 '
1350 PRINT:PRINT "Wages for 40 hour week":PRINT
1360 TOTAL.WAGES = 0                         'Initialize total wages
1370 FOR I = 1 TO NO.EMP
1380    EMP.EARN! = EMP.RATE!(I)*8           'Compute employee earnings
1390    PRINT USING FORMAT$;EMP.NM$(I);EMP.EARN!
1400    TOTAL.WAGES! = TOTAL.WAGES! + EMP.EARN! 'Total employee wages
1410 NEXT I
1420 PRINT STRING$(LEN(FORMAT$),"-")
1430 PRINT USING FORMAT$;"Total wages";TOTAL.WAGES!
1440 RETURN
1450 '
1460 'Insert employee name EMP.NM$ at INDEX
1470 'We assume NO.EMP < MAX.EMP
1480 '
1490 NO.EMP = NO.EMP + 1
1500 FOR I = NO.EMP TO INDEX + 1 STEP -1
1510    EMP.NM$(I) = EMP.NM$(I - 1)          'Slide names up one
1520    EMP.RATE!(I) = EMP.RATE!(I - 1)      'Move pay rates with names
1530 NEXT I
1540 EMP.NM$(INDEX) = EMP.NM$                'Insert name at propper spot
1550 RETURN
1560 '
1570 'Binary search for EMP.NM$.  FOUND = TRUE if name is found otherwise
1580 'FOUND = FALSE.  If the name is found INDEX will point to the name.
1590 'If the name is not found INDEX will point where the name should go.
1600 '
1610 LOW = 1: HIGH = NO.EMP: FOUND = FALSE
1620 WHILE LOW <= HIGH AND FOUND = FALSE
1630    INDEX = (LOW + HIGH)\2
1640    IF EMP.NM$ = EMP.NM$(INDEX) THEN FOUND = TRUE
1650    IF EMP.NM$ < EMP.NM$(INDEX) THEN HIGH = INDEX - 1 ELSE LOW = INDEX + 1
1660 WEND
1670 IF EMP.NM$ > EMP.NM$(INDEX) THEN INDEX = INDEX + 1
1680 RETURN
```

The subroutine starting at line 1210 first checks to see whether the maximum number of employees has already been entered into the program. If not, you can enter the new employee name. The program then calls the binary search subroutine that starts at line 1610.

At line 1610 the flag variable **FOUND** is initialized to the variable **FALSE**. The program then proceeds with the binary search to determine whether or not the name is already in the file. If it is, the flag **FOUND** is set equal to **TRUE**. If the name is not found, then the variable **INDEX** will contain the subscript indicating the correct place in the list to add the new employee.

It is important that you understand the conditional branch at 1250. If the name has been found, the name does not have to be inserted in the list since it is already there. You therefore proceed to 1290, where you are given the opportunity to change the pay rate. If the name has not been found, line 1260 transfers you to the subroutine at 1490. This subroutine opens up a space in the list of employees so that the new name may be inserted in the proper alphabetical position. (Remember that the list must always be kept in alphabetical order if the binary search routine is to work properly.) You are then returned to line 1270, where pay rates may be entered, and then back to line 1210, where a new employee name may be entered. You can also press RETURN if you wish to go back to the menu.

At line 1670 there is an important addition to the binary search routine. If the name has not been found on the list when the program exits the WHILE loop at line 1660, the pointer (INDEX) may either be at the name before or at the name after the correct name. Line 1670 ensures that the pointer is always moved to the name following the point where insertion should take place.

When the program runs it looks like this:

```
RUN

-=< M E N U >=-
1) Enter names and pay rates
2) Compute wages
3) End

Select? 1

Enter employee name or <RETURN> for done: Foster, Tina
Enter pay rate for Foster, Tina: ? 5.75

Enter employee name or <RETURN> for done: Hall, George
Enter pay rate for Hall, George: ? 5.00
```

(***Tutorial** 12-2: Continued*)

```
Enter employee name or <RETURN> for done: Billings, Jennifer
Enter pay rate for Billings, Jennifer: ? 5.50

Enter employee name or <RETURN> for done:

-=< M E N U >=-
1) Enter names and pay rates
2) Compute wages
3) End

Select? 2

Wages for 40 hour week

Billings, Jennifer          $44.00
Foster, Tina                $46.00
Hall, George                $40.00
----------------------------------
Total wages                $130.00

-=< M E N U >=-
1) Enter names and pay rates
2) Compute wages
3) End

Select? 3
Ok
```

EXERCISES

1. Use the random number generator to generate 50 words. Count the number of words that begin with each letter of the alphabet. Then print out the list in alphabetical order and the count for each letter.

2. Generate three random numbers in the range 50 to 150 and print them out in descending order.

3. Consider a simple guessing game in which a computer chooses a random number between 1 and 100 and you try to guess what the number is. The computer will tell you if your guess is too low, too high, or correct. If you

were to use a binary search in this game, what would be the maximum number of guesses required to pick the correct number? If the computer were to pick a random number from 1 to 1000, what would be the maximum number of guesses required to pick the correct number?

4. Use the linear search routine to write a program to find how many times a given number occurs in a list of 100 random numbers. Find the position of each occurrence.

13

Debugging Your Programs

Statements:	ERROR, ON ERROR, RESUME, STOP
Variables:	ERL, ERR
Commands:	TRON, TROFF, CONT

The process of writing a program can be divided into three major steps: planning, writing, and debugging. Before you start typing code into the computer, you have to decide what information the program is going to use, what algorithms or rules will manipulate that information, and what format the output will take. Debugging is the act of finding all the problems that can cause a program to malfunction. These problems can be as simple as a syntax error. Longer programs with many branching statements may have logic errors that only show up when program flow is carefully traced.

As a rule of thumb, the planning, writing, and debugging phases of program development each require approximately the same amount of time. If the planning stage is shortchanged, you will probably have to make up for this false economy in the debugging portion of development.

Why do programs need to be debugged at all? The reason is that programming is a very exact art and programmers are not perfect. So much precision is required that as your programs become longer and more involved, errors are almost inevitable.

There are two general categories of errors, both of which you will encounter frequently when you are programming. They are *run time errors* and *program logic errors*. Let's consider each in turn.

Run Time Errors

Run time errors are the most common and usually the easiest errors to correct. Listed in two groups in Figure 13-1 are some of MBASIC's more common error messages. You have probably encountered most of these error messages in your programming.

The run time errors in Group 1 all point to two-part statements that have been left incomplete. Although such errors are generally easy to find, spotting them in multiple nested loops is more difficult. For this reason, in FOR/NEXT loops you should always specify the appropriate variable following the NEXT (for example, NEXT I).

The run time errors in Group 2 cover a wider variety of programming mistakes. Let's consider each of the errors in this group in turn.

SYNTAX ERRORS

Syntax errors generally occur for one of the following reasons: either you have misspelled a word or you have used a keyword as a

GROUP 1	GROUP 2
NEXT without FOR	Syntax error
RETURN without GOSUB	Out of data
FOR without NEXT	Type mismatch
WHILE without WEND	Undefined line
WEND without WHILE	Division by zero
	Illegal function call

Figure 13-1.
Common run time errors

variable or you have used an incorrect format for the particular keyword you are working with. When MBASIC encounters a syntax error, the program immediately terminates and places you in edit mode. The line number that contains the error is then shown on the screen. Press L if you wish to see the complete line. You now have full use of the editor to correct any syntax errors.

OUT OF DATA

Out of data errors occur when you try to read past the end of the statement's data. This is usually caused by READ statements in an endless loop.

TYPE MISMATCH

A type mismatch error usually means that you have used a string variable or constant where a numeric variable or constant is required, or vice versa. Type mismatch errors occur in functions if an argument for the function is of the wrong type. For example, the command PRINT ASC(32) will generate a type mismatch error because the ASC function requires a string, not a number, as its argument. Note that if a function has more than one argument, a type mismatch error may refer to any of the arguments.

A type mismatch error can also occur in an assignment statement. Setting a numeric variable equal to a string or vice versa constitutes a type mismatch error.

Finally, using a double-precision variable for the counter in a FOR/NEXT loop will give a type mismatch error.

UNDEFINED LINE NUMBER

An undefined line number error indicates that a program-branching statement attempted to transfer control to a nonexistent line number.

DIVISION BY ZERO

Division by zero is undefined in mathematics and, of course, will give an error if attempted in MBASIC. MBASIC assigns all variables to a value of 0 unless you explicitly assign a value to the variable. For example:

```
10 PRINT A/B
20 PRINT B
```

```
RUN
Division by zero
 1.70141E+38
 0
Ok
```

Since we did not assign a value to **B**, it has the value 0, which is assigned by MBASIC. The cure, of course, is to be sure that a divisor always has a value assigned to it before it is used. Note that the program continues to run after the error message is printed.

ILLEGAL FUNCTION CALL

An illegal function call error generally occurs when the argument for the function is outside the legal range. For instance, both of the following lines will generate an "Illegal function call" error message.

```
10 PRINT SQR(-1)        ' Can not take square root of negative number
20 PRINT CHR$(300)      ' ASCII code must be less than 256
```

The errors are easy to see in these examples but may be hard to spot if the arguments are complex algebraic expressions or other functions.

Now consider the following program. It contains several errors. Try running the program each time we fix an error.

```
10 REM  BUG.C13
20 READ A(X)
30    IF A$(X)="END" THEN 100
40    X=X+1
50    GOTO 20
60 DATA "SMITH, SAM","LYONS, MIKE","JONES, MARY","END"
200 FOR Y=1 TO 4
210    COMMA=INSTR(A$(Y),", ")
220    PRINT MID$(A$(Y),COMMA+2);" ";LEFT$(A(Y),COMMA-1)
230 NEXT Y
```

```
RUN
Syntax error in 60
Ok
60
```

According to the computer, the first error is in line 60. But if you look closely, you will see that the first error is actually in line 20. It should read

```
20 READ A$(X)
```

The point is that MBASIC cannot determine whether the variable or the data is wrong. Therefore, although you might have expected a type mismatch error, the error message only indicates the syntax error in line 60.

Now that we have corrected the first error, we will run the program again.

```
RUN
Undefined line number in 30
Ok
```

We change line 30 to read

```
30 IF A$(X)= "END" THEN 200
```

Run the program once again.

```
RUN
MIKE
Type mismatch in 220
Ok
```

Again, a $ has been omitted in the first parameter, **A(Y)**, of LEFT$. To correct this error, change **A(Y)** to **A$(Y)** in line 220. In this case, the type mismatch error is given because a string variable is required with the LEFT$ function. Run the program again.

```
RUN
MIKE LYONS
MARY JONES
ND
Illegal function call in 220
Ok
```

There are really two errors here that you should notice: first, the first name in the list should be **SAM SMITH**; and second, an illegal function call occurs in line 220. Sam is left out because we did not initialize the subscript **X** when the list was read. Remember that the default value for a variable is 0. To correct this, enter the following as line 15:

```
15 X = 1
```

An illegal function call error is usually not immediately apparent.

If you do not see it right away, print out the parameters for any functions that occur in the line that contains the error in direct mode.

Here is how we do this for line 220:

```
Ok
PRINT COMMA
 0
Ok
```

We know now that **COMMA** has the value 0. Look at the end of line 220 and notice the expression **COMMA−1**. The value for **COMMA−1** is −1. This is outside of the legal range (0-255).

To correct the error, look back at line 210 where **COMMA** is assigned. Its job is to search for the position of the comma and space characters between the last and first names. When the INSTR function cannot find this in the dummy data, "**END**", **COMMA** is assigned the value 0. Thus the correction in this case is to change line 200 to read

```
200 FOR Y = 1 TO 3
```

An even better solution would be to substitute **X−1** for the 3 in line 200. This solution is better because it makes the program more general. It allows you to enter additional names into the DATA statement without changing any other portion of the program. The new program now reads

```
10 REM  BUGC.C13
15 X=1
20 READ A$(X)
30 IF A$(X)="END" THEN 200
40     X=X+1
50     GOTO 20
60 DATA "SMITH, SAM","LYONS, MIKE","JONES, MARY","END"
200 FOR Y=1 TO X-1
210     COMMA=INSTR(A$(Y),", ")
220     PRINT MID$(A$(Y),COMMA+2);" ";LEFT$(A$(Y),COMMA-1)
230 NEXT Y

RUN
SAM SMITH
MIKE LYONS
MARY JONES
Ok
```

Program Logic Errors

The second category of common MBASIC errors is program logic errors. Program logic errors are generally the more difficult to correct because when a program logic error has occurred, the program runs through to completion but the output is incorrect.

In order to minimize these errors, careful preplanning is required. Long programs should be developed in *modules*, and each module should be tested before it is combined with the rest of the program. A module is a section of a program that performs a specific task. For example, a simple program might contain just three modules: an input module in which data is entered into the program, a section in which the data is manipulated, and finally a module that formats and prints the results. Test each module with sample data that has known results.

A useful technique for developing a program is to use PRINT statements between modules. These statements show your output at each stage. When the program is finished and the output is verified, these extra PRINT statements can be removed.

Remember that the most damaging assumption a programmer can make is that the output of the computer is always correct. Always keep in mind the computer aphorism, "Garbage in, garbage out."

Six important guidelines can save you time in program development. First, understand the problem; second, identify input and output; third, formulate a precise statement of the problem; fourth, develop your algorithm; fifth, translate the algorithm to MBASIC; and sixth, test the algorithm with simple data.

Trapping Errors
[ON ERROR, ERROR, ERR, ERL, RESUME]

As we have just seen, MBASIC detects many errors. When one of these errors is detected, MBASIC either places you back in direct mode or, in the case of a syntax error, it puts you in edit mode.

But MBASIC has another error feature that allows you to define and then detect errors in your program. This is called *error trapping* and may be defined as the process of handling errors that occur in a program. For example, suppose you maintained a mailing list in which all the people lived within a limited number of ZIP codes. You could design an error trap that would call to the computer operator's attention any ZIP code that was entered that was outside the designated area.

You can design this trap not only to detect the errors you define, but also to help you decide what action to take when an error is detected. What is more, you are not limited to trapping the errors you design; you may also trap any of the errors MBASIC automatically detects.

The following section will explain how to make a program handle certain types of errors so that program execution may continue. The section of the program that decides what to do when an error occurs is called the *error-trapping routine* or just the *error routine*.

AN ERROR ROUTINE AS A SUBROUTINE

An error routine is similar to a subroutine (subroutines were discussed in Chapter 10). Three statements (ON ERROR, ERROR, and RESUME) and two variables (ERR, ERL) form the basis for error-trapping routines.

The ON ERROR GOTO statement is used to select an error-trapping routine. You may have as many error routines as you wish, but only one error routine may be used at a time. Assuming line 100 is the first line of an error-trapping routine, the statement ON ERROR GOTO 100 causes your program to branch to the error routine when there is an error. What happens in the error routine is entirely up to you.

Let's start with a simple example that transfers control to an error routine.

```
10 ON ERROR GOTO 100
20 PRINT "See you at:"
30 PRNT "Line 30"
40 PRINT "Line 40"
90 END
100 PRINT "BOO"
```

```
RUN
See you at:
BOO
No RESUME in 100
Ok
```

In line 10 we tell MBASIC where the error trap is located. The program then proceeds normally until it encounters the error in line 30 (the **I** missing from **PRNT**). It then transfers control to line 100 and takes whatever action the program designates.

Notice the statement END at line 90. Since an error trap is a subroutine, it should be preceded by either END or a branching statement to prevent accidental entry into the subroutine. Do not be concerned about the message "No RESUME in 100" yet; we will discuss this message shortly.

IDENTIFYING THE ERROR AND LINE

Just printing **BOO** in our error trap is not very productive. We can use the MBASIC variables ERR and ERL to print out the error code and line number of the error. The variables ERR and ERL are generally used together. ERR is the variable that holds the *error number*, while ERL holds the *line number* of the line that contains the error. Each MBASIC error has a code number. These codes are listed in Appendix C along with the corresponding error message. Examples of error codes are listed in Table 13-1.

Let's return to the example of an error-trapping routine. Replace line 100 with the following:

```
100 PRINT ERL,ERR
```

Run the program and you have

```
RUN
See you at:
 30            2
No RESUME in 100
Ok
```

ERR and ERL are used by the error-trapping routine to tell the user what error has occurred and where it occurred. In the output here,

Table 13-1.
Examples of Error Code Numbers

Error Message	Error Code
Syntax error	2
Illegal function call	5
Type mismatch	13
Disk full	61

the **30** informs you that the error occurred in line 30 and the 2 tells you the error is a syntax error. Now we will take care of the "No RESUME" message.

CONTINUING THE PROGRAM AFTER AN ERROR

After an error-trapping routine has taken appropriate action, such as informing the user of the error or adjusting some variables to remedy the error condition, the RESUME statement is used to continue the program. RESUME is to an error trap what RETURN is to a standard subroutine, except that with RESUME you may resume at any line number in the program.

There are three formats for RESUME. The first, RESUME or RESUME 0, resumes at the statement that caused the error. The second, RESUME NEXT, resumes at the statement following the one that caused the error. And the third, RESUME linenumber, resumes program execution at the *linenumber.* Which format you use, of course, depends on your program. For the example we are working with, add the following at line 110:

```
110 RESUME NEXT
```

Run the program and you have

```
RUN
See you at:
 30            2
Line 40
Ok
```

In this example, after printing the error code and line number, the program resumes at line 40. The program prints **Line 40** and then ends.

Note that MBASIC initially has error trapping turned off. This means that MBASIC does not branch to an error-trapping routine when an error occurs, but instead simply prints an error message and stops, leaving you in either direct or edit mode. When you use the ON ERROR GOTO statement to specify an error-trapping routine, you have turned on the error trapping. Once the error trapping has been turned on, it remains on until you turn it off.

ERROR TRAPPING IN DIRECT MODE

Since the error trapping in the last example was not turned off when the program ended in line 90, the error trapping remains on even in the direct mode. If you attempt to run the program again and make a direct mode error, such as typing **RUM** instead of **RUN**, you will get the following output:

```
RUM
 65535          2
Ok
```

Typing **RUM** instead of **RUN** generated a syntax error and therefore the error code 2. The line number 65535 is the way MBASIC informs you that the error occurred in direct mode.

TURNING OFF AN ERROR ROUTINE

The command used to turn off an error trap is ON ERROR GOTO 0. This command has two uses, depending on where the command is executed.

If ON ERROR GOTO 0 is executed in any portion of the program outside of the error-trapping routine, all subsequent errors will cause MBASIC to stop and print the appropriate error message. It is used in this manner simply to turn off error trapping and to let MBASIC handle any errors in its usual manner.

If, however, ON ERROR GOTO 0 is executed inside an error-trapping routine, MBASIC will stop execution and print the error message for the error which caused the error-trapping routine to be executed. An error-trapping routine should use ON ERROR GOTO 0 whenever there is an error that the error routine is not equipped to handle.

As an example of turning off error trapping, change line 100 and run the following:

```
100 IF ERR <= 90 THEN ON ERROR GOTO 0
```

```
RUN
See you at:
Syntax error in 30
Ok
30
```

Since the error is a syntax error (code 2), line 100 turns error trapping off and the error is handled in the standard manner.

With error trapping now off, a direct mode error will be handled in the usual way. Type **RUM** now and you will get the following:

```
RUM
Syntax error
Ok
```

RENUMBERING PROGRAMS WITH ERR AND ERL

In an assignment statement, ERR and ERL must be on the right of the equal sign since ERR and ERL are reserved words. If you use the RENUM command to renumber your program and if a relational operator is used with ERL and a line number, the number must be on the right in order for it to be renumbered correctly.

For example, change line 100 in our example:

```
100 IF ERL<100 AND ERR=2 THEN PRINT "Line";ERL;"has a syntax error"
```

This line will print the message **Line XX has a syntax error** if a syntax error (code 2) occurred in a line number less than line 100. Run the program and you have

```
RUN
See you at:
Line 30 has a syntax error
Line 40
Ok
```

If the program is renumbered with the RENUM command, the expression **ERL<100** will automatically be changed to reflect the renumbered line 100. On the other hand, if we use the expression **100>ERL** instead (which is equivalent to **ERL<100**), the RENUM command will not change the 100 to reflect any renumbered lines. You will most often want to place line numbers to the right of ERL so that they can be renumbered. Try renumbering the preceding program and notice that the expression **ERL<100** has changed.

```
RENUM
Ok
LIST
10 ON ERROR GOTO 60
20 PRINT "See you at:"
30 PRNT "Line 30"
40 PRINT "Line 40"
50 END
60 IF ERL<60 AND ERR=2 THEN PRINT "Line";ERL;"has a syntax error"
70 RESUME NEXT
Ok
```

SIMULATING AN ERROR

If you look at Appendix C, you will notice that the highest error code listed there is code 67 (for "Too many files"). Actually, there are 255 different error codes (1 to 255). It is possible to assign the extra 188 error codes for your own use. For instance, a program might use error code 200 to mean "Invalid ZIP code entry". Using your own error codes becomes increasingly useful as your programs become longer and more complex.

To allow you to define your own error codes, the ERROR statement simulates the occurrence of an error. The syntax for the ERROR command is

```
ERROR errornumber
```

where the *errornumber* is the number of the error you want to simulate.

Since MBASIC uses the smallest numbers for its codes (1 through 67), the safest idea is to start at the top (255) and work down when assigning your error codes. This way there will be less chance of conflicting error codes with later versions of MBASIC.

Now consider the following program.

```
10 ON ERROR GOTO 500
20 INPUT "What is your zip";ZIP$
30 IF ZIP$="94520" OR ZIP$="94522" THEN PRINT ZIP$ ELSE ERROR 255
40 END
500 IF ERR <> 255 OR ERL <> 30 THEN ON ERROR GOTO 0
510 PRINT "That is not a valid zip code; try again."
520 RESUME 20
```

ZIP codes are to be entered, but the program accepts only the two ZIP codes 94520 and 94522 and rejects any others. Line 10 selects the error-trapping routine; when any error is encountered, MBASIC will branch to line 500. Line 30 checks to see if the proper ZIP code was entered. If it was not, line 30 sets the error code to 255 with the ERROR statement. Line 500 determines whether the error that invoked the error-trapping routine was a result of a wrong ZIP code entry. If it was, the program informs the user of this by printing line 510. The program then transfers execution back to line 20 for the ZIP code to be reentered. If the error occurred for some other reason, the ON ERROR GOTO 0 statement at the end of line 500 causes the program to stop and print an appropriate error message.

Running the program gives the following output:

```
RUN
What is your zip? 94533
That is not a valid zip code; try again.
What is your zip? 94522
94522
Ok
```

Note that you may use the ERROR statement even when the error trapping is off. If you use ERROR with the error trapping off, MBASIC will print the message "Unprintable error" for those error codes with no available error message (that is, error codes greater than 67). As an example, run the following:

```
20 INPUT "What is your zip";ZIP$
30 IF ZIP$="94520" OR ZIP$="94522" THEN PRINT ZIP$ ELSE ERROR 255
40 END
```

```
RUN
What is your zip? 94533
Unprintable error in 30
Ok
```

ERRORS NOT HANDLED BY THE ERROR TRAP

To illustrate the full use of the ON ERROR GOTO 0, add line 25 to our earlier ZIP code example:

```
25 INPUT "What is  your name"
```

The variable that is required after an INPUT statement has been omitted. An error not handled by the error trap has been encountered.

Run the program again:

```
RUN
What is your zip? 94520
Syntax error in 25
Ok
25
```

The ON ERROR GOTO 0 in line 500 turned the error trapping off and caused MBASIC to report the error in the normal way. Since line 25 contains a syntax error, MBASIC automatically entered the edit mode.

Here are two more examples of error trapping. They illustrate a couple of important points. Consider the output from the following:

```
10 ON ERROR GOTO 100
20 A$ = 838
30 PRINT "BOO"
40 ON ERROR GOTO 0
50 PRINT CHR$(-1)
60 END
100 PRINT ERR, ERL
110 RESUME NEXT

RUN
 13            20
BOO
Illegal function call in 50
Ok
```

When the program is run, line 10 turns the error trapping on, and line 20 generates an error. The program then transfers to 100. Line 100 prints out the error number for a type mismatch (13) and the line number (20). The program resumes on line 30, which prints the output **BOO**. In line 40 error trapping is turned off with the ON ERROR GOTO 0 command.

Notice that this use of ON ERROR GOTO 0 did not do the same thing as it did in the previous set of examples. In particular, it did not cause the program to stop and print the error that occurred in line 20 because the ON ERROR GOTO 0 was executed outside of the error-trapping routine (that is, after the RESUME statement was executed). Since the error trapping is turned off in line 40, program execution halts when the error in line 50 is reached, and MBASIC handles the error in the normal way with the message "Illegal function call in 50".

AN ERROR TRAP AS AN INTERNAL TRAP

When you debug longer programs, you will want to put internal checking into your program. An internal check is a statement in your program that checks one or more variables to see that they are within the proper range.

For instance, a subroutine that prints out totals for an employee's income may want to check to see that the totals are actually positive numbers. A negative total income in this case is obviously a programming error, which might be caused by a bug in a pay deductions routine. In such a situation, you could use error code 255 to signal an "Internal error". Your error-trapping routine could then detect these types of internal errors and instruct the user to call a programmer. In Chapter 14 you will see an application of this kind of internal checking with an error-trapping routine.

It takes some practice to get used to error trapping. Used properly, however, error trapping is a very useful programming tool.

Other Debugging Techniques

There are other methods for debugging your programs. MBASIC allows you to trace your program step-by-step or to exit to command level at appropriate moments to check the values of variables.

TRACING YOUR PROGRAMS [TRON, TROFF]

MBASIC has another versatile command, TRON, that is useful when program errors persist. The TRON command, which stands for "trace on," prints on the screen the line numbers of your program in the sequence in which they are executed.

The TRON command is particularly useful in a program that has several subroutines. The program runs in the normal manner, except that a line number is printed as each line is executed. You can then check whether or not branching has occurred as you intended. You may use the command from the direct mode by giving the TRON command and then running your program, or you can use TRON as a statement in your program at a particular line number in order to trace a limited section of your program.

Once the TRON command has been issued, it stays in effect until the TROFF command ("trace off") is used; in other words, TROFF turns TRON off. The TROFF command may also be given in direct mode or used as a statement in the program.

The following program is the first sorting routine introduced in Chapter 12. We have made two minor changes in the program so that you may test your debugging skills. You might first look through the program to see if you can spot any errors. Then run the program and repair the errors that MBASIC reports. Finally, use TRON to see if the program follows the sequence you expect. It is possible that after one correction, the program may appear to run correctly if you make a lucky choice for the random number seed. Try three or four different values for the seed before you decide that the program is fully debugged.

```
100 RANDOMIZE
110 DEFINT A-Z
120 FOR X=1 TO 5
130    A(X)=INT(RND*100)+1
140 NEXT X
150 GOSUB 270
160 PRINT
170 DONE=0
180 WHILE DONE=0
190    DONE=1
200    FOR X=1 TO 4
210       IF A(X) > A(X+1) THEN SWAP A(X),A(X+1):DONE=1
220    NEXT X
230 GOSUB 270
240 WEND
260 '
270 FOR X=1 TO 5
280    PRINT A(X);
290 NEXT X
300 PRINT
310 RETURN
```

USING THE COMMAND MODE FOR DEBUGGING [STOP,CONT]

A powerful tool in debugging a program is the STOP statement. This statement is used to stop execution of a program. When program execution reaches the line containing the STOP statement, the program halts and gives the message "Break in line nn", where *nn* is the line number. The program then returns you to direct mode.

Enter and run the following:

```
10 X=5
20 PRINT X
30    X=X+5
40    IF X=100 THEN END
45    STOP
50 GOTO 20

RUN
 5
Break in 45
Ok
```

From direct mode, you may print the value held by any of the variables in your program, such as

```
PRINT X
 10
Ok
```

When you have finished inspecting the variables, you can continue the program with the CONT command. Program execution will continue at the line number following the line number indicated by the break message.

```
CONT
 10
Break in 45
Ok
```

You may also change the value of any of your variables. In the following example, we change the value of the variable **X** and continue the program with the CONT command:

```
X=35
Ok
CONT
 35
Break in 45
Ok
```

You cannot, however, continue the program with CONT after using the editor or adding or deleting program lines. Only program variables may be altered if you wish to continue the program.

You may place as many STOP statements in your program as you think are necessary in order to inspect the results at any particular point in the program. You can do this at the beginning of modules, at the end of modules, or within modules. When the program is completely debugged, these STOP statements may be removed.

DEBUGGING BY MODULES

As mentioned earlier, longer programs should be developed in modules. For instance, you might have a section of the program that prints the menu, another that controls input, and a third that controls output. When you are working with these modules, keep in mind that all variables in MBASIC are global. In other words, a variable used in one subroutine will continue to retain its value in another subroutine. You should therefore be careful when you use the same variable name in two different subroutines. If two subroutines use the same variable name, be sure that one subroutine does not allow the other accidentally or unexpectedly to alter the value of the variable.

It is also important to ensure that the program does not enter subroutines accidentally. Subroutines should always be preceded by a GOTO, RETURN, or END statement, so that the program cannot accidentally move into these areas.

EXERCISES

1. Write a program that allows names, birth dates, and phone numbers to be entered with an INPUT statement. Incorporate into the program an error trap that will force the user to reenter the phone number or birth date if any character other than the numerals 0 through 9, –, or / is entered. Enter both phone number and birth date as strings.
2. Write a program to read and print out the following names: "RITA FRYBURGER", "SUZAN BLOND", "JOE SIMPLE", "EGBERT ZZT", "VLADIMIR PUF". Use error trapping instead of dummy data to determine and print the length of the list.

14

Working With Sequential Files

Statements:	OPEN, WRITE#, PRINT#, CLOSE, INPUT#, CHAIN
Functions:	EOF

Until this point, we have only worked with small amounts of data. The information to be processed in programs has been stored in DATA statements. In many cases, this is a good method of storing information, but in other cases, the computer's memory may not be able to hold all the information required. This is especially likely to happen when programs are very long or when the amount of data is very large or when both these conditions exist.

The alternative to storing information in DATA statements is to use *data files.* A data file is a collection of information that is stored on disk and that can be called in by your program when it is ready to process the data. The only limit to the amount of data that can be stored in this manner is the capacity of your disk system.

Using Data Files

MBASIC supports two types of data files: *sequential* and *random-access* files. The word "file" has a variety of meanings in computer terminology. For example, all the programs you have written are called files when they are saved on the disk. What is more, the MBASIC program itself is a file. Here we are specifically concerned only with data files of the sequential and random-access type.

It is important to know that a data file is made up of a collection of *records*. A record, in turn, is a collection of data; all records in the data file contain similar types of data. For example, each record in a file might consist of the name, age, and telephone number of a person. Data files may consist of only a few records or of thousands of records.

One difference between sequential and random-access files is that sequential files have records of variable lengths, while random-access files have fixed-length records. This means that each record in a sequential file can have a different number of characters. In a random file, however, all the records have the same length. In both types of files, MBASIC reads and writes an entire record at a time.

A second difference is that if you are working with a sequential file and you want to find some information in one of these records, you must start at the beginning of the file (record number 1) and move in sequence through the records, checking the data in each one until you find the information you are interested in. On the other hand, if your file is random-access, each record in your data file has a record number, and you can move directly to any record in your file by specifying this record number.

Both types of data file have their advantages and disadvantages. The type of file you choose should be determined by the practical requirements of the application you are working with. We will consider sequential files in this chapter and random-access files in the next.

Naming Data Files

Data files are given names just like any other file you work with in MBASIC. The rules for naming data files are the same as for other files: the file name may have up to eight letters plus an optional three-letter extension. The data file name always remains the same unless, of course, you use the RENAME command to change the file name or the KILL command to get rid of the file completely.

Sequential Files

The major advantage of the sequential file is efficiency of data storage; in effect, there is less wasted disk space. Figure 14-1 illustrates the concept of a sequential file.

A sequential file can consist of records of many different sizes. A record is usually a set of related items: for example, names, addresses, and telephone numbers. Each item within a record is called a *field* of the record. The fields are separated by commas. Significantly, there is no wasted space between the fields; although fields may vary in length, all of the space in the file is used.

A sequential file must be read in sequence. This means that the file is read consecutively beginning with the first field of the first record and continuing to the end. If you are interested in the data fields in record number 199, you must pass through the first 198 records in order to look at that record.

Writing to a Sequential File [OPEN, CLOSE, WRITE#, PRINT#]

There are three steps to entering data in a sequential file: opening the file, writing the data, and closing the file.

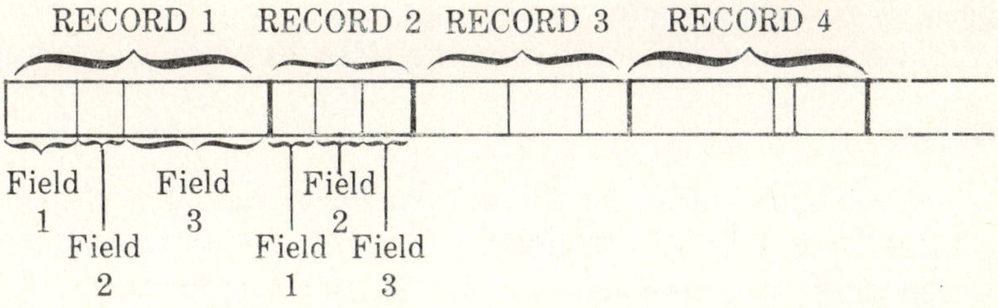

Figure 14-1.
Records in a sequential file

To open a file you use the OPEN command. The syntax for the OPEN command for sequential files is

```
OPEN mode$, #filenumber, filename$
```

where *mode$* is either "O" or "I", *filenumber* is a number between 1 and 14, and *filename$* is the name of the file that you are opening. The number sign (#) is optional, although it is commonly used. You can open sequential files either in output mode (O) or input mode (I). If you open a file in output mode, you are telling MBASIC that you do not care about the current contents of the file and that you only want to write to the file. You cannot write to a file that has been opened in input mode.

As many as three data files may be opened at the same time by default. Be sure to assign a different number to each data file opened. MBASIC then does any further writing to or reading from the file by referring to the file number.

In addition, each file you write to must have a name. This is the name that will appear on the disk when you use the DIR command from CP/M or the FILES command from MBASIC. The extension ".DAT" is commonly used for data files.

Here is an example of the OPEN command:

```
OPEN "O", #1, "CALORIE.DAT"
```

The **"O"** stands for output and tells MBASIC that data is to be written to the disk. If the file already exists, its current contents will be lost. The **#1** is the number of the file, and **CALORIE.DAT** is the file name.

If you want to open more than three files at one time, you must specify the number of files in the MBASIC command as **/F:nnn**, when *nnn* is the maximum number of files you are using. For example, to use as many as five files, invoke MBASIC with the command

```
MBASIC /F:5
```

Once you have opened the file, you can write data to it with either the PRINT# or WRITE# command. We will explain the difference between these two commands shortly. The formats for them are

```
PRINT#filenumber, expressions

WRITE#filenumber, expressions
```

where *filenumber* is the number you assigned the file in the OPEN command. These two commands work just like the PRINT command, except that they write a record to a file, not to the screen. For example:

```
PRINT #1, FOOD$;TYPE$;UNIT$;CAL
```

In this example our records consist of four fields: **FOOD$**, **TYPE$**, **UNITS$**, and **CAL**.

To close a file you use the CLOSE command. The syntax for this command is

```
CLOSE #filenumber
```

where *filenumber* is the number you assigned with the OPEN command. If you give the CLOSE command without a *filenumber*, MBASIC closes all files that are open. After a file has been closed, its number can be reused in another OPEN command.

Now let's construct a program that will write data into a sequential file. We will write a program that will store the following items in a file: foods, type of food, serving unit, and number of calories per serving unit. Use the data from Table 14-1.

Keep in mind that when you are through entering data into a file, the file must be closed.

```
100 OPEN "O",#1,"CTABLE.DAT"
110 PRINT:INPUT "Food name: ",FOOD$
120 IF FOOD$="" THEN GOTO 180
130    INPUT "Type: ",TYPE$
140    INPUT "Unit serving: ",UNIT$
```

Table 14-1.
Sequential File Data

Food	Type	Unit	Calories
Apricots	Dried	3 oz.	260
Beans	Green	3 oz.	33
Beef	Sirloin	1 oz.	110
Chocolate	Sweet	1 oz.	150
Carrots	Fresh	1 oz.	12
Fruit cocktail	Canned	1 cup	91
Noodles	Egg	8 oz.	881
Rice	Brown	1 cup	232

```
150    INPUT "Calories per unit: ",CAL
160    WRITE #1,FOOD$;TYPE$;UNIT$;CAL
170    GOTO 110
180 CLOSE #1
190 END
```

When the user presses RETURN with no other entry in response to the prompt in line 110, the program transfers to line 180, where the file is closed.

Now enter each item when the program is run:

```
RUN

Food name: Apricots
Type: Dried
Unit serving: 3 oz.
Calories per unit: 260

Food name: Beans
Type: Green
Unit serving: 3 oz.
Calories per unit: 33

Food name:
Ok
```

After entering a portion of this data, save your program and exit to CP/M with the SYSTEM command. Use the TYPE command to display the file on the screen:

```
A>TYPE CTABLE.DAT
"Apricots","Dried","3 oz.",260
"Beans","Green","3 oz.",33
A>
```

Each line is a record, and each record contains three strings and one number, while each of these items is a field of the record. Notice that the records have different lengths and that the fields begin at different columns in the record.

Now return to MBASIC and load the program again. Change the WRITE# statement in line 160 into a PRINT# statement with the same variables, and then run the program and enter the data exactly as you did before. This time when you return to CP/M and display the file, you will have

```
A>TYPE CTABLE.DAT
ApricotsDried3 oz. 260
BeansGreen3 oz. 33
A>
```

The PRINT# statement does not separate fields with quotation marks and commas. In most cases you will therefore want to use the WRITE# statement so that you can determine where the fields in each record are. The PRINT# statement is used for advanced or specialized applications in which the data file is to be considered as one big string of characters.

Reading a Sequential File
[EOF, INPUT#]

Now let's read the data that is in our file. To do this we need to open the file, read the data, and close the file.

First, open the file with the OPEN command. This is the same command you used when you wrote to the file, except that now you must use input ("I") for the *mode$*. For example:

```
OPEN "I", #1, "CALORIE.DAT"
```

If the file is not on the disk, you will get a "File not found" error message.

Read the data from the file with the INPUT# statement. This statement is analogous to the WRITE# statement, in that it reads the expressions the way that WRITE# wrote them out. The syntax is

```
INPUT #filenumber, expressions
```

For example, the following statement

```
INPUT #1, FOOD$;TYPE$;UNIT$;CAL
```

could be used to read records from our previous program.

In many cases, we will have to continue reading records until we find the one we want or until we reach the end of the file. The EOF (end of file) function is used to let you know when you have reached the end of the file. Attempting to read beyond the end of a sequential file will give the error message "Input past end".

The EOF function is commonly used with a conditional branch, such as

```
10 IF EOF(1) THEN 60
```

The number inside the parentheses is the file number. Note that in this case the number sign must *not* be used in front of the file number. This is an inconsistency in MBASIC. A number sign is optional with OPEN and CLOSE and is required with PRINT#, WRITE#, and INPUT#, but the number sign is not allowed with EOF.

Remember to close any files with the CLOSE command when you are through reading from them.

The following program will read and print out the data from the file we previously created with the WRITE# statement. Remember to recreate the file in order to get rid of the data that we wrote with the PRINT# statement.

```
100 OPEN "I",#1,"CTABLE.DAT"
110 WHILE NOT EOF(1)
120     INPUT #1,FOOD$,TYPE$,UNIT$,CAL
130     PRINT:PRINT FOOD$;", ";TYPE$
140     PRINT CAL;"Calories per ";UNIT$
150 WEND
160 CLOSE #1
170 END
```

Running this program displays the file CTABLE.DAT created by the previous program. The program would not work if the file were written with the PRINT# statement.

```
RUN

Apricots, Dried
 260 Calories per 3 oz.

Beans, Green
 33 Calories per 3 oz.
Ok
```

Adding to a Sequential File

If you wish to add records to an already existing sequential file, you cannot simply open the file and begin writing to it. If you open a preexisting file in output mode, all information in the file is automatically lost. We will use our file CTABLE.DAT to go through the steps necessary to add data.

1. Open a new file called COPY.DAT in the output or O mode. Open the existing file CTABLE.DAT in the input or I mode.
2. Read the data from CTABLE.DAT and then write it to the file COPY.DAT.
3. Close the file CTABLE.DAT and then erase it with the KILL command.
4. Write the new data to the file COPY.DAT.
5. Close the file.
6. Rename the file COPY.DAT to CTABLE.DAT.

Now you have a file on the disk that has the same name as the original and that contains all the data from the original plus the data you added. At this point, examine the following program carefully and see how each of these tasks is accomplished. Notice that error trapping is used to check whether CTABLE.DAT exists on the disk. If CTABLE.DAT does not exist, we can skip the second and third steps in the preceding list. You will need to use error trapping often when adding to a sequential file, since there is no way for MBASIC to see whether or not a file exists on the disk.

```
100 ON ERROR GOTO 350
110 OPEN "O",#1,"COPY.DAT"
120 OPEN "I",#2,"CTABLE.DAT"
130 '
140 'The following WHILE loop is skipped if the OPEN statement
150 'for CTABLE.DAT caused an error 53 (File not found on disk)
160 '
170 WHILE NOT EOF(2)
180    INPUT #2,FOOD$,TYPE$,UNIT$,CAL
190    WRITE #1,FOOD$;TYPE$;UNIT$;CAL
200 WEND
210 CLOSE #2
220 KILL "CTABLE.DAT"
230 '
240 PRINT:INPUT "Food name: ",FOOD$
250 IF FOOD$="" THEN 310
260    INPUT "Type: ",TYPE$
270    INPUT "Unit serving: ",UNIT$
280    INPUT "Calories per unit: ",CAL
290    WRITE #1,FOOD$;TYPE$;UNIT$;CAL
300    GOTO 240
310 CLOSE #1
```

```
320 NAME "COPY.DAT" AS "CTABLE.DAT"
330 END
340 '
350 IF ERR = 53 AND ERL = 120 THEN 380
360    CLOSE
370 ON ERROR GOTO 0
380    CLOSE #2
390 RESUME 240
```

You may use this program to add additional data from Table 14-1 to the file CTABLE.DAT. The data may then be displayed using the INPUT# example program.

In line 170, we control our WHILE/WEND loop by reading the file until the EOF (end of file) mark is encountered. When the EOF mark is reached, the loop terminates and CTABLE.DAT is closed and erased by the KILL command in line 220. Notice that the CLOSE statement is absolutely necessary here because if you delete a file before closing it, unpredictable (and almost assuredly bad) things can happen to your files. MBASIC will not give you an error message if you delete an open file.

Finally, in line 350, error 53 stands for "File not found". If some error other than error 53 in line 120 occurs, line 360 closes all files, and line 370 prints the error message and stops.

TUTORIALS

Tutorial 14-1: Calorie Counter [CHAIN]

The calorie counter application programs use sequential files to determine the number of calories consumed during a meal. Four programs are used in this application. They are named MENU, ENTER, MERGE, and MEAL. Each of the programs is relatively short. Our main purpose here is to illustrate another of MBASIC's commands: CHAIN. The CHAIN command invokes a program from the disk that replaces the program in the computer's memory.

The program MENU gives you a choice of either entering new data into file CTABLE.DAT or of calculating the number of calories that you consume during a meal. After making your choice, a second program is "chained" into the computer to do the actual calculating or to enter new data.

The program ENTER is similar to a program you used earlier in this chapter. It allows you to enter data on various foods. After the data has been entered, the program uses quicksort to place all the foods you entered in alphabetical order. The sorted data is contained

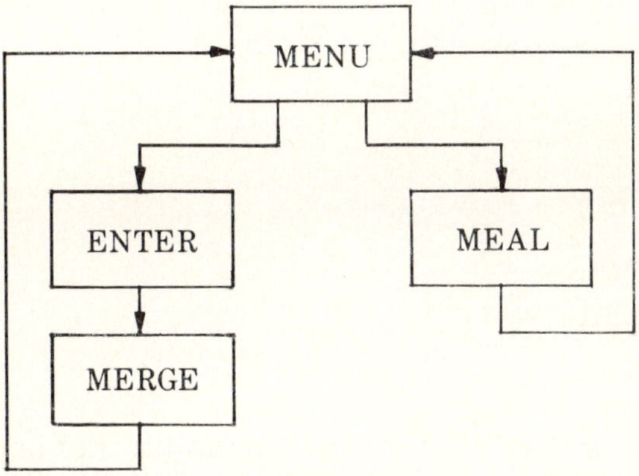

Figure 14-2.
Chain of programs for the calorie counter

in a sequential file named ADDITION.DAT. When this task is completed, the program automatically chains in the next program, MERGE.

The MERGE program combines the data from the file ADDITION.DAT and the file CTABLE.DAT into a single alphabetized file named COPY.DAT. When this task is completed, the program deletes the ADDITION.DAT and CTABLE.DAT files and then renames the file COPY.DAT to CTABLE.DAT.

The final program, MEAL, allows you to enter the foods you eat during a meal, searches through the file for the data on that food, and calculates the calories that you consumed during that meal. The diagram in Figure 14-2 shows how the four programs are connected.

Now let's take a look at the pertinent lines or sections of each program.

```
10 REM -                    -=*MENU.C14*=-
20 REM -                    Menu program for calorie file system
30 REM -                    2/13/83
40 REM -
100 DEFINT A-Z
110 PRINT
120 PRINT "Choose one of the following:"
130 PRINT "   1 ... Enter new data into table"
140 PRINT "   2 ... Compute total calories for a meal"
150 PRINT "   3 ... End"
160 PRINT
170 INPUT "Enter your selection: ",SEL
180 IF SEL = 3 THEN END
190 IF SEL >=1 AND SEL <=2 THEN 220
200     PRINT "Invalid selection, enter a number form 1 to 2."
210     GOTO 170
220 FOR I = 1 TO SEL
230     READ PGM$
240 NEXT I
250 CHAIN PGM$
260 '
270 'Program name data
280 '
290 DATA "ENTER.C14","MEAL.C14"
```

In the program MENU, two different programs can be chained in. They are entered as data in line 290. When the CHAIN command in line 230 is reached, the program will chain in from the disk the program whose name is held in the variable **PGM$**. Selecting program 1 on the menu will chain in and run the program ENTER.

The longest portion of the ENTER program contains quicksort and record addition.

```
10 REM -                -=*ENTER.C14*=-
20 REM -                Enter calorie table data
30 REM -                2/15/83
40 REM -
100 DEFINT A-Z
110 MAXSIZE = 50         'Maximum number of entries per sitting
120 DIM FOOD$(MAXSIZE),TYPE$(MAXSIZE),UNIT$(MAXSIZE),CAL(MAXSIZE)
130 DIM STK(INT(LOG(MAXSIZE)/LOG(2))+1,2)       'Stack for Quicksort
140 SIZE = 0
150 '
160 'Begin main program
170 '
180 PRINT : INPUT "Food name or <RETURN> to end: ",F$
190 IF F$="" THEN 280
200    SIZE = SIZE + 1
210    FOOD$(SIZE) = F$
220    INPUT "Type: ",TYPE$(SIZE)
230    INPUT "Unit serving: ",UNIT$(SIZE)
240    INPUT "Calories per unit: ",CAL(SIZE)
250    IF SIZE < MAXSIZE THEN 180
260 PRINT "You have entered all I can hold right now."
270 PRINT "Take a break while I sort the list."
280 IF SIZE = 0 THEN CHAIN "MENU.C14"   'No entries, don't bother merging
290 GOSUB 430   'Sort the list
300 '
310 'Write sorted list to file ADDITION.DAT to be merged later
320 '
330 OPEN "O",#1,"ADDITION.DAT"
340 FOR I = 1 TO SIZE
350    WRITE #1,FOOD$(I);TYPE$(I);UNIT$(I);CAL(I)
360 NEXT I
370 WRITE #1,"zzzzz","","",0    'Write sentinel record to end
380 CLOSE #1
390 CHAIN "MERGE.C14"   'Now merge list into CTABLE.DAT
400 '
410 'Quicksort
420 '
430 PRINT "Quicksorting array: ";
440 SP=1:STK(SP,1)=1:STK(SP,2)=SIZE
450 WHILE SP>0
460    PRINT "*";
470    L=STK(SP,1):R=STK(SP,2):SP=SP-1
480    WHILE L<R
490       I=L:J=R:S=1
500       WHILE I<J
510          IF FOOD$(I)<=FOOD$(J) THEN 550
520             SWAP FOOD$(I),FOOD$(J) : SWAP TYPE$(I),TYPE$(J)
530             SWAP UNIT$(I),UNIT$(J) : SWAP CAL(I),CAL(J)
```

(Tutorial 14-1: Continued)

```
540             S=-S
550          IF S=1 THEN I=I+1 ELSE J=J-1
560       WEND
570       IF R-I>J-L THEN 610
580          IF J-1>L THEN SP=SP+1:STK(SP,1)=L:STK(SP,2)=J-1
590          L=I+1
600       GOTO 630
610          IF I+1<R THEN SP=SP+1:STK(SP,1)=I+1:STK(SP,2)=R
620          R=J-1
630    WEND
640 WEND
650 PRINT
660 RETURN
```

After completing the quicksort in lines 430 through 660, the program returns to line 330 where the file ADDITION.DAT is opened. Then, in the following FOR/NEXT loop, the data is placed alphabetically in the file. Line 370 writes the last record in the file as dummy data, which will be used by later programs. Do not worry about the fact that this record will be added each time you run the program; MEAL will still work. Line 390 chains in the next program, MERGE.

In the MERGE program, three files are opened—two for input and one for output.

```
10 REM -                    -=*MERGE.C14*=-
20 REM -                    Merge MERGE.FIL into CTABLE.DAT
30 REM -                    2/15/83
40 REM -
100 DEFINT A-Z
110 ON ERROR GOTO 440
120 REM - Open files
130 OPEN "I",#1,"CTABLE.DAT"
140 OPEN "I",#2,"ADDITION.DAT"
150 OPEN "O",#3,"COPY.DAT"
160 REM - Diminsion records for files 1 and 2
170 DIM FOOD$(2),TYPE$(2),UNIT$(2),CAL(2)
180 IF EOF(1) THEN FIL = 2 : GOTO 310    'There are no records in CTABLE.DAT
190 IF EOF(2) THEN ERROR 255             'Should not be merging if no additions
200 PRINT "Merging files: ";
210 FIL=2
220 INPUT #1,FOOD$(1),TYPE$(1),UNIT$(1),CAL(1)
230 WHILE NOT EOF(FIL)
240     INPUT #FIL,FOOD$(FIL),TYPE$(FIL),UNIT$(FIL),CAL(FIL)
250     PRINT "*";
260     IF FOOD$(1) < FOOD$(2) THEN FIL = 1 ELSE FIL = 2
270     WRITE #3,FOOD$(FIL),TYPE$(FIL),UNIT$(FIL),CAL(FIL)
280 WEND
```

(Tutorial 14-1: Continued)

```
290 IF FIL = 1 THEN FIL = 2 ELSE FIL = 1     'Switch FIL to other value
300 WRITE #3,FOOD$(FIL),TYPE$(FIL),UNIT$(FIL),CAL(FIL) 'Clear current record
310 WHILE NOT EOF(FIL)      'Flush the file that still has records
320     INPUT #FIL,FOOD$(FIL),TYPE$(FIL),UNIT$(FIL),CAL(FIL)
330     WRITE #3,FOOD$(FIL),TYPE$(FIL),UNIT$(FIL),CAL(FIL)
340 WEND
350 PRINT                         'Done merging the files
360 CLOSE
370 KILL "CTABLE.DAT"
380 KILL "ADDITION.DAT"
390 NAME "COPY.DAT" AS "CTABLE.DAT"
400 CHAIN "MENU.C14"
410 '
420 'Error trap routine
430 '
440 IF ERR <> 53 OR ERL <> 130 THEN ON ERROR GOTO 0
450 CLOSE
460 NAME "ADDITION.DAT" AS "CTABLE.DAT"
470 RESUME 400
```

The actual merge takes place in lines 200 through 340. After the files have been merged into a single file, the program uses the CHAIN command to return you back to MENU, where you can either terminate the program or select the program MEAL.

Now to our final program, MEAL.

```
10 REM -                    -=*MEAL.C14*=-
20 REM -                    Compute calories per meal
30 REM -                    2/15/83
40 REM -
100 DEFINT A-Z
110 MAXMEAL = 20          'Maximum meal size
120 MAXTYPE = 10          'Maximum numer of types per given food
130 DIM FOOD$(MAXMEAL),TYPE$(MAXMEAL),UNIT$(MAXMEAL),CAL(MAXMEAL),AMT(MAXMEAL)
140 DIM T$(MAXTYPE),U$(MAXTYPE),C(MAXTYPE)
150 FOOD$ = "zzzzz"      'Initialize file pointer to end
160 MSIZE = 0            'This is the meal size (number of foods)
170 PRINT : PRINT "Enter food #";MSIZE+1;"or <RETURN> to end: ";
180 INPUT "",F$
190 IF F$="" THEN 300
200    GOSUB 480           'Choose food type
210    IF SEL = 0 THEN 290       'SEL = 0 if not found or no selection
220       MSIZE = MSIZE + 1
230       FOOD$(MSIZE) = F$
240       TYPE$(MSIZE) = T$(SEL)
250       UNIT$(MSIZE) = U$(SEL)
260       CAL(MSIZE) = C(SEL)
270       PRINT "How many ";UNIT$(MSIZE);" servings? ";
```

(Tutorial 14-1: Continued)

```
280        INPUT "",AMT(MSIZE)
290     IF SIZE < MAXMEAL THEN 170
300 PRINT
310 PRINT TAB(17);"-*= Food calorie chart =*-"
320 PRINT "Food, type                    amount units    cal/unit total"
330 PRINT "------------------------    ------ -----    -------- -----"
340 SL$ = "\                          \  ###   \      \  ####   #####"
350 TL$ = "Total calories consumed:                             #####"
360 TOTAL = 0
370 FOR I = 1 TO MSIZE
380     SUBT = AMT(I)*CAL(I)
390     PRINT USING SL$;FOOD$(I)+", "+TYPE$(I);AMT(I),UNIT$(I),CAL(I),SUBT
400     TOTAL = TOTAL + SUBT
410 NEXT I
420 PRINT USING TL$;TOTAL
430 PRINT : INPUT "Press <RETURN> to return to menu. ",A$
440 CHAIN "MENU.C14"
450 '
460 'Look up F$ in CTABLE and get appropriate type.
470 '
480 IF FOOD$ < F$ THEN 510       'Check if F$ is before or after file pointer
490     CLOSE #1                 'If F$ is before file pointer then
500     OPEN "I",#1,"CTABLE.DAT" 'Restore to beginning of file
510 INPUT #1,FOOD$,TYPE$,UNIT$,CAL       'Search for F$
520 IF FOOD$ < F$ THEN 510
530 TSIZE = 0               'This is the number of types for F$
540 WHILE FOOD$ = F$ AND TSIZE < MAXTYPE
550     TSIZE = TSIZE + 1
560     PRINT USING "##) &";TSIZE;TYPE$
570     T$(TSIZE) = TYPE$ : U$(TSIZE) = UNIT$ : C(TSIZE) = CAL
580     INPUT #1,FOOD$,TYPE$,UNIT$,CAL
590 WEND
600 IF TSIZE > 0 THEN 640
610     PRINT F$;" not found in file."
620     SEL = 0
630     RETURN
640 INPUT "Enter your selection or 0 for none of the above: ",SEL
650 IF SEL >= 0 AND SEL <= TSIZE THEN 680
660     PRINT "Invalid selection, enter a number between 0 and";TSIZE
670     GOTO 640
680 RETURN
```

Note that line 150 sets the pointer to the end of the file by setting the variable **FOOD$** equal to "**zzzzz**". After making your first choice of food, the program transfers to the subroutine at 480. Since **FOOD$** is "**zzzzz**", the file will be opened the first time through in line 500, which automatically sets the pointer to the beginning of the file. The program then searches through the file sequentially to find the food that you indicated in line 180. On finding your entry, the program determines how many types are in the file. For instance, if your choice was milk, type might be "whole," "2%," and "non-fat." The program then indicates on the screen these types and allows you to make your selection by number. After selecting the appropriate type of the food, lines 220 through 280 record the information in arrays so that it can be printed out later. You then go to line 170 to make your next selection.

On your second selection, when the program reaches line 480, it checks to see if the file pointer is before or after your selection. If the file pointer is before, MEAL does not close the file but continues to search through for your next selection. If the file pointer is after the second selection, MEAL must close the file in order to reset the pointer to the beginning of the file. If your food choices were entered in alphabetical order, the file would only be opened once. If they were entered in reverse alphabetical order, the file would have to be closed and reopened on each selection.

Each program contains a DEFINT A-Z statement in line 100. Since none of the programs requires single-precision numbers, the DEFINT statement at line 100 is used to make all variables default to integer type unless otherwise specified.

Here is an example of running the program:

```
RUN

Choose one of the following:
   1 ... Enter new data into table
   2 ... Compute total calories for a meal
   3 ... End

Enter your selection: 1

Food name or <RETURN> to end: Beef
Type: Sirloin
Unit serving: 1 oz.
Calories per unit: 110

Food name or <RETURN> to end: Chocolate
Type: Sweet
Unit serving: 1 oz.
Calories per unit: 150
```

*(**Tutorial 14-1:** Continued)*

```
Food name or <RETURN> to end:
Quicksorting array: *
Merging files: *******

Chose one of the following:
   1 ... Enter new data into table
   2 ... Compute total calories for a meal
   3 ... End

Enter your selection: 2

Enter food # 1 or <RETURN> to end: Beef
 1) Sirloin
Enter your selection or 0 for none of the above: 1
How many 1 oz. servings? 8

Enter food # 2 or <RETURN> to end: Apricots
 1) Dried
Enter your selection or 0 for none of the above: 1
How many 3 oz. servings? 2

Enter food # 3 or <RETURN> to end: Chocolate
 1) Sweet
Enter your selection or 0 for none of the above: 1
How many 1 oz. servings? 3

Enter food # 4 or <RETURN> to end:

                -*= Food calorie chart =*-
Food, type                  amount units    cal/unit total
-------------------------   ------ -----    -------- -----
Beef, Sirloin                    8  1 oz.      110     880
Apricots, Dried                  2  3 oz.      260     520
Chocolate, Sweet                 3  1 oz.      150     450
Total calories consumed:                              1850

Press <RETURN> to return to menu.

Chose one of the following:
   1 ... Enter new data into table
   2 ... Compute total calories for a meal
   3 ... End

Enter your selection: 3
Ok
```

EXERCISES

1. Write a program that will allow you to enter names and addresses into a sequential file.

2. For the sequential file of the first problem, write a program that will print out, in mailing label format, only those names that have a specific ZIP code.

15

Working With Random-Access Files

Statements:	LSET, PUT, RSET, GET, FIELD, MERGE
Functions:	MKI$, CVI, MKS$, CVS, MKD$, CVD, LOF

The second file structure used by MBASIC for data is *random access.* Just as with sequential files, a random file consists of a group of records or even of a single record, although this would not be practical. Most files will consist of a hundred or more records.

Working with Random Files

Figure 15-1 is a diagram of how a random-access file is set up. Compare it to Figure 14-1, which shows a sequential file.

The advantage of random access is that if we wish to read record number 199, MBASIC goes directly to that record without needing to

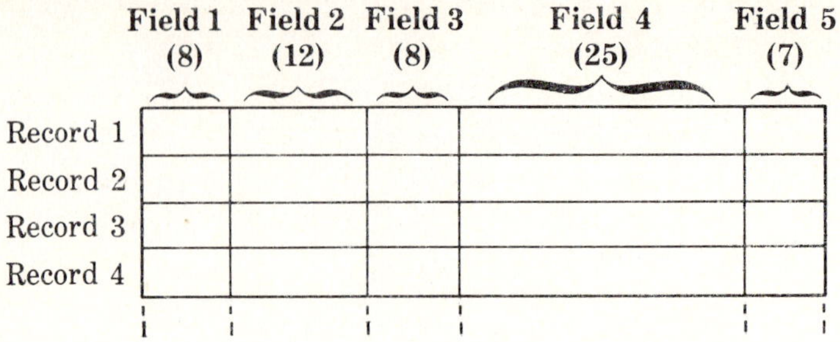

Figure 15-1.
Records in a random file

read the first 198 records. The disadvantage of the random-access file is the waste of space. For example, if the fourth field is to contain names and we specify that the length of the field is 25 bytes, this will be the maximum length for any name entered into the field. Many names will be shorter than this, but 25 bytes of storage are allocated and will be used for each name whether or not 25 bytes are required.

OPENING A RANDOM-ACCESS FILE [OPEN, FIELD]

Before you can work with random-access files, you must always use two statements. They are the OPEN statement and the FIELD statement. Let's look at each of these.

The OPEN statement is similar to the OPEN statement in Chapter 14, except that the *mode$* is "R". This allows you to both read and write in the file. In addition, you must indicate the length of each record at the end of the command. When you are working with a random-access file, the record length is determined by the sum of the lengths of the individual fields of the record. For example, if field one has a length of 4 and field two has a length of 12, then the record length would be 16. An example of an OPEN command for a random-access file is

```
OPEN "R", #1, "CHKBOOK.DAT", 38
```

The 38 is the record length.

A **FIELD** statement is needed in the program to set the length for each field. The syntax is

```
FIELD #filenumber, width1 AS varible1, width2 AS variable2, ...
```

where *filenumber* is the number of the file we are describing, *width1* is the number of bytes in the first field, which is stored in *variable1$*, and so on. All of the variables must be strings, and these strings must be filled only by the GET, LSET, or RSET statements. Do not assign the strings specified in the FIELD statement with either INPUT or LET, since this will mix up MBASIC's internal memory. An example of a FIELD command is

```
FIELD #1, 25 AS F.PAYTO$, 8 AS F.DATE$, 4 AS F.AMOUNT$,1 AS F.STATUS$
```

The **#1** indicates the number of the file that contains the records with these fields. Following the file number is a comma-separated list of field lengths and the name of each field. In our example **25 AS F.PAYTO$** indicates that the first field in our record has a length of 25 characters and is assigned to the variable name **F.PAYTO$**. The second field has a length of 8 and is assigned to **F.DATE$**. The third field has a length of 4 and is assigned the variable name **F.AMOUNT$**. You will see in a moment why we chose to put F. before each variable name.

LOF FUNCTION
[LOF]

The LOF function returns the approximate number of records in a random-access file. Depending on your record length, LOF will be accurate within about seven records. Since LOF is only an approximation, it is usually used to determine whether a random-access file contains any records at all. For example,

```
IF LOF(1)=0 THEN 200
```

will branch to line 200 if file number one contains no records. Notice that when you use the LOF function, you must not put the number sign in front of the file number. The application in Tutorial 15-1 at the end of this chapter will use the LOF function.

PREPARING STRING DATA FOR A FILE
[LSET,RSET]

Variables that are used in a FIELD statement need special attention. The only safe way to assign a value to a variable in a FIELD statement is to use the LSET or RSET statement. Because fields in a record are a specified length and the data is usually shorter than this length, you must either left- or right-justify the data.

For example, suppose a customer name field has a length of 25, and we enter the name **Wallace, David**. The name requires only 14 spaces, including the comma and the space between last and first names. LSET will left-justify the data within the field and RSET will right-justify the name within the field, as shown in Figure 15-2.

The LSET and RSET statements are used to store the data in the fields for the file, but they do not actually store the data in the file. This is done with the PUT statement, which is described later in the chapter. If the strings being stored by LSET and RSET are longer than the variables, LSET and RSET will eliminate the rightmost excess characters. If the strings are shorter than the variables, the string is padded with spaces.

Notice that we started all our variables in the FIELD example with **F.**, for example, **F.PAYTO$**. This particular notation is not essential, but because field variables are treated in a special way (they must be LSET or RSET), it is worthwhile to develop some notation to readily distinguish them from other string variables. Since you cannot assign field variables with a LET or INPUT statement, a two-step process is necessary. The data is entered into a standard string variable, and then it is assigned to the field variable using RSET or LSET.

For example, to assign the field variable **F.PAYTO$** with data entered from the keyboard, you could use

```
100 INPUT "Payment to: ",PAYTO$
110 LSET F.PAYTO$ = PAYTO$
```

If the variable **F.PAYTO$** were used in line 100, the data would not be placed properly in the field. No error message is printed if you assign data to a field variable without using LSET or RSET. It is easy to forget to use LSET and RSET when you are first working

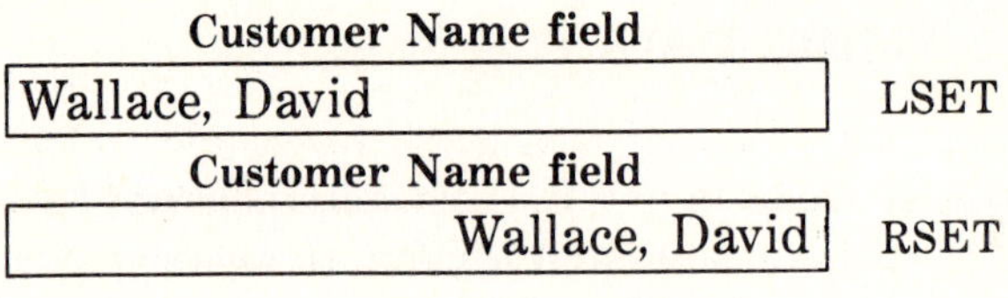

Figure 15-2.
Filling a field with LSET and RSET

with random-access files. If a field variable is assigned without LSET or RSET, however, it can no longer be used to place data into a field of a record.

STORING NUMBERS IN RANDOM FILES [CVI, CVS, CVD, MKI$, MKS$, MKD$]

Since only string variables may appear in a FIELD statement, numbers need special attention. To write numbers to a random-access file, you must first convert them to strings.

The MBASIC functions that are used for this purpose are MKI$, MKS$, and MKD$. MKI$ converts an *integer* into a two-byte string, MKS$ converts a *single-precision number* into a four-byte string, and MKD$ converts a *double-precision number* into an eight-byte string. Once the numeric values have been converted to strings, LSET or RSET is used to place them in the field variables.

When numbers that have been converted to strings are read from a random-access file, they must be reconverted to numeric values before they can be processed by your program. The MBASIC functions that are used for this purpose are CVI, CVS, and CVD.

CVI converts a two-byte string to an *integer*, CVS converts a four-byte string to a *single-precision number*, and CVD converts an eight-byte string to a *double-precision number*.

In addition to the specific functions designed for this conversion, you can also use the CHR$ and ASC functions to convert numbers in the range of 0 through 255. This can be useful if space is a consideration, since only one byte of storage is required for each number.

For example, if in our previous FIELD example, you wished to store the number 235 in the **F.STATUS$** field, which has a length 1, you would use

```
LSET F.STATUS$ = CHR$(235)
```

To extract a number stored in the **F.STATUS$** field, you would use

```
NUM = ASC(F.STATUS$)
```

It is also worth noting that numbers that do not require any mathematical manipulation (such as phone numbers, ZIP codes, and so on) may be stored and treated as strings throughout a program. You can also use the STR$ and VAL functions that were introduced in Chapter 9. The field length required will depend on the maximum value you wish to store. For example, the FIELD statement for numbers in the range 0 to 9999 will require four bytes of storage.

General Requirements for Random-Access Files

In addition to the preceding rules governing number and string conversion, there are some other general requirements for random files.

First of all, each time a random-access file is to be used, it must be opened with the same record length. MBASIC locates an individual record in a random-access file by using the record length to compute the exact location of the record in the file. For example, if the record length is 40 and you want to retrieve the thirtieth record, MBASIC moves directly to byte 1200 in the file and reads the next 40 bytes.

Second, the maximum record length is set by default at 128 bytes. This can be changed when you load MBASIC from CP/M. To change this maximum, add /**S:nnn**, where *nnn* is the maximum record size, to the MBASIC command. For example, to allow for 300-byte record lengths, give the command

```
MBASIC /S:300
```

Finally, the total length of all the fields specified in the FIELD statement must be less than or equal to the record size specified in the OPEN command. Note that the error message **FIELD overflow** will be given if the combined length of the field variables in a FIELD statement is greater than the record length specified for the file.

You may, however, want to specify a record length that is greater than the total length of all the fields. If your record contains extra room not used up by the fields, you may easily add fields to your FIELD statement at a later time without having to recreate the entire data file. You must decide how much extra room to set aside for future expansion by weighing the amount of wasted room against the importance of being able to add fields to your record.

Writing to a Random File
[PUT,GET]

When all the fields of a record have been filled with LSET or RSET, use the PUT statement to write the record to the file. The syntax of the PUT statement is

```
PUT #filenumber, recordnumber
```

where *filenumber* is the number of the desired file and *recordnumber* is the record in the file that will be filled in.

For example, to write to record number six of file number one, you would use

```
PUT #1, 6
```

More commonly, a variable will appear as the record number, as in

```
PUT #1, RECNUM
```

You do not have to include a list of field variables in the PUT statement as you did with the PRINT# or WRITE# statements. The FIELD statement has already specified which variables are to be written to each record of the file.

To optimize the time required to write data to a disk file, the PUT statement actually places the data in a buffer instead of on the disk. A *buffer* is a section of the computer memory that is managed internally by MBASIC and that is used to hold information temporarily. When the buffer is full, or when the file is closed with the CLOSE statement, the data is written to the disk. It is therefore very important to be sure that the program closes the file when it has finished reading from or writing to the file. If this is not done, data may be lost.

Since the RUN, END, SYSTEM, LOAD, NEW, and EDIT commands will automatically close all files, the problem of lost data rarely arises. Of course, it is still possible to lose data accidentally if you prematurely exit from MBASIC. If you turn the power off or reset the computer before closing a file, you may lose some of your latest file updates. These warnings also apply to sequential files opened with the output or "O" mode.

Reading from a random file is very similar to writing to it. The syntax of the GET statement is

```
GET #filenumber, recordnumber
```

where *filenumber* and *recordnumber* are the same as for the PUT statement. When the GET statement reads a record from a file, it automatically assigns all of the field variables specified in the FIELD statement for that file. You do not specify which variables to read as you did with the INPUT# statement.

Organizing Your Data Records

The main function of files is to store a lot of data. For this reason, the time spent planning the structure of data within a file is well worthwhile. It is very frustrating, for example, to find that a particular field should be longer or that an additional field is required after entering a hundred records.

Our first random-access file program will allow us to input data for a personal checkbook. Table 15-1 shows that fields are provided for the following data: who the check is paid to; the date; the amount; and the check's status, which indicates whether or not the check has cleared the bank. The status will be either "O" for "outstanding" (the check has not cleared the bank) or "C" for "clear" (the check has cleared the bank). The check number will be the same as the record number. This means that we will not actually store the check number, since it is already known.

Type in and run the following program:

```
10 REM - CHKBOOK1
100 OPEN "R",#1,"CHKBOOK.DAT",38
110 FIELD #1,25 AS F.PAYTO$,8 AS F.DATE$,4 AS F.AMOUNT$,1 AS F.STATUS$
120 CHKNUM = 1
130 PRINT:PRINT "Check number";CHKNUM
140    LINE INPUT "Payment to: ",PAYTO$
150    IF PAYTO$ = "" THEN 250
160    LINE INPUT "Date: ",DATE$
170    INPUT "Amount of payment: ",AMOUNT
180    LSET F.PAYTO$ = PAYTO$
190    LSET F.DATE$ = DATE$
200    LSET F.AMOUNT$ = MKS$(AMOUNT)
210    LSET F.STATUS$ = "O"
220    PUT #1,CHKNUM
```

Table 15-1.
Random File Data

Check # (3)	Payto (25)	Date (8)	Amount (4)	Status (1)
1	Eric Crum	1/3/83	93.30	O
2	P.G. & E.	1/3/83	192.50	O
3	Macy's	1/7/83	147.30	O
4	Slug, Fred	1/14/83	45.50	O
5	CP/M/83	1/14/83	20.00	O

```
230    CHKNUM = CHKNUM + 1
240    GOTO 130
250 CLOSE #1
260 END
```

Notice that each of the variables assigned in the FIELD statement in line 110 has the prefix **F.**, so that when you inspect your program, you can quickly distinguish the field variables from other variables.

```
RUN

Check number 1
Payment to: Eric Crum
Date: 1/3/83
Amount of payment: 93.90

Check number 2
Payment to: P. G. & E.
Date: 1/3/83
Amount of payment: 192.50

Check number 3
Payment to:
Ok
```

In lines 180 through 200 the field variables—those prefixed with **F.**—are set equal to the variables you input. In line 200 the single-precision numeric variable **AMOUNT** is converted to a four-byte string with MKS$ so that it may be stored in the field **F.AMOUNT$**. (Remember, **AMOUNT** is a single-precision variable by default.) In line 210 the field variable **F.STATUS$** is set equal to the constant "**O**" since the checks have not cleared the bank yet. The PUT statement of line 220 writes the information that was LSET in lines 180 through 210 to the file.

In this next program, we will use the GET command to read the data we wrote to the CHKBOOK.DAT file in the previous program. In addition to reading the file, the program will also allow us to post whether or not a check has been cleared. When a check is posted as clear, the **F.STATUS$** field is set to "C" for "clear."

```
10 REM - CHKBOOK2
100 OPEN "R",#1,"CHKBOOK.DAT",38
110 FIELD #1,25 AS F.PAYTO$,8 AS F.DATE$,4 AS F.AMOUNT$,1 AS F.STATUS$
120 PRINT:INPUT "Enter check number to clear: ",CHKNUM
130    IF CHKNUM = 0 THEN 210
```

```
140    GET #1,CHKNUM
150    AMOUNT = CVS(F.AMOUNT$)
160    PRINT:PRINT USING "Check number: ###  date: &";CHKNUM;F.DATE$
170    PRINT USING "Pay to: & for $$###.##";F.PAYTO$;AMOUNT
180    INPUT "Post check as cleared (Y/N)? ",ANS$
190    IF ANS$ = "Y" THEN LSET F.STATUS$ = "C" : PUT #1,CHKNUM
200    GOTO 120
210 CLOSE #1
220 END
```

Running the program produces the following:

```
RUN

Enter check number to clear: 2

Check number:   2  date: 1/3/83
Pay to: P. G. & E.                for  $192.50
Post check as cleared (Y/N)? Y

Enter check number to clear: 1

Check number:   1  date: 1/3/83
Pay to: Eric Crum                 for   $93.90
Post check as cleared (Y/N)? Y

Enter check number to clear:
Ok
```

The GET statement in line 140 reads in the record number specified in the variable **CHKNUM** from file number 1. In line 150, the CVS function converts the amount of each check from the string data held in **F.AMOUNT$** to single-precision numeric data and places it in the single-precision variable **AMOUNT**. In lines 160 and 170, **F.DATE$** and **F.PAYTO$** are used as strings in the program so that they do not need to be converted. In line 190, the LSET command is used to set the status of the check to be cleared if the answer to the question in line 190 is **Y** for yes.

Line 190 also writes the record back to the file with the PUT statement if **F.STATUS$** is changed. Here we are *updating* a record; that is, we are rewriting a record that already exists. Even though we are only changing one field, **F.STATUS$**, the PUT statement writes the entire record back to the file.

Notice that in the run of the program, check numbers 2 and 1 were read out of order. Because your checks will generally come back from the bank out of order, your program should be able to post checks in a *random* order. Since we have conveniently made the check number the same as the record number, we can select any check from our random-access file. A sequential file would not be suitable for this application because it would restrict your program to posting checks in sequential order.

Now run the program again and enter check number 100:

```
RUN

Enter check number to clear: 100

Check number: 100  date:
Pay to:  for    $0.00
Post check as cleared (Y/N)? Y
```

Our file only contains two records—one for check number 1 and one for check number 2—yet the program allowed us to read record number 100. Reading past the end of a random-access file does not generate an error in MBASIC. It is up to your program to make sure that you use the GET statement to read in only those record numbers that have been previously written to with the PUT statement.

Now let's see what happens if we answer **Y** to clear the check. This will write to record 100 even though we have not written to any of the records between record 3 and record 99. After writing record 100, use the program to look at record 90.

```
Enter check number to clear: 90

Check number:  90  date: s:. /
Pay to:    ++sc::                   for    $0.00
Post check as cleared (Y/N)?
```

Your results will be different from this example's but equally unpredictable. In general, reading a record that does not exist will give incorrect data.

If you have been working with these examples on your own computer, you should stop now and delete the CHKBOOK.DAT file with the KILL command since clearing check 100 inadvertently filled records 3 through 99 with garbage. The following three lines will check to see if we are reading past the end of the file:

```
142    IF NOT EOF(1) THEN 150
144        PRINT "Bad check number, reading past end of file"
146        GOTO 120
```

The EOF function works for random-access files almost the same way it does for sequential files. The EOF function returns true if the last GET statement executed read a record past the end of the file.

In the following example, the program reads through the entire file and determines whether or not each check has been cleared. It then prints out the total amount outstanding for the uncleared checks.

```
10 REM - CHKBOOK3
100 OPEN "R",#1,"CHKBOOK.DAT",38
110 FIELD #1,25 AS F.PAYTO$,8 AS F.DATE$,4 AS F.AMOUNT$,1 AS F.STATUS$
120 TOTAL = 0 : CHKNUM = 1
130 GET #1,CHKNUM
140 WHILE NOT EOF(1)
150    IF F.STATUS$ <> "0" THEN 200
160       AMOUNT = CVS(F.AMOUNT$)
170       PRINT:PRINT USING "Check number: ###  date: &";CHKNUM;F.DATE$
180       PRINT USING "Pay to: & for $$####.##";F.PAYTO$;AMOUNT
190       TOTAL = TOTAL + AMOUNT
200    CHKNUM = CHKNUM + 1
210    GET #1,CHKNUM
220 WEND
230 PRINT:PRINT USING "Total for outstanding checks: $$#####.##";TOTAL
240 CLOSE #1
250 END
```

The EOF function in line 140 checks to see whether we have read a record past the end of the file. The GET statement in line 30 reads the first record. If there are no records in the file, the WHILE loop starting at line 140 is not executed. Otherwise, the WHILE loop continues to read records until the GET statement in line 210 reads beyond the end of the file. In the tutorials section of this chapter, we will introduce another method of finding the last record in a random-access file.

Line 150 determines whether or not a check has been cleared by looking at **F.STATUS$**. If the check has not been cleared, it is printed and the amount is added to the variable **TOTAL**.

We have written three separate programs that illustrate the use of random-access files to deal with checkbook entries. The purpose of the first program was to enter data; the second program was used to read the data and clear checks; and the last program listed the outstanding checks. When you are used to working with random files, you will be able to incorporate all three of these functions into a single program.

Merging Programs
[MERGE]

Let's see how the MERGE command can be used to combine these three programs into a single program. The MERGE command is used to combine separate programs that are stored on the disk as individual files into a single program stored in the computer's memory. In order to combine separate programs in this way, we will have to do some preliminary planning, then renumber the existing programs.

First we should begin our program with a menu that will allow us to implement each of these functions. Recall that using a menu was explained in Chapter 8. Enter the following, which will be the beginning of our combined program:

```
10 REM - CHKBOOK.C15 (MERGED)
100 OPEN "R",#1,"CHKBOOK.DAT",38
110 FIELD #1,25 AS F.PAYTO$,8 AS F.DATE$,4 AS F.AMOUNT$,1 AS F.STATUS$
120 PRINT
130 PRINT "Choose one of the following functions:"
140 PRINT "   1 ... Add checks to file"
150 PRINT "   2 ... Clear checks"
160 PRINT "   3 ... List outstanding checks"
170 PRINT "   4 ... End/close files"
180 PRINT
190 INPUT "What is your selection? ",SEL
200 IF SEL < 1 OR SEL > 4 THEN PRINT "Invalid selection.":GOTO 190
210 ON SEL GOSUB 1000,2000,3000,4000
220 GOTO 120
4000 CLOSE
4010 END
```

In effect, each of our previous programs will be a subroutine of this program. Line 210 indicates the beginning line numbers of each of these subroutines. Line 1000 will be the start of the subroutine that allows us to add checks to our data file. Line 2000 is the beginning of the subroutine to clear checks and line 3000 is the beginning of the subroutine that lists the outstanding checks. The last subroutine, which begins at 4000, closes the files and ends the program.

At this point, let's save this program with the file name **CHKBOOK.C15** and begin the modifications of the three checkbook programs that will be subroutines. First load the program CHKBOOK1, delete the lines that we are not interested in, and renumber the program beginning at line 1000. Also add a RETURN statement to the end of the first subroutine, and replace the END statement with a REM statement. Then save the program under the name **FILE1**.

```
LOAD "CHKBOOK1"
Ok
DELETE 10-110
Ok
120 INPUT "What is the next check number? ",CHKNUM
250 RETURN
260 REM
RENUM 1000
Ok
SAVE "FILE1",A
Ok
```

In order to use the MERGE command, it is necessary to save the program in the ASCII format. This is done with the A option of the SAVE command. Note the change in line 120 that will allow check numbers to start where the last session left off.

The same procedure is followed in the programs CHKBOOK2 and CHKBOOK3.

```
LOAD "CHKBOOK2"
Ok
DELETE 10-110
Ok
210 RETURN
220 REM
RENUM 2000
Ok
SAVE "FILE2",A
Ok
LOAD "CHKBOOK3"
Ok
DELETE 10-110
Ok
240 RETURN
250 REM
RENUM 3000
Ok
SAVE "FILE3",A
Ok
```

Now that our menu program is written and our three checkbook programs are modified and renumbered, we can proceed to merge them into a single program by following these steps:

```
LOAD "CHKBOOK.C15"
Ok
MERGE "FILE1"
Ok
MERGE "FILE2"
Ok
MERGE "FILE3"
Ok
```

Here is the final result:

```
10 REM - CHKBOOK.C15 (MERGED)
100 OPEN "R",#1,"CHKBOOK.DAT",38
110 FIELD #1,25 AS F.PAYTO$,8 AS F.DATE$,4 AS F.AMOUNT$,1 AS F.STATUS$
120 PRINT
130 PRINT "Choose one of the folowing functions:"
140 PRINT "   1 ... Add checks to file"
150 PRINT "   2 ... Clear checks"
160 PRINT "   3 ... List outstanding checks"
170 PRINT "   4 ... End/close files"
180 PRINT
190 INPUT "What is your selection? ",SEL
200 IF SEL < 1 OR SEL > 3 THEN PRINT "Invalid selection.":GOTO 190
210 ON SEL GOSUB 1000,2000,3000,4000
220 GOTO 120
1000 INPUT "What is the next check number? ",CHKNUM
1010 PRINT:PRINT "Check number";CHKNUM
1020    INPUT "Payment to: ",PAYTO$
1030    IF PAYTO$ = "" THEN 1130
1040    INPUT "Date: ",DATE$
1050    INPUT "Amount of payment: ",AMOUNT
1060    LSET F.PAYTO$ = PAYTO$
1070    LSET F.DATE$ = DATE$
1080    LSET F.AMOUNT$ = MKS$(AMOUNT)
1090    LSET F.STATUS$ = "0"
1100    PUT #1,CHKNUM
1110    CHKNUM = CHKNUM + 1
1120    GOTO 1010
1130 RETURN
1140 REM
2000 PRINT:INPUT "Enter check number to clear: ",CHKNUM
2010    IF CHKNUM = 0 THEN 2120
2020    GET #1,CHKNUM
2030    IF NOT EOF(1) THEN 2060
2040       PRINT "Bad check number, reading past end of file"
2050       GOTO 2000
2060    AMOUNT = CVS(F.AMOUNT$)
2070    PRINT:PRINT USING "Check number: ###  date: &";CHKNUM;F.DATE$
2080    PRINT USING "Pay to: & for $$###.##";F.PAYTO$;AMOUNT
```

```
2090    INPUT "Post check as cleared (Y/N)? ",ANS$
2100    IF ANS$ = "Y" THEN LSET F.STATUS$ = "C" : PUT #1,CHKNUM
2110    GOTO 2000
2120 RETURN
2130 REM
3000 TOTAL = 0 : CHKNUM = 1
3010 GET #1,CHKNUM
3020 WHILE NOT EOF(1)
3030    IF F.STATUS$ <> "O" THEN 3080
3040       AMOUNT = CVS(F.AMOUNT$)
3050       PRINT:PRINT USING "Check number: ###  date: &";CHKNUM;F.DATE$
3060       PRINT USING "Pay to: & for $$###.##";F.PAYTO$;AMOUNT
3070       TOTAL = TOTAL + AMOUNT
3080    CHKNUM = CHKNUM + 1
3090    GET #1,CHKNUM
3100 WEND
3110 PRINT:PRINT USING "Total for outstanding checks: $$####.##";TOTAL
3120 RETURN
3130 REM
4000 CLOSE
4010 END
```

Notice that lines 4000 and 4010, which were part of the first menu program CHKBOOK.C14, appear at the end of the listing following the three subroutines FILE1, FILE2, and FILE3.

Here is a sample RUN of the program:

```
RUN

Choose one of the following functions:
   1 ... Add checks to file
   2 ... Clear checks
   3 ... List outstanding checks
   4 ... End/close files

What is your selection? 1
What is the next check number? 23

Check number 23
Payment to: Senior House
Date: 1/24/83
Amount of payment: 15.50

Check number 24
Payment to: Sigma Delta
Date: 1/25/83
Amount of payment: 6.66
```

```
Check number 25
Payment to:

Choose one of the following functions:
   1 ... Add checks to file
   2 ... Clear checks
   3 ... List outstanding checks
   4 ... End/close files

What is your selection? 3

Check number:  23  date: 1/24/83
Pay to: Senior House              for   $15.50

Check number:  24  date: 1/25/83
Pay to: Sigma Delta               for    $6.66

Total for outstanding checks:    $22.16

Choose one of the following functions:
   1 ... Add checks to file
   2 ... Clear checks
   3 ... List outstanding checks
   4 ... End/close files

What is your selection? 4
Ok
```

TUTORIALS

Tutorial 15-1: Inventory

This tutorial, which is an inventory program, is the longest single program we have worked with to this point. Before we go into the specific details, let's take a look at the problem as a whole and observe how it is organized.

```
10 REM -                -=*INVENTRY*=-
20 REM -                Inventry program
30 REM -                2/6/83
40 REM -
1000 DEFINT A-Z
1010 BELL$ = CHR$(7)
1020 REM *=- Open inventory file
```

(Tutorial 15-1: Continued)

```
1030 OPEN "R",#1,"INVENTRY.DAT",38
1040 REM *=- Field the header record with status and number of parts.
1050 FIELD #1.1 AS STAT$,2 AS NUMPTS$
1060 REM *=- Field data records with description, quantity, reorder level,
1070 REM *=- and price per unit.
1080 FIELD #1,30 AS DESC$,2 AS QTY$,2 AS REDR$,4 AS PRICE$
1090 IF LOF(1) = 0 THEN 1150     'Check file size
1100    GET #1,1                  Get old header record
1110    IF STAT$ = "C" THEN 1130
1120       PRINT BELL$;">>--> WARNING: file not previously closed properly."
1130    NUMPTS = CVI(NUMPTS$)
1140 GOTO 1170
1150    NUMPTS = 0      'New file, initialize header record
1160    LSET NUMPTS$ = MKI$(0)
1170 LSET STAT$ = "O"   'Set file to (O)pen status
1180 PUT #1,1           'Write out header record
1190 PRINT : PRINT
1200 PRINT "There are";NUMPTS;"parts on file."
1210 PRINT
1220 PRINT "Choose one of the following functions:"
1230 PRINT "   1 ... Query an existing part"
1240 PRINT "   2 ... Enter a new part"
1250 PRINT "   3 ... Edit an existing part"
1260 PRINT "   4 ... Sales transaction"
1270 PRINT "   5 ... Purchase transaction"
1280 PRINT "   6 ... List parts below reorder level"
1290 PRINT "   7 ... End program/close file"
1300 PRINT
1310 INPUT "Selection number: ",SEL
1320 IF SEL >= 1 AND SEL <= 7 THEN 1350
1330    PRINT "Please enter a selection between 1 and 7."
1340    GOTO 1310
1350 IF NUMPTS > 0 OR SEL = 2 OR SEL = 7 THEN 1380
1360    PRINT BELL$;">>--> No parts on file."
1370    GOTO 1310
1380 ON SEL GOSUB 1430,1510,1620,1710,1770,1830,2010
1390 GOTO 1190
1400 '
1410 'Query an existing part
1420 '
1430 TRNS$ = "query"
1440 GOSUB 2090          'Get part number
1450 GOSUB 2190          'Print part
1460 PRINT : INPUT "Press <RETURN> to continue... ",A$
1470 RETURN
1480 '
1490 'Enter a new part
1500 '
1510 PRINT
```

(Tutorial 15-1: Continued)

```
1520 NUMPTS = NUMPTS + 1 : PART = NUMPTS     'This is the new part number
1530 LSET DESC$ = "NEW PART"
1540 LSET QTY$ = MKI$(0) : LSET REDR$ = MKI$(0) : LSET PRICE$ = MKS$(0)
1550 GOSUB 2280          'Edit new part
1560 PRINT : INPUT "More parts to enter (Y/N)? ",A$
1570 IF A$="Y" THEN 1510
1580 RETURN
1590 '
1600 'Edit an existing part
1610 '
1620 TRNS$ = "edit"
1630 GOSUB 2090          'Get part number
1640 GOSUB 2280          'Edit part
1650 PRINT : INPUT "More parts to edit (Y/N)? ",A$
1660 IF A$="Y" THEN 1630
1670 RETURN
1680 '
1690 'Sell a part
1700 '
1710 TRNS$ = "sell" : SIGN = -1
1720 GOSUB 2420          'Carry out sales transaction
1730 RETURN
1740 '
1750 'Purchase transaction
1760 '
1770 TRNS$ = "purchase" : SIGN = 1
1780 GOSUB 2420          'Carry out purchase transaction
1790 RETURN
1800 '
1810 'List parts below reorder level
1820 '
1830 COUNT = 0
1840 FOR PART = 1 TO NUMPTS
1850    GET #1,PART + 1
1860    QTY = CVI(QTY$) : REDR = CVI(REDR$)
1870    IF QTY > REDR THEN 1930
1880       COUNT = COUNT + 1
1890       GOSUB 2190    'Print part
1900       PRINT ">>-->";
1910       IF QTY = REDR THEN PRINT " At"; ELSE PRINT REDR-QTY;"bellow";
1920       PRINT " reorder level"
1930 NEXT PART
1940 IF COUNT = 0 THEN PRINT "No "; ELSE PRINT:PRINT COUNT;
1950 PRINT "parts below reorder level
1960 PRINT : INPUT "Press <RETURN> to continue... ",A$
1970 RETURN
1980 '
1990 'End/Close files
2000 '
```

(Tutorial 15-1: Continued)

```
2010 LSET STAT$ = "C"           'Set file status to closed
2020 LSET NUMPTS$ = MKI$(NUMPTS)
2030 PUT #1,1
2040 CLOSE #1
2050 END
2060 '
2070 'Get part number
2080 '
2090 PRINT : PRINT "Enter part number to ";TRNS$; : INPUT ": ",PART
2100 IF PART >= 1 AND PART <= NUMPTS THEN 2140
2110    PRINT BELL$;"Invalid part number."
2120    PRINT "Part number must be in the range 1 to";NUMPTS
2130    GOTO 2090
2140 GET #1,PART + 1
2150 RETURN
2160 '
2170 'Print a part
2180 '
2190 PRINT
2200 PRINT "Part number";PART;TAB(18);"Description: ";DESC$
2210 PRINT "Quantity on hand:";CVI(QTY$)
2220 PRINT "Reorder level:";CVI(REDR$)
2230 PRINT "Price per unit:";CVS(PRICE$)
2240 RETURN
2250 '
2260 'Edit part entry
2270 '
2280 PRINT "Part number:";PART;"  (Push return for no change)"
2290 PRINT "Description: ";DESC$;TAB(45); : INPUT ": ",A$
2300 IF A$<>"" THEN LSET DESC$ = A$
2310 PRINT "Quantity on hand:";CVI(QTY$);TAB(45); : INPUT ": ",A$
2320 IF A$<>"" THEN LSET QTY$ = MKI$(VAL(A$))
2330 PRINT "Reorder level:";CVI(REDR$);TAB(45); : INPUT ": ",A$
2340 IF A$<>"" THEN LSET REDR$ = MKI$(VAL(A$))
2350 PRINT "Price per unit:";CVS(PRICE$);TAB(45); : INPUT ": ",A$
2360 IF A$<>"" THEN LSET PRICE$ = MKS$(VAL(A$))
2370 PUT #1,PART + 1
2380 RETURN
2390 '
2400 'Do sales or purchase transaction
2410 '
2420 GOSUB 2090          'Get part number
2430 GOSUB 2190          'Print part
2440 QTY = CVI(QTY$) : REDR = CVI(REDR$) : PRICE! = CVS(PRICE$)
2450 PRINT : PRINT "Enter number of units to ";TRNS$; : INPUT ": ",A
2460 IF QTY + SIGN*A >= 0 THEN 2490
2470    PRINT "Can not sell more than";QTY;"units."
2480    GOTO 2450
2490 QTY = QTY + SIGN*A
```

(Tutorial 15-1: Continued)

```
2500 PRINT "There are now";QTY;"units in stock."
2510 LSET QTY$ = MKI$(QTY)
2520 PUT #1,PART + 1
2530 PRINT : PRINT "More parts to ";TRNS$; : INPUT " (Y/N)? ",A$
2540 IF A$="Y" THEN 2420
2550 RETURN
```

The lines from 1000 through 1390 constitute the main program, which includes the menu in lines 1190 through 1390. The second portion of the program, lines 1400 through 2050, contains the main subroutines. The final section of the program, lines 2060 through 2550, contains the primitive subroutines of the program. These primitive subroutines are called only by the main subroutines.

The main menu gives you a good idea of the function of the program:

```
1 ... Query an existing part
2 ... Enter a new part
3 ... Edit an existing part
4 ... Sales transaction
5 ... Purchase transaction
6 ... List parts below reorder level
7 ... End program/close file
```

This program uses one new method that you should be aware of: namely, the two FIELD statements in lines 1050 and 1080. The existence of two FIELD statements means that each time a record is read from the file, the variables in *both* FIELD statements will be filled in by MBASIC. We do this because we are using a *header record*, which is a special record in the file with a different format than the rest of the file.

Line 1050 describes only the header record, while line 1080 describes the data records. When we read and write the header record, we will use **STAT$** and **NUMPTS$** from line 1050. The header record is the first record in the file, and contains information about the *entire* file.

The first field of the header record is the file status (**STAT$**) and will contain either the letter O for "open" or C for "closed." This field is used to tell whether or not the file had been closed properly on its previous use. If the file has not been closed properly (that is, with menu selection 7), the number of parts (**NUMPTS$**) may not be accurate. In particular, if you add some parts to the file and then exit the program without using selection 7 (for example, by typing CTRL-C), the header record will not reflect the additional parts. When the file is opened, a warning message is printed by line 1120 if **STAT$** does not equal C. When selection 7 is chosen from the menu, line 2010 sets the file status to C for "closed" just before closing the file.

The second field of the header record, **NUMPTS$**, contains the number of parts in the file. Storing this number in the header record allows the program to accurately check for reading past the end of the file, as well as to know what the next available part number is. This number is stored with the two-byte integer, which allows for a maximum of 32,767 records (provided that your disk has the room). Recall that the Checkbook program had no way of knowing how many checks were in the file without asking the user.

The FIELD statement in line 1080 describes the data records for each part in the inventory. We have decided that the part number will be the same as the record number. Each part number has a description (**DESC$**), quantity (**QTY$**), reorder level (**REDR$**), and price (**PRICE$**). The combined length of each of these fields is 38, which is also the record length.

Note that even though the combined length of the fields of the header record is only three bytes, the record itself is 38 bytes long. Remember that in a random-access file, all the records must be the same length.

Line 1090 is our first use of the LOF function. If LOF(1) is 0, then file number one contains no records. Lines 1150 and 1160 initialize the header record in this case.

```
RUN


There are 8 parts on file.

Choose one of the following functions:
   1 ... Query an existing part
   2 ... Enter a new part
   3 ... Edit an existing part
   4 ... Sales transaction
   5 ... Purchase transaction
   6 ... List parts below reorder level
   7 ... End program/close file

Selection number: 1

Enter part number to query: 1
```

(Tutorial 15-1: Continued)

```
Part number 1    Description: OSBORNE
Quantity on hand: 1
Reorder level: 2
Price per unit: 1500

Press <RETURN> to continue...


There are 8 parts on file.

Choose one of the following functions:
   1 ... Query an existing part
   2 ... Enter a new part
   3 ... Edit an existing part
   4 ... Sales transaction
   5 ... Purchase transaction
   6 ... List parts below reorder level
   7 ... End program/close file

Selection number: 2

Part number: 9   (Push return for no change)
Description: NEW PART                     : TERMINAL
Quantity on hand: 0                       : 8
Reorder level: 0                          : 3
Price per unit: 0                         : 600

More parts to enter (Y/N)? N


There are 9 parts on file.

Choose one of the following functions:
   1 ... Query an existing part
   2 ... Enter a new part
   3 ... Edit an existing part
   4 ... Sales transaction
   5 ... Purchase transaction
   6 ... List parts below reorder level
   7 ... End program/close file

Selection number: 4

Enter part number to sell: 2

Part number 2    Description: Z-19
Quantity on hand: 5
Reorder level: 3
Price per unit: 696.5
```

*(**Tutorial 15-1:** Continued)*

```
Enter number of units to sell: 3
There are now 2 units in stock.

More parts to sell (Y/N)? N



There are 9 parts on file.

Choose one of the following functions:
   1 ... Query an existing part
   2 ... Enter a new part
   3 ... Edit an existing part
   4 ... Sales transaction
   5 ... Purchase transaction
   6 ... List parts below reorder level
   7 ... End program/close file

Selection number: 7
Ok
```

EXERCISES

1. Write a program that will allow you to enter names and addresses into a random-access file. Use a header record to record the total number of names and addresses.

2. Write a program that will print out, in mailing label format, only those names that have a specified ZIP code from the file created in the first question.

3. Write a separate program that will allow you to edit any data in the file from the first question. Use MERGE to merge these two programs into one.

4. Write an error-trapping subroutine for Tutorial 15-1 that will properly close the file and terminate the program if any error is encountered.

5. Explain why a PUT, GET, INPUT#, or WRITE# command might not cause the disk to move each time one of these commands is executed.

16

Using Boolean Operators

Statements:	POKE
Operators:	NOT, XOR, IMP, EQV
Functions:	PEEK, OCT$, HEX$

Consider the following problem. The agricultural department of a university requires a program that will maintain a mailing list for their 60,000 subscribers. They produce 500 different publications on various agricultural problems each year. The subscribers range from farmers who may be interested in only one publication to other universities that are interested in all 500 publications. Of course, subscribers may alter their subscriptions at any time.

If we use only one byte of memory per publication for each subscriber in our data base, that will be 500 bytes for each subscriber. With 60,000 names in the data base, that would be 30 million bytes (60,000×500). Notice that this is a conservative figure because we have not included the memory required for the names and addresses.

Let's examine an alternate method of storing this data. Each byte that we use only determines whether or not a subscriber requests a certain publication; it therefore records only "yes" or "no." Now consider that a byte is made up of 8 bits, with each bit being a 1 or a 0. If we can use these bits themselves to represent "yes" or "no," we will need only one eighth the storage of the previous method, or 3.75 million bytes.

This alternative method could be very useful if it saved you from buying an extra hard disk. On a smaller scale, using this procedure could eliminate the need for another floppy disk drive. The idea of using bits to store data is called *bit mapping;* it will be developed at the end of this chapter.

In order to program the type of problem just described, you need to know first how information is stored in the computer, and second, how to use Boolean operators as logical operators.

Before we begin working with logical operators, we need to be sure you have the necessary background for working with the binary number system. If you are familiar with the binary system, skip to the next section. If this is new to you, or if you are rusty in this area, read on.

How Computers Store Numbers

All computers work with the binary number system, which is also known as *base 2.* A byte (the storage unit that holds an individual ASCII character) consists of an eight-place binary number. An example of a binary number is 11010110_2. Each of these eight places is known as a bit. When we talk about binary and decimal numbers in the same context, we will distinguish between them with the subscript "2" for binary (base 2) and the subscript "10" for decimal (base 10).

If working with other number bases is new to you, consider the following comparisons between the decimal and binary number systems.

In the decimal system we use ten digits (0 through 9). In the binary system there are two digits (0 and 1).

In the decimal system, a number is represented by digits that stand for multiples of powers of 10. For example:

$$437 = 4\times10^2 + 3\times10^1 + 7\times10^0 = 400+30+7 = 437$$

Each digit in the number is multiplied by 10, with an increase of 1 in the exponent as we move to the left.

The same idea applies to the binary system. For example:

$$1110_2 = 1\times2^3 + 1\times2^2 + 1\times2^1 + 0\times2^0 = 8+4+2+0 = 14_{10}$$

Note that any number raised to the 0 power is equal to 1 (for example, $10^0 = 1$, $8^0 = 1$, $2^0 = 1$).

If a decimal number is multiplied by 10, the effect is to move the digits one place to the left in respect to the decimal point. For example:

$$437\times10 = 4370$$

$$4370\times10 = 43700$$

The same is true for binary numbers. When they are multiplied by 2, the digits are shifted one place to the left. For example:

$$1110_2\times2_{10} = 11100_2$$

$$11100_2\times2_{10} = 111000_2$$

Since this is not so obvious in binary, let's verify it by using the decimal system. As we have already seen, 1110_2 in binary equals 14_{10} in decimal. Therefore,

$$11100_2 = 1\times2^4 + 1\times2^3 + 1\times2^2 + 0\times2^1 + 0\times2^0 = 16+8+4+0+0 = 28_{10}$$

$$111000_2 = 1\times2^5 + 1\times2^4 + 1\times2^3 + 0\times2^2 + 0\times2^1 + 0\times2^0 = 32+16+8+0+0+0 = 56_{10}$$

And last of all, dividing a decimal number by 10 moves the digits one place to the right (for example, 680/10 = 68). It follows that dividing a binary number by 2 also moves (shifts) the digits one place to the right.

LARGEST NUMBER STORED BY A BYTE

If all the eight positions or bits of a byte are filled with 1's (for example, 11111111), the binary number then represents 255_{10} in decimal notation.

$$11111111_2 = 1\times2^7 + 1\times2^6 + 1\times2^5 + 1\times2^4 + 1\times2^3 + 1\times2^2 + 1\times2^1 + 1\times2^0 = 128+64+32+16+8+4+2+1 = 255_{10}$$

Notice that 255_{10} is the largest number that can be represented by a byte.

Working With Operators [NOT, XOR, IMP, EQV]

The NOT, XOR (Exclusive OR), IMP (Imply), EQV (Equivalence), AND, and OR operators can be used as either *Boolean* or *logical operators*.

The term Boolean is derived from the name of the English mathematician George Boole. He did much of the early development of these types of operators in the late nineteenth century.

BOOLEAN OPERATORS

Boolean operators are used to test whether the comparison of statements is true or false. For example, consider the following program:

```
10 A=3:B=2
20 FOR D= -2 TO 2
30   IF A>B AND D<>0 THEN PRINT "TRUE" ELSE PRINT "FALSE"
40 NEXT D

RUN
TRUE
TRUE
FALSE
TRUE
TRUE
Ok
```

In this example **A** equals 3 and **B** equals 2. Therefore, **A** is always greater than **B**. **D** has the successive values −2, −1, 0, 1, and 2. Therefore, **D** is not equal to 0 except on the third pass of the FOR/NEXT loop. The Boolean operator AND is used to judge when both comparisons are true at the same time.

The relational operators (=, <, >, <>, <=, and >=) are actually Boolean operators. This means that they return the values TRUE or FALSE. The equal sign (=) plays a dual role: it is both an assignment statement (as in LET A = 3) and a Boolean operator.

As an example, consider the following:

```
10 A = 5 : B = 5
20 P = (A = B)
30 PRINT P
```

```
RUN
-1
Ok
```

The first equal sign in line 20 is for assignment. It assigns to **P** the TRUE or FALSE value returned by the comparison (A = B). The parentheses are unnecessary; they are used to help visually separate the assignment from the comparison. When you run this program, since **A** and **B** are equal to 5, the comparison is TRUE and **P** is assigned the value −1, which MBASIC uses to designate TRUE. MBASIC uses 0 to designate FALSE.

Enter and run this example:

```
10 B = 0
20 FOR A = -2 TO 2
30      P = (A = B)
40      PRINT P
50 NEXT A

RUN
 0
 0
-1
 0
 0
Ok
```

If you change the **A=B** in line 30 to **A>B**, what will be the result?

In a somewhat more practical example, let's use this idea to control a WHILE/WEND loop. Enter and run the following:

```
10 A=5 : POSITIVE = (A>0)
20 WHILE POSITIVE
30      PRINT A;
40      A=A-1
50      POSITIVE = (A>0)
60 WEND

RUN
 5  4  3  2  1
Ok
```

Notice that as soon as **A** becomes 0, the variable **POSITIVE** becomes FALSE and the loop terminates.

If Boolean operators are used to compare the individual bits in a byte, then they are considered logical operators. We'll look at this procedure shortly.

TRUTH TABLES
[NOT, AND]

A common way of thinking of logical or Boolean operators is in the form of true/false statements. For example, if X represents a true expression, then **NOT X** will be a false expression, and conversely, if X represents a false expression, then **NOT X** represents the true expression. A *truth table* is a shorthand way of representing this relationship. The truth table for NOT is given in Table 16-1.

The truth tables for the remaining logical operators involve the relationship between two true/false expressions. Here's the way the AND operator works: if X is true and Y is true, then **X AND Y** is true.

The complete list of truth tables for the logical operators supported by MBASIC is shown in Table 16-2.

LOGICAL OPERATORS

Now we're getting to the interesting part of this chapter—manipulating the individual bits in a byte. Remember that our purpose here is to save memory by using what is known as "bit mapping."

Logical operators work with the individual bits in each byte. Thus, instead of comparing two bytes, we are comparing two bits. The truth tables we saw in the last section are still valid, but now instead of comparing true and false values, we are comparing 1's and 0's. In Table 16-2, simply replace the *T*s with 1's and the *F*s with 0's.

Remember that in MBASIC each integer is actually two bytes long, so there are 16 bits in each integer variable. For example, 0 is stored as $00000000\ 00000000_2$, 1_{10} is stored as $00000000\ 00000001_2$, and 18_{10} is stored as $00000000\ 00010010_2$.

Negative numbers are a bit trickier. If the far left bit of the binary number is a 1, the number is negative. To determine what the value of the negative number is, you must change all the remaining

Table 16-1.
Truth Table for NOT

X	NOT X
T	F
F	T

Table 16-2.
Truth Tables

NOT	X	NOT X
	T	F
	F	T

AND	X	Y	X AND Y
	T	T	T
	T	F	F
	F	T	F
	F	F	F

OR	X	Y	X OR Y
	T	T	T
	T	F	T
	F	T	T
	F	F	F

XOR	X	Y	X XOR Y
	T	T	F
	T	F	T
	F	T	T
	F	F	F

IMP	X	Y	X IMP Y
	T	T	T
	T	F	F
	F	T	T
	F	F	T

EQV	X	Y	X EQV Y
	T	T	T
	T	F	F
	F	T	F
	F	F	T

1's to 0's and 0's to 1's, then add 1 to the result (this is called the *one's complement* of the number). For example, the number 11111111 10100101 is the same as negative 00000000 01011010 plus 1, or negative 00000000 01011011, or −91 (decimal). The number −1 is represented as 11111111 11111111.

When we compare two integers with the Boolean operators, we compare them bit-by-bit. Thus, to determine the result of **12 AND 10**, write out the bit maps of each, and use the AND operation on each pair of bits:

12	= 00000000 00001100
10	= 00000000 00001010
12 AND 10	= 00000000 00001000

The result, 00000000 00001000, is equal to 8 (decimal). To perform this same operation with an MBASIC program, enter and run the following:

```
10 X = 12 : Y = 10
20 PRINT X AND Y

RUN
 8
Ok
```

Now add line 30 to the preceding program.

```
30 PRINT X OR Y

RUN
 8
 14
Ok
```

The result is found the same way as before—that is, by using OR on each pair of bits:

12	= 00000000 00001100
10	= 00000000 00001010
12 OR 10	= 00000000 00001110

The result is equal to 14 (decimal), as the program reported.

Setting Bits

The following program uses the logical operators to look at the bits in a random byte:

```
100 DEFINT A-Z
110 RANDOMIZE
120 ORANGE=1
130 BANANA=2
140 APPLE=4
150 KIWI=8
160 PEACH=16
170 BOWL=INT(RND*32)
180 PRINT "BOWL = ";BOWL;" has the following:"
190 IF (BOWL AND ORANGE)<>0 THEN PRINT "ORANGE"
200 IF (BOWL AND BANANA)<>0 THEN PRINT "BANANA"
210 IF (BOWL AND APPLE)<>0 THEN PRINT "APPLE"
220 IF (BOWL AND KIWI)<>0 THEN PRINT "KIWI"
230 IF (BOWL AND PEACH)<>0 THEN PRINT "PEACH"
```

In lines 120 through 160, each fruit is set equal to a bit.

ORANGE	$= 1_{10}$	(00000001_2)
BANANA	$= 2_{10}$	(00000010_2)
APPLE	$= 4_{10}$	(00000100_2)
KIWI	$= 8_{10}$	(00001000_2)
PEACH	$= 16_{10}$	(00010000_2)

In line 170, **BOWL** is set to **INT (RND*32)**. The number generated will be a byte with any combination of 1's and 0's for the last five bits. If **BOWL** is 17, it is stored in the computer as 00000000 00010001. Lines 180 through 220 determine if these bits are set (equal to 1) or not set (equal to 0) in **BOWL**.

Now run the program:

```
RUN
Random number seed (-32768 to 32767)? 98
BOWL =  3  has the following:
ORANGE
BANANA
Ok
RUN
Random number seed (-32768 to 32767)? 456
BOWL =  23  has the following:
ORANGE
BANANA
APPLE
PEACH
Ok
```

In the first run, the random number seed 98 produced the random number 3. Therefore, **BOWL** was $00000000\ 00000011_2$.

Since the two rightmost bits are set to 1, you can see from the table following the listing that the fruits chosen are **ORANGE** and **BANANA**. Lines 190 and 200 determine this and print the appropriate results. In the second run, the random number chosen, 23, has the binary value $00000000\ 00010111_2$. Again, inspecting the table following the listing shows that the fruits selected are **ORANGE, BANANA, APPLE,** and **PEACH**.

Shifting Bits Left or Right

The following program changes any decimal number in the range 0 through 255 into a binary number. Enter and run the program.

```
100 DEFINT A-Z
110 INPUT "Enter an integer from 0 to 255: ",BYTE
115 PRINT BYTE;"= ";
120 FOR I = 1 TO 8
130     PRINT USING "#";(BYTE AND 128)/128;
140     BYTE = (BYTE AND 127)*2
150 NEXT I

RUN
Enter an integer from 0 to 255: 16
 16 = 00010000
Ok
RUN
Enter an integer from 0 to 255: 137
 137 = 10001001
Ok
```

The key part of this program is the FOR/NEXT loop in lines 120 through 150. In line 130, we have the expression **(BYTE AND 128)/128**; 128_{10} is equal to the binary number 10000000_2. The AND operation is being used to test whether a bit is on. Since 128_{10} has 0's in all but the leftmost column, the result of **BYTE AND 128** will have only this bit turned on, or no bits on. Since this result is either 128 or 0, **(BYTE AND 128)/128** is either 1 or 0.

Line 140 performs the function of shifting the bits in **BYTE** to the left. As we discussed earlier, multiplying a decimal number by 10 moves the digits to the left (437×10=4370). In the binary system, multiplying the number by 2 has the same effect.

The purpose of line 140 is to move the bits left while preventing an overflow error. **BYTE AND 127** removes the leftmost bit from our number by setting it to 0. Therefore, we never get a number greater than 255 in the loop.

To demonstrate the program, let's use our second run, with 137 as our value. The number 137 (decimal) is equal to 10001001 (binary). The first time through the FOR/NEXT loop, line 130 prints a 1, since the left bit in **BYTE** is 1, and thus **(BYTE AND 128)/128** is 1. Line 140 then computes **(BYTE AND 127)** as follows:

BYTE	= 00000000 10001001
127	= 00000000 01111111
BYTE AND 127	= 00000000 00001001

The result, 00001001 (binary) or 9 (decimal), is multiplied by 2 to shift the bits one position to the left. The next time through the FOR/

NEXT loop, line 130 prints a 0 since the left bit in the new **BYTE** is 0, and thus **(BYTE AND 128)/128** is 0.

The loop continues, each time printing a 0 or 1, depending on whether the value of **(BYTE AND 128)** is 0 or 128.

Using Octal and Hexadecimal Numbers [OCT$, HEX$]

Computers work only in binary. Unfortunately, binary is a difficult number system for humans to work with since working only with 1's and 0's makes it very easy to make mistakes. Although MBASIC works with the decimal number system, decimal is not convenient for many applications.

Fortunately, MBASIC allows you to work with two other number bases: *octal*, which is also known as base 8, and *hexadecimal* (or *hex*), which is base 16. These number systems are a compromise between computers and humans; it is easy for the computer to convert to these systems from binary, and they are more resistant to human error than binary. Of the two, hexadecimal is much more commonly used than octal by microcomputer programmers.

MBASIC assumes that any number you enter into a program will be a decimal number, and you must specifically tell the program if you are using any other type. To designate a number as octal, preface the number with an ampersand (&) and the letter O (for example, 255_{10} is also written &O377). Preface hexadecimal numbers with an ampersand and the letter H (for example, 1114_{10} is also written &H45A). Table 16-3 shows some decimal numbers and their hexadecimal equivalents.

The OCT$ and HEX$ functions are used by MBASIC to convert the output of a program from the standard decimal notation to octal

Table 16-3.
Decimal-to-Hexadecimal Conversion

Decimal	0	1	2	8	9	10	11	12	13	14	15	16	17	18	19	30	31	32
Hexadecimal	0	1	2	8	9	A	B	C	D	E	F	10	11	12	13	1E	1F	20
Decimal	33	34	159	160	161	254	255	256	257	1023	1024	1025						
Hexadecimal	21	22	9F	A0	A1	FE	FF	100	101	3FF	400	401						

and hexadecimal notation. As an example, enter and run the following:

```
10 PRINT " Decimal        Octal          Hexadecimal"
20 PRINT "-------------------------------------------"
30 FOR X= 100 TO 500 STEP 50
40   PRINT X,OCT$(X),HEX$(X)
50 NEXT X
```

```
RUN
 Decimal        Octal          Hexadecimal
-------------------------------------------
 100            144            64
 150            226            96
 200            310            C8
 250            372            FA
 300            454            12C
 350            536            15E
 400            620            190
 450            702            1C2
 500            764            1F4
Ok
```

Converting Binary Numbers to Hexadecimal

An eight-bit binary number always converts to a two-place hexadecimal number. Consider 1111_2, which is the largest four-bit binary number:

$$1111_2 = 2^3 + 2^2 + 2^1 + 2^0 = 8 + 4 + 2 + 1 = 15_{10}.$$

The smallest four-place binary number is:

$$0000_2 = 0_{10}$$

Notice that a four-bit binary number gives us 16 possible values, 0 through 15 (decimal). In hexadecimal, these values are written as 0 through F. So in one byte, the four rightmost digits of a binary number represent the single rightmost digit of a hexadecimal number. Furthermore, the four leftmost digits of an eight-bit binary number represent the left digit of a two-digit hexadecimal number.

To convert a binary number to hex, treat the first four bits and the last four bits as separate units. For example, separate the number 10110011_2 into

First part: $1011 = 2^3 + 2^1 + 2^0 = 8 + 2 + 1 = B_{16}$

Second part: $0011 = 2^1 + 2^0 = 2 + 1 = 3_{16}$

Therefore, $10110011_2 = B3_{16}$. You may verify this by converting both numbers to decimal:

$$10110011_2 = 2^7 + 2^5 + 2^4 + 2^1 + 2^0 = 128 + 32 + 16 + 2 + 1 = 179_{10}$$
$$B3_{16} = B\times16^1 + 3\times16^0 = 176 + 3 = 179_{10}$$

The program we used earlier to convert from decimal to binary may also be used to convert from octal or hexadecimal to binary. Simply type in the numbers with the appropriate MBASIC prefix (&H for hexadecimal and &O for octal). Let's rewrite the program slightly.

```
100 DEFINT A-Z
110 INPUT "Enter an integer from 0 to 255: ",BYTE
115 PRINT BYTE;"= ";
120 FOR I = 1 TO 8
130     PRINT USING "#";(BYTE AND &H80)/128;
140     BYTE = (BYTE AND &H7F)*2
150 NEXT I
```

Running the program with hexadecimal and octal numbers produces the following:

```
RUN
Enter an integer from 0 to 255: &H10
 16 = 00010000
Ok
RUN
Enter an integer from 0 to 255: &O20
 16 = 00010000
Ok
```

Notice that in lines 130 and 140 the decimal numbers 128 and 127 have been converted to hexadecimal. This makes no difference to MBASIC. You will find that when you work with a program that produces binary output, using hexadecimal numbers in the program is often more convenient.

Talking to the Computer
[PEEK, POKE]

You have already talked to the computer through MBASIC since MBASIC is actually an interpreter. But with the PEEK function and the POKE statement, you can also speak directly to the computer; in effect, you can see what is on its mind.

Let's look at a byte stored in a given place in the computer's memory. To do this, we use the PEEK function. PEEK can tell us what is stored in any memory location in the computer.

From the direct mode, give the command

```
PRINT PEEK (100)
 32
Ok
```

In this case, PEEK has returned 32, but it could have been any number in the range 0 through 255, depending on the memory location you looked at. PEEK has told us that the value stored in memory location 100 is 32. It is always safe to use PEEK to look at any point in the computer's memory. Using PEEK in this way does not disturb what is there but only displays it for you on the screen.

PEEK's counterpart, the POKE statement, is an entirely different story in that POKE places a number in memory. POKE is used to place the number you specify at a particular memory location. This, of course, can have unpredictable results if you do not know the function of the byte at that address in memory.

Let's illustrate the use of PEEK and POKE.

```
PRINT PEEK(100)
 32
Ok
POKE 100,65
Ok
PRINT PEEK(100)
 65
Ok
```

Now we will use POKE to put the original value back into location 100.

```
POKE 100,32
Ok
```

You can verify that 32 is at address 100 by again using PEEK to print the value.

The ideas presented in this chapter may be new to you, and some are rather difficult. But you now have at your disposal the tools to handle the bit-mapping concept we used at the beginning of this chapter. Bit mapping can reduce the memory requirements of your programs dramatically.

It is important to note that the tools presented in this chapter are not limited only to bit mapping. Boolean and logical operators have many applications. The more tools you have available to you, the more easily you can handle your programming challenges.

TUTORIALS

Tutorial 16-1: Dump Memory

Our first application is a program that allows you to display on the screen any portion of the computer's memory that you wish. The program prompts you to enter the first and last addresses of the section of memory you wish to examine. The addresses may be entered in decimal, hexadecimal, or octal.

```
10 REM -                  -=*DUMP.C16*=-
20 REM -                  Hexadecimal memory dump
30 REM -                  2/15/83
40 REM -
100 DEFINT A-Z
110 INPUT "Enter start addresses: ",ADDR
120 INPUT "Enter last address: ",LAST
130 PRINT
140 WHILE ADDR <= LAST
150     PRINT RIGHT$("000"+HEX$(ADDR),4);":";
160     FOR I = ADDR TO (ADDR OR &HF)
170         PRINT " ";RIGHT$("0"+HEX$(PEEK(I)),2);
180     NEXT I
190     PRINT "   ";
200     FOR I = ADDR TO (ADDR OR &HF)
210         CH = PEEK(I)
220         IF CH < 32 OR CH > 126 THEN PRINT "."; ELSE PRINT CHR$(CH);
230     NEXT I
240     PRINT
250     ADDR = (ADDR OR &HF) + 1
260 WEND
270 END
```

Now let's consider the main points of interest in the program. The WHILE/WEND loop in lines 140 through 260 controls the output from the initial address to the final address. Line 150 prints out the address for the first byte of memory shown in each row. The FOR/NEXT loop in lines 160 through 180 uses the PEEK function to print the hex value held in memory for up to 16 successive locations.

The effect of using **(ADDR OR &HF)** as the upper bound of the FOR/NEXT loops is purely cosmetic. The purpose is to make each line end on an address that is 1 less than an even multiple of 16, thus causing all lines after the first to start on an even multiple of 16. This produces a dump that is easier to read.

To verify this action, remember that **&HF** is 1111_2. **(ADDR OR &HF)** forces the last four bits of **ADDR** to be all 1's, and the next number (the beginning of the new line) will have all 0's for the last four bits.

The second FOR/NEXT loop in lines 200 through 230 prints the character represented by the ASCII code for each of the memory locations as long as the code is in the range 32 to 126; otherwise, a period is printed. Line 250 sets **ADDR** to the address of the next 16-byte block of memory. The output looks like this:

```
RUN
Enter start addresses: &H250
Enter last address: &H350

0250: C5 C3 4F 4E D4 9A 4C 45 41 D2 92 49 4E D4 1C 53  ..ON..LEA..IN..S
0260: 4E C7 1D 44 42 CC 1E 56 C9 2B 56 D3 2C 56 C4 2D  N..DB..V.+V..V.-
0270: 4F D3 0C 48 52 A4 16 41 4C CC B6 4F 4D 4D 4F CE  O..HR..AL..OMMO.
0280: B8 48 41 49 CE B9 00 45 4C 45 54 C5 AA 41 54 C1  .HAI...ELET..AT.
0290: 84 49 CD 86 45 46 53 54 D2 AD 45 46 49 4E D4 AE  .I..EFST..EFIN..
02A0: 45 46 53 4E C7 AF 45 46 44 42 CC B0 45 C6 98 00  EFSN..EFDB..E...
02B0: 4C 53 C5 A2 4E C4 81 52 41 53 C5 A6 44 49 D4 A7  LS..N..RAS..DI..
02C0: 52 52 4F D2 A8 52 CC D6 52 D2 D7 58 D0 0B 4F C6  RRO..R..R..X..O.
02D0: 2F 51 D6 FA 00 4F D2 82 49 45 4C C4 C0 49 4C 45  /Q...O..IEL..ILE
02E0: D3 C6 CE D3 52 C5 0F 49 D8 1F 00 4F 54 CF 89 4F  ....R..I...OT..O
02F0: 20 54 CF 89 4F 53 55 C2 8D 45 D4 C1 00 45 58 A4   T..OSU..E...EX.
0300: 1A 00 4E 50 55 D4 85 C6 8B 4E 53 54 D2 DA 4E D4  ..NPU....NST..N.
0310: 05 4E D0 10 4D D0 FB 4E 4B 45 59 A4 DD 00 00 49  .N..M..NKEY....I
0320: 4C CC C8 00 50 52 49 4E D4 9E 4C 49 53 D4 9F 50  L...PRIN..LIS..P
0330: 4F D3 1B 45 D4 88 49 4E C5 B1 4F 41 C4 C4 53 45  O..E..IN..OA..SE
0340: D4 C9 49 53 D4 93 4F C7 0A 4F C3 30 45 CE 12 45  ..IS..O..O.OE..E
0350: 46 54 A4 01 4F C6 31 00 45 52 47 C5 C5 4F C4 FC  FT..O.1.ERG..O..
Ok
RUN
Enter start addresses: &H61D0
Enter last address: &H62D0
```

*(**Tutorial 16-1:** Continued)*

```
61D0: 2D 09 09 2D 3D 2A 44 55 4D 50 2E 43 31 36 2A 3D  -..-=*DUMP.C16*=
61E0: 2D 00 03 62 14 00 8F 20 2D 09 09 48 65 78 61 64  -..b... -..Hexad
61F0: 65 63 69 6D 61 6C 20 6D 65 6D 6F 72 79 20 64 75  ecimal memory du
6200: 6D 70 00 14 62 1E 00 8F 20 2D 09 09 32 2F 31 35  mp..b... -..2/15
6210: 2F 38 33 00 1C 62 28 00 8F 20 2D 00 26 62 64 00  /83..b(.. -.&bd.
6220: AE 20 41 F3 5A 00 4B 62 6E 00 85 20 22 45 6E 74  . A.Z.Kbn.. "Ent
6230: 65 72 20 73 74 61 72 74 20 61 64 64 72 65 73 73  er start address
6240: 65 73 3A 20 22 2C 41 44 44 52 00 6D 62 78 00 85  es: ",ADDR.mbx..
6250: 20 22 45 6E 74 65 72 20 6C 61 73 74 20 61 64 64   "Enter last add
6260: 72 65 73 73 3A 20 22 2C 4C 41 53 54 00 73 62 82  ress: ",LAST.sb.
6270: 00 91 00 87 62 8C 00 B4 F2 20 41 44 44 52 20 F1  ....b.... ADDR .
6280: F0 20 4C 41 53 54 00 AA 62 96 00 20 20 20 91 20  . LAST..b..    .
6290: FF 82 28 22 30 30 30 22 F2 FF 9A 28 41 44 44 52  ..("000"...(ADDR
62A0: 29 2C 15 29 3B 22 3A 22 3B 00 CB 62 A0 00 20 20  )..);":";..b..
62B0: 20 82 20 49 20 F0 20 41 44 44 52 20 CE 20 28 41   . I . ADDR . (A
62C0: 44 44 52 20 F8 20 0C 0F 00 29 00 F0 62 AA 00 20  DDR . ...)..b..
62D0: 20 20 20 20 20 91 20 22 20 22 3B FF 82 28 22 30       . " ";..("0
Ok
```

The two sections of memory displayed here contain code that may be of interest. The first section of memory shows part of MBASIC's symbol table. If you look at the right-hand section of the output carefully, you might recognize a portion of MBASIC's commands and functions. They are shown in the shorthand method of MBASIC, with the first and last letter of each missing. The second section of memory displayed shows a portion of the program DUMP. It is shown in the partially compiled form, which is the way MBASIC stores a program in memory.

There is a small problem with the program. If the address &H8000 lies within the range you want to dump, the program will not dump any memory. In addition, if &H7FFF is your last address entry, the program will get an overflow error in line 180. This problem arises because the hexadecimal addresses &H8000 to &HFFFF are interpreted as negative numbers by MBASIC.

Tutorial 16-2: Subscriber List

This program maintains a list of periodical subscribers. It keeps track of which among the 80 periodicals available each subscriber is to receive.

The program allows you to inspect existing subscribers' records and see what periodicals they take; to enter new subscribers into the list and assign them periodicals; and to add to, delete, or change the periodicals taken by an existing subscriber. The program uses ten bytes to keep track of a subscriber's choices among 80 different periodicals.

```
10 REM -                    -=*SUBSCRIB.C16*=-
20 REM -                    Subscribtion program
30 REM -                    2/15/83
40 REM -
1000 DEFINT A-Z
1010 BELL$ = CHR$(7)
1020 REM *=- Open subscribtion file
1030 OPEN "R",#1,"SUBSCRIB.DAT",89
1040 REM *=- Field the header record with status and number of subscribers.
1050 FIELD #1,1 AS STAT$,2 AS NOSBC$
1060 REM *=- Field data records with description, quantity, reorder level,
1070 REM *=- and price per unit.
1080 FIELD #1,20 AS NM$,25 AS ADR1$,25 AS ADR2$,9 AS ZIP$,10 AS BMAP$
1090 IF LOF(1) = 0 THEN 1150    'Check file size
1100    GET #1,1                'Get old header record
1110    IF STAT$ = "C" THEN 1130
1120       PRINT BELL$;">>--> WARNING: file not previously closed properly."
1130    NOSBC = CVI(NOSBC$)
1140 GOTO 1170
1150    NOSBC = 0         'New file, initialize header record
1160    LSET NOSBC$ = MKI$(0)
1170 LSET STAT$ = "O"    'Set file to (O)pen status
1180 PUT #1,1            'Write out header record
1190 PRINT : PRINT
1200 PRINT "There are";NOSBC;"subscribers on file."
1210 PRINT
1220 PRINT "Choose one of the following functions:"
1230 PRINT "   1 ... Query an existing subscriber."
1240 PRINT "   2 ... Enter a new subscriber."
1250 PRINT "   3 ... Edit an existing subscriber."
1260 PRINT "   4 ... End program/close file."
1270 PRINT
1280 INPUT "Selection number: ",SEL
1290 IF SEL >= 1 AND SEL <= 4 THEN 1320
1300    PRINT "Please enter a selection between 1 and 4."
1310    GOTO 1280
1320 IF NOSBC > 0 OR SEL = 2 OR SEL = 4 THEN 1350
1330    PRINT BELL$;">>--> No subscribers on file."
1340    GOTO 1280
1350 ON SEL GOSUB 1400,1480,1600,1690
1360 GOTO 1190
1370 '
1380 'Query an existing subscriber
1390 '
1400 TRNS$ = "query"
1410 GOSUB 1770          'Get subscriber number
1420 GOSUB 1870          'Print subscriber
```

(Tutorial 16-2: Continued)

```
1430 PRINT : INPUT "Press <RETURN> to continue... ",A$
1440 RETURN
1450 '
1460 'Enter a new subscriber
1470 '
1480 PRINT
1490 NOSBC = NOSBC + 1 : SBCNO = NOSBC  'This is the new subscriber number
1500 LSET NM$ = "NEW NAME"
1510 LSET ADR1$ = "" : LSET ADR2$ = "" : LSET ZIP$ = ""
1520 LSET BMAP$ = STRING$(10,0)         'Set to no subscriptions (all bits 0)
1530 GOSUB 1970         'Edit new subscriber
1540 PRINT : INPUT "More subscribers to enter (Y/N)? ",A$
1550 IF A$="Y" THEN 1480
1560 RETURN
1570 '
1580 'Edit an existing subscriber
1590 '
1600 TRNS$ = "edit"
1610 GOSUB 1770         'Get subscriber number
1620 GOSUB 1970         'Edit subscriber
1630 PRINT : INPUT "More subscribers to edit (Y/N)? ",A$
1640 IF A$="Y" THEN 1610
1650 RETURN
1660 '
1670 'End/Close files
1680 '
1690 LSET STAT$ = "C"           'Set file status to closed
1700 LSET NOSBC$ = MKI$(NOSBC)
1710 PUT #1,1
1720 CLOSE #1
1730 END
1740 '
1750 'Get subscriber number
1760 '
1770 PRINT : PRINT "Enter subscriber number to ";TRNS$; : INPUT ": ",SBCNO
1780 IF SBCNO >= 1 AND SBCNO <= NOSBC THEN 1820
1790    PRINT BELL$;"Invalid subscriber number."
1800    PRINT "Numbers must be in the range 1 to";NOSBC
1810    GOTO 1770
1820 GET #1,SBCNO + 1
1830 RETURN
1840 '
1850 'Print a subscriber
1860 '
1870 PRINT
1880 PRINT "Subscriber number";SBCNO;TAB(25);"Name: ";NM$
1890 PRINT "Address line 1: ";ADR1$
1900 PRINT "Address line 2: ";ADR2$
1910 PRINT "Zip code: ";ZIP$
```

(Tutorial 16-2: Continued)

```
1920 GOSUB 2230         'Print subscriptions
1930 RETURN
1940 '
1950 'Edit subscriber entry
1960 '
1970 PRINT "Subscriber number:";SBCNO;"  (Push return for no change)"
1980 PRINT "Name: ";NM$;TAB(45); : INPUT ": ",A$
1990 IF A$<>"" THEN LSET NM$ = A$
2000 PRINT "Address line 1: ";ADR1$;TAB(45); : INPUT ": ",A$
2010 IF A$<>"" THEN LSET ADR1$ = A$
2020 PRINT "Address line 2: ";ADR2$;TAB(45); : INPUT ": ",A$
2030 IF A$<>"" THEN LSET ADR2$ = A$
2040 PRINT "Zip code: ";ZIP$;TAB(45); : INPUT ": ",A$
2050 IF A$<>"" THEN LSET ZIP$ = A$
2060 GOSUB 2230         'Print subscribtions
2070 PRINT : PRINT "Enter publication numbers to add or delete:"
2080 GOSUB 2450         'Input publication number
2090 WHILE NOT(PNO = 0)
2100    BYTE = (BYTE XOR MASK)          'Toggle the bit on or off
2110    IF (BYTE AND MASK) = 0 THEN 2140        'Test if bit is 0
2120       PRINT "Added publication";PNO;"to the list."
2130    GOTO 2150
2140       PRINT "Removed publication";PNO;"from the list."
2150    LSET BMAP$ = LEFT$(BMAP$,BPOS-1) + CHR$(BYTE) + MID$(BMAP$,BPOS+1)
2160    GOSUB 2450      'Input next publication number
2170 WEND
2180 PUT #1,SBCNO + 1
2190 RETURN
2200 '
2210 'Print subscribtions for one subscriber
2220 '
2230 IF BMAP$ = STRING$(10,0) THEN PRINT:PRINT "No subscribtions.":RETURN
2240 PRINT "Subscriptions to the folowing publication numbers:"
2250 COUNT = 0
2260 FOR I = 1 TO 10
2270    BYTE = ASC(MID$(BMAP$,I,1))
2280    FOR J = 0 TO 7                  'Examen all 8 bits for each byte
2290       IF (BYTE AND 2^J) = 0 THEN 2330      'Test bit J for 0
2300          PRINT USING " ##";(I-1)*8 + J + 1;        'Print publication #
2310          COUNT = COUNT + 1
2320          IF COUNT MOD 20 = 0 THEN PRINT
2330    NEXT J
2340 NEXT I
2350 PRINT : PRINT "Printed";COUNT;"subscribtions."
2360 RETURN
2370 '
2380 'Input publication number.
2390 '   BYTE is set to the binary value of the byte in BMAP$ containing
2400 '      the corresponding bit of the publication.
2410 '   MASK is set to the binary value of the bit in question.
```

(Tutorial 16-2: Continued)

```
2420 '      MASK takes on values 1, 2, 4, 8, 16, 32, 64, or 128
2430 '   BPOS is the position of BYTE in BMAP$
2440 '
2450 INPUT "Publication number or 0 to end: ",PNO
2460 IF PNO >= 0 AND PNO <= 80 THEN 2490
2470    PRINT "Invalid number.  Enter a number between 0 and 80."
2480    GOTO 2450
2490 IF PNO = 0 THEN 2530
2500    BPOS = (PNO-1)\8 + 1              'BYTE position in BMAP$
2510    BYTE = ASC(MID$(BMAP$,BPOS,1))    'BYTE contains the PNO bit
2520    MASK = 2^((PNO - 1) MOD 8)        'This is the bit mask
2530 RETURN
```

This program is very similar to the inventory program in Tutorial 15-1, except for the lines that implement the bit mapping. First of all, let's consider line 1520. This line sets the variable **BMAP$** (which holds the bit map) equal to a string of ten bytes all set to 0's. This means there are 80 bits (each bit handles one periodical) set to 0, since each byte contains eight bits. The key to the program is in the lines 2500 through 2520.

Line 2500 determines the byte position of the byte that will contain the code for the periodical to which we are going to subscribe. A portion of the **BMAP$** string is shown in Figure 16-1. Remember that each byte is read from right to left.

Let's run through these three lines assuming a subscriber is interested in the twentieth periodical in the list. **BPOS** is the byte position in **BMAP$** of the byte with the periodical; **PNO** is the periodical number (1 to 80). In line 2500, we have

$$\text{BPOS} = (20-1)\backslash 8+1 = 19\backslash 8+1 = 2+1 = 3$$

Thus, the third byte contains the 20th bit.

In line 2510, the variable **BYTE** is the byte in position **BPOS**. In line 2520 the variable **MASK** has the bit corresponding to the appropriate periodical.

$$\begin{aligned}\text{MASK} &= 2\hat{\ }((20-1)\ \text{MOD}\ 8)\\ &= 2\hat{\ }((19)\ \text{MOD}\ 8)\\ &= 2\hat{\ }(3) = 2^3 = 8\\ &= 00001000_2\end{aligned}$$

We now know that periodical 20 is the fourth bit of the third byte. The variables **BPOS** and **MASK** can now be used either to set or to

	Byte 1	Byte 2	Byte 3	Byte 4	---
	00000000	00000000	00000000	00000000	---
Bits	87654321	16 · · · 9	24 · · · 17	32 · · · 25	---

Figure 16-1.
The BMAP$ string

clear the bit in **BMAP$** corresponding to publication number 20. **MASK** is used with the XOR logical operator in line 2100 to *toggle* the **PNO** bit. Toggle means to switch the value of the bit; that is, to set the bit to 0 if it is 1, or set it to 1 if it is 0. This has the effect of removing the publication if it was in the list or adding the publication if it was not in the list. Note also that since **MASK** has only one bit set, the XOR operator will not affect any of the other bits in **BYTE**. **MASK** is used again in lines 2110 through 2140 to determine the outcome of line 2100 and report the result to the user. **BYTE** is inserted back into **BMAP$** in line 2150.

The program looks like this when run:

```
RUN


There are 0 subscribers on file.

Choose one of the following functions:
   1 ... Query an existing subscriber.
   2 ... Enter a new subscriber.
   3 ... Edit an existing subscriber.
   4 ... End program/close file.

Selection number: 2

Subscriber number: 1   (Push return for no change)
Name: NEW NAME                                : Mike Smith
Address line 1:                               : 12 Ace Street
Address line 2:                               : Concord, CA
Zip code:                                     : 94554

No subscribtions.

Enter publication numbers to add or delete:
Publication number or 0 to end: 13
Added publication 13 to the list.
Publication number or 0 to end: 33
Added publication 33 to the list.
Publication number or 0 to end: 0

More subscribers to enter (Y/N)? N
```

(Tutorial 16-2: Continued)

```
There are 1 subscribers on file.

Choose one of the following functions:
   1 ... Query an existing subscriber.
   2 ... Enter a new subscriber.
   3 ... Edit an existing subscriber.
   4 ... End program/close file.

Selection number: 1

Enter subscriber number to query: 1

Subscriber number 1     Name: Mike Smith
Address line 1: 12 Ace Street
Address line 2: Concord  CA
Zip code: 94554
Subscriptions to the folowing publication numbers:
 13 33
Printed 2 subscribtions.

Press <RETURN> to continue...


There are 1 subscribers on file.

Choose one of the following functions:
   1 ... Query an existing subscriber.
   2 ... Enter a new subscriber.
   3 ... Edit an existing subscriber.
   4 ... End program/close file.

Selection number: 4
Ok
```

EXERCISES

1. Convert the following binary numbers to decimals:

   a. 10010001   *c.* 00001001
   b. 11001100   *d.* 11011111

2. Convert the binary numbers of the first problem to hexadecimal and to octal.

3. Complete the truth tables for the following:

   a.

X	Y	NOT(X AND Y)
1	1	
1	0	
0	1	
0	0	

   b.

X	Y	NOT(X) OR NOT(Y)
1	1	
1	0	
0	1	
0	0	

4. Write a program to convert a binary number in the range 0 to 255 into decimals.

5. The memory capacity of a microcomputer is usually given in multiples of 1K. This figure, 1K, is actually 2^{10} bytes. How many bytes of memory, in decimal, is this? Write a program to give the actual number of bytes of memory, in decimal, for a microcomputer. Do this in multiples of 4K, starting with 4K and ending with 64K.

6. Use the program in Tutorial 16-1 to print out memory from $4A0_{16}$ to 780_{16}. Can you guess what part of MBASIC this is?

7. How will the following line change the output when added to the DUMP.C15 program?

```
155 PRINT SPC((addr adn &hf)*3);
```

17

Defining Your Own Functions

Statements: DEF FN

MBASIC provides you with approximately 40 built-in functions, such as the math functions SQR and SIN and the string functions MID$, RIGHT$, and so on. But it also provides you with the DEF FN statement, which allows you to define your own functions. Recall that functions are like small programs inside of MBASIC that make your programming task easier. Like the built-in functions, the user-defined functions of MBASIC fall into the general areas of math and string functions.

Our first example is a user-defined function to generate random numbers. Recall from Chapter 8 that in order to generate random numbers between 1 and 10 we used the formula

```
X = INT(RND*9)+1
```

In general, to produce a random number between A and B, we would use this formula:

```
X = INT(RND*(B-A+1))+A
```

With the DEF FN statement, we can create our own function which uses this formula. We will call our function FNRAND. Before we explain how to construct this function, let's look at how our function can be used in a program. For example, the line

```
PRINT FNRAND(1,10)
```

will print a random number between 1 and 10. Similarly, the statement

```
LET X = FNRAND(10,20)
```

will assign a random number between 10 and 20 to **X**.

Figure 17-1 shows how to construct a function in MBASIC. There are three things to notice about this example of defining a function. First, the function name can be any legal variable name that starts with the letters FN. Second, the parameter list is a list of variables used in the definition of the function. In this case, the parameter **A** is the lower bound of the range and **B** is the upper bound of the range. The parameters are separated by commas. Third, the function definition is an expression that performs the operation of your function. All the variables that appear in the parameter list can be used in the function definition.

Now let's look at a program that uses our defined function.

```
100 DEF FNRAND(A,B) = INT(RND*(B-A+1))+A
110 PRINT "Random numbers between 1 and 10"
120 FOR I = 1 TO 5
130    PRINT FNRAND(1,10);
140 NEXT I
150 PRINT
160 PRINT "Random numbers between 10 and 20"
170 FOR I = 1 TO 5
180    PRINT FNRAND(10,20);
190 NEXT I
```

```
RUN
Random numbers between 1 and 10
 3  4  4  6  1
Random numbers between 10 and 20
 18  15  14  20  19
Ok
```

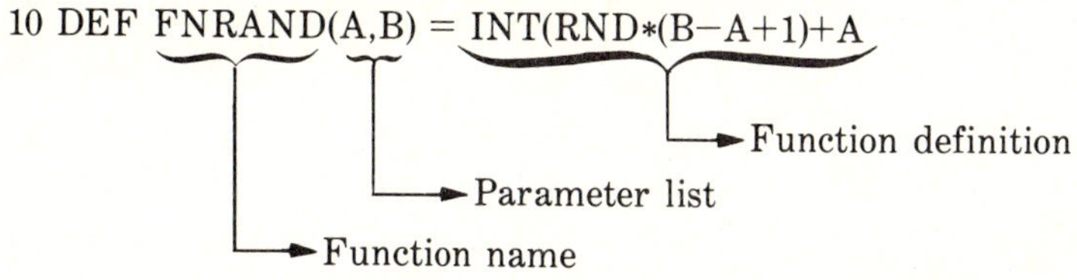

Figure 17-1.
Parts of a user-defined function

When we use a defined function in a program, we are *calling* the function. In line 130, MBASIC calls the function FNRAND with the arguments 1 and 10. When line 130 calls FNRAND, the arguments 1 and 10 are substituted for the parameters **A** and **B** of the function definition in line 100. The equation **INT(RND*(B−A+1))+A** is then evaluated as **INT(RND*(10−1+1))+1**, which is the proper formula for generating a random number between 1 and 10. Similarly, when line 180 calls FNRAND, the arguments 10 and 20 are substituted for the parameters **A** and **B**. The equation is then evaluated as **INT(RND*(20−10+1))+10**, which is the proper formula for generating a random number between 10 and 20.

Once you have written the defined function FNRAND, you can generate random numbers in any range simply by specifying the range in arguments to the function. You will never have to write out the equation for generating random numbers again.

In Chapter 9 we emphasized the built-in string functions. In this chapter we will focus on user-defined string functions. One common application of user-defined string functions is providing fancy screen output.

Defining String Functions

Frequently, programs have elaborate screen displays that provide the user with information or that request some input from the user. Such a display will have a title at the top of the screen. The title can vary in length depending on the display, as can the line on which you wish to place the title.

Let's develop a user-defined function that will allow us to center a title of any length on the screen, in any line we choose. We will call our function FNTITLE$. Once you have a definite function like FNTITLE$, you will no longer have to count spaces or guess at the correct TAB position to center any particular string on a line. For example, the line

```
PRINT FNTITLE$(2,"RETURN OF THE JEDI")
```

will center the title **RETURN OF THE JEDI** on line 2. What happens here is that the function FNTITLE$ returns a string that contains the proper control characters to center the title on line 2. We could use

```
100 A$ = FNTITLE$(2,"RETURN OF THE JEDI")
110 PRINT A$
```

to produce the same results.

In order to construct the FNTITLE$ function, we must first develop two other functions. First, we will write a function called FNCENTER$ to center a message on the current line. As with the FNTITLE$ function, we will use FNCENTER$ with a PRINT statement. For example, the statement

```
PRINT FNCENTER$("Hello there")
```

will center the message **Hello there** on the current line. Notice that FNCENTER$ does not allow you to choose which line to center the message on; this is what the function FNTITLE$ will do.

Look at the DEF FN statement for the function FNCENTER$:

```
110 DEF FNCENTER$(M$)=SPACE$((80-LEN(M$))\2)+M$
120 PRINT FNCENTER$("Hello there")
```

Tracing through the function, we notice first that MBASIC sets the parameter M$ in line 110 equal to the argument **Hello there** in line 120. The message takes up 11 spaces. Therefore, the expression **(80−LEN(M$))\2** is equal to **(80−11)\2 = 69\2 = 34**. The function will return **SPACE$(34)+"Hello there"**. (Recall from Chapter 9 that SPACE$(34) returns a string of 34 spaces.) Line 120 will then print a string 45 characters long. The first 34 characters are spaces, and the last 11 characters are **Hello there**. Now run the program:

```
RUN
                                  Hello there
Ok
```

In this example the centering is for an 80-column screen. If your terminal is different, substitute the appropriate value for 80.

Next let's define a function that will direct the cursor to any position on the screen. We will call this function FNCP$ (the CP is for "cursor position"). Again we will use FNCP$ with a PRINT statement. For example, the statement

```
PRINT FNCP$(2,10);
```

will position the cursor on line 2 in column 10. Note that the semicolon suppresses the carriage return so that the cursor actually stays at this position. To position **RETURN OF THE JEDI** at column 10 of line 2, we could say

```
PRINT FNCP$(2,10);"RETURN OF THE JEDI"
```

Now let's look at the DEF FN statement for our function.

```
10 DEF FNCP$(L,C) = CHR$(27)+"Y"+CHR$(31+L)+CHR$(31+C)
```

This example is for the Heath/Zenith Z-19 terminal. Consult your computer's or terminal's operations manual for the proper format and codes for positioning the cursor on your terminal. These instructions are usually given in a section on cursor control.

The parameters **L** and **C** designate the line and column at which you wish to position the cursor for the next character you want to print. The **CHR$(27)+"Y"** is the *cursor lead-in sequence* for the Z-19 terminal. **CHR$(27)** is the ASCII ESCAPE character. Many terminals use this character for cursor commands. The manual for your terminal will specify which character or characters to use for direct cursor positioning. Following the cursor lead-in sequence are the characters that specify the line and column. Since CHR$(32) represents line 1 and column 1 of our terminal, we must add 31 to **L** and **C** (for example, CHR$(35)+CHR$(38) corresponds to line 4 column 7). Some terminals do not require that you add a number like this, and your manual will specify the offset to use, if any.

Here is an example of how FNCP$ is used:

```
100 DEF FNCP$(L,C)=CHR$(27)+"Y"+CHR$(31+L)+CHR$(31+C)
110 PRINT FNCP$(3,20);"HELLO"

RUN



                    HELLO
Ok
```

The output from line 110 appears on the screen in line 3, column 20.

To get a better idea of how defined functions work, try running this next program:

```
100 DEF FNRAND(A,B) = INT(RND*(B-A+1))+A
110 DEF FNCP$(L,C)=CHR$(27)+"Y"+CHR$(31+L)+CHR$(31+C)
120 FOR L=1 TO 50
130    PRINT FNCP$(FNRAND(1,24), FNRAND(1,70));"HELLO"
140 NEXT L
```

When this program is run, it will print **HELLO** 50 times, each at a random cursor position. There are two things you should notice about this example. First, we have used **FNRAND(1,24)** and **FNRAND(1,70)** for the line and column number arguments of **FNCP$**. **FNRAND(1,24)** selects a random line number from 1 to 24, and **FNRAND(1,70)** selects a random column position between 1 and 70. Second, notice that line 120 uses the variable **L** for the FOR/NEXT loop. This variable has no effect on the variable **L** used in the parameter list of FNCP$. The variables in the parameter list of a DEF FN statement are *local* to the DEF FN statement. In other words, variables in the parameter list of a DEF FN statement are not related to other variables of the same name in the program.

Using Functions Within Functions

You can incorporate the previously defined functions into the definition of a new function. We will illustrate this with the DEF FN statement for the FNTITLE$ function described earlier. FNTITLE$ first positions the cursor at the beginning of the appropriate line with the FNCP$ function and then centers the line with FNCENTER$.

```
100 DEF FNCP$(L,C)=CHR$(27)+"Y"+CHR$(31+L)+CHR$(31+C)
110 DEF FNCENTER$(M$)=SPACE$((80-LEN(M$))/2)+M$
120 DEF FNTITLE$(L,M$)=FNCP$(L,1)+FNCENTER$(M$)
130 PRINT FNTITLE$(2,"Hello There")
```

If you run this program, the message **Hello There** will be centered on the screen in line 2.

```
RUN

                                  Hello There
Ok
```

We will use these functions in the tutorials section of this chapter and in subsequent chapters.

Defining Boolean Functions

The Boolean operators we discussed in the last chapter lend themselves very nicely to many applications using the DEF FN statement. Let's consider three examples that all accomplish the same thing: namely, determining whether a number is even.

EVEN NUMBERS: EXAMPLE ONE

The most common method of checking for an even number in a program is to use an IF/THEN statement either in the form

```
IF X/2 = INT(X/2) THEN ...
```

or in the form

```
IF X/2 = X\2 THEN ...
```

An example of this is

```
10 FOR X = 1 TO 5
20   IF X/2 = X\2 THEN PRINT X;
30 NEXT X

RUN
 2  4
Ok
```

When **X** equals 5, 5/2 equals 2.5 and 5\2 equals 2. Since 2.5 is not equal to 2, the program determines that the number 5 is not even. For any even number, the results would be equal. For example, 4/2 and 4\2 both equal 2.

EVEN NUMBERS: EXAMPLE TWO

The same method can be used with a DEF FN statement:

```
10 DEF FNEVEN(N) = (N/2=N\2)
20 FOR X=1 TO 5
30    IF FNEVEN(X) THEN PRINT X
40 NEXT X
```

The FNEVEN function returns the Boolean TRUE or FALSE value for the comparison **(N/2=N\2)**. This program produces the same result as the preceding example.

```
RUN
 2  4
Ok
```

EVEN NUMBERS: EXAMPLE THREE

Another method of defining FNEVEN is to use the logical AND operator. We have incorporated this function into the following program:

```
10 DEF FNEVEN(N) = ((N AND 1)=0)
20 FOR X = 1 TO 5
30    IF FNEVEN(X) THEN PRINT X;
40 NEXT X
```

```
RUN
 2  4
Ok
```

This function relies on the fact that if the first (rightmost) bit of the binary representation of a number is 1, then the number is odd, and if the first bit is 0, the number is even. The expression **(N AND 1)** will return 0 if the first bit is 0 and will return 1 if the first bit is 1. Therefore, the comparison **((N AND 1)=0)** will be true if the first bit is 0 and false if the first bit is 1.

This method is not as obvious as the previous one, so why use it? Speed is the answer. Whenever you are writing a program that you expect to be used by someone else, a prime consideration should be how quickly a program performs its operations. The two divisions required in the previous examples necessitate many more machine cycles than does the use of the logical operator AND. For a single statement, this time difference would not be noticed. But if the program were performing several operations before returning to the user, the added time factor might make AND worth using.

Functions Without Parameters

Next we will write a DEF FN statement that will stop output to the printer at any time you press either **X** or **x**. For programs that produce long printer listings, this function is a convenience, since it means that you do not have to wait for the entire printout to be completed or to break the program by pressing CTRL-C if you want to stop the output.

Recall from Chapter 9 that the INKEY$ function will return the last character typed at the terminal or a null string if no character has been typed. We can check whether the letters **X** or **x** have been typed at the keyboard by comparing INKEY$ to these characters. In particular, if at any point in the program INKEY$ is a character in the string "**Xx**", we know that the user has typed **X** or **x**. The program can then take the appropriate action.

At first, we might try to use the INSTR function to see if INKEY$ is the string "**Xx**" as follows:

```
IF INSTR("Xx", INKEY$) > 0 THEN ...
```

However, if you use this statement in a program, you will find that it will not work properly. The reason is that when no key has been pressed at the keyboard, INKEY$ is a null string. In this case, the INSTR function will return 1 because the string to search for, INKEY$, is a null string. The program will therefore stop printing whether or not an **X** or **x** has been typed.

To correct this problem, we might try the following:

```
IF INSTR("Xx", INKEY$) > 1 THEN ...
```

We have solved the problem of the printer stopping when no key has been pressed. Now, however, we find that the printer will stop if we press **x** but will not stop when we press **X**. This is because **X** is in the first position of the string "**Xx**". We need the INSTR function to return a value greater than 1 when **X** is pressed. To fix this problem we can simply insert a space before the **Xx**.

```
IF INSTR(" Xx", INKEY$) > 1 THEN ...
```

We have put **X** and **x** in the second and third positions of the string " **Xx**". Now, when **X** is pressed, INSTR will return 2. The only time **INSTR(" Xx", INKEY$)** will be greater than 1 is when the letter **X** or **x** has been pressed.

In the next program we have incorporated INSTR and INKEY$ into the defined function FNSTOPPRT%.

```
10 DEFSNG A-Z
20 WIDTH LPRINT 42
30 DEF FNSTOPPRT% = (INSTR(" Xx",INKEY$) > 1)
40 J%=1
50 WHILE J% <= 450 AND NOT FNSTOPPRT%
60    LPRINT USING "####.##";J%;
70    J% = J% + 1
80 WEND
90 WIDTH LPRINT 80
100 END
```

After leaving the WHILE/WEND loop, your program can take action to stop the printer or to offer whatever options you wish. Notice that FNSTOPPRT% has no parameters. FNSTOPPRT% simply checks to see if an appropriate key has been pressed. If you wanted to pass the " **Xx**" as a parameter, you would have to make the FNSTOPPRT% function check for characters other than **X** and **x**. The definition would look like this:

```
DEF FNSTOPPRT%(C$) = (INSTR(C$, INKEY$) > 1)
```

Passing " **Xx**" would check for **X** and **x** as in the previous example. However, you could set **C$** equal to " **Qq**" or any other letters you wish.

The percent sign (%) at the end of FNSTOPPRT% means the function returns an integer. For speed and memory considerations, it is a good idea to declare as integer all functions and variables that will take on Boolean TRUE or FALSE values (−1 or 0).

As you write programs and make use of the DEF FN command, save your definitions in a special program. You will soon have a *library* of these functions that you can use in future programs. All you will have to do is merge this library with your current application and delete those that do not apply. A great deal of programming time can be saved in this manner.

Defining Numeric Functions

If the type of programming you do does not deal with mathematical formulas, you may want to skip this section. Of course, it is not our intention to derive any of the mathematics used in this section, but rather to illustrate how to use the DEF FN statement with mathematical equations.

Let's consider a program using DEF FN to find the *Y* values for a quadratic function. The formula for the general quadratic equation is

$$Y = AX^2 + BX + C$$

Our program will input the coefficients *A*, *B*, and *C* through the keyboard with the INPUT statement. The program will then use the defined function FNQUAD to determine the values of *Y*.

The DEF FN statement is

```
DEF FNQUAD(X) = A*X^2 + B*X + C
```

Notice that **X** is the only variable in the parameter list. **A**, **B**, and C are used in the function definition but are not listed in the parameter list. If a variable in the function definition is not listed in the parameter list, its value will be whatever value you assign in the program.

To see how this works, enter and run the following:

```
100 DEF FNQUAD(X) = A*X^2 + B*X + C
110 INPUT "Enter the coefficients for X^2, X and the constant C: ",A,B,C
120 FOR Z = -5 TO 5
130     PRINT USING "X = ##  Y = ###.##";Z,FNQUAD(Z)
140 NEXT Z
150 END

RUN
Enter the coefficients for X^2, X and the constant C: 2,1,-3
X = -5  Y =  42.00
X = -4  Y =  25.00
X = -3  Y =  12.00
X = -2  Y =   3.00
X = -1  Y =  -2.00
X =  0  Y =  -3.00
X =  1  Y =   0.00
X =  2  Y =   7.00
X =  3  Y =  18.00
X =  4  Y =  33.00
X =  5  Y =  52.00
Ok
```

For our next example, let's define a function that will help us print the SIN, COS, and TAN for angles from 0 to 45 with increments of 1 degree. Because MBASIC only accepts angles in radian measure, we will have to convert from degrees to radians.

Our function, FNRAD, which converts degrees to radians, can be written as

```
DEF FNRAD(A) = (A/180)*3.14159
```

Incorporating this into the program we have

```
10 DEF FNRAD(A) = (A/180)*3.14159
20 FOR J = 1 TO 45
30   PRINT USING "SIN(##) = #.###### COS(##) = #.###### TAN(##) = #.######";
          J,SIN(FNRAD(J)),J,COS(FNRAD(J)),J,TAN(FNRAD(J))
40 NEXT J

RUN
SIN( 1) = 0.017452 COS( 1) = 0.999848 TAN( 1) = 0.017455
SIN( 2) = 0.034899 COS( 2) = 0.999391 TAN( 2) = 0.034921
SIN( 3) = 0.052336 COS( 3) = 0.998630 TAN( 3) = 0.052408
SIN( 4) = 0.069756 COS( 4) = 0.997564 TAN( 4) = 0.069927
SIN( 5) = 0.087156 COS( 5) = 0.996195 TAN( 5) = 0.087489
SIN( 6) = 0.104528 COS( 6) = 0.994522 TAN( 6) = 0.105104
SIN( 7) = 0.121869 COS( 7) = 0.992546 TAN( 7) = 0.122784
SIN( 8) = 0.139173 COS( 8) = 0.990268 TAN( 8) = 0.140541
SIN( 9) = 0.156434 COS( 9) = 0.987688 TAN( 9) = 0.158384
SIN(10) = 0.173648 COS(10) = 0.984808 TAN(10) = 0.176327
SIN(11) = 0.190809 COS(11) = 0.981627 TAN(11) = 0.194380
              .
              .
              .
              .
SIN(43) = 0.681998 COS(43) = 0.731354 TAN(43) = 0.932514
SIN(44) = 0.694658 COS(44) = 0.719340 TAN(44) = 0.965687
SIN(45) = 0.707106 COS(45) = 0.707107 TAN(45) = 0.999999
Ok
```

The advantages of using DEF FN increase as the number of calls to it increases. This not only requires less programming, but also allows a function that is changed in one line to affect the entire program.

TUTORIALS

Tutorial 17-1: Screen Mask

Normally when you work with a files program, you repeatedly enter large quantities of similar data. For example, you might enter many employees' names, social security numbers, phone numbers, street addresses, and so on. Entering this type of data is often easier for the computer operator if a screen mask is provided. An illustration of a screen mask is shown in Figure 17-2.

This screen mask lists the data items to be entered, along with a set of brackets for filling in each item. The brackets indicate the length of the fields.

Some of the properties of our screen masks are that the cursor moves only within the field; that you can move the cursor backward in the field with the BACKSPACE key; that characters can be deleted within the field; that the cursor can be moved easily to the next or to the previous field; and that pressing the ESCAPE key causes the cursor to return to the first field in the mask.

Screen masks can, of course, be more elaborate. In this example, however, we will program the functions just mentioned. Note that the cursor position codes used in this program are for the Z-19 terminal. Check the manual for your terminal to see if there are differences, and modify the program if there are.

```
ENTER EMPLOYEE NUMBER OR '00' FOR NEW EMPLOYEE

Employee number [  ]

Employee name    [                  ]  S.S. number    [           ]
Employee title   [                  ]  Phone number   [             ]
Street address   [                  ]
City/state       [                  ]  ZIP code       [     ]
```

Figure 17-2.
Example of a screen mask

```
10 REM -        -=*SCRMASK.C17*=-
20 REM -        Screen mask demonstration
30 REM -        2/15/83
40 REM -
1000 '
1010 'Screen mask data
1020 '
1030 DATA 7
1040 DATA 5,1,16,25,"Employee name"
1050 DATA 5,45,58,11,"S.S. Number"
1060 DATA 6,1,16,25,"Empolyee title"
1070 DATA 6,45,58,15,"Phone number"
1080 DATA 7,1,16,25,"Street address"
1090 DATA 8,1,16,25,"City/State"
1100 DATA 8,45,58,9,"Zip code"
1110 '
1120 'Program initialization
1130 '
1140 CLEAR ,,500
1150 DEFINT A-Z
1160 WIDTH 255
1170 DEF FNCP$(L,C) = ESC$+"Y"+CHR$(L+31)+CHR$(C+31)
1180 DEF FNCL$(L) = FNCP$(L,1) + ESC$ + "l"  'Clear line
1190 DEF FNMS$(M$) = FNCL$(1)+FNCP$(1,(80-LEN(M$))\2)+M$
1200 DEF FNBKT$(L,C,M$) = FNCP$(L,C)+"["+M$+"]"
1210 DEF FNINBOUND(X,L,H) = (X >= L AND X <= H)
1220 '
1230 ESC$ = CHR$(27)     'Escape character
1240 CLS$ = ESC$+"E"     'Clear screen code
1250 BELL$ = CHR$(7)
1260 BS$ = CHR$(8)       'Back space code
1270 REM - Input command string CMD$ consists of all special function
1280 REM - characters for input editing:
1290 REM - 1) Backspace, 2) Delete, 3) Back-up (^K), 4) <RETURN>, 5) Escape
1300 CMD$ = CHR$(8) + CHR$(127) + CHR$(11) + CHR$(13) + ESC$
1310 '
1320 'Initialize screen and variables
1330 '
1340 PRINT CLS$
1350 READ NOFLDS
1360 NOEMP = 0 : MAXEMP = 20
1370 DIM FL(NOFLDS),FC(NOFLDS),FLN(NOFLDS),F$(MAXEMP,NOFLDS)
1380 FOR I = 1 TO NOFLDS
1390    READ FL(I),C,FC(I),FLN(I),FD$
1400    A$ = SPACE$(FLN(I))
1410    PRINT FNCP$(FL(I),C);FD$;FNBKT$(FL(I),FC(I),A$)
1420 NEXT I
1430 '
1440 'Begin main program
```

(Tutorial 17-1: Continued)

```
1450 '
1460 PRINT FNMS$("ENTER EMPOLYEE NUMBER OR '00' FOR NEW ENTRY")
1470 PRINT FNCL$(3);"Employee number ";
1480 A$="  " : L = 3 : C = 17
1490 GOSUB 1900          'Field input A$
1500 IF RC = -1 THEN END          'Program ends here
1510 EMPNO = VAL(A$)
1520 IF FNINBOUND(EMPNO,0,NOEMP) THEN 1550
1530    PRINT FNMS$("INVALID ENTRY.  THERE ARE ONLY"+STR$(NOEMP)+" EMPLOYEES")
1540    GOTO 1490
1550 IF EMPNO > 0 THEN 1630      'Check for new employee
1560    PRINT FNMS$("** NEW EMPLOYEE **")
1570    EMPNO = NOEMP + 1
1580    FOR FLD = 1 TO NOFLDS   'Clear fields for new employee
1590       F$(EMPNO,FLD) = SPACE$(FLN(FLD))
1600    NEXT FLD
1610    RSET A$ = STR$(EMPNO)
1620    PRINT FNBKT$(L,C,A$)
1630 GOSUB 1700          'Edit fields
1640 IF RC = -1 THEN 1460        'Check for back-up
1650 IF EMPNO > NOEMP THEN NOEMP = EMPNO        'Check if Emp was new entry
1660 GOTO 1460
1670 '
1680 'Edit fields for employee EMPNO.
1690 '
1700 GOSUB 1830          'Print fields
1710 FLD = 1
1720 WHILE FNINBOUND(FLD,1,NOFLDS)
1730    A$ = F$(EMPNO,FLD)
1740    L = FL(FLD) : C = FC(FLD)
1750    GOSUB 1900       'Field input A$
1760    LSET F$(EMPNO,FLD)=A$
1770    FLD = FLD + RC  'Return code (RC) determines next field to edit
1780 WEND
1790 RETURN
1800 '
1810 'Print fields
1820 '
1830 FOR FLD = 1 TO NOFLDS
1840    PRINT FNBKT$(FL(FLD),FC(FLD),F$(EMPNO,FLD))
1850 NEXT FLD
1860 RETURN
1870 '
1880 'Input routine
1890 '
1900 PRINT FNBKT$(L,C,A$);FNCP$(L,C+1);
1910 I = 1       'Index position in A$
1920 CH$ = INPUT$(1)
1930 ON INSTR(CMD$,CH$) GOTO 1980,2000,2030,2050,2070
```

(Tutorial 17-1: Continued)

```
1940    IF CH$ < " " THEN PRINT BELL$; : GOTO 1920       'No control chars.
1950    MID$(A$,I,1) = CH$ : PRINT CH$:
1960    IF I < LEN(A$) THEN I = I + 1 ELSE PRINT BS$;   'Check bounds
1970 GOTO 1920
1980    IF I > 1 THEN I = I - 1:PRINT CH$;       'Backspace char. trap
1990 GOTO 1920
2000    MID$(A$,I)=MID$(A$,I+1)+" "              'Delete char. trap
2010    PRINT MID$(A$,I);FNCP$(L,C+I);
2020 GOTO 1920
2030    RC = -1         'Backup char. trap
2040 RETURN
2050    RC = 1          '<RETURN> char. trap
2060 RETURN
2070    RC = NOFLDS     'Escape char. trap
2080 RETURN
```

Now let's go through the program and consider the main points. Line 1030 specifies the number of fields that will be displayed. In the remaining data statements (lines 1040-1100), each of the seven fields is described. Each of these data statements contains the following: the line that the field will be on, the column position for the field title, the beginning column of the bracketed field, the length of the field, and the title of the field. Encoding the screen mask in data statements like this makes it very easy to change the format of the screen mask. For instance, you can change the line and column positions for any field simply by changing the appropriate data statement. You can also easily add more fields by changing line 1030 and adding another data statement with the information on the new field.

Lines 1170 through 1210 contain the user-defined function statements that will be used in this program. You may need to change the first two DEF FN statements for your terminal. You have seen FNCP$ earlier in the chapter. FNCL$ returns a string that, when printed, clears a line. This may also be referred to in your terminal's manual as *clear line* or *clear to end of line.* Line 1240 defines the character sequence to clear the screen. This sequence may also be different on your terminal.

The function FNMS$ centers a message on line 1. This function is similar to the FNTITLE$ function introduced earlier. The function FNBKT$ in line 1200 positions the brackets for the field and inserts the data when required. In line 1210, the function INBOUND returns TRUE or FALSE if the value of **X** is between the low and high values indicated by **L** and **H**.

Line 1300 defines the user commands that are implemented in this program. The definition of each is contained in the REMARK statements in line 1290. CMD$ defines which keys will be used for each of the five commands. The FOR/NEXT loop in lines 1380 through 1420 displays the screen mask with empty fields. Notice the use in line 1520 of the function INBOUND to check to see if the employee number is within the legitimate range (between 0 and the number of employees entered). The loop in lines 1550 through 1620 clears the brackets of old data in preparation for entering the information on a new employee.

In lines 1630 through 1870, notice the use of nested GOSUB commands. Line 1630 sends the program to 1700, which in turn sends it to 1830. The RETURN in 1860 sends the program back to 1710, and the RETURN at 1790 returns the program to 1640.

The last section of the program, lines 1900 through 2080, is the section that interprets the command string defined in line 1300. In line 1920, a character is input and held in the variable **CH$**. In line 1930, the program transfers to the appropriate subroutine, which interprets one of the five commands of line 1300. For example, when you press BACKSPACE (CTRL-H), line 1930 will send you to line 1980. At line 1980 the program checks to make sure that you do not backspace out of the brackets. Then the program goes back to line 1920 for more input.

When you run the program, it first places the mask on the screen with the cursor in the first field, **Employee number**. Press RETURN to add a new employee and a 1 will be placed in the field, letting you know that the new employee number is number 1. The cursor will then automatically move to the beginning of the next field. Enter the data requested and press RETURN when you are finished. When RETURN is pressed for the last field, the cursor returns to the employee number field. You may now enter **1** to review the data previously entered, or press RETURN to enter data for a new employee.

At any time during data entry, you may use the DELETE or BACKSPACE keys. If your keyboard is missing these keys, use whatever control codes you want to define them and place them in line 1300. When CTRL-K is pressed, the cursor moves directly to the beginning of the previous field. The only way to end the program is to press CTRL-K when the cursor is in the first field. Pressing ESCAPE at any time in the lower portion of the screen moves the cursor to the first field. This program does not use files, and therefore each time the program is run, new data must be entered.

EXERCISES

1. Write a DEF FN statement that will find the value of *t* in the following equations:

   a. $t = P(1 + r)^n$
   (**P**, **r**, and **n** are all parameters.)

   b. $t = AX^3 + BX^2 + C$
   (Enter **A**, **B**, and **C** as variables using INPUT, and **X** as a parameter.)

2. Write a defined function similar to the STR$ function that always returns a four-place number in the range 0 to 9999. For example, 34 would be converted to 0034.

3. Modify the STOPPRT% function so that, after stopping, the program will continue if C or **c** is pressed and will terminate if **Q** or **q** is pressed.

4. Write a defined function FNBIT(BYTE,BITNO) to test a bit, where **BYTE** is a byte value in the range 0 to 255 and **BITNO** is a bit number in the range 0 to 7. The function should return the value 1 or 0 of the bit in position **BITNO** in **BYTE**.

III.

Power Tools

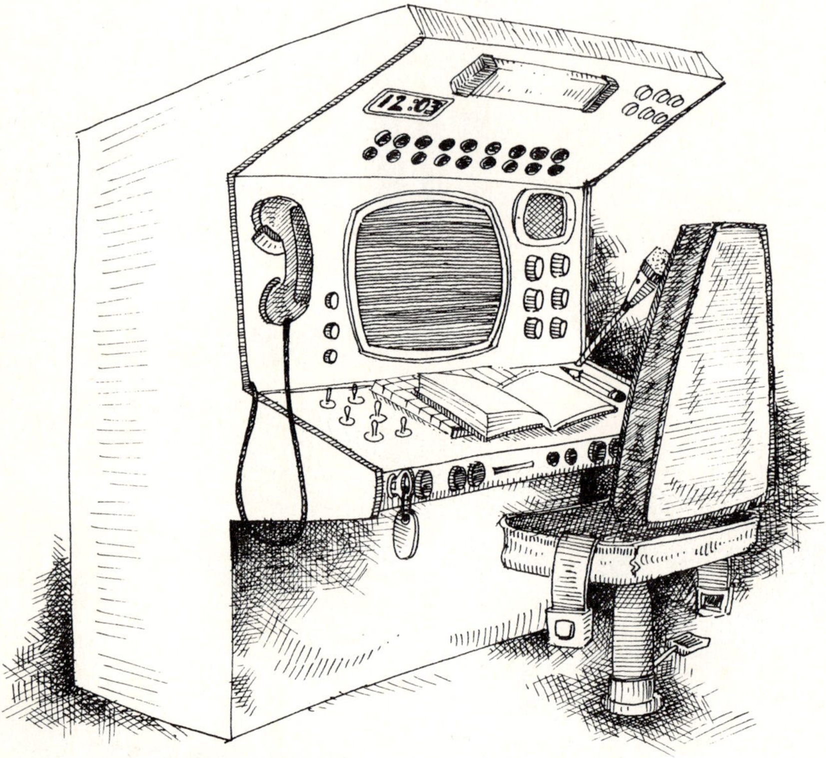
12.03

18

Programming With Software Tools

Once you become serious about programming, you will want to avail yourself of several commercial programs that can greatly increase your productivity. Among the most useful are a word processor, a cross-referencing program, a file-access routine, and a compacting program. First let's consider the word processor.

Editing BASIC Programs with A Word Processor

At this point, you have had many opportunities to use MBASIC's excellent line editor. Frequently, however, the global editing features of a word processor make it far superior to MBASIC's editor for many of the editing tasks you need to perform when you are working with longer programs. We use WordStar (from MicroPro International) for this purpose, but there are now many excellent word processors on the market, and most of them (though not all) are capable of being used as editors for MBASIC programs.

If you do not yet have a word processor and you are in the market for one, you should be sure that the word processor you purchase can be used to write MBASIC programs as well as letters and other documents. Features such as right justification and paragraph reforming are necessary for writing documents such as letters, but these same features can have disastrous effects on MBASIC programs. For example, most word processors will insert control characters into the text wherever you use features such as paragraph reforming. A word processor suitable for writing MBASIC programs, however, will allow you to enter text into the computer without inserting control characters in the text. For instance, WordStar's nondocument mode can be used to edit MBASIC programs because it does not automatically reform paragraphs or insert control characters in the text. Other highly desirable features in a word processor for editing MBASIC programs are global search, find-and-replace, block move, and block delete.

A word processor is particularly useful for longer programs because it allows you to make corrections in spelling or other typographical errors and thus can greatly speed up the initial entry of a program. A word processor can also be used to modify programs written for other versions of BASIC so that they will run on your computer.

The find-and-replace function of a word processor is an especially useful tool for performing this conversion. Suppose, for example, that you wish to convert a program written in Radio Shack's version of BASIC so that the program can run in MBASIC on your computer and terminal. Since Radio Shack uses the CLS command for clearing the screen and MBASIC does not have this command, you could use the find-and-replace feature of a word processor to change all the CLS commands to PRINT CLS$. Then at the beginning of the program, you would assign CLS$ to whatever control codes are required to clear the screen.

The find-and-replace feature is also helpful in the process of extracting modules from an existing program and moving them elsewhere. For example, you might have written a very nice quicksort routine for one program that you later want to use in another. You can remove this portion of the program, save it to a disk, and combine it with your new program. Then, with a find-and-replace command, you can quickly change the variables so that they satisfy the requirements of your new program.

Using a Cross-Reference Program

A cross-reference program produces an alphabetical list of the keywords, variables, numeric constants, and string constants used in a program, along with the line number for each. The primary purpose of using a cross-reference program is to obtain a list of all the variables used in your program. The line numbers listed in the cross-reference tell you where each variable is used.

Figure 18-1 is an example of the output from the cross-reference program PMAP from Software House. The program used for this example is DUMP.C16 from Chapter 16.

A cross-reference is a very powerful debugging tool to help you when problems arise in your program. For instance, it is easy to tell if you misspelled a variable name by looking at the cross-reference. A secondary use is in the conversion of a program from one BASIC to another. For instance, a cross-reference listing will help you in determining the compatibility of a program written in MBASIC with one written in another BASIC, such as Apple or Altair.

A Program to Index Files

One of the common problems of working with large files is that of sorting and searching. The sorting routines described in this book, bubble sort and quicksort, are very useful, but each has its limitations. Bubble sort is useful as long as the number of items in the list is relatively small—say, less than 50. Quicksort is very fast with several hundred items in a file; but if your file has several thousand items, the sorting time required becomes too great to make quicksort an efficient programming tool. The binary search described in Chapter 12 is much faster than a linear search, but requires the list to be sorted after any additions to the file.

When there are thousands of records in a file, another method of sorting and searching a file becomes necessary. One such method is the *b-tree file-access routines.* These routines can find any one of 10,000 records on a floppy disk in around two to three seconds.

Micro B+ from Faircom is a commercial program that you can incorporate into an MBASIC program. The Micro B+ program does not actually rearrange your files in any particular order. What it does is build *key files* that establish pointers to the various records in your file. For example, if you have a file that contains names, addresses,

DUMP.BAS	
WORD	**LINES CONTAINING WORD**
Variable Names	
A	100
ADDR	110 140 150 160 160 200 200 250 250
CH	210 220 220 220
I	160 170 180 200 210 230
LAST	120 140
Z	100
Commands, Statements, and Functions	
CHR$	220
DEFINT	100
ELSE	220
END	270
FOR	160 200
HEX$	150 170
IF	220
INPUT	110 120
NEXT	180 230
OR	160 200 220 250
PEEK	170 210
PRINT	130 150 170 190 220 220 240
REM	10 20 30 40
RIGHT$	150 170
THEN	220
TO	160 200
WEND	260
WHILE	140
Numeric Constants	
&HF	160 200 250
1	250
126	220
2	170
32	220
4	150
Quoted Strings	
“ ”	190
“ ”	170
“.”	220
“0”	170
“000”	150
“:”	150
“Enter last address:”	120
“Enter start addresses:”	110

Figure 18-1.
Program map of DUMP.C16

telephone numbers, and occupations, you can enter the data in any order you wish. As you enter the data, the Micro B+ program can build a key on names alphabetically, on ZIP codes, on telephone number area codes, or on any other basis that may be useful to you.

After you enter data into the file, you can search the file for any of the keys you have established with the Micro B+ program. For example, if you had established a key for telephone number area codes, you could quickly search the file for each record associated with a particular area code. If you have a key on names, you can produce an alphabetical list by reading the name keys sequentially. What is more, each time you add a new record to the file, all of the keys associated with that record are added to the key files, with the result that you never have to actually sort the file.

Using a Compacting Program

The last tool we will discuss is a compacting program. This program removes all unnecessary material from another program, such as remark statements and extra spaces, leaving only the code that is essential to run the program.

There are two purposes for compacting a program. One is to save memory space. Obviously, after compacting larger programs, there is more free space in the computer's memory for data. The second purpose is to increase the speed of the program. A compacted program with all the extraneous material removed runs faster than an uncompacted program. Note, however, that it is a good idea to use the original program as a guide for all editing and debugging even though you use the compacted program for the actual runs.

Here is an example of a compacting program:

```
0 REM -                 COMPACTED: 3/25/83
10 REM =-               -=*COMPACT*=-
20 REM =-               Ascii Format Program Compacter
30 REM =-               Ver. 1.0  03/13/82
40 REM =-
1010 DEFINT A-Z
1030 WIDTH 80 : WIDTH LPRINT 80
1040 ON ERROR GOTO 3360
1050 PRINT:LINE INPUT "Today's date? ",DATE$
1060 LINE INPUT "Source program name to compact? ";SRC$
1070 IF INSTR(SRC$,".") = 0 THEN 1110
1080 IF RIGHT$(SRC$,4) = ".SRC" THEN 1100
1090 PRINT "File name must end in '.SRC'" : GOTO 1060
1100 GOTO 1120
```

```
1110 SRC$ = SRC$ + ".SRC"
1120 OBJ$ = LEFT$(SRC$,INSTR(SRC$,".")) + "BAS"
1140 OPEN "I",1,SRC$
1150 OPEN "O",2,OBJ$
1155 LINE INPUT "Do you want a printer listing (Y/N)? ";PRT$
1160 QUOTE$ = CHR$(34)
1170 TAB$ = CHR$(9)
1180 WHITE$ = TAB$+" "
1190 SRCCNT! = 0
1200 OBJCNT! = 0
1210 PRINT : PRINT : PRINT "--COMPACTING PROGRAM--" : PRINT
1220 SRCLNE$ = "0 REM -" + STRING$(3,TAB$) + "COMPACTED: " + DATE$
1230 LASTLNO$ = "-1"
1240 WHILE NOT EOF(1)
1250 PRINT SRCLNE$
1260 IF PRT$ = "Y" THEN LPRINT SRCLNE$
1270 IF SRCLNE$ = "" THEN 1340
1280 IF SRCLNE$ < " " OR SRCLNE$ > CHR$(126) THEN ERROR 200
1290 GOSUB 3070
1300 IF OBJLNE$ = "" THEN 1330
1310 OBJCNT! = OBJCNT! + LEN(OBJLNE$)
1320 PRINT #2,OBJLNE$
1330 LASTLNE$ = LNO$
1340 LINE INPUT #1,SRCLNE$
1350 SRCCNT! = SRCCNT! + LEN(SRCLNE$)
1360 WEND
1370 PRINT : PRINT : PRINT "COMPACT COMPLETED"
1380 PRINT USING "######&";SRCCNT!;" Bytes read from " + SRC$
1390 PRINT USING "######&";OBJCNT!;" Bytes written to " + OBJ$
1400 PRINT USING "######&";SRCCNT! - OBJCNT!;" Bytes recovered"
1410 PRINT USING "###.##&";(SRCCNT! - OBJCNT!)/SRCCNT!*100;" Percent recovered."
1420 IF PRT$ = "Y" THEN LPRINT CHR$(11);
1430 CLOSE
1440 END
3070 I = 1 : LENGTH = LEN(SRCLNE$)
3080 WHILE INSTR("0123456789",MID$(SRCLNE$,I,1)) > 0 AND I <= LENGTH
3090 I = I + 1
3100 WEND
3110 IF I > LENGTH THEN ERROR 201
3120 LNO$ = LEFT$(SRCLNE$,I-1)
3130 IF VAL(LNO$) <= VAL(LASTLNO$) THEN ERROR 202
3140 WHILE INSTR(WHITE$,MID$(SRCLNE$,I,1)) AND I <= LENGTH
3150 I = I + 1
3160 WEND
3170 IF I > LENGTH THEN ERROR 203
3180 IF MID$(SRCLNE$,I,1) = "'" THEN 3310
3190 OBJLNE$ = MID$(SRCLNE$,I)
3200 I = INSTR(OBJLNE$,"'") : RPOS = 0
3210 WHILE I <> RPOS
3220 QPOS = INSTR(I,OBJLNE$,QUOTE$)
3230 IF QPOS > 0 THEN I = INSTR(QPOS,OBJLNE$,"'") ELSE RPOS = I
```

```
3240 WEND
3250 IF RPOS = 0 THEN I = LEN(OBJLNE$) ELSE I = I - 1
3260 WHILE INSTR(WHITE$,MID$(OBJLNE$,I)) > 0
3270 I = I - 1
3280 WEND
3290 OBJLNE$ = LNO$ + " " + LEFT$(OBJLNE$,I)
3300 GOTO 3320
3310 OBJLNE$ = ""
3320 RETURN
3360 CLOSE
3370 PRINT:PRINT "ERROR: ";
3380 IF NOT(ERR=52 AND ERL=1140) THEN 3410
3390 PRINT "PROGRAM ";SRC$;" DOES NOT EXIST."
3400 STOP
3410 IF ERR <> 200 THEN 3440
3420 PRINT "PROGRAM ";SRC$;" NOT SAVED IN ASCII FORMAT."
3430 STOP
3440 IF ERR <> 201 THEN 3470
3450 PRINT "DIRECT STATEMENT IN PROGRAM."
3460 STOP
3470 IF ERR <> 202 THEN 3500
3480 PRINT "LINE NUMBERS OUT OF SEQUENCE."
3490 STOP
3500 IF ERR <> 203 THEN  3530
3510 PRINT "BLANK LINE NUMBER."
3520 STOP
3530 PRINT:PRINT "BASIC ERROR";ERR;" IN LINE";ERL
```

EXAMPLE OF COMPACTING A PROGRAM

Now we will compact the Screen Mask program from Tutorial 17-1. In order to use the program COMPACT, you must save the program that you wish to compact in the ASCII mode. To do this, use the SAVE command with the A option.

```
SAVE "SCRMASK.SRC",A
```

The extension .SRC stands for "source." The compacted version of program SCRMASK.SRC will be named SCRMASK.BAS. When you run COMPACT, it will ask for the date, the name of the program to compact, and whether or not you want a listing on the printer. The date is placed in a REM statement in the compacted version of the program. When COMPACT asks for the program name, enter the name without the extension .SRC. As COMPACT runs, the listing of your source program is shown on the screen. If you answered yes to the question about printer listing, a listing of your source program will also be sent to the printer.

```
RUN

Today's date? 7/10/83
Source program name to compact? SCRMASK
Do you want a printer listing (Y/N)? N


--COMPACTING PROGRAM--

     (Listing of SCRMASK.SRC)

COMPACT COMPLETED
  3419 Bytes read from SCRMASK.SRC
  2651 Bytes written to SCRMASK.BAS
   768 Bytes recovered
 22.46 Percent recovered.
Ok
```

For the average well-documented program, the savings in bytes will be between 15% and 20%. If you look ahead in this book to Chapter 20, you will see the MLEDIT program, which was run through COMPACT. Since MLEDIT is a very extensively documented program, the savings turned out to be greater than 50%.

When writing a program to be compacted, keep in mind that remark statements that begin with REM are not removed from the program. Only remark statements that begin with a single quotation mark (') are removed from the program. For this reason, be sure that branching statements never transfer to a line that begins with a single quotation mark.

SPEED VERSUS FREE SPACE

The speed of execution of a program is related to the amount of available free memory, although it is difficult to give any hard and fast rule on this. For applications involving a large number of string manipulations, a program that has about 1500 bytes of free memory may run 10 to 15 times faster than a program that has only 200 bytes of free memory. However, increasing the amount of free space beyond this amount—say, from 1500 to 2500—may make little or no difference in the speed of operation. In general, though, you want as much free memory as possible when you are working with programs that deal with string manipulation or files.

19

Menu Driver

Statements: COMMON

A small business is likely to use its computer to operate several different MBASIC programs. For example, it may have separate programs that handle the mailing list, the inventory, the payroll, and the accounts receivable. And the business may use other programs as well.

A convenient way of accessing these various programs is to use a menu driver. The diagram in Figure 19-1 illustrates how program flow is controlled by a menu driver. The diagram illustrates a simple Main Menu that provides an option of three submenus. The Main Menu and the Mailing List submenu are shown in Figures 19-2 and 19-3 as they would actually appear on the screen.

From the Main Menu you can call up the Mailing List menu, the Payroll menu, or **END**. If you choose either Mailing List or Payroll, you are presented with the submenus for these programs. If you choose **END**, you are returned to CP/M.

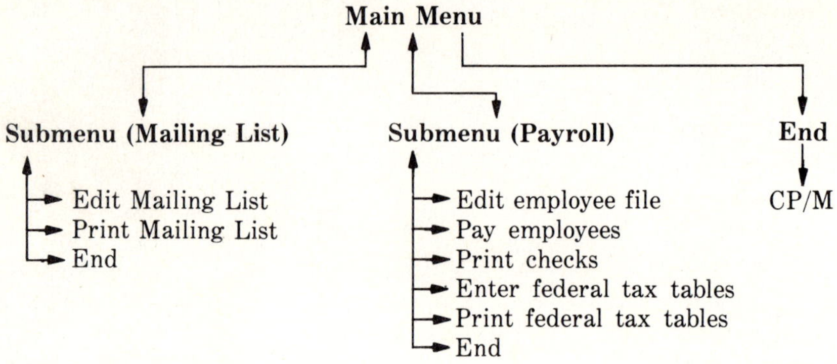

Figure 19-1.
The Main Menu

—Main Menu—

MLS = Mailing List—submenu
PRL = Payroll—submenu
END = End

Enter selection [ ]

Figure 19-2.
The Main Menu screen

—Mailing List—

EML = Edit Mailing List
PML = Print Mailing List
END = End

Enter selection [ ]

Figure 19-3.
The Mailing List menu screen

From either the Mailing List submenu or the Payroll submenu, you may transfer control to any specific program that you are interested in. For example, suppose that from the Mailing List submenu, you chose to print the Mailing List by entering **PML**. Once the Mailing List printing program was completed, the program would automatically return you to the Mailing List submenu. You could then choose to edit the Mailing List, and when you had finished editing, you would again return to the submenu. If you chose **END**, you would be returned to the Main Menu.

The point is that whatever path you choose, you follow that path to completion and then return along that same path to your starting point, the Main Menu. The only way to leave the menu driver is from the Main Menu by making the choice **END**.

The menu driver consists of three programs plus a file for each menu. The files for the menus are MAIN.MEN for the Main Menu, MAIL.MEN for the Mailing List menu, and PAYROLL.MEN for the Payroll menu.

Each menu file contains a title and a list of selections. The exact format of these files will be discussed later.

Initializing the System

The first program, INIT, is the system initialization program.

```
1 GOTO 10
2 SAVE "INIT":END
4 SAVE "INIT",A:END
6 SAVE "INIT":RUN
10 REM -                    -=*INIT*=-
20 REM -                    System initializaiion
30 REM -                    ver. 1.0  06/05/83
40 REM -
50 COMMON CLI$,CS$,HC$,SF$,SB$,CL$,BS$,BELL$,FF$,CC$,PLNK$,MLNK$,DATE$,DR$
1000 '
1010 '                      **********************************
1020 '                      *       SYSTEM INITIALIZAION     *
1030 '                      **********************************
1040 '
1050 CLEAR ,,500            'Set stack space for DEF FN statements
1060 WIDTH 255              'Turn off width checking
1070 WIDTH LPRINT 255
1080 DR$=""                 'CP/M data drive
1090 ESC$=CHR$(27)          'Escape char. for Heath codes
1100 CLI$=ESC$+"Y"          'Cursor lead in
1110 CS$=ESC$+"E"           'Clear screen
```

```
1120 HC$=ESC$+"H"          'Home cursor
1130 SF$=ESC$+"p"          'Set forground (inverse video)
1140 SB$=ESC$+"q"          'Set background (normal)
1150 CL$=ESC$+"K"          'Clear line
1160 BS$=CHR$(8)           'Back space
1170 BELL$=CHR$(7)         'CRT bell
1180 FF$=CHR$(12)          'Printer form feed character
1190 CC$=CHR$(8)+CHR$(12)+CHR$(127)+CHR$(22)    'Cursor control characters
1200 PLNK$="MENU    .BAS"        'Program linkage string
1210 MLNK$="MAIN    .MEN"        'Menu linkage string
1220 PRINT
1230 PRINT "System initialization:"
1240 PRINT
1250 LINE INPUT "Input today's date (up to 8 characters, any style): ",DATE$
1260 PRINT
1270 CHAIN LEFT$(PLNK$,12)       'Chain to menu proram
```

TRANSFERRING VARIABLES BETWEEN PROGRAMS [COMMON]

We will refer to the menu driver and all of the programs listed on the submenus as the "system." The system initialization program, INIT, assigns a set of *common variables.* These variables are called "common" because all of the programs in the system use them. All variables listed in a COMMON statement are transferred to the program chosen from the menu. If you have more common variables than will fit on one line, you may use more than one COMMON statement to list them all. The COMMON statement is always used in conjunction with the CHAIN command, which was introduced in Chapter 14.

The advantage of using the COMMON statement is that important variables do not have to be reassigned in every program. For instance, the variable **CS$** (used to clear the screen) assigned in line 1110 of INIT contains the control codes to clear the screen on our computer. If you want to run your programs on another terminal, you will have to change only the INIT program, not each program in the system. While in this example not all of the variables are used in every program, they are used frequently enough to make it worthwhile to define them once and carry them to each program with the COMMON statement.

The key part of the menu driver is contained in lines 1200 and 1210. These are the string variables **PLNK$** and **MLNK$** (standing for "program link" and "menu link"). They are the strings that contain the names of the programs or menus that are chained in. These strings grow or diminish in length as you move back and forth from the Main Menu to the submenus and programs you are using. Just how these strings change in length will be shown in the MENU program.

When INIT is run and all the common variables have been assigned, line 1270 chains to the MENU program, whose name is contained in the variable **PLNK$**.

Before we proceed with this menu driver, take a look at the top four lines of INIT. Have you ever been involved in debugging a long program and, after completing the job, saved it under the wrong name? If the name you used was the name of another program on your disk, then you would have lost that other program. By using the four lines shown at the beginning of INIT in every program you write (with the appropriate name, of course), you will eliminate this problem.

For instance, giving the **RUN 2** command saves the program, and you return to MBASIC. Giving the **RUN 4** command saves the program in the ASCII mode, and you return to MBASIC. The ASCII mode is necessary if you intend to edit your program with a word processor or run the COMPACT program presented in Chapter 18. The **RUN 6** command saves the program and runs it automatically so that you may check for possible bugs. Finally, the purpose of line 1 is to skip over the SAVE options when you wish to run the program in the normal manner.

Now let's consider the program MENU, which is the main program of this chapter.

```
1 GOTO 10
2 SAVE "MENU":END
4 SAVE "MENU",A:END
6 SAVE "MENU":RUN "INIT"
10 REM -                    -=*MENU*=-
20 REM -                    Menu Driver
30 REM -                    03/21/83
40 REM -
50 COMMON CLI$,CS$,HC$,SF$,SB$,CL$,BS$,BELL$,FF$,CC$,PLNK$,MLNK$,DATE$,DR$
1000 '
1010 '                      ************************************
1020 '                      *      PROGRAM INITIALIZATION      *
1030 '                      ************************************
1040 '
1050 'Initialize screen and variables
1060 '
1070 GOSUB 4660             'Define functions
```

```
1080 T=(0=0):F=NOT(T)     'Boolean true and false
1090 PRINT CS$;FNMS$("ONE MOMENT PLEASE....");PRINT
1100 RC$ = CHR$(13) + CHR$(11)                '2 Return characters
1110 DIM RC(2) : RC(1) = 0 : RC(2) = -1       '2 Return codes
1120 MAXSIZE = 15                        'Maximum number of menu selections
1130 DIM NMC$(MAXSIZE),PNM$(MAXSIZE),PDS$(MAXSIZE)
3000 '
3010 '                ****************************
3020 '                *       MAIN PROGRAM       *
3030 '                ****************************
3040 '
3050 MS$=""              'Clear error message
3060 WHILE MLNK$<>""
3070    GOSUB 4070       'Print menu
3080    SEL$="   "
3090    PRINT FNMS$(MS$+"ENTER SELECTION")
3100    PRINT FNCP$(7+NPGM,1);"Enter selection ";
3110    L=0:A$=SEL$:GOSUB 4400:SEL$=A$          'Input selection
3120    IF RC=-1 OR SEL$="END" THEN 3230
3130       GOSUB 4200                           'Search for selection
3140       IF NOT FOUND THEN MS$="INVALID SELECTION, RE-":GOTO 3090
3150       PRINT FNCP$(4+PGM,34);SF$;PDS$(PGM);SB$
3160       IF RIGHT$(PNM$(PGM),3)="MEN" THEN 3210
3170          PRINT FNMS$("LOADING PROGRAM")
3180          PLNK$=FNPNM$(PNM$(PGM))+PLNK$
3190          CHAIN LEFT$(PLNK$,12)
3200       GOTO 3220
3210          MLNK$=FNPNM$(PNM$(PGM))+MLNK$
3220    GOTO 3240
3230       MLNK$=MID$(MLNK$,13)
3240    MS$=""
3250 WEND
3260 PRINT CS$;FNMS$("EXITING")
3270 SYSTEM
4000 '
4010 '                ***************************
4020 '                *       SUBROUTINES       *
4030 '                ***************************
4040 '
4050 'Print menu selections
4060 '
4070 OPEN "I",1,LEFT$(MLNK$,12)
4080 INPUT #1,NPGM,TTL$                  'Read in no. of programs and title
4090 PRINT CS$;FNCE$(3,TTL$):PRINT
4100 FOR PGM=1 TO NPGM
4110    INPUT #1,MNC$(PGM),PNM$(PGM),PDS$(PGM)
4120    PRINT TAB(28);NMC$(PGM);" = ";PDS$(PGM)
4130 NEXT PGM
4140 PRINT TAB(28);"END = End"
4150 CLOSE 1
4160 RETURN
4170 '
```

```
4180 'Search for selection
4190 '
4200 PGM=1:FOUND=F
4210 WHILE PGM<=NPGM AND NOT FOUND
4220    FOUND = (MNC$(PGM) = SEL$)
4230    PGM=PGM+1
4240 WEND
4250 PGM=PGM-1
4260 RETURN
4270 '
4280 'Bracket input
4290 '   Input:
4300 '      A$  = String to input (Length must be set)
4310 '      L,C = Line and column for input.  (L=0 for current position)
4320 '      CC$ = Cursor command characters
4330 '      RC$ = Return characters
4340 '      RC() = Return codes (one for each char. in RC$)
4350 '
4360 '   Output:
4370 '      A$ = New input is same length.
4380 '      RC = Return code specified in RC() array.
4390 '
4400 SL=LEN(A$):I=1
4410 IF L>0 THEN PRINT FNCP$(L,C);               'Position cursor for input
4420 PRINT "[";A$;"]";STRING$(SL+1,BS$);         'Print string for input
4430 CH$=INPUT$(1)                               'Get one char. of input
4440 ON INSTR(CC$,CH$) GOTO 4530,4550,4570,4600 'Search for cursor control
4450 IF INSTR(RC$,CH$) > 0 THEN 4500             'Search for return code
4460    IF CH$<" " THEN PRINT BELL$;:GOTO 4430   'No control chars.
4470    MID$(A$,I,1)=CH$:PRINT CH$;              'Char to A$ and screen
4480    IF I<LEN(A$) THEN I=I+1 ELSE PRINT BS$;  'Check bounds
4490 GOTO 4430
4500    RC = RC(INSTR(RC$,CH$))                  'Get return code
4510    PRINT CHR$(13);                          'Show some response
4520 RETURN
4530    IF I>1 THEN I=I-1:PRINT BS$;             'Backspace char. trap
4540 GOTO 4430
4550    IF I<LEN(A$) THEN PRINT MID$(A$,I,1);:I=I+1     'Right character
4560 GOTO 4430
4570    MID$(A$,I)=MID$(A$,I+1)+" "              'Delete char. trap
4580    PRINT MID$(A$,I);STRING$(SL-I+1,BS$);
4590 GOTO 4430
4600    MID$(A$,I)=" "+MID$(A$,I)                'Insert character
4610    PRINT MID$(A$,I);STRING$(SL-I+1,BS$);
4620 GOTO 4430
4630 '
4640 'Define functions
4650 '
4660 DEFINT A-Z
4670 ON ERROR GOTO 4770
4680 DEF FNCP$(L,C)=CLI$+CHR$(L+31)+CHR$(C+31)
```

```
4690 DEF FNCE$(L,M$)=FNCP$(L,(80-LEN(M$))\2)+M$
4700 DEF FNMS$(M$)=HC$+CL$+SPACE$((80-LEN(M$))\2)+SF$+M$+SB$
4710 DEF FNPNM$(P$)=LEFT$(P$+SPACE$(12),12)
4720 DEF FNBKT$(L,C,M$) = FNCP$(L,C)+"["+M$+"]"
4730 RETURN
4740 '
4750 'Error trapping
4760 '
4770 IF NOT(ERR=53 AND (ERL=3190 OR ERL=4070)) THEN CHAIN "ERROR",,ALL
4780 MS$="SORRY, THAT ONE HASN'T BEEN WRITTEN YET RE-"
4790 IF RIGHT$(PNM$(PGM),3)="MEN" THEN MLNK$=MID$(MLNK$,13)
        ELSE PLNK$=MID$(PLNK$,13)
4800 CLOSE
4810 RESUME 3060
```

Line 50 occurs in all the programs that can be called in from any of the submenus. This line contains all the common variables that were assigned in the INIT program. Each program must have this COMMON statement so that the common variables will be transferred to the other programs chained by the menu driver.

INITIALIZING SCREEN AND VARIABLES

Lines 1050 through 1130 of the program take care of dimensioning and defining variables that are used only in this program. If the variables are to be used in more than one program, they must be assigned in the INIT program and carried to other programs with the COMMON statement.

MAIN PROGRAM

The function of the main program, which occurs in lines 3000 through 3270, is to control program flow by calling in the subroutines at the appropriate time. In lines 3180 and 3210 the names of the programs or menus are added to the strings **PLNK$** and **MLNK$**. These strings are then carried to the next program through the COMMON statement. The next program chained in takes care of adding an additional name to these strings if subsequent programs are chained. When you transfer back through the programs and menus you are working with, these names are removed from the **PLNK$** and **MLNK$** strings. Since the MENU program is always the last stop before returning to CP/M, no code is required in the program to remove names from **PLNK$** or **MLNK$**.

For example, to get to the program that edits the Mailing List, the **MLNK$** and **PLNK$** strings are first assigned the names **MAIN.MEN** and **MENU.BAS** in the program INIT. When you choose the Mailing List submenu from the Main Menu, **MAIL.MEN** is added to **MLNK$** and the new menu is printed on the screen. Then, when you choose to edit the Mailing List from the Mailing List submenu, **MAILEDIT.BAS** is added to **PLNK$** and the program is chained in. **MLNK$** is then "**MAIL.MEN**" + "**MAIN.MEN**" and **PLNK$** is "**MAILEDIT.BAS**" + "**MENU.BAS**".

When the Edit Mailing List program is finished, it removes its name from **PLNK$** and chains the next program in the new **PLNK$** entry, **MENU.BAS**. The menu program then prints the Mailing List menu because **MAIL.MEN** is first on the **MLNK$** list. When you select **END** on the Mailing List menu, the program removes **MAIL.MEN** from **MLNK$** and then prints the Main Menu because **MAIN.MEN** is next on the **MLNK$** list. Selecting **END** from the Main Menu returns you to CP/M since there are no more menu entries in **MLNK$**.

MLNK$** and **PLNK$ become even more useful when programs and submenus become more deeply nested. For example, it is possible for a submenu to be a menu of still more submenus. In this case **MLNK$** would allow you to go back and forth through the menus without losing the path.

Reading and Printing Menu Selections

Lines 4050 through 4180 open the file for the menu that is to be presented on the screen and print it out. The menu is read from a file and stored in the arrays **MNC$** (which holds the mnemonics), **PNM$** (which holds the program names), and **PDS$** (which holds the program descriptions).

The subroutine in lines 4180 through 4260 searches the **MNC$** array for the selection you made from the menu. The subroutine then transfers back to the main program, where it determines if another menu is to be loaded.

The input subroutine in lines 4280 through 4620 handles character input and is similar to the character-handling routine in the Screen Mask program in Chapter 17. In addition, there is an insert-character key (CTRL-V) and a key to move right (CTRL-L). These codes are added to the string **CC$**. The insert-character key allows you to insert a character when typing input, and the move-right key moves the cursor one character to the right. Lines 1100 and 1110 contain the return codes defined for this program. The RETURN key has the return code 0, and the backup key (CTRL-K) has the return code −1.

The initializing subroutine (lines 4640 through 4730) contains all of the DEF FN statements used in this program. Defined functions must be defined in each program where they are to be used; they cannot be chained from one program to another with the COMMON statement. Error trapping is also turned on in this subroutine.

The only defined function that is new in this program is **FNPNM$** in line 4710. It pads the names of the programs used in **PLNK$** and **MLNK$** so that they always contain 12 characters.

The error trap routine in lines 4770 through 4810 checks for a **File not found** (code 53) error in lines 3190 or 4070. If this is the error, line 4780 sets **MS$** to the message **SORRY, THAT ONE HASN'T BEEN WRITTEN YET**. If the error was some other error, the ERROR program is chained in. This program then prints an appropriate error message. More will be said about this program at the end of the chapter.

Although this example has only two choices in the Main Menu, it could contain any number of choices without lengthening the program. The only addition needed would be to the Menu files. Each Menu file ends with the extension .MEN. Figure 19-4 shows two examples of files containing menus used by this program.

The number at the beginning of each file (in this case 2) represents the number of choices from the menu. The following string is the menu title that will be displayed. The following lines contain the

---

Main Menu file MAIN.MEN

```
2,"—M A I N   M E N U—"
"MLS","MAIL.MEN","Mailing List—submenu"
"PRL","PAYROLL.MEN","Payroll—submenu"
```

Mailing List file MAIL.MEN

```
2,"—M A I L I N G   L I S T—"
"EML","MLEDIT.BAS","Edit Mailing List"
"PML","MLPRINT.BAS","Print Mailing List"
```

Figure 19-4.
Contents of the MAIN.MEN and MAIL.MEN files

mnemonic that you will type in, the name of the program or submenu, and the description of the program or submenu. The mnemonics for the title and the description of the mnemonics are printed on the screen when you enter that menu. Of course, each menu shows **END**, which is contained in the program, not in the menu files.

Here is an example of a simple MBASIC program that can be used to write this type of menu to the disk. You can also create these files with a text editor.

```
10 OPEN "O",1,"MAIL.MEN"
20 WRITE #1,2;" - M A I L    L I S T - "
30 WRITE #1,"EML";"MLEDIT.BAS";"Edit Mail List"
40 WRITE #1,"PML";"MLPRINT.BAS";"Print Mail List"
50 CLOSE
```

Using an Error-Handling Program

An error-handling program is very useful when you are dealing with a group of programs that act as a unit, like this menu program group. If an error occurs that the error trap within the program cannot handle, the error-handling program is chained in. It prints **ERROR** on the screen in large letters and tells the operator the name of the program in which the error occurred, along with the code number for the error and the number of the line in which the error occurred. The name of the program is easily obtained from the **PLNK$** string.

```
1 GOTO 10
2 SAVE "ERROR":END
4 SAVE "ERROR",A:END
6 SAVE "ERROR":RUN"INIT"
10 REM =-                    -=*ERROR*=-
20 REM =-                    Error Trapping Report
30 REM =-                    Ver 1.0  03/12/83
40 REM =-
50 COMMON CLI$,CS$,HC$,SF$,SB$,CL$,BS$,BELL$,FF$,CC$,PLNK$,MLNK$,DATE$,DR$
1000 '
1010 '                       ************************************
1020 '                       *       PROGRAM INITIALIZATION     *
1030 '                       ************************************
1040 '
1050 DEFINT A-Z
1060 DEF FNCP$(L,C)=CLI$+CHR$(L+31)+CHR$(C+31)
1070 DEF FNCE$(L,M$)=FNCP$(L,(80-LEN(M$))\2)+M$
1080 DEF FNMS$(M$)=HC$+CL$+SPACE$((80-LEN(M$))/2)+SF$+M$+SB$
1090 FORMAT$ = ">>>-->>  Error ### in line ##### of \          \  <<--<<<"
```

```
1100 COL = 10
1110 '
1120 PRINT CS$;FNCE$(3,"ERROR REPORT")
1130 PRINT FNMS$("PLEASE TAKE NOTE OF ERROR CODES")
3000 '
3010 '                  *****************************
3020 '                  *       MAIN PROGRAM        *
3030 '                  *****************************
3040
3050 PRINT FNCP$(4,1)
3060 PRINT TAB(COL);"************************************************************"
3070 PRINT TAB(COL);"*********************                  *********************"
3080 PRINT TAB(COL);"**********                                        **********"
3090 PRINT TAB(COL);"*****     ######   #####   #####     ###   #####       *****"
3100 PRINT TAB(COL);"****      ##       ##  ##  ##  ##   ## ##  ##  ##       ****"
3110 PRINT TAB(COL);"***       #####    #####   #####    #   #  #####         ***"
3120 PRINT TAB(COL);"****      ##       ## ##   ## ##    ## ##  ## ##        ****"
3130 PRINT TAB(COL);"*****     ######   ##  ##  ##  ##    ###   ##  ##      *****"
3140 PRINT TAB(COL);"**********                                        **********"
3150 PRINT TAB(COL);"*********************                  *********************"
3160 PRINT TAB(COL);"************************************************************"
3170 PRINT
3180 PRINT TAB(COL);USING FORMAT$;ERR;ERL;PLNK$
3190 PRINT
```

Notice the use of the ALL option in the CHAIN statement on line 4770 of Menu. This has the effect of transferring *all* of the variables used in the program to the ERROR program. The ALL option has the same effect as listing all the variables used in a program in a COMMON statement. You may wish to expand the ERROR program to examine both the error codes ERR and ERL and the **PLNK$** string in order to determine and report what corrective action the operator should take. Since all of the variables from the program containing the error have been transferred to the ERROR program, it is possible, at least in theory, to determine the cause of any error.

20

Payroll

Our purpose here is twofold. First, we want to show how the menu driver of Chapter 19 functions with a set of programs. Second, we want to illustrate how a set of several programs can function as a unit. The programs contained in the Payroll program set include the following:

PREDIT.BAS	Used to enter and edit employee data
POSTHRS.BAS	Keeps track of hours for pay period
PRTCHK.BAS	Prints the employees' checks
ENTFTT.BAS	Used to enter federal tax table
PRTFTT.BAS	Prints out the federal tax table.

For each of these programs, we will give an overview of the program operation and show the program's screen mask, where appropriate.

This set of programs can be used as a basis for a small business payroll. The programming skills you will have gained in using this book will allow you to modify these programs and also to add additional programs to the set according to your specific needs. By adding or deleting fields, you can modify the programs to suit your requirements. For example, the federal tax table could be extended to include other classes of employees. State tax tables could also be added. If your payroll includes employees on commission or employees with different pay periods, the program could be altered accordingly.

The Payroll Menu

In order to run the Payroll programs, you will need not only the five programs shown above, but also INIT.BAS, MENU.BAS, MAIN.MEN, and MAIL.MEN from the previous chapter. These should be on your disk. In addition, you will need the menu file PAYROLL.MEN, shown in Figure 20-1.

The program MENU.BAS presents you with a menu that includes a Mailing List option, which you should not try at this point, since that option is presented and discussed in the next chapter. From the Main Menu, enter the Payroll selection by typing **PRL**. You are then presented with the Payroll menu shown in Figure 20-2. Included in this menu are three programs left for you to write as an exercise. These programs are EOQ, EOY, and PER.

Entering Employee Data

Enter in the brackets **EPR**. This chains to the PREDIT program. The message **Program Loading** appears and remains on the screen for two or three seconds. Then you are prompted with

```
Enter Social Security number, to search for or add: [           ]
```

Payroll file PAYROLL.MEN

```
7,"  — P A Y R O L L   M E N U — "
"EPR","PREDIT.BAS","Edit/enter employee data"
"PEH","POSTHRS.BAS","Post employees' hours"
"PCH","PRTCHK.BAS","Print checks"
"EOQ","ENDQTR.BAS","End of quarter (form 941)"
"EOY","ENDOYR.BAS","End of year (form W2)"
"PER","PRTROST.BAS","PRINT employee roster"
"ETT","ENTFTT.BAS","Enter federal tax table"
"PTT","PRTFTT.BAS","Print federal tax table"
```

Figure 20-1.
Contents of the PAYROLL.MEN file

```
                —PAYROLL MENU—
          EPR = Edit/enter employee data
          PEH = Post employees' hours
          PCH = Print checks
          EOQ = End of quarter (form 941)
          EOY = End of year (form W2)
          PER = Print employee roster
          ETT = Enter federal tax table
          PTT = Print federal tax table
          END = End
          Enter selection [   ]
```

Figure 20-2.
The Payroll menu screen

After you enter the Social Security number (with or without dashes), the program will search the array. If the number you entered is not found, you will receive the message

```
Number not found in file; do you want to add it (Y/N)? [Y]
```

The **Y** is automatically placed in the brackets, assuming you want to add the number to your file. If not, you may enter the response **N** and press RETURN. If you respond with a "no," you return to the initial question to enter a new Social Security number. If you press RETURN with **Y** in the field, the full screen mask, as shown in Figure 20-3, will be displayed on the screen.

The Social Security number you just entered will be in the appropriate field. The cursor will be in field one, **Employee name**. After entering data in a field, press RETURN and the cursor will advance to the next field. When you have finished entering the desired data, press the ESCAPE key and the following command line will be displayed:

```
Field number to edit, delete, save, or exit without save (#/D/S/E)? [ ]
```

Make whatever choice you wish and press RETURN.

While the cursor is in any of the screen mask fields, you may move to the previous field by pressing CTRL-K. Pressing CTRL-K when the cursor is in the first field (Social Security number) will return you to the Payroll menu. Pressing CTRL-K from the Payroll menu will return you to the Main Menu.

```
1. Employee name          [                         ]
2. Social security #      [           ]
3. Pay rate               [      ]
4. Number of dependents   [ ]
5. Deductions:
   Savings [      ]  Dental    [      ]
   Medical [      ]  Union     [      ]
              6. Hours                7. Quarter to date   8. Year to date
Regular      [   ] Gross pay          [        ]           [        ]
Over time    [   ] Deductions         [        ]           [        ]
Double time  [   ] Fed tax            [        ]           [        ]
                   Social security    [        ]           [        ]
```

Figure 20-3.
The Payroll screen mask

Here is the PREDIT program:

```
1 GOTO 10
2 SAVE "PREDIT":END
4 SAVE "PREDIT",A:END
6 SAVE "PREDIT":RUN "INIT"
10 REM =-                    -=*PREDIT*=-
20 REM =-                    Payroll file editor
30 REM =-                    3/22/83
40 REM =-
50 COMMON CLI$,CS$,HC$,SF$,SB$,CL$,BS$,BELL$,FF$,CC$,PLNK$,MLNK$,DATE$,DR$
1000 '
1010 '                       *****************************
1020 '                       *       PROGRAM DATA        *
1030 '                       *****************************
1040 '
1050 'Data for field bracket locations:  line, column, length
1060 '
1070 DATA 19
1080 DATA 5,25,25, 6,25,11, 7,25,6,  8,25,2
1090 DATA 11,12,6, 12,12,6, 11,32,6, 12,32,6
1100 DATA 15,14,6, 16,14,6, 17,14,6
1110 DATA 15,42,8, 16,42,8, 17,42,8, 18,42,8
1120 DATA 15,62,8, 16,62,8, 17,62,8, 18,62,8
1130 '
1140 'Data for field descriptions: line, column, string
1150 '
1160 DATA 5,1,"1) Employee name",6,1,"2) Social Security #",7,1,"3) Pay rate"
1170 DATA 8,1,"4) Number of dependants",10,1,"5) Deductions"
1180 DATA 11,4,"Savings",12,4,"Medical",11,25,"Dental",12,25,"Union"
```

```
1190 DATA 14,13,"6) Hours",14,38,"7) Quarter to date",14,59,"8) Year to date"
1200 DATA 15,1,"Regular",16,1,"Overtime",17,1,"Double time"
1210 DATA 15,26,"Gross pay",16,26,"Deductions",17,26,"Fed. tax"
1220 DATA 18,26,"Social Security",0,0,""
1230 '
1240 '                    ***********************************
1250 '                    *      PROGRAM INITIALIZATION     *
1260 '                    ***********************************
1270 '
1280 DEFINT A-Z
1290 ON ERROR GOTO 4070
1300 DEF FNCP$(L,C) = CLI$+CHR$(L+31)+CHR$(C+31)
1310 DEF FNCE$(L,S$) = FNCP$(L,(80-LEN(S$))\2)+S$
1320 DEF FNCES$(L) = FNCP$(L,1)+MID$(CES$,(L-1)*(LEN(CL$)+1)+1)+FNCP$(L,1)
1330 DEF FNMG$(M$) = HC$+CL$+SPACE$((80-LEN(M$))\2)+SF$+M$+SB$
1340 DEF FNBKT$(L,C,M$) = FNCP$(L,C)+"["+M$+"]"
1350 DEF FNMKDI$(N#) = MKI$(INT(N#/256)-32768#) + CHR$(N#-INT(N#/256)*256)
1360 DEF FNCVDI#(N$) = (CVI(N$)+32768#)*256 + ASC(MID$(N$,3,1))
1370 DEF FNXSS$(S$) = LEFT$(S$,3) + "-" + MID$(S$,4,2) + "-" + MID$(S$,6,4)
1380 DEF FNCSS$(S$) = LEFT$(S$,3) + MID$(S$,5,2) + RIGHT$(S$,4)
1390 '
1400 TTL$ = CS$ + FNCE$(3,"PAYROLL FILE EDITOR")
1410 RC$=CHR$(13)+CHR$(11)+CHR$(27)            '3 Return characters
1420 DIM RC(3):RC(1)=1:RC(2)=-1:RC(3)=999      '3 Return codes
1430 READ NO.FLDS                    'Read # of fields
1440 NO.PAY.TYPE = 3                 'Number of pay types
1450 NO.DEDUC = 4                    'Number of deductions
1460 NO.TO.DATE = 4                  'Number of to-date fields
1470 DIM F$(NO.FLDS),FL(NO.FLDS),FC(NO.FLDS),DED$(NO.DEDUC)
1480 DIM HRS$(NO.PAY.TYPE),QTD$(NO.TO.DATE),YTD$(NO.TO.DATE)
1490 FOR I = 1 TO NO.FLDS
1500    READ FL(I),FC(I),FLN         'Line, column, and length of screen field
1510    F$(I) = SPACE$(FLN)          'Set screen field length
1520 NEXT I
1530 '
1540 MAXSIZE = 300                   'Maximun number of employees
1550 DIM SSKEY(300)                  'This is a list of partial SS numbers
1560 '
1570 OPEN "R",1,"PREMP.DAT",81
1580 FIELD 1,1 AS STATUS$,2 AS FSIZE$   'Header record
1590 FIELD 1,25 AS EMPNAME$,9 AS SS$,3 AS RATE$,2 AS NODEP$
1600 DUMMY = 25 + 9 + 3 + 2          'DUMMY will skip over first 4 fields
1610 FOR I = 1 TO NO.DEDUC           'Field deductions
1620    FIELD 1,DUMMY AS DUMMY$,3 AS DED$(I)
1630    DUMMY = DUMMY + 3
1640 NEXT I
1650 FOR I = 1 TO NO.PAY.TYPE        'Field current hours
1660    FIELD 1,DUMMY AS DUMMY$,2 AS HRS$(I)
1670    DUMMY = DUMMY + 2
1680 NEXT I
1690 FOR I = 1 TO NO.TO.DATE         'Field quarter and year to date totals
```

```
1700     FIELD 1,DUMMY AS DUMMY$,3 AS QTD$(I),3 AS YTD$(I)
1710     DUMMY = DUMMY + 6
1720 NEXT I
1730
1740 IF LOF(1)=0 THEN 1780                 'Check if file is new
1750     GET 1,1                           'Get header record of old file
1760     BADFILE = (STATUS$ <> "C")        'Check if file was closed
1770 GOTO 1790
1780     LSET FSIZE$ = MKI$(1)             'New file, initialize header record
1790 FSIZE = CVI(FSIZE$)                   'Get Last Record for program use
1800 LSET STATUS$ = "O"                    'Set file to (O)pen mode
1810 PUT 1,1                               'Write header record
1820 '
1830 FOR RN = 2 TO FSIZE                   'Read partial SS numbers
1840     GET 1,RN
1850     IF STATUS$ = CHR$(255) THEN 1880
1860        SSKEY(RN) = VAL(RIGHT$(SS$,4))
1870     GOTO 1890
1880        SSKEY(RN) = -1                 '-1 for deleted record
1890 NEXT RN
3000 '
3010 '                    ****************************
3020 '                    *       MAIN PROGRAM       *
3030 '                    ****************************
3040 '
3050 PRINT TTL$
3060 IF BADFILE THEN PRINT FNMS$("WARNING: FILE WAS NOT CLOSED PROPERLY")
3070 LSET F$(2) = ""
3080 PRINT FNCP$(5,1);"Enter social security number to search or add: ";
3090 L=0 : A$ = F$(2) : GOSUB 5300:F$(2) = A$
3100 IF RC<>-1 THEN 3150
3110     PRINT FNMS$("EXITING")
3120     GOSUB 4120               'Close files
3130     PLNK$=MID$(PLNK$,13)     'Strip of program name
3140     CHAIN LEFT$(PLNK$,12)    'Return to chaining program
3150 IF MID$(F$(2),4,1) = "-" THEN 3180
3160     SEARCH$ = LEFT$(F$(2),9):F$(2) = FNXSS$(F$(2))
3170 GOTO 3190
3180     SEARCH$ = FNCSS$(F$(2))
3190 GOSUB 4200                   'Search for SS number in SEARCH$
3200 IF FOUND THEN 3300
3210     PRINT FNCP$(6,1);
3220     IF RN > 0 THEN 3250
3230        PRINT "Number is not found and there is no more room in the file."
3240        GOTO 3080
3250     PRINT "Number not found in file, do you want to add it (Y/N)? ";
3260     L = 0 : A$ = "Y" : GOSUB 5300   'Input A$
3270     IF A$ <> "Y" OR RC = -1 THEN PRINT CL$ : GOTO 3080
3280     GOSUB 4610               'Initialize new employee
3290 GOTO 3310
3300     GOSUB 4690               'Read in existing employee
```

```
3310 GOSUB 4470                  'Print edit screen mask
3320 IF FOUND THEN 3350
3330    PRINT FNMS$("NEW EMPLOYEE")
3340    FLD=1 : GOSUB 4380       'Edit fields now if new employee
3350 PRINT FNCP$(24.1);
3360 PRINT "Field number to edit, delete, save,";
3365 PRINT " or exit without save (#/D/S/E)? ";
3370 L = 0:A$ = " ":GOSUB 5300  'Field input A$
3380 IF RC = -1 THEN A$ = "E"   'Backup treated same as Exit
3390 IF VAL(A$) = 0 THEN 3460
3400    FLD=VAL(A$)
3410    IF FLD = 8 THEN FLD = 16
3420    IF FLD = 7 THEN FLD = 12
3430    IF FLD = 6 THEN FLD = 9
3440    GOSUB 4380               'Edit fields
3450    GOTO 3350
3460 SEL = INSTR("DSE",A$)       'SEL = 1 for delete, 2 for save, 3 for exit
3470 IF SEL = 0 THEN PRINT FNMS$("INVALID SELECTION"):GOTO 3350
3480 ON SEL GOSUB 4880,4990      'Delete or Save (No action for Exit)
3490 GOTO 3050
4000 '
4010 '                  **************************
4020 '                  *      SUBROUTINES       *
4030 '                  **************************
4040 '
4050 'Error trapping
4060 '
4070 GOSUB 4120            'Close files
4080 CHAIN "ERROR",,ALL
4090 '
4100 'Close files
4110 '
4120 LSET STATUS$ = "C"          'Set file status as (C)losed
4130 LSET FSIZE$ = MKI$(FSIZE)   'Set total number of records
4140 PUT 1,1                     'Write out header record
4150 CLOSE 1
4160 RETURN
4170 '
4180 'Search for SS number SEARCH$
4190 '
4200 RN = 1:FOUND = F
4210 KEY = VAL(RIGHT$(SEARCH$,4))
4220 WHILE RN < FSIZE AND NOT FOUND
4230    RN = RN + 1
4240    IF SSKEY(RN) <> KEY THEN 4270   'Check on last 4 digits
4250       GET 1,RN
4260       FOUND = (SEARCH$ = SS$)      'Check entire SS number
4270 WEND
4280 IF FOUND THEN RETURN
4290 RN = 2                             'If not found, find an unused record
4300 WHILE RN < FSIZE AND SSKEY(RN) <> -1
```

```
4310    RN = RN + 1
4320 WEND
4330 IF SSKEY(RN) <> -1 THEN IF FSIZE < MAXSIZE THEN RN = FSIZE + 1 ELSE RN = 0
4340 RETURN
4350 '
4360 'Edit fields
4370 '
4380 WHILE FLD >= 1 AND FLD <= NO.FLDS
4390    L = FL(FLD):C = FC(FLD)             'Get line and column for input
4400    A$ = F$(FLD):GOSUB 5300:LSET F$(FLD) = A$          'Input F$(FLD)
4410    FLD = FLD + RC            'Return code determines next field to edit
4420 WEND
4430 RETURN
4440 '
4450 'Print edit screen mask
4460 '
4470 PRINT TTL$
4480 RESTORE 1160
4490 READ L,C,S$
4500 WHILE L<>0                          'L = 0 is dummy data
4510    PRINT FNCP$(L,C);S$
4520    READ L,C,S$
4530 WEND
4540 FOR FLD=1 TO NO.FLDS
4550    PRINT FNBKT$(FL(FLD),FC(FLD),F$(FLD))
4560 NEXT FLD
4570 RETURN
4580 '
4590 'Initialize new employee
4600 '
4610 LSET F$(1) = ""
4620 FOR FLD = 3 TO NO.FLDS
4630    LSET F$(FLD) = ""          'Clear all fields (except field 2)
4640 NEXT FLD
4650 RETURN
4660 '
4670 'Initialize for existing employee
4680 '
4690 GET 1,RN
4700 LSET F$(1) = EMPNAME$
4710 LSET F$(2) = FNXSS$(SS$)
4720 LSET F$(3) = MID$(STR$(FNCVDI#(RATE$)/1000),2)
4730 LSET F$(4) = NODEP$
4740 FOR I = 1 TO NO.DEDUC        'Convert deductions
4750    LSET F$(I+4) = MID$(STR$(FNCVDI#(DED$(I))/100),2)
4760 NEXT I
4770 FOR I = 1 TO NO.PAY.TYPE    'Convert pay type hours
4780    LSET F$(I+8) = MID$(STR$(CVI(HRS$(I))/100),2)
4790 NEXT I
4800 FOR I = 1 TO NO.TO.DATE     'Convert quarter- and year-to-date totals
4810    LSET F$(I+11) = MID$(STR$(FNCVDI#(QTD$(I))/100),2)
```

```
4820    LSET F$(I+15) = MID$(STR$(FNCVDI#(YTD$(I))/100),2)
4830 NEXT I
4840 RETURN
4850 '
4860 'Delete employee
4870 '
4880 IF SSKEY(RN) = -1 THEN RETURN          'Employee not in file yet
4890 SSKEY(RN)=-1                           'Remove from key array
4900 IF RN < FSIZE THEN 4930
4910    FSIZE = FSIZE - 1                   'Delete last record
4920 GOTO 4950
4930    LSET STATUS$ = CHR$(255)            'Set deleted flag
4940    PUT 1,RN
4950 RETURN
4960 '
4970 'Save employee
4980 '
4990 LSET EMPNAME$ = F$(1)
5000 LSET SS$ = FNCSS$(F$(2))
5010 LSET RATE$ = FNMKDI$(VAL(F$(3))*1000)
5020 LSET NODEP$ = F$(4)
5030 FOR I = 1 TO NO.DEDUC        'LSET deductions
5040    LSET DED$(I) = FNMKDI$(VAL(F$(I+4))*100)
5050 NEXT I
5060 FOR I = 1 TO NO.PAY.TYPE    'LSET pay type hours
5070    LSET HRS$(I) = MKI$(VAL(F$(I+8))*100)
5080 NEXT I
5090 FOR I = 1 TO NO.TO.DATE      'LSET quarter- and year-to-date totals
5100    LSET QTD$(I) = FNMKDI$(VAL(F$(I+11))*100)
5110    LSET YTD$(I) = FNMKDI$(VAL(F$(I+15))*100)
5120 NEXT I
5130 SSKEY(RN) = VAL(RIGHT$(SS$,4))
5140 IF RN > FSIZE THEN FSIZE = RN
5150 PUT 1,RN
5160 RETURN
5170 '
5180 'Bracket input
5190 '    Input:
5200 '       A$  = String to input (Length must be set)
5210 '       L,C = Line and column for input.  (L=0 for current position)
5220 '       CC$ = Cursor control characters
5230 '       RC$ = Return characters
5240 '       RC() = Return codes (one for each char. in RC$)
5250 '
5260 '    Output:
5270 '       A$ = New input is same length.
5280 '       RC = Return code specified in RC() array.
5290 '
5300 SL=LEN(A$):I=1
5310 IF L>0 THEN PRINT FNCP$(L,C);                 'Position cursor for input
5320 PRINT "[";A$;"]";STRING$(SL+1,BS$);           'Print string for input
```

```
5330 CH$=INPUT$(1)                              'Get one char. of input
5340 ON INSTR(CC$,CH$) GOTO 5430,5450,5470,5500 'Search for cursor control
5350 IF INSTR(RC$,CH$) > 0 THEN 5400            'Search for return code
5360     IF CH$<" " THEN PRINT BELL$;:GOTO 5330  'No control chars.
5370     MID$(A$,I,1)=CH$:PRINT CH$;            'Char to A$ and screen
5380     IF I<LEN(A$) THEN I=I+1 ELSE PRINT BS$; 'Check bounds
5390 GOTO 5330
5400     RC = RC(INSTR(RC$,CH$))                'Get return code
5410     PRINT CHR$(13);                        'Show some response
5420 RETURN
5430     IF I>1 THEN I=I-1:PRINT BS$;           'Backspace char. trap
5440 GOTO 5330
5450     IF I<LEN(A$) THEN PRINT MID$(A$,I,1);:I=I+1     'Right character
5460 GOTO 5330
5470     MID$(A$,I)=MID$(A$,I+1)+" "            'Delete char. trap
5480     PRINT MID$(A$,I);STRING$(SL-I+1,BS$);
5490 GOTO 5330
5500     MID$(A$,I)=" "+MID$(A$,I)              Insert character
5510     PRINT MID$(A$,I);STRING$(SL-I+1,BS$);
5520 GOTO 5330
```

PROGRAM DATA

The data section of the program (lines 1000 through 1220) contains all the information necessary for the correct placement of the brackets on the screen. The numbers represent the screen line number, column number, and field length. The field titles are also contained in the DATA statements.

PROGRAM INITIALIZATION

Lines 1230 through 1380 take care of setting the error trap and defining the user functions for this program, since these cannot be transferred from one program to another by the use of the COMMON statement.

Four new user-defined functions are included in this section. The DEF FN statements in lines 1350 and 1360 increase the size of the number that may be stored in the field for an employee's annual earnings. **FNMKDI$** uses three bytes to store the numbers instead of the eight that would be required if we went to double-precision numbers.

The functions **FNMKDI$** and **FNCVDI#** work in the same way as **MKI$** and **CVI** (the DI stands for "double integer"). The range for these functions is the integers from 0 to 16,777,215. This means that the program can handle an employee's annual income of up to $167,772.15. Note that our "double integers" are only positive integers. It is possible to modify the functions to handle negative numbers (for some other application) simply by adding or subtracting an offset before making or converting the number. The only real limitation is that the "double integer" functions can store 2^{24} different numbers.

The next DEF FN statement, line 1370, places the dashes in the appropriate positions of the Social Security number when the program prints the number in the designated field. Line 1380 strips the dashes from the numbers when they are stored in the file, which saves two bytes for each record. The next portion of the initialization section, lines 1400 through 1520, takes care of defining the character codes and return codes used in the program. It also handles all of the dimensioning for the arrays.

The FIELD statements for the files are also contained in this section. The maximum number of records for the file is set, and the status for the header record is determined to ensure that the files have been properly closed and to determine the number of records in the file. This header record is similar to the one described in Tutorial 15-1.

Now let's consider a variation on the traditional use of the FIELD statement. Study, for a moment, lines 1570 through 1720. Line 1580 sets the fields for the header record for the PREMP.DAT file. Line 1590 sets the first four fields for the remainder of the records. Lines 1610 through 1640 set the field length for the four possible deductions. The variable **DUMMY** is used to skip over fields that have been previously set in 1620. Lines 1690 through 1720 set the remaining fields for regular hours and overtime (time-and-a-half and double time) and for the cumulative totals (quarter-to-date and year-to-date). The variable **DUMMY** is again used to pass over the previously set fields.

The use of the FOR/NEXT loop to set field lengths means that only one variable has to be changed to affect several FIELD lengths. If you want to set the fields in a large array in a single record, using a FOR/NEXT loop may be the only way to set all the field lengths with one FIELD statement.

A specialized characteristic of this program is the method used to search the file for the name or Social Security number of an employee. Consider lines 1830 through 1890. During the initialization of the program, this section reads through the entire file sequentially and stores (in an integer array) the last four digits of each employee's

Social Security number. Then, when a request is made for an employee's data, the computer can quickly search the array for a match on the last four digits of the Social Security number.

The variable **SSKEY(RN)** has the same subscript as the employee's record number. When a partial match is made, the disk is accessed and a check of the full Social Security number is made. In the unlikely event that there are two Social Security numbers with the same last four digits, the search would continue through the array, checking against the full Social Security number until an exact match is found. If no match is found, the program asks if you wish to add that employee.

Lines 1830 through 1890 also have another function: they determine whether a record is unused and then store this information in the array by setting **SSKEY(RN)** equal to −1. When a new employee is entered, his or her data goes to the first empty record, thus minimizing wasted space on the disk.

This procedure makes for fast searching, but it has a limitation. The limitation is that you have to have sufficient memory in the computer to contain both the program and the array. In line 1540 the maximum size for the array is set to 300. Since two bytes are used for each employee, the array utilizes 600 bytes. Although 600 bytes is not very much memory for 300 employees, the need for this much memory is a limiting factor.

MAIN PROGRAM

The primary purpose of the main program (lines 3000 through 3490) is to handle all transfers to the subroutines. Additional functions, like that in line 3110, print messages such as **EXITING** when you leave the program. It is important that the operator should always be kept aware of what is happening. Line 3130 strips the name of the program from the **PLNK$** string when control returns to the Payroll submenu.

SUBROUTINES

Lines 4050 through 4080 contain the chain to the error trap program and take care of closing the data file when an error occurs. When a Social Security number is entered, the subroutine in lines 4180 through 4340 makes a sequential search of the array created in the program initialization to determine whether the number already exists in the files or whether it is a new number. The WHILE/

WEND loop in lines 4380 through 4430 allows you to edit the fields allotted to new and existing employees. Lines 4450 through 4570 print the brackets for the fields and the field titles for the screen mask.

Setting up the fields for a new employee requires that they all be blanked. Lines 4590 through 4650 handle this. For an existing employee, all of the data has to be read and converted into the appropriate fields. This is handled by lines 4670 through 4840. When an employee is deleted from the file, the record number has to be marked as empty. The subroutine in lines 4860 through 4950 sets the status of the record to 255, indicating an unused record. A value of −1 is also placed in the Social Security array for this record. After all of an employee's information has been entered and you have chosen to save the data, lines 4970 through 5160 write the information to the file.

The input subroutine (lines 5180 through 5520) handles all of the bracket input. All of the character codes and return codes implemented in this program are handled by the primitive subroutines of this section. This routine is identical to the one in the MENU program in Chapter 19.

Posting Employees' Hours

Choosing to post employees' hours from the Payroll menu chains to the PAYEMP.BAS program. You are prompted with

```
Enter regular hours for this pay period: [     ]
```

When you enter the number of hours and press RETURN, the screen then shows this message:

```
Working on:
```

The employees' names from the data file now flash on the screen rapidly. The purpose of this rapid flashing is to let the computer operator know that the program is working. When the hours for all employees in the data file have been posted, the program automatically returns to the Payroll menu. You may then use the EPR menu selection to edit the data of any employees with nonstandard hours.

```
1 GOTO 10
2 SAVE "POSTHRS":END
4 SAVE "POSTHRS",A:END
6 SAVE "POSTHRS":RUN "INIT"
10 REM =-                  -=*POSTHRS*=-
20 REM =-                  Post employees' hours
30 REM =-                  3/25/83
40 REM =-
50 COMMON CLI$,CS$,HC$,SF$,SB$,CL$,BS$,BELL$,FF$,CC$,PLNK$,MLNK$,DATE$,DR$
1000 '
1010 '                     ***********************************
1020 '                     *       PROGRAM INITIALIZATION      *
1030                       ***********************************
1040 '
1050 DEFINT A-Z
1060 ON ERROR GOTO 4070
1070 DEF FNCP$(L,C) = CLI$+CHR$(L+31)+CHR$(C+31)
1080 DEF FNCE$(L,S$) = FNCP$(L,(80-LEN(S$))\2)+S$
1090 DEF FNMS$(M$) = HC$+CL$+SPACE$((80-LEN(M$))\2)+SF$+M$+SB$
1100 DEF FNBKT$(L,C,M$) = FNCP$(L,C)+"["+M$+"]"
1110 '
1120 TTL$ = CS$ + FNCE$(3,"PAY EMPLOYEES")
1130 PRINT TTL$;FNMS$("ONE MOMENT PLEASE...")
1140 RC$ = CHR$(13) + CHR$(11)           '2 Return characters
1150 DIM RC(2):RC(1) = 1:RC(2) = -1:     '2 Return codes
1160 NO.PAY.TYPE = 3              'Number of pay rates
1170 NO.DEDUC = 4                 'Number of deductions
1180 NO.TO.DATE = 4               'Number of to-date fields
1190 DIM HRS$(NO.PAY.TYPE)
1200 '
1210 'Open employee data file
1220 '
1230 OPEN "R",1,"PREMP.DAT",81
1240 FIELD 1,1 AS STATUS$,2 AS FSIZE$             'Header record
1250 FIELD 1,25 AS EMPNAME$
1260 DUMMY = 25 + 9 + 3 + 2 + NO.DEDUC*3
1270 FOR I = 1 TO NO.PAY.TYPE                     'Field current hours
1280    FIELD 1,DUMMY AS DUMMY$,2 AS HRS$(I)
1290    DUMMY = DUMMY + 2
1300 NEXT I
1310 '
1320 IF LOF(1)=0 THEN 1360               'Check if file is new
1330    GET 1,1                          'Get header record of old file
1340    BADFILE = (STATUS$ <> "C")       'Check if file was closed
1350 GOTO 1390
1360    PRINT FNCP$(5,1);"WARNING: no employees on file."
1370    INPUT "Press <RETURN> to return to the menu. ";A$
1380    GOTO 3280                        'Exit program
1390 FSIZE = CVI(FSIZE$)                 'Get Last Record for program use
1400 LSET STATUS$ = "O"                  'Set file to (O)pen mode
1410 PUT 1,1                             'Write header record
```

```
3000 '
3010 '                  ***************************
3020 '                  *      MAIN PROGRAM       *
3030 '                  ***************************
3040 '
3050 IF BADFILE THEN PRINT FNMS$("WARNING: FILE WAS NOT CLOSED PROPERLY")
3060 A$="
3070 PRINT FNCP$(5,1);"Enter regular hours for this pay period: ";
3080 L=0:GOSUB 4300            'Input A$
3090 IF RC=-1 THEN 3280        'Exit program
3100 IF VAL(A$) > 0 THEN 3130
3110    PRINT FNMS$("INVALID NUMBER, PLEASE RE-ENTER")
3120    GOTO 3070
3130 REGHRS$ = MKI$(VAL(A$)*100)         'Standard hours for regular pay rate
3140 ZERO$ = MKI$(0)                     '0 for non-regular pay rates
3150 PRINT FNMS$("ONE MOMENT PLEASE...");FNCP$(5,1);CL$
3160 FOR RN = 2 TO FSIZE
3170    GET #1,RN
3180    IF STATUS$ = CHR$(255) THEN 3240
3190       PRINT FNCP$(5,1);"Working on: ";EMPNAME$
3200       LSET HRS$(1) = REGHRS$        'Set regular hours
3210       FOR I = 2 TO NO.PAY.RATES
3220          LSET HRS$(I) = ZERO$       'Set non-regular hrs. to 0
3230       NEXT I
3240    PUT #1,RN
3250 NEXT RN
3260 PRINT FNCP$(5,1);CL$;"Done."
3270 '
3280 PRINT FNMS$("EXITING")
3290 GOSUB 4120                 'Close employee data file
3300 PLNK$=MID$(PLNK$,13)       'Strip of program name
3310 CHAIN LEFT$(PLNK$,12)      'Return to chaining program
4000 '
4010 '                  **************************
4020 '                  *      SUBROUTINES       *
4030 '                  **************************
4040 '
4050 'Error trapping
4060 '
4070 GOSUB 4120          'Close employee data file
4080 CHAIN "ERROR",,ALL
4090 '
4100 'Close employee data file
4110 '
4120 LSET STATUS$ = "C"          'Set file status as (C)losed
4130 LSET FSIZE$ = MKI$(FSIZE)   'Set total number of records
4140 PUT 1,1                     'Write out header record
4150 CLOSE 1
4160 RETURN
4170 '
4180 'Bracket input
```

```
4190 '   Input:
4200 '      A$  = String to input (Length must be set)
4210 '      L,C = Line and column for input.  (L=0 for current position)
4220 '      CC$ = Cursor control characters
4230 '      RC$ = Return characters
4240 '      RC() = Return codes (one for each char. in RC$)
4250 '
4260 '   Output:
4270 '      A$ = New input is same length.
4280 '      RC = Return code specified in RC() array.
4290 '
4300 SL=LEN(A$):I=1
4310 IF L>0 THEN PRINT FNCP$(L,C);                  'Position cursor for input
4320 PRINT "[";A$;"]";STRING$(SL+1,BS$);            'Print string for input
4330 CH$=INPUT$(1)                                  'Get one char. of input
4340 ON INSTR(CC$,CH$) GOTO 4430,4450,4470,4500 'Search for cursor control
4350 IF INSTR(RC$,CH$) > 0 THEN 4400               'Search for return code
4360    IF CH$<" " THEN PRINT BELL$;:GOTO 4330  'No control chars.
4370    MID$(A$,I,1)=CH$:PRINT CH$;                 'Char to A$ and screen
4380    IF I<LEN(A$) THEN I=I+1 ELSE PRINT BS$;  'Check bounds
4390 GOTO 4330
4400    RC = RC(INSTR(RC$,CH$))                     'Get return code
4410    PRINT CHR$(13);                             'Show some response
4420 RETURN
4430    IF I>1 THEN I=I-1:PRINT BS$;                'Backspace char. trap
4440 GOTO 4330
4450    IF I<LEN(A$) THEN PRINT MID$(A$,I,1);:I=I+1      'Right character
4460 GOTO 4330
4470    MID$(A$,I)=MID$(A$,I+1)+" "                 'Delete char. trap
4480    PRINT MID$(A$,I);STRING$(SL-I+1,BS$);
4490 GOTO 4330
4500    MID$(A$,I)=" "+MID$(A$,I)                   'Insert character
4510    PRINT MID$(A$,I);STRING$(SL-I+1,BS$);
4520 GOTO 4330
```

Printing Checks

The Printing Checks option of the Payroll menu chains to the PRTCHK.BAS program. You are prompted with

```
Print (C)hecks or (A)lignment mask (C/A)? [ ]
```

An alignment mask is useful any time a preprinted form such as a check is to be filled in. It prints dummy data on the form so that you may check that the forms are positioned properly in the printer. If you choose to print the checks, the program indicates the totals for wages, taxes, and the various deductions, and then returns to the Payroll menu.

You will most likely have to modify the check printing subroutine of this program to suit your check forms. You may also wish to print additional information (like year-to-date totals) on the check stub.

```
1 GOTO 10
2 SAVE "PRTCHK":END
4 SAVE "PRTCHK",A:END
6 SAVE "PRTCHK":RUN "INIT"
10 REM =-                    -=*PRTCHK*=-
20 REM =-                    Print checks
30 REM =-                    3/25/83
40 REM =-
50 COMMON CLI$,CS$,HC$,SF$,SB$,CL$,BS$,BELL$,FF$,CC$.PLNK$,MLNK$,DATE$.DR$
1000 '
1010 '                       ****************************
1020 '                       *       PROGRAM DATA       *
1030 '                       ****************************
1040 '
1050 DATA ONE,TWO,THREE,FOUR,FIVE,SIX,SEVEN,EIGHT,NINE,TEN,ELEVEN,TWELVE
1060 DATA THIRTEEN,FOURTEEN,FIFTEEN,SIXTEEN,SEVENTEEN.EIGHTEEN,NINETEEN
1070 DATA TWENTY,THIRTY,FORTY,FIFTY,SIXTY,SEVENTY,EIGHTY,NINETY
1080 '
1090 'Deduction titles
1100 '
1110 DATA Savings,Medical,Dental,Union
1120 '
1130 '                       *************************************
1140 '                       *       PROGRAM INITIALIZATION      *
1150 '                       *************************************
1160 '
1170 DEFINT A-Z
1180 ON ERROR GOTO 4070
1190 DEF FNCP$(L,C) = CLI$+CHR$(L+31)+CHR$(C+31)
1200 DEF FNCE$(L,S$) = FNCP$(L,(80-LEN(S$))\2)+S$
1210 DEF FNMS$(M$) = HC$+CL$+SPACE$((80-LEN(M$))\2)+SF$+M$+SB$
1220 DEF FNBKT$(L,C,M$) = FNCP$(L,C)+"["+M$+"]"
1230 DEF FNMKDI$(N#) = MKI$(INT(N#/256)-32768#) + CHR$(N#-INT(N#/256)*256)
1240 DEF FNCVDI#(N$) = (CVI(N$)+32768#)*256 + ASC(MID$(N$,3,1))
1250 '
1260 TTL$ = CS$ + FNCE$(3,"PAY EMPLOYEES")
1270 PRINT TTL$;FNMS$("ONE MOMENT PLEASE...")
1280 RC$ = CHR$(13) + CHR$(11)           '2 Return characters
1290 DIM RC(2):RC(1) = 1:RC(2) = -1:     '2 Return codes
1300 NO.PAY.TYPE = 3               'Number of pay rates
1310 NO.DEDUC = 4                  'Number of deductions
1320 NO.TO.DATE = 4                'Number of to-date fields
1330 FICARATE# = 6.23#             'Social security rate (in percent)
1340 DIM DED$(NO.DEDUC),HRS$(NO.PAY.TYPE),TD$(2,NO.TO.DATE)
1350 DIM DED#(NO.DEDUC),TOTDED#(NO.DEDUC)
1360 DIM NUMBER$(27)
```

```
1370 FOR I = 1 TO 27
1380    READ NUMBER$(I)         'Read long hand numbers
1390 NEXT I
1400 FOR I = 1 TO NO.DEDUC
1410    READ DEDNAME$(I)        'Read deduction descriptions
1420 NEXT I
1430 '
1440 'Read in federal tax table
1450 '
1460 OPEN "I",#1,"FEDTAX.DAT"
1470 IF NOT EOF(1) THEN 1510
1480    PRINT FNCP$(5,1);"WARNING: No federal tax table has been entered."
1490    PRINT "Press any key to return to menu. ";:A$ = INPUT$(1)
1500    GOTO 3200                'Exit program
1510 INPUT #1,FTSIZE,MAXDEP,EXPRCT!
1520 DIM FTAX#(FTSIZE,MAXDEP),INDEX#(FTSIZE)
1530 FOR I = 1 TO FTSIZE
1540    INPUT #1,INDEX#(I)
1550    FOR J = 0 TO MAXDEP
1560       INPUT #1,FTAX#(I,J)
1570    NEXT J
1580 NEXT I
1590 CLOSE #1
1600 '
1610 'Open employee data file
1620 '
1630 OPEN "R",#1,"PREMP.DAT",81
1640 FIELD #1,1 AS STATUS$,2 AS FSIZE$           'Header record
1650 FIELD #1,25 AS EMPNAME$,9 AS SS$,3 AS RATE$,2 AS NODEP$
1660 DUMMY = 25 + 9 + 3 + 2
1670 FOR I = 1 TO NO.DEDUC       'Field deductions
1680    FIELD #1,DUMMY AS DUMMY$,3 AS DED$(I)
1690    DUMMY = DUMMY + 3
1700 NEXT I
1710 FOR I = 1 TO NO.PAY.TYPE   'Field pay type hours
1720    FIELD #1,DUMMY AS DUMMY$,2 AS HRS$(I)
1730    DUMMY = DUMMY + 2
1740 NEXT I
1750 FOR I = 1 TO NO.TO.DATE    'Field to-date totals
1760    FIELD #1,DUMMY AS DUMMY$,3 AS TD$(1,I),3 AS TD$(2,I)
1770    DUMMY = DUMMY + 6
1780 NEXT I
1790 '
1800 IF LOF(1)=0 THEN 1840              'Check if file is new
1810    GET #1,1                        'Get header record of old file
1820    BADFILE = (STATUS$ <> "C")      'Check if file was closed
1830 GOTO 1870
1840    PRINT FNCP$(5,1);"WARNING: no employees on file."
1850    INPUT "Press <RETURN> to return to the menu. ";A$
1860    GOTO 3200                       'Exit program
1870 FSIZE = CVI(FSIZE$)                'Get Last Record for program use
```

```
1880 LSET STATUS$ = "O"                  'Set file to (O)pen mode
1890 PUT #1,1                            'Write header record
3000 '
3010 '                 ***************************
3020 '                 *      MAIN PROGRAM       *
3030 '                 ***************************
3040 '
3050 IF BADFILE THEN PRINT FNMS$("WARNING: FILE WAS NOT CLOSED PROPERLY")
3060 PRINT FNCP$(5,1);"Print (C)hecks or (A)lignment mask (C/A)? ";
3070 L=0:A$=" ":GOSUB 5150               'Input A$
3080 IF RC = -1 THEN 3200                'Exit program
3090 IF A$ = "A" THEN GOSUB 4660         'Print alignment mask
3100 IF A$ <> "C" THEN 3060
3110 ZERO$ = MKI$(0)
3120 PRINT FNMS$("PRINTING CHECKS....");FNCP$(5,1);CL$
3130 FOR RN = 2 TO FSIZE
3140    GET #1,RN
3150    IF STATUS$ <> CHR$(255) THEN GOSUB 4240 'Compute pay
3160 NEXT RN
3170 GOSUB 4940                 'Print totals
3180 PRINT FNCP$(5,1);CL$;"Done."
3190 '
3200 PRINT FNMS$("EXITING")
3210 GOSUB 4160                 'Close employee data file
3220 PLNK$=MID$(PLNK$,13)       'Strip of program name
3230 CHAIN LEFT$(PLNK$,12)      'Return to chaining program
4000 '
4010 '                 **************************
4020 '                 *      SUBROUTINES       *
4030 '                 **************************
4040 '
4050 'Error trapping
4060 '
4070 IF ERR <> 53 OR ERL <> 1460 THEN 4110
4080    PRINT FNCP$(5,1);"WARNING: Federal tax tables have not been entered."
4090    PRINT "Press any key to return to menu. "::A$ = INPUT$(1)
4100    GOTO 3220        'Exit program
4110 IF FSIZE > 0 THEN GOSUB 4160        'Close employee data file if open
4120 STOP:CHAIN "ERROR",,ALL
4130 '
4140 'Close employee data file
4150 '
4160 LSET STATUS$ = "C"         'Set file status as (C)losed
4170 LSET FSIZE$ = MKI$(FSIZE)  'Set total number of records
4180 PUT #1,1                   'Write out header record
4190 CLOSE 1
4200 RETURN
4210 '
4220 'Compute pay for employee
4230 '
4240 PRINT FNCP$(5,1);"Working on: ";EMPNAME$
```

```
4250 RATE# = FNCVDI#(RATE$)/1000#          'Pay rate
4260 NODEP = VAL(NODEP$)
4270 GROSSPAY# = 0                    'This will be employee's gross pay
4280 FOR I = 1 TO NO.PAY.TYPE
4290    GROSSPAY# = GROSSPAY# + INT(CVI(HRS$(I))*RATE#*(I*.5+.5) + .5#)/100#
4300 NEXT I
4310 GROSSDED# = 0                    'This will be the gross deductions
4320 FOR I = 1 TO NO.DEDUC
4330    DED#(I) = FNCVDI#(DED$(I))/100#
4340    GROSSDED# = GROSSDED# + DED#(I)
4350 NEXT I
4360 FICA# = INT(FICARATE#*GROSSPAY# + .5)/100# 'Social security
4370 ENTRY = 1                        'Search table for federal tax
4380 WHILE ENTRY < FTSIZE AND GROSSPAY# >= INDEX#(ENTRY)
4390    ENTRY = ENTRY + 1
4400 WEND
4410 FED# = FTAX#(ENTRY,NODEP)
4420 IF ENTRY=FTSIZE THEN
        FED#=FED#+INT(EXPRCT!*(GROSSPAY#-INDEX#(ENTRY-1))+.5)/100
4430 NETPAY# = GROSSPAY# - GROSSDED# - FED# - FICA#
4440 IF NETPAY# <= 0 THEN 4620  'Do nothing if NETPAY# is not positive
4450    TOTPAY# = TOTPAY# + GROSSPAY#    'Keep gross pay total
4460    FOR I = 1 TO NO.DEDUC             'Total deductions
4470       TOTDED#(I) = TOTDED#(I) + DED#(I)
4480    NEXT I
4490    TOTFICA# = TOTFICA# + FICA#       'Total social security
4500    TOTFED# = TOTFED# + FED#          'Total federal tax
4510    FOR I = 1 TO NO.PAY.TYPE          'Set hours to zero
4520       LSET HRS$(I) = ZERO$
4530    NEXT I
4540    FOR I = 1 TO 2              'Set totals in employee's file
4550       LSET TD$(I,1) = FNMKDI$(FNCVDI#(TD$(I,1)) + GROSSPAY#*100)
4560       LSET TD$(I,2) = FNMKDI$(FNCVDI#(TD$(I,2)) + GROSSDED#*100)
4570       LSET TD$(I,3) = FNMKDI$(FNCVDI#(TD$(I,3)) + FED#*100)
4580       LSET TD$(I,4) = FNMKDI$(FNCVDI#(TD$(I,4)) + FICA#*100)
4590    NEXT I
4600    GOSUB 4720                  'Print check
4610    PUT #1,RN
4620 RETURN
4630 '
4640 'Print alignment mask
4650 '
4660 LSET EMPNAME$ = "THIS CHECK IS VOID": NETPAY# = 123.45
4670 GOSUB 4720                     'Print a check
4680 RETURN
4690 '
4700 'Print a check
4710 '
4720 LPRINT:LPRINT:LPRINT TAB(60);DATE$
4730 LPRINT:LPRINT "Pay to the order of: ";EMPNAME$;
4740 LPRINT TAB(60) USING "$$###.##";NETPAY#:LPRINT:LPRINT "The sum: ";
```

```
4750 X = INT(NETPAY#)
4760 IF X >= 1000 THEN LPRINT NUMBER$(X\1000);" THOUSAND ";: X = X MOD 1000
4770 IF X >= 100 THEN LPRINT NUMBER$(X\100);" HUNDRED ";: X = X MOD 100
4780 IF X > 20 THEN LPRINT NUMBER$(X\10 + 18);" ";: X = X MOD 10
4790 IF X >= 1 AND X <= 20 THEN LPRINT NUMBER$(X);" ";
4800 LPRINT USING "AND ##/100 DOLLARS";(NETPAY# - INT(NETPAY#))*100
4810 LPRINT:LPRINT                    'Line feed down to check stub
4820 LPRINT USING "Gross pay:          $$###.##";GROSSPAY#
4830 LPRINT "Deductions:"
4840 FOR I = 1 TO NO.DEDUC
4850    LPRINT USING "  \               \ $$###.##";DEDNAME$(I);DED#(I)
4860 NEXT I
4870 LPRINT USING "Federal tax:        $$###.##";FED#
4880 LPRINT USING "FICA:               $$###.##";FICA#
4890 LPRINT:LPRINT
4900 RETURN
4910 '
4920 'Print totals
4930 '
4940 LPRINT USING "Total gross pay:   $$####.##";TOTPAY#
4950 LPRINT "Total deductions:"
4960 FOR I = 1 TO NO.DEDUC
4970    LPRINT USING "  \               \ $$####.##";DEDNAME$(I);TOTDED#(I)
4980 NEXT I
4990 LPRINT USING "Total federal tax: $$####.##";TOTFED#
5000 LPRINT USING "Total FICA:        $$####.##";TOTFICA#
5010 RETURN
5020 '
5030 'Bracket input
5040 '    Input:
5050 '       A$  = String to input (Length must be set)
5060 '       L,C = Line and column for input.  (L=0 for current position)
5070 '       CC$ = Cursor control characters
5080 '       RC$ = Return characters
5090 '       RC() = Return codes (one for each char. in RC$)
5100 '
5110 '    Output:
5120 '       A$ = New input is same length.
5130 '       RC = Return code specified in RC() array.
5140 '
5150 SL=LEN(A$):I=1
5160 IF L>0 THEN PRINT FNCP$(L,C);              'Position cursor for input
5170 PRINT "[";A$;"]";STRING$(SL+1,BS$);        'Print string for input
5180 CH$=INPUT$(1)                              'Get one char. of input
5190 ON INSTR(CC$,CH$) GOTO 5280,5300,5320,5350 'Search for cursor control
5200 IF INSTR(RC$,CH$) > 0 THEN 5250            'Search for return code
5210    IF CH$<" " THEN PRINT BELL$;:GOTO 5180  'No control chars.
5220    MID$(A$,I,1)=CH$:PRINT CH$;             'Char to A$ and screen
5230    IF I<LEN(A$) THEN I=I+1 ELSE PRINT BS$; 'Check bounds
5240 GOTO 5180
5250    RC = RC(INSTR(RC$,CH$))                 'Get return code
```

```
5260    PRINT CHR$(13);                          'Show some response
5270 RETURN
5280    IF I>1 THEN I=I-1:PRINT BS$;             'Backspace char. trap
5290 GOTO 5180
5300    IF I<LEN(A$) THEN PRINT MID$(A$,I,1);:I=I+1     'Right character
5310 GOTO 5180
5320    MID$(A$,I)=MID$(A$,I+1)+" "              'Delete char. trap
5330    PRINT MID$(A$,I);STRING$(SL-I+1,BS$);
5340 GOTO 5180
5350    MID$(A$,I)=" "+MID$(A$,I)                'Insert character
5360    PRINT MID$(A$,I);STRING$(SL-I+1,BS$);
5370 GOTO 5180
```

Entering Federal Tax Tables

Choosing to enter federal tax tables from the Payroll menu chains the ENTFTT.BAS program.

```
Note: This program will overwrite the existing federal tax tables.
Do you wish to continue (Y/N)?
```

If you proceed, the program will create a file for the new tax table to store the data you enter.

```
1 GOTO 10
2 SAVE "ENTFTT":END
4 SAVE "ENTFTT",A:END
6 SAVE "ENTFTT":RUN "INIT"
10 REM =-                 -=*ENTFTT*=-
20 REM =-                 Enter federal tax tables
30 REM =-                 3/21/83
40 REM =-
50 COMMON CLI$,CS$,HC$,SF$,SB$,CL$,BS$,BELL$,FF$,CC$,PLNK$,MLNK$,DATE$,DR$
1000 '
1010 '                    ***************************************
1020 '                    *       PROGRAM INITIALIZATION        *
1030 '                    ***************************************
1040 '
1050 DEFINT A-Z
1060 ON ERROR GOTO 4070
1070 DEF FNCP$(L,C) = CLI$+CHR$(L+31)+CHR$(C+31)
1080 DEF FNCE$(L,S$) = FNCP$(L,(80-LEN(S$))\2)+S$
1090 DEF FNMS$(M$) = HC$+CL$+SPACE$((80-LEN(M$))\2)+SF$+M$+SB$
1100 MAXSIZE = 50       'Maximum # of entries for tax table
1110 '
1120 PRINT CS$;FNCE$(3,"FEDERAL TAX TABLE ENTRY")
3000 '
3010 '                    *****************************
3020 '                    *       MAIN PROGRAM        *
3030 '                    *****************************
```

```
3040 '
3050 PRINT FNMS$("");FNCP$(5,1);
3060 PRINT "NOTE: this program will overwrite the existing federal tax table."
3070 INPUT "Do you wish to continue (Y/N)? ",A$
3080 IF A$<>"Y" THEN 3390                  'Exit program
3090 PRINT:INPUT "Enter maximum number dependents: ",MAXDEP
3100 DIM TAX#(MAXSIZE,MAXDEP),HIGH#(MAXSIZE)
3110 ENTRY = 1:LOW# = 0:DONE = (1=2)     'Variable DONE is initialized to false
3120 WHILE NOT DONE
3130    PRINT:PRINT "Table entry";ENTRY
3140    PRINT "Income at least";LOW#;
3150    INPUT "but less than (Enter 0 for final entry): ",HIGH#(ENTRY)
3160    PRINT "Withholding for:"
3170    FOR I = 0 TO MAXDEP
3180       PRINT I;"Dependents: ";:INPUT "",TAX#(ENTRY,I)
3190    NEXT I
3200    DONE = (HIGH#(ENTRY) = 0)          'DONE is set to true on final entry
3210    IF DONE THEN 3250
3220       LOW# = HIGH#(ENTRY)
3230       ENTRY = ENTRY + 1
3240    GOTO 3270
3250       PRINT "Percentage of the amount over";LOW#;"is? ";
3260       INPUT "",EXPRCT!
3270 WEND
3280 PRINT:PRINT "Writing tax file....";
3290 OPEN "O",#1,"FEDTAX.DAT"
3300 WRITE #1,ENTRY,MAXDEP,EXPRCT!
3310 FOR I = 1 TO ENTRY
3320    WRITE #1,HIGH#(I)
3330    FOR J = 0 TO MAXDEP
3340       WRITE #1,TAX#(I,J)
3350    NEXT J
3360 NEXT I
3370 CLOSE #1                         'Close tax file
3380 '
3390 PRINT:PRINT "Done, exiting program";FNMS$("EXITING")
3400 PLNK$=MID$(PLNK$,13)            'Strip of program name
3410 CHAIN LEFT$(PLNK$,12)           'Return to chaining program
4000 '
4010 '                  **************************
4020 '                  *      SUBROUTINES       *
4030 '                  **************************
4040 '
4050 'Error trapping
4060 '
4070 CLOSE #1                         'Close tax file
4080 CHAIN "ERROR",,ALL
```

Printing Federal Tax Tables

Printing the federal tax tables chains in PRTFTT.BAS. You are prompted with

```
Press <RETURN> when printer is ready.
```

The program then prints out the tax table that you entered in the previous selection so that it may be verified. After printing the table, the program returns to the Payroll menu.

```
1 GOTO 10
2 SAVE "PRTFIT":END
4 SAVE "PRTFTT",A:END
6 SAVE "PRTFTT":RUN "INIT"
10 REM =-                    -=*PRTFTT*=-
20 REM =-                    Print  federal tax table
30 REM =-                    3/21/83
40 REM =-
50 COMMON CLI$,CS$,HC$,SF$,SB$,CL$,BS$,BELL$,FF$,CC$,PLNK$,MLNK$,DATE$,DR$
1000 '
1010 '                       ***************************************
1020 '                       *      PROGRAM INITIALIZATION         *
1030 '                       ***************************************
1040 '
1050 DEFINT A-Z
1060 ON ERROR GOTO 4070
1070 DEF FNCP$(L,C) = CLI$+CHR$(L+31)+CHR$(C+31)
1080 DEF FNCE$(L,S$) = FNCP$(L,(80-LEN(S$))\2)+S$
1090 DEF FNMS$(M$) = HC$+CL$+SPACE$((80-LEN(M$))\2)+SF$+M$+SB$
1100 FMT$ = " $$##.## |"
1110 '
1120 PRINT CS$;FNMS$("");FNCE$(3,"PRINT FEDERAL TAX TABLE")
3000 '
3010 '                       *****************************
3020 '                       *      MAIN PROGRAM         *
3030 '                       *****************************
3040 '
3050 PRINT FNCP$(5,1);
3060 OPEN "I",#1,"FEDTAX.DAT"
3070 INPUT "Press <RETURN> when printer is ready. ",A$
3080 PRINT FNMS$("PRINTING TAX TABLE....")
3090 INPUT #1,SIZE,MAXDEP,EXPRCT!
3100 LPRINT:LPRINT TAB(25);"FEDERAL WITHHOLDING TAX TABLE":LPRINT
3110 LPRINT "|";TAB(10);"RANGE";TAB(29);"|";TAB(40);"NUMBER OF DEPENDENTS";
3120 LPRINT TAB(MAXDEP*10 + 39);"|"
3130 LPRINT "| At least  | but less than |";
3140 FOR I = 0 TO MAXDEP
3150    LPRINT USING "    ##   |";I;
3160 NEXT I
```

```
3170 LPRINT:LPRINT "¦-----------¦---------------¦";
3180 FOR I = 0 TO MAXDEF
3190    LPRINT "---------¦";
3200 NEXT I
3210 LPRINT
3220 LOW# = 0
3230 FOR I = 1 TO SIZE
3240    LPRINT USING "¦ $$###.##  ¦";LOW#;
3250    IF I = SIZE THEN 3290
3260       INPUT #1,HIGH#
3270       LPRINT TAB(17) USING "$$###.##";HIGH#;
3280    GOTO 3300
3290       LPRINT TAB(17) USING "+##.##%";EXPRET!;
3300    LPRINT TAB(29);"¦";
3310    FOR J = 0 TO MAXDEF
3320       INPUT #1,TAX#
3330       LPRINT USING FMT$;TAX#;
3340    NEXT J
3350    LPRINT
3360    LOW# = HIGH#
3370 NEXT I
3380 LPRINT:LPRINT "Printed: ";DATE$
3390 LPRINT FF$;                    'Form feed the printer
3400 '
3410 CLOSE #1                       'Close tax file
3420 PRINT:PRINT "Done, exiting program";
3430 PLNK$=MID$(PLNK$,13)           'Strip of program name
3440 CHAIN LEFT$(PLNK$,12)          'Return to chaining program
4000 '
4010 '                    ***************************
4020 '                    *       SUBROUTINES       *
4030 '                    ***************************
4040 '
4050 'Error trapping
4060 '
4070 CLOSE #1                       'Close tax file
4080 IF ERR <> 53 OR ERL <> 3060 THEN CHAIN "ERROR",,ALL
4090 PRINT "WARNING: Tax tables have not been entered yet."
4100 INPUT "Press <RETURN> to return to menu. ",A$
4110 GOTO 3410
```

21

Mailing Labels

Our final program is a lengthy and sophisticated mailing list program. Our purpose here is to tie in a complete program with the menu driver of Chapter 19. In addition, this program will exemplify the use of keyed files. Those who need such a program and have the patience to type it in will find it very practical, especially for maintaining a customer mailing list with a data base of about 500. If you wish to maintain a larger data base, it would be desirable to incorporate a commercial machine language search routine like Micro B+, which was discussed in Chapter 18.

The program presented in this chapter could be used by a small business to maintain a list of customers. The program stores the names, addresses, and attributes of customers in a file. When you enter a customer's name, the program searches the file and displays the data for that customer on the screen.

Using Key Files

The main feature of this program is the use of *keys* to search the file for the requested information. As an illustration of the principle of key files, consider the simple example presented in Figure 21-1. In

Data File:			Key File:	
Record #	Names in File	Age	Key	Record #
1	Smith, Sam	21	AD	4
2	Jones, Mike	18	BA	5
3	Wilson, Sally	33	JO	2
4	Adams, Jane	24	SM	1
5	Baker, Alfred	27	WI	3

Figure 21-1.
Key file structure

this example the data file contains an individual's name and age. A separate file, the key file, is maintained by the program. Each time a new record is added to the data file, a key is constructed that contains the first two letters of the last name and the record number that contains that name. The key is then placed in the proper alphabetical position in the key file, while the names go into the next available record in the data file.

The record number after the first two letters of the last name in the key file is referred to as the *pointer* because it points to the record number of the data file that contains the complete data. Then, anytime a request is made for the data associated with a name, a binary search is made of the key file and the pointer tells the program which record to read. The advantage of this procedure is that records in the data file, which may be quite lengthy, do not have to be shuffled. Only the three-byte records of the key file have to be rearranged to maintain the pointer so that it keeps track of the names in alphabetical order.

Mailing List Overview

The purpose of this chapter is not to have you write a program with a keyed file but to give you access to a prewritten keyed-file subroutine that you can use with a mailing list program.

In addition to a key based on names, the programs MLEDIT.BAS and MLPRINT.BAS also maintain and use a key based on ZIP codes. This ensures that when you print mailing labels, the list will be printed out in ZIP code order, which is what the post office requires for bulk and lower-cost first-class mailings.

Note that you must append the program discussed in the section "Key File System" at the end of this chapter to *both* MLEDIT.BAS and MLPRINT.BAS.

HIT SELECT

Another feature of the mailing list program is a technique called *hit select*, which consists of searching the file to find a group of records with similar names. For example, if you enter only the letter **L** for the customer name, all of the customers' names that begin with *L* will be presented on the screen, with each name numbered. You may then select by number the name that you wish. The data for that customer will automatically be shown in the screen mask.

In this particular application of hit select, you may enter any number of letters you like up to the complete name.

Customizing the Mailing List Programs

The largest portion of the MLEDIT.BAS program (the file handling section) maintains the key file. Although this topic is not covered in this book, you can still make limited modifications to the program for your application.

```
1 GOTO 10
2 SAVE "MLEDIT":END
4 SAVE "MLEDIT",A:END
6 SAVE "MLEDIT":RUN "INIT"
10 REM =-                    -=*MLEDIT*=-
20 REM =-                    Mail List Editor
30 REM =-                    Ver 1.0  03/22/83
40 REM =-
50 COMMON CLI$,CS$,HC$,SF$,SB$,CL$,BS$,BELL$,FF$,CC$,PLNK$,MLNK$,DATE$,DR$
1000 '
1010 '                       ****************************
1020 '                       *       PROGRAM DATA       *
1030 '                       ****************************
1040 '
1050 'Screen mask data: Line number, Column for description,
1060 '  Column for brackets, Length of field, Field type, Field description
1070 '
1080 'Field type: 0 = Field does not belong in file buffer
1090 '            1 = Field gets FIELDed into file buffer
1100 '
1110 DATA 13
1120 DATA 5,1,20,25,1,"1) Customer name",6,1,20,20,1,"2) Title"
```

```
1130 DATA 7,1,20,25,1,"3) Address line 1",8,1,20,25,1,"4) Address line 2
1140 DATA 9,1,20,9,1,"5) Zip code",13,1,14,1,0,"6)  Credit"
1150 DATA 13,19,34,1,0,"7)  Check card",13,39,52,1,0,"8)  Cash only"
1160 DATA 13,57,73,1,0,"9)  Employee",14,1,14,1,0,"10) Courtesy"
1170 DATA 14,19,34,1,0,"11) Products",14,39,52,1,0,"12) Services"
1180 DATA 14,57,73,1,0,"13) Time"
1190 '
1200 '                    *************************************
1210 '                    *       PROGRAM INITIALIZATION       *
1220 '                    *************************************
1230 '
1240 'Define functions
1250 '
1260 DEFINT A-Z
1270 ON ERROR GOTO 4070
1280 DEF FNCP$(L,C)=CLI$+CHR$(L+31)+CHR$(C+31)
1290 DEF FNCE$(L,M$)=FNCP$(L,(80-LEN(M$))\2)+M$
1300 DEF FNCES$(L)=FNCP$(L,1)+MID$(CES$,(L-1)*(LEN(CL$)+1)+1)+FNCP$(L,1)
1310 DEF FNMS$(M$)=HC$+CL$+SPACE$((80-LEN(M$))\2)+SF$+M$+SB$
1320 DEF FNBKT$(L,C,M$)=FNCP$(L,C)+"["+M$+"]"
1330 '
1340 'Initialize variables and open files
1350 '
1360 PRINT CS$;FNCE$(3,"-- M A I L    L I S T    E D I T O R --")
1370 PRINT FNMS$("ONE MOMENT PLEASE...."):PRINT
1380 RC$=CHR$(13)+CHR$(11)+CHR$(27)      '3 Return characters
1390 MAXHIT = 15                         'Maximum # of hits per screen
1400 DIM RC(3),HRN(MAXHIT)               '3 Return codes, 15 hits per screen
1410 RC(1)=1:RC(2)=-1:RC(3)=999          '3 Return codes
1420 READ NF                             'Read # of fields
1430 DIM FL(NF),FDC(NF),FC(NF),FLN(NF),F$(NF),FD$(NF)
1440 CES$ = CL$                    'Construct clear to end of screen string
1450 FOR I=1 TO 23:CES$=CES$+CHR$(10)+CL$:NEXT I
1460 NMKF = 1 : ZIPKF = 5          'Name key from field 1, zip key from field 5
1470 NKF=2:NDF=1:MRL=105:GOSUB 6250      'Initialize file system
1480 '
1490 '                    Name key file
1500 LKN=1:KFNM$=DR$+"NAME.KEY":KL(1)=6
1510 GOSUB 7300            'Open name key file
1520 '
1530 '                    Zip key file
1540 LKN=2:KFNM$=DR$+"ZIP.KEY":KL(2)=5
1550 GOSUB 7300            'Open zip key file
1560 '
1570 '                    Mail list data
1580 LDN=1:DFNM$=DR$+"ML.DAT":RL(1)=105
1590 GOSUB 6450            'Open link list data file
1600 DMY=0
1610 FOR I = 1 TO NF
1620    READ FL(I),FDC(I),FC(I),FLN(I),FT,FD$(I)
1630    IF FT=0 THEN 1670                'Check field type
1640       FIELD DFN(LDN),DMY AS DMY$,FLN(I) AS F$(I)
```

```
1650        DMY = DMY + FLN(I)
1660    GOTO 1680
1670        F$(I) = SPACE$(FLN(I))          'Field types 0 don't go in the buffer
1680 NEXT I
1690 FIELD DFN(LDN),DMY AS DMY$,1 AS ATTRIB$     'ATTRIB$ is a bit map
3000 '
3010 '                    ****************************
3020 '                    *       MAIN PROGRAM       *
3030 '                    ****************************
3040 '
3050 GOSUB 4190                      'Get customer to edit (hit select)
3060 IF RC<>-1 THEN 3110
3070    PRINT FNMS$("EXITING")
3080    GOSUB 4120                   'Close files
3090    PLNK$=MID$(PLNK$,13)         'Strip of program name
3100    CHAIN LEFT$(PLNK$,12)        'Return to chaining program
3110 IF DRN=0 THEN GOSUB 4790 ELSE GOSUB 4890    'Init new or existing entry
3120 GOSUB 4700                              'Print edit screen mask
3130 IF DRN=0 THEN FLD=1:GOSUB 4600         'Edit fields now if new customer
3140 PRINT FNMS$(MS$+", SELECT OPTION")
3150 PRINT FNCP$(24,1);
3160 PRINT "Field number to edit, Delete, Save, or Exit (#/D/S/E)? ";
3170 L=0:A$=" ":GOSUB 5480          'Field input A$
3180 IF RC=-1 THEN A$="E"           'Backup treated same as Exit
3190 IF VAL(A$)=0 THEN 3220
3200    FLD=VAL(A$):GOSUB 4600      'Edit fields
3210    GOTO 3140
3220 IF LEFT$(A$,1)=" " THEN A$=RIGHT$(A$,1) ELSE A$=LEFT$(A$,1)
3230 SEL = INSTR("DSE",A$)          'SEL = 1 for delete, 2 for save, 3 for exit
3240 IF SEL=0 THEN PRINT FNMS$("INVALID SELECTION"):GOTO 3150
3250 ON SEL GOSUB 5020,5140         'Delete or Save (No action for Exit)
3260 GOTO 3050
4000 '
4010 '                    **************************
4020 '                    *       SUBROUTINES      *
4030 '                    **************************
4040 '
4050 'Error trapping
4060 '
4070 GOSUB 4120             'Close files
4080 CHAIN "ERROR..ALL
4090
4100 'Close files
4110
4120 IF KFN(1)>0 THEN LKN=1:GOSUB 8800  'Close name key file
4130 IF KFN(2)>0 THEN LKN=2:GOSUB 8800  'Close zip key file
4140 IF DFN(1)>0 THEN LDN=1:GOSUB 7100  'Close mail list data file
4150 RETURN
4160 '
4170 'Hit select
4180
4190 NM$=SPACE$(FLN(NMKF))
```

```
4200 PRINT FNCES$(5);FNMS$("")
4210 PRINT FNCP$(5,1);"Enter customer name to search or add: ";
4220 L=0:A$=NM$:GOSUB 5480:NM$=A$                   'Input NM$ (name)
4230 IF RC=-1 THEN RETURN
4240 IF NM$=SPACE$(FLN(NMKF)) THEN 4210
4250 CLN = FLN(NMKF)                               'CLN = Compare Length for Name
4260 WHILE CLN>1 AND MID$(NM$,CLN,1)=" "           'Get real length of name
4270    CLN=CLN-1
4280 WEND
4290 IF CLN>KL(1) THEN CLK=KL(1) ELSE CLK=CLN    'CLK = Compare Length for Key
4300 LKN=1:SKV$=LEFT$(NM$,KL(1)):SKP=0:GOSUB 7580       'Search name for key
4310 PRINT FNMS$("SELECT NAME FROM LIST"):GOSUB 4450   'Print hits on name key
4320 PRINT FNCP$(6,1);"Enter selection number or 0 to add new name: ";
4330 L=0:A$="0 ":GOSUB 5480     'Input A$
4340 IF RC=-1 THEN 4200
4350 SEL=VAL(A$)
4360 IF SEL=99 THEN 4310        'Print next page
4370 IF SEL>=0 AND SEL<=NHIT THEN 4400
4380    PRINT FNMS$("INVALID SELECTION")
4390    GOTO 4320
4400 IF SEL=0 THEN DRN=0 ELSE DRN=HRN(SEL)      'Set DRN=0 if a new customer
4410 RETURN
4420 '
4430 'Print hits on the name entry
4440 '
4450 NHIT=0:PRINT FNCES$(8);
4460 WHILE LEFT$(FKV$,CLK)=LEFT$(SKV$,CLK) AND NHIT<MAXHIT
4470    GET DFN(1),FKP          'FKP = found key pointer
4480    IF LEFT$(NM$,CLN)<>LEFT$(F$(NMKF),CLN) THEN 4520'Compare entire name
4490       NHIT=NHIT+1
4500       PRINT USING "## & &";NHIT;F$(NMKF);F$(2)     'Print name and title
4510       HRN(NHIT)=FKP
4520    LKN=1:GOSUB 8670         'Get next key (FKP is returned)
4530 WEND
4540 IF LEFT$(FKV$,CLK)=LEFT$(SKV$,CLK) THEN PRINT "99 See next page"
4550 IF NHIT=0 THEN PRINT "No matches, type '0' to enter a new name."
4560 RETURN
4570 '
4580 'Edit fields
4590 '
4600 PRINT FNMS$(MS$+", EDIT FIELDS")
4610 WHILE FLD>=1 AND FLD<=NF
4620    L=FL(FLD):C=FC(FLD)       'Get line and column for input
4630    A$=F$(FLD):GOSUB 5480:LSET F$(FLD)=A$    'Input F$(FLD)
4640    FLD=FLD+RC       'Return code determins next field to edit
4650 WEND
4660 RETURN
4670 '
4680 'Print edit screen mask
4690 '
4700 PRINT FNCES$(5);FNCP$(11,1);"Customer attributes (Y/N):"
4710 FOR FLD = 1 TO NF
```

```
4720    PRINT FNCP$(FL(FLD),FDC(FLD));FD$(FLD)
4730    PRINT FNBKT$(FL(FLD),FC(FLD),F$(FLD))
4740 NEXT FLD
4750 RETURN
4760 '
4770 'Initialize new customer
4780 '
4790 FOR FLD = 1 TO NF
4800    LSET F$(FLD) = ""          'Set all fields to spaces
4810 NEXT FLD
4820 LSET F$(NMKF) = NM$           'Assume new name
4830 ONMK$=SPACE$(KL(1)):OZK$=SPACE$(KL(2))      'Set old keys to blanks
4840 MS$ = "NEW CUSTOMER"          'Message for top line
4850 RETURN
4860 '
4870 'Initialize for existing customer
4880 '
4890 GET DFN(1),DRN                'Read in customer
4900 ATTRIB=ASC(ATTRIB$)           'Get bit mask
4910 FOR FLD=6 TO 13               'Convert bit mask to fields 6 thru 13
4920    IF (ATTRIB AND 1)=1 THEN LSET F$(FLD)="Y" ELSE LSET F$(FLD)=""
4930    ATTRIB=ATTRIB\2            'Right shift one bit position
4940 NEXT FLD
4950 ONMK$ = LEFT$(F$(NMKF),KL(1))         'Set old name key
4960 OZK$ = LEFT$(F$(ZIPKF),KL(2))         'Set old zip key
4970 MS$ = "CUSTOMER FOUND"                'Message for top line
4980 RETURN
4990 '
5000 'Delete customer
5010 '
5020 IF DRN=0 THEN RETURN          'Customer not in file yet
5030 GOSUB 6900                    'Delete customer from data file
5040 IF ONMK$=SPACE$(KL(1)) THEN 5070
5050    LKN=1:OKV$=ONMK$:OKP=DRN
5060    GOSUB 8090                 'Delete name key
5070 IF OZK$=SPACE$(KL(1)) THEN 5100
5080    LKN=2:OKV$=OZK$:OKP=DRN
5090    GOSUB 8090                 'Delete zip key
5100 RETURN
5110 '
5120 'Save customer
5130 '
5140 ATTRIB=0
5150 FOR FLD=13 TO 6 STEP -1       'Convert fields 6 thru 13 to bit map
5160    ATTRIB=ATTRIB*2            'Left shift one bit position
5170    IF F$(FLD)="Y" THEN ATTRIB=(ATTRIB OR 1)         'Set bit = 1 for "Y"
5180 NEXT FLD
5190 LSET ATTRIB$=CHR$(ATTRIB)
5200 IF DRN=0 THEN LDN=1:GOSUB 6710      'Get a new record if new customer
5210 PUT DFN(1),DRN
5220 OKP=DRN:NKP=DRN    'Set Old and New Key Pointers for next two GOSUBs
5230 LKN=1:OKV$=ONMK$:NKV$=LEFT$(F$(NMKF),KL(1))         'Set new name key
```

```
5240 IF OKV$<>NKV$ THEN GOSUB 5310                        'Save name key
5250 LKN=2:OKV$=OZK$:NKV$=LEFT$(F$(ZIPKF),KL(2))          'Set new zip key
5260 IF OKV$<>NKV$ THEN GOSUB 5310                        'Save zip key
5270 RETURN
5280 '
5290 'Save key
5300 '
5310 IF OKV$=SPACE$(KL(LKN)) THEN SEL=0 ELSE SEL=1
5320 IF NKV$<>SPACE$(KL(LKN)) THEN SEL=SEL+2
5330 ON SEL GOSUB 8090,8260,7870        'Delete, Insert, or Update key
5340 RETURN
5350 '
5360 'Bracket input
5370 '    Input:
5380 '       A$  = String to input (Length set)
5390 '       L,C = Line and column form input.  (L=0 for current position)
5400 '       CC$ = Cursor command characters
5410 '       RC$ = Return characters
5420 '       RC() = Return codes (one for each char. in RC$)
5430 '
5440 '    Output:
5450 '       A$ = New input is same length.
5460 '       RC = Return code specified in RC() array.
5470 '
5480 SL=LEN(A$):I=1
5490 IF L>0 THEN PRINT FNCP$(L,C);                  'Position cursor for input
5500 PRINT "[";A$;"]";STRING$(SL+1,BS$);            'Print string for input
5510 CH$=INPUT$(1)                                  'Get one char. of input
5520 ON INSTR(CC$,CH$) GOTO 5610,5630,5650,5680 'Search for cursor control
5530 IF INSTR(RC$,CH$) > 0 THEN 5580               'Search for return code
5540    IF CH$<" " THEN PRINT BELL$;:GOTO 5510     'No control chars.
5550    MID$(A$,I,1)=CH$:PRINT CH$;                'Char to A$ and screen
5560    IF I<LEN(A$) THEN I=I+1 ELSE PRINT BS$; 'Check bounds
5570 GOTO 5510
5580    RC = RC(INSTR(RC$,CH$))                    'Get return code
5590    PRINT CHR$(13);                            'Show some response
5600 RETURN
5610    IF I>1 THEN I=I-1:PRINT BS$;               'Backspace char. trap
5620 GOTO 5510
5630    IF I<LEN(A$) THEN PRINT MID$(A$,I,1);:I=I+1      'Right character
5640 GOTO 5510
5650    MID$(A$,I)=MID$(A$,I+1)+" "                'Delete char. trap
5660    PRINT MID$(A$,I);STRING$(SL-I+1,BS$);
5670 GOTO 5510
5680    MID$(A$,I)=" "+MID$(A$,I)                  'Insert character
5690    PRINT MID$(A$,I);STRING$(SL-I+1,BS$);
5700 GOTO 5510
```

All that is necessary to change the number of fields in the records is to change the data in line 1110. This line must reflect the number of fields you added or deleted. In addition, if you change the order of the fields, you will have to change the values of **NMKF** ("name key field") and **ZIPKF** ("ZIP code key field") in line 1460. You can change the three constants **NKF** ("number of key files"), **NDF** ("number of data files"), and **MRL** ("maximum record length") if you modify the program.

The number of customer attributes may be reduced or enlarged, and, of course, the attributes themselves may be changed by changing the program data section. As many as 15 attributes can be handled without much modification. If more than eight attributes are used, the **ATTRIB$** field will have to be two bytes in length. You will also need to change the CHR$-ASC conversions to MKI$-CVI conversions whenever **ATTRIB$** appears. Figure 21-2 shows the screen mask used with this program.

Program Analysis

The first section of the program (lines 1110 through 1180) contains all the data for the placement of the brackets. It also designates the field titles for each set of brackets.

Just as with the menu driver, the next section, lines 1260 through 1690, initializes the variables that are used exclusively in this program. There is only one new user-defined function in this program. Line 1300 contains the function **FNCES$**, or "clear to end of screen." This function clears the screen from line **L** through line 24. Line 1470 takes care of initializing the keyed-file system section of the program.

```
                    — Mail List Editor —
 1) Customer name     [                    ]
 2) Title             [                 ]
 3) Address line 1    [                    ]
 4) Address line 2    [                    ]
 5) ZIP code          [     ]
Customer attributes (Y/N):
  6) Credit     [ ]   7) Check card [ ]   8) Cash only [ ]
  9) Employee   [ ]  10) Courtesy   [ ]  11) Products  [ ]
 12) Services   [ ]  13) Time       [ ]
Field number to edit, delete, save, or exit without saving (#/D/S/E)? [ ]
```

Figure 21-2.
Screen mask for Mailing List editing

The main program controls the transfers to the subroutines for the implementation of the various tasks required by the program. Notice that line 3090 strips the name of this program from the **PLNK$** string when returning to the menu.

SUBROUTINES

Many of the subroutines in this program are essentially those in the Payroll menu in Chapter 20.

First of all, the subroutine in lines 4100 through 4150 determines which files are open and then closes them and returns to the main program. Lines 4170 through 4560 constitute the subroutine that carries out the hit select that was briefly described earlier in this chapter. The subroutine matches all names in the file that begin with your entry. The Print subroutine of this section (lines 4430 through 4560) prints the names that were found by the hit select subroutine.

The subroutine in lines 5000 through 5100 deletes a current customer from the file. Note that the file system routines are used to delete both the data record and the two associated keys. Deleted records are reused when new customers are added.

The subroutine in lines 5110 through 5340 writes the data for a new or existing customer to the files. If the customer already exists in the file, the new data is written back to the file. If the customer is new, the file system is called to return a new record number. Deleted records are used before the data file is expanded in length through the addition of a new record. The name and ZIP keys may also be added to or updated by the file system. Lines 5290 through 5340 save new or updated customer data. They determine which of four possible actions needs to be taken in regard to a given key: do nothing, delete the old key, insert a new key, or update the current key.

Mailing List Print Program

The Mailing List Print program (MLPRINT.BAS) prints the mailing labels from the data maintained by the program MLEDIT.BAS. As usual, we will go through the programs by modules, but this time we will look only at those lines that must be changed when the program is modified. We will also briefly examine modules that are new to this program. Much of this program is similar to the Mailing List Editor.

```
1 GOTO 10
2 SAVE "MLPRINT":END
4 SAVE "MLPRINT",A:END
6 SAVE "MLPRINT":RUN "INIT"
10 REM =-                    -=*MLPRINT*=-
20 REM =-                    Mail List Label Printer
30 REM =-                    Ver 1.0  06/11/83
40 REM =-
50 COMMON CLI$,CS$,HC$,SF$,SB$,CL$,BS$,BELL$,FF$,CC$,PLNK$,MLNK$,DATE$,DR$
1000 '
1010 '                       ****************************
1020 '                       *       PROGRAM DATA       *
1030 '                       ****************************
1040 '
1050 DATA 7,1,10,"Prefered",7,15,30,"Pays cash"
1060 DATA 7,35,48,"Deadbeat",7,53,69,"Sap"
1070 DATA 8,1,10,"Human",8,15,30,"Cro-Magnon"
1080 DATA 8,35,48,"I-Magnin",8,53,69,"Neanderthal"
1090 '
1100 '                       ************************************
1110 '                       *      PROGRAM INITIALIZATION      *
1120 '                       ************************************
1130 '
1140 'Define functions
1150 '
1160 DEFINT A-Z
1170 ON ERROR GOTO 4070
1180 DEF FNCP$(L,C)=CLI$+CHR$(L+31)+CHR$(C+31)
1190 DEF FNCE$(L,M$)=FNCP$(L,(80-LEN(M$))\2)+M$
1200 DEF FNMS$(M$)=HC$+CL$+SPACE$((80-LEN(M$))\2)+SF$+M$+SB$
1210 DEF FNBKT$(L,C,M$)=FNCP$(L,C)+"["+M$+"]"
1220 DEF FNSTOPPRT = (INSTR(" Xx",INKEY$) > 1)
1230 '
1240 'Initialize variables and open files
1250 '
1260 PRINT CS$;FNCE$(3,"- M A I L   L I S T   L A B E L   P R I N T E R -")
1270 PRINT FNMS$("ONE MOMENT PLEASE...."):PRINT
1280 RC$=CHR$(13)+CHR$(11)+CHR$(27)             '3 Return characters
1290 DIM RC(3):RC(1)=1:RC(2)=-1:RC(3)=999       '3 Return codes
1300 DIM FL(8),FC(8),F$(8)        'Dimension to 8 attributes
1310 ACROSS = 2                   'Number of labels across
1320 VERTICAL = 6                 'Line spacing from top to top of labels
1330 DIM COL(ACROSS)              'Set up tab locations for each label
1340 FOR I = 1 TO ACROSS
1350    COL(I) = (I-1)*35 + 5     'Initialize column positions for labels
1360 NEXT I
1370 NKF=1:NDF=1:MRL=105:GOSUB 6250     'Initialize the file system
1380 '
1390 '                    Zip key file
1400 LKN=1:KFNM$=DR$+"ZIP.KEY":KL(1)=5
1410 GOSUB 7300           'Open zip key file
1420 '
```

```
1430 '                    Mail list data
1440 LDN=1:DFNM$=DR$+"ML.DAT":RL(1)=105
1450 GOSUB 6450           'Open link list data file
1460 FIELD DFN(LDN),25 AS CNM$,25 AS CTTL$,25 AS ADR1$,
                   20 AS ADR2$,9 AS ZIP$,1 AS ATRIB$
1470 '
1480 PRINT FNCP$(5,1);"Print customers with any of the attributes marked Y"
1490 FOR FLD = 1 TO 8
1500    READ FL(FLD),FDC,FC(FLD),FD$
1510    PRINT FNCP$(FL(FLD),FDC);FD$      'Print screen mask
1520    F$(FLD) = " "                     'Initialize attribute fields
1530    PRINT FNBKT$(FL(FLD),FC(FLD),F$(FLD))
1540 NEXT FLD
3000 '
3010 '                    ***************************
3020 '                    *       MAIN PROGRAM      *
3030 '                    ***************************
3040 '
3050 PRINT FNMS$("SPECIFY (Y)ES OR (N)O")
3060 GOSUB 4320                 'Edit attributes to be printed
3070 IF RC = -1 THEN 3430       'Exit program
3080 IF ATRIB>0 THEN 3110
3090    PRINT FNMS$("YOU MUST HAVE AT LEAST ONE ATTRIBUTE MARKED AS [Y]")
3100    GOTO 3060
3110 PRINT FNMS$("SELECT OPTION")
3120 PRINT FNCP$(24,1);
3130 PRINT "(A)lignment mask, (E)dit attributes or (P)rint labels (A/E/P)? ";
3140 L=0:A$=" ":GOSUB 4770      'Field input A$
3150 IF RC = -1 THEN A$="E"     'Backup treated same as (E)dit attributes
3160 IF A$ = "E" THEN GOTO 3050                'Edit fields
3170 IF A$ = "A" THEN GOSUB 4180:GOTO 3120     'Print alignment mask
3180 IF A$ <> "P" THEN PRINT FNMS$("INVALID SELECTION"):GOTO 3120
3190 '
3200 PRINT FNCP$(24,1);CL$;FNMS$("PRINTING LABELS, PRESS 'X' TO STOP PRINT")
3210 LKN=1:GOSUB 8520    'Get first zip key (FKP is returned)
3220 ABORT = 0
3230 WHILE FKP <> 0 AND NOT ABORT
3240    COUNT = 0
3250    WHILE COUNT < ACROSS AND FKP <> 0          'FKP = 0 at end of key file
3260       GET DFN(LDN),FKP
3270       IF (ATRIB AND ASC(ATRIB$)) = 0 THEN 3360
3280          COUNT = COUNT + 1
3290          LBL$(1,COUNT) = CNM$
3300          IF CTTL$=SPACE$(LEN(CTTL$)) THEN 3330      'Check if no title
3310             OFSET = 1:LBL$(2,COUNT) = CTTL$
3320          GOTO 3340
3330             OFSET = 0:LBL$(4,COUNT)=""
3340          LBL$(2+OFSET,COUNT) = ADR1$
3350          LBL$(3+OFSET,COUNT) = ADR2$+" "+ZIP$
3360       LKN=1:GOSUB 8670     'Get next key (FKP is returned)
3370    WEND
3380    GOSUB 4470              'Print labels across
```

```
3390    IF FNSTOPPRT THEN GOSUB 4580    'Stop print or continue?
3400 WEND
3410 IF ABORT THEN 3110
3420 '
3430 PRINT FNMS$("EXITING")
3440 GOSUB 4120                 'Close files
3450 PLNK$=MID$(PLNK$,13)       'Strip of program name
3460 CHAIN LEFT$(PLNK$,12)      'Return to chaining program
4000 '
4010 '                    **************************
4020 '                    *      SUBROUTINES       *
4030 '                    **************************
4040 '
4050 'Error trapping
4060 '
4070 GOSUB 4120         'Close files
4080 CHAIN "ERROR",,ALL
4090 '
4100 'Close files
4110 '
4120 IF KFN(1)>0 THEN LKN=1:GOSUB 8800  'Close zip key file
4130 IF DFN(1)>0 THEN LDN=1:GOSUB 7100  'Close mail list data file
4140 RETURN
4150 '
4160 'Print alignment mask
4170 '
4180 ZZ$ = STRING$(25,".")                  'Use dots for alignment
4190 LSET CNM$ = "NAME"+ZZ$:LSET CTTL$ = "TITLE"+ZZ$
4200 LSET ADR1$ = "ADDRESS 1"+ZZ$:LSET ADR2$ = "ADDRESS 2"+ZZ$
4210 LSET ZIP$ = "ZIP"+ZZ$
4220 COUNT = ACROSS
4230 FOR I = 1 TO COUNT
4240   LBL$(1,I) = CNM$:LBL$(2,I) = CTTL$
4250   LBL$(3,I) = ADR1$:LBL$(4,I) = ADR2$+" "+ZIP$
4260 NEXT I
4270 GOSUB 4470         'Print labels across
4280 RETURN
4290 '
4300 'Edit fields
4310 '
4320 FLD = 1
4330 WHILE FLD>=1 AND FLD<=8
4340    L=FL(FLD):C=FC(FLD)     'Get line and column for input
4350    A$=F$(FLD):GOSUB 4770:LSET F$(FLD)=A$   'Input F$(FLD)
4360    FLD=FLD+RC       'Return code determines next field to edit
4370 WEND
4380 ATRIB = 0
4390 FOR FLD=8 TO 1 STEP -1
4400    ATRIB = ATRIB*2                         'Shift bits left
4410    IF F$(FLD)="Y" THEN ATRIB=(ATRIB OR 1)  'Bit = 1 for "Y", 0 otherwise
4420 NEXT FLD
4430 RETURN
```

```
4440 '
4450 'Print labels across
4460 '
4470 FOR I = 1 TO 4
4480    FOR J = 1 TO COUNT
4490       LPRINT TAB(COL(J));LBL$(I,J);
4500    NEXT J
4510    LPRINT
4520 NEXT I
4530 LPRINT STRING$(VERTICAL-5,10)      'Line feed down to next label
4540 RETURN
4550 '
4560 'Stop print or continue?
4570 '
4580 PRINT FNCP$(24,1);"(S)top print or (C)ontinue (S/C)? ";
4590 L=0:A$=" ":GOSUB 4770       'Input A$
4600 IF RC = -1 THEN A$="S"      'Backup treated same as Stop
4610 IF A$ = " " THEN 4580
4620 ABORT = (A$="S")            'Set abort flag true or false
4630 RETURN
4640 '
4650 'Bracket input
4660 '   Input:
4670 '      A$  = String to input (Length set)
4680 '      L,C = Line and column form input.  (L=0 for current position)
4690 '      CC$ = Cursor command characters
4700 '      RC$ = Return characters
4710 '      RC() = Return codes (one for each char. in RC$)
4720 '
4730 '   Output:
4740 '      A$ = New input is same length.
4750 '      RC = Return code specified in RC() array.
4760 '
4770 SL=LEN(A$):I=1
4780 IF L>0 THEN PRINT FNCP$(L,C);                'Position cursor for input
4790 PRINT "[";A$;"]";STRING$(SL+1,BS$);          'Print string for input
4800 CH$=INPUT$(1)                                'Get one char. of input
4810 ON INSTR(CC$,CH$) GOTO 4900,4920,4940,4970 'Search for cursor control
4820 IF INSTR(RC$,CH$) > 0 THEN 4870              'Search for return code
4830    IF CH$<" " THEN PRINT BELL$;:GOTO 4800    'No control chars.
4840    MID$(A$,I,1)=CH$:PRINT CH$;               'Char to A$ and screen
4850    IF I<LEN(A$) THEN I=I+1 ELSE PRINT BS$;  'Check bounds
4860 GOTO 4800
4870    RC = RC(INSTR(RC$,CH$))                   'Get return code
4880    PRINT CHR$(13);                           'Show some responce
4890 RETURN
4900    IF I>1 THEN I=I-1:PRINT BS$;              'Backspace char. trap
4910 GOTO 4800
4920    IF I<LEN(A$) THEN PRINT MID$(A$,I,1);:I=I+1     'Right character
4930 GOTO 4800
4940    MID$(A$,I)=MID$(A$,I+1)+" "               'Delete char. trap
4950    PRINT MID$(A$,I);STRING$(SL-I+1,BS$);
```

```
4960 GOTO 4800
4970     MID$(A$,I)=" "+MID$(A$,I)                    'Insert character
4980     PRINT MID$(A$,I);STRING$(SL-I+1,BS$);
4990 GOTO 4800
```

In order to change the mailing label spacing requirements to fit your own label format, you only need to change **ACROSS** in line 1310 and **VERTICAL** in line 1320. The FOR/NEXT loop in lines 1340 through 1360 assigns the tab locations for the horizontal spacing.

The WHILE/WEND loop in lines 3220 through 3390 sets up the array in preparation for printing the labels. Lines 3290 through 3350 set up three address lines instead of four if no title or company name is contained in a customer's record.

As in the Payroll program, it is worthwhile to print an alignment mask to verify that the printer output has the correct format. This subroutine prints one row of labels to allow you to adjust your printer accordingly.

Finally, the subroutine in lines 4450 through 4540 does the actual printing. The values for all variables are assigned in the main program. Lines 4560 through 4630 interrupt the printing when either the capital or lowercase **X** key is pressed. The variable **ABORT** is then set to **TRUE** if you choose to stop printing. This causes the WHILE/WEND loop of the main program to terminate.

Key File System

This section, lines 6000 through 8840, contains the file subroutines for both the MLEDIT.BAS and MLPRINT.BAS programs. It must be appended to each of the programs with the exact line numbers shown.

The comment lines at the beginning of each subroutine describe the input and output parameters for that particular subroutine. The remaining portion of each subroutine is also explained with the extensive use of remark statements. Those of you who wish to use these subroutines for your own applications will have to pay close attention to the input and output parameters for each of the subroutines.

Our purpose here is to give you a ready-made tool to use in an existing program, not to have you write a program using key files. Here is the listing of the file system subroutines:

```
6000 '
6010 'Set up data file and key file variables
6020 '   Input:
6030 '      NDF = Number of data files to be used.
6040 '      NKF = Number of key files to be used.
6050 '      MRL = Maximum record length for data files.
6060 '   Output (Following variables are dimensioned):
6070 '      DFN(NDF) = Data File Numbers.
6080 '      RL(NDF)  = Record length for data files.
6090 '      R$(NDF)  = Fielded as entire data file Record.
6100 '      FS$(NDF) = Header field for File Status.
6110 '      DS$(NDF) & DS(NDF) = Header field for Deleted record Stack.
6120 '      LR$(NDF) & LR(NDF) = Header field for Last Record in file.
6130 '      NU$(NDF) & NU(NDF) = Header field for Number of Used records.
6140 '
6150 '      KFN(NKF) = Key File Numbers.
6160 '      KL(NKF)  = Key length
6170 '      KR$(NKF) = Fielded as entire key file Record.
6180 '      NK$(NKF) & NK(NKF) = Header field for Number of keys in file.
6190 '      KV$(NKF) = Fielded as Key Value.
6200 '      KP$(NKF) = Fielded as Key Pointer.
6210 '
6220 '      FIN = File number counter (Initialized at 1)
6230 '      TB$ = Temporary storage buffer (length set to MRL)
6240 '
6250 DIM DFN(NDF),RL(NDF),R$(NDF),FS$(NDF),DS$(NDF),DS(NDF)
6260 DIM LR$(NDF),LR(NDF),NU$(NDF),NU(NDF)
6270 DIM KFN(NKF),KL(NKF),KR$(NKF),NK$(NKF),NK(NKF),KV$(NKF),KP$(NKF)
6280 FIN=1:TB$=SPACE$(MRL)
6290 RETURN
6300 '
6310 'Open data file (field buffer contents are lost)
6320 '   Input:
6330 '      LDN     = Logical Data file Number 1 <= LDN <= NDF
6340 '      DFNM$   = File name
6350 '      RL(LDN) = Record length 7 <= RL(LDN) <= MRL
6360 '   Output:
6370 '      ERROR 200 if file was not closed properly.
6380 '      DS(LDN) = Top of Deleted record Stack.
6390 '      LR(LDN) = Last Record number in file.
6400 '      NU(LDN) = Number of Used (not deleted) records
6410 '
6420 '   DS(LDN), LR(LDN), and NU(LDN) are updated by each of the
6430 '      data file subroutines.
6440 '
6450 DFN(LDN)=FIN:FIN=FIN+1                'Assign a data file number
6460 OPEN "R",DFN(LDN),DFNM$,RL(LDN)      'Open file
6470 FIELD DFN(LDN),1 AS FS$(LDN),2 AS DS$(LDN),2 AS LR$(LDN),2 AS NU$(LDN)
```

```
6480 FIELD DFN(LDN),RL(LDN) AS R$(LDN)   'R$ is the whole field buffer
6490 IF LOF(DFN(LDN))=0 THEN 6520         'Check if file is new
6500    GET DFN(LDN),1                    'Get header record of old file
6510 GOTO 6560
6520    LSET FS$(LDN)="C"           'Set new file as closed properly
6530    LSET LR$(LDN)=MKI$(1)       'New file, initialize header record
6540    LSET DS$(LDN)=MKI$(0)       'Set Deleted record Stack (0=none)
6550    LSET NU$(LDN)=MKI$(0)       'Set # records in use to 0
6560 LR(LDN)=CVI(LR$(LDN))          'Get Last Record for program use
6570 DS(LDN)=CVI(DS$(LDN))          'Get record from Deleted Stack.
6580 NU(LDN)=CVI(NU$(LDN))          'Get Number Used data records
6590 IF FS$(LDN)<>"C" THEN ERROR 200     'Make sure file was (C)losed
6600 LSET FS$(LDN)="O"              'Set file to (O)pen mode
6610 PUT DFN(LDN),1                 'Write header record
6620 RETURN
6630 '
6640 'Get a new record returned in DRN (field buffer saved)
6650 '   Input:
6660 '      LDN = Logical Data file Number
6670 '   Output:
6680 '      ERROR 201 if new record is already in use.
6690 '      DRN = New record number for use
6700 '
6710 IF DS(LDN)=0 THEN 6790         'Check if any delete records to use
6720    LSET TB$=R$(LDN)            'Save buffer
6730    GET DFN(LDN),DS(LDN)        'Read delete record
6740    IF FS$(LDN)<>CHR$(255) THEN ERROR 201    'Check deleted flag
6750    DRN=DS(LDN)                 'New record number goes in DRN
6760    DS(LDN)=CVI(DS$(LDN))       'Get new DR from link in record
6770    LSET R$(LDN)=TB$            'Restore buffer
6780 GOTO 6810
6790    LR(LDN)=LR(LDN)+1           'No records for re-use, add on to the end
6800    DRN=LR(LDN)
6810 NU(LDN)=NU(LDN)+1              'Increment # of utilized records
6820 RETURN
6830 '
6840 'Delete a record number (field buffer saved)
6850 '   Input:
6860 '      DRN = Record number to delete
6870 '   Output:
6880 '      ERROR 202 if record DRN is already deleted
6890 '
6900 IF DRN=LR(LDN) THEN 7000       'Check if deleting last record
6910    LSET TB$=R$(LDN)            'Save file buffer
6920    GET DFN(LDN),DRN            'Get record to delete
6930    IF FS$(LDN)=CHR$(255) THEN ERROR 202    'Check if already deleted
6940    LSET FS$(LDN)=CHR$(255) 'Flag record as deleted
6950    LSET DS$(LDN)=MKI$(DS(LDN))      'Store deleted record number link
6960    PUT DFN(LDN),DRN                 'Delete record
6970    DS(LDN)=DRN                 'Set DR = last delete record
6980    LSET R$(LDN)=TB$            'Restore file buffer
6990 GOTO 7010
```

```
7000    LR(LDN)=LR(LDN)-1          'Delete last record in file
7010 NU(LDN)=NU(LDN)-1             'Decrement # of utilized records
7020 RETURN
7030 '
7040 'Close data file (field buffer lost)
7050 '   Input:
7060 '      LDN = Logical Data file Number to close.
7070 '   Ouput:
7080 '      DS$(LDN), LR$(LDN), and NU$(LDN) are written to header record
7090 '
7100 LSET FS$(LDN)="C"                   'Set file status as (C)losed
7110 LSET DS$(LDN)=MKI$(DS(LDN))         'Set top of delete record stack
7120 LSET LR$(LDN)=MKI$(LR(LDN))         'Set last record in use
7130 LSET NU$(LDN)=MKI$(NU(LDN))         'Set number of utilized records
7140 PUT DFN(LDN),1                      'Write out header record
7150 CLOSE DFN(LDN)
7160 RETURN
7170 '
7180 'Open key file
7190 '   Input:
7200 '      LKN     = Logical key file number to open.
7210 '      KFNM$   = Data File Name
7220 '      KL(LKN) = Key length.  KL(LKN) >= 3
7230 '   Output:
7240 '      ERROR 203 if file was not closed properly.
7250 '      NK(LKN) = Number of Keys in file.
7260 '      KRN     = Internal key record pointer initialized
7270 '
7280 '   NK(LKN) is updated by each of the key file subroutines.
7290 '
7300 KFN(LKN)=FIN:FIN=FIN+1              'Assign a key file number
7310 OPEN "R",KFN(LKN),KFNM$,KL(LKN)+2   'Open file (+2 is for key pointer)
7320 FIELD KFN(LKN),1 AS KFS$(LKN),2 AS NK$(LKN)          'Header record
7330 FIELD KFN(LKN),KL(LKN) AS KV$(LKN),2 AS KP$(LKN)     'Key and key pointer.
7340 FIELD KFN(LKN),KL(LKN)+2 AS KR$(LKN)                 'KR$ is entire record.
7350 IF LOF(KFN(LKN))=0 THEN 7380                'Check if file is new
7360    GET KFN(LKN),1                           'Get header record of old file
7370 GOTO 7400
7380    LSET KFS$(LKN)="C"          'Set new file as closed properly
7390    LSET NK$(LKN)=MKI$(0)       'New file, set No. Keys to 0
7400 NK(LKN)=CVI(NK$(LKN))          'Get Number of Keys for program use
7410 IF KFS$(LKN)<>"C" THEN ERROR 203   'Make sure file was (C)losed
7420 LSET KFS$(LKN)="O"             'Set file to (O)pen mode
7430 PUT KFN(LKN),1                 'Write header record
7440 LSET KV$(LKN)="":LSET KP$(LKN)=MKI$(0):KRN=0       'Initialize key fields
7450 RETURN
7460 '
7470 'Search for a key
7480 '   Input:
7490 '      LKN  = Logical Key file Number to search.
7500 '      SKV$ = Search Key Value.
```

```
7510 '       SKP  = Search Key Pointer.
7520 '    Output:
7530 '       FKV$ = Found Key Value (blank if not found).
7540 '       FKP  = Found Key Pointer (zero if not found).
7550 '       KRN  = Current key Record Number points to key found or
7560 '              points to where key should be if it is not found.
7570 '
7580 SKR$=SKV$+MKI$(SKP)                      'Search on key value + key pointer
7590 LSET KV$(LKN)="":LSET KP$(LKN)=MKI$(0)
7600 LB=2:HB=NK(LKN)+1:FKP=0                  'Set binary search bounds
7610 WHILE LB<=HB AND FKP=0                   'Binary search the key file for SKR$
7620    KRN=(LB+HB)\2
7630    GET KFN(LKN),KRN
7640    IF SKR$=KR$(LKN) THEN FKP=KRN
7650    IF SKR$<KR$(LKN) THEN HB=KRN-1 ELSE LB=KRN+1
7660 WEND
7670 IF SKR$<=KR$(LKN) THEN 7730           'If no exact match we must point to
7680    KRN=KRN+1                          'the smallest key greater than SKR$
7690    IF KRN>NK(LKN)+1 THEN 7720         'Check if SKR$ greater than all keys
7700       GET KFN(LKN),KRN
7710    GOTO 7730
7720       LSET KV$(LKN)="":LSET KP$(LKN)=MKI$(0) 'Search found end of file
7730 FKV$=KV$(LKN):FKP=CVI(KP$(LKN))     'Set returned variables
7740 RETURN
7750 '
7760 'Update key and pointer
7770 '    Input:
7780 '       LKN  = Logical key file Number to update.
7790 '       OKV$ = Old Key Value to be updated.
7800 '       OKP  = Old Key Pointer to be updated.
7810 '       NKV$ = New key Value after update.
7820 '       NKP  = New Key Pointer after update.
7830 '    Output:
7840 '       ERROR 204 if key to update was not found in key file.
7850 '       KRN will point to the updated key.
7860 '
7870 OKR$=OKV$+MKI$(OKP):NKR$=NKV$+MKI$(NKP)     'Construct key records
7880 SKV$=OKV$:SKP=OKP:GOSUB 7500                'Search for old key
7890 IF OKR$<>KR$(LKN) THEN ERROR 204            'Error if Old key not found.
7900 IF OKR$>NKR$ THEN DIR=-1 ELSE DIR=1         'Set direction for WHILE loop
7910 GET KFN(LKN),KRN+DIR                        'Slide a block of keys over
7920 WHILE KRN+DIR>1 AND KRN+DIR<NK(LKN)+2 AND (KR$(LKN)>NKR$ XOR DIR>0)
7930    PUT KFN(LKN),KRN
7940    KRN=KRN+DIR:GET KFN(LKN),KRN+DIR
7950 WEND
7960 LSET KR$(LKN)=NKR$          'Write new key
7970 PUT KFN(LKN),KRN
7980 RETURN
7990 '
8000 'Delete key
8010 '    Input:
```

```
8020 '       LKN  = Logical Key file Number.
8030 '       OKV$ = Old Key Value to delete.
8040 '       OKP  = Old Key Pointer to delete.
8050 '    Output:
8060 '       ERROR 205 if key to delete was not found in key file.
8070 '       KRN = Will point one past end of key file.
8080 '
8090 SKV$=OKV$:SKP=OKP
8100 GOSUB 7580           'Search for old key
8110 IF OKV$<>FKV$ OR OKP<>FKP THEN ERROR 205   'Error if Old key not found.
8120 FRN=KRN:LRN=NK(LKN):DIR=1             'DIR is direction to move block.
8130 GOSUB 8380           'Move block left one position
8140 NK(LKN)=NK(LKN)-1   'One less key in key file
8150 RETURN
8160 '
8170 'Insert key
8180 '    Input:
8190 '       LKN  = Logical Key file Number.
8200 '       NKV$ = New Key Value to insert.
8210 '       NKP  = New Key Pointer to insert.
8220 '    Output:
8230 '       ERROR 206 if key and pointer already exist in key file.
8240 '       KRN = Will point to the inserted key.
8250 '
8260 SKV$=NKV$:SKP=NKP
8270 GOSUB 7580           'Search for old key
8280 IF KV$(LKN)=SKV$ AND CVI(KP$(LKN))=SKP THEN ERROR 206
8290 FRN=NK(LKN)+2:LRN=KRN+1:DIR=-1      'DIR is direction to move block
8300 GOSUB 8380           'Move block right one position
8310 LSET KV$(LKN)=NKV$:LSET KP$(LKN)=MKI$(NKP)
8320 PUT KFN(LKN),KRN   'Write out new key
8330 NK(LKN)=NK(LKN)+1  'One more key in key file
8340 RETURN
8350 '
8360 'Move block (used by delete and insert only)
8370 '
8380 FOR KRN=FRN TO LRN STEP DIR
8390    GET KFN(LKN),KRN+DIR
8400    PUT KFN(LKN),KRN
8410 NEXT KRN
8420 RETURN
8430 '
8440 'Get first key
8450 '    Input:
8460 '       LKN = Logical Key file Number.
8470 '    Output:
8480 '       FKV$ = Found Key Value of first key in file (blank if no keys).
8490 '       FKP  = Found Key Pointer of first key in file (0 if no keys).
8500 '       KRN  = Points to first key (if any).
8510 '
8520 IF NK(LKN)=0 THEN 8550                'Check for no keys in file
8530    KRN=2:GET KFN(LKN),KRN
```

```
8540 GOTO 8560
8550    LSET KV$(LKN)="":LSET KP$(LKN)=MKI$(0)  'First key is end of key file
8560 FKV$=KV$(LKN):FKP=CVI(KP$(LKN))
8570 RETURN
8580 '
8590 'Get next key
8600 '    Input:
8610 '       LKN = Logical Key file Number.
8620 '    Output:
8630 '       FKV$ = Found Key Value of next key in file (blank if no more keys)
8640 '       FKP  = Found Key Pointer of next key in file (0 if no more keys)
8650 '       KRN  = Points to next key (if any)
8660 '
8670 IF KRN>NK(LKN)+1 THEN 8700          'Check if for end of key file
8680    KRN=KRN+1:GET KFN(LKN),KRN
8690 GOTO 8710
8700    LSET KV$(LKN)="":LSET KP$(LKN)=MKI$(0)  'Next key is end of key file
8710 FKV$=KV$(LKN):FKP=CVI(KP$(LKN))
8720 RETURN
8730 '
8740 'Close key file
8750 '    Input:
8760 '       LKN = Logical Key file Number to close.
8770 '    Output:
8780 '       Key file status and size are written to header record
8790 '
8800 LSET KFS$(LKN)="C"                 'Set file status as (C)losed
8810 LSET NK$(LKN)=MKI$(NK(LKN))        'Set last delete record
8820 PUT KFN(LKN),1                     'Write out header record
8830 CLOSE KFN(LKN)
8840 RETURN
```

22

User Documentation

When the term "documentation" has been used in this book up to this point, it has always meant the comments the programmer makes in describing the purpose of a single line or section of code in a program. MBASIC requires that these comments be prefaced by the REM statement or its abbreviation, the single quotation mark ('). This type of documentation is intended for a programmer—that is, either for the one who wrote the program or for another programmer who may have to modify the program.

Another equally important type of documentation is that intended for the program user. More often than not, users of programs have little or no interest in how or why a program works. To users, the program is only a tool for getting results.

Imagine that you have finished your first program intended for use by someone else. You have spent hours entering every possible combination of data, and you have done the systematic debugging so that the last bug has been eradicated. Now you are ready to write the user documentation.

The first step is to think of your audience, the person who will use the program. Normally, this will not be another programmer or technical person familiar with computer terminology. Unless you know the specific audience, you should assume no background in computers on the part of your audience when you write your documentation.

Documentation varies depending on the complexity of the program, but in all cases, it will have at least three parts: first, an introduction giving an overview explaining what the program does and what results to expect; second, an explanation of how to use the program, including how to load, start, and end the program; and third, examples of the screen and program output.

To illustrate how you might go about writing these three parts, we will write the user documentation for the inventory program from Tutorial 15-1.

Introduction

INVENTRY.BAS is a program that allows you to maintain an inventory. This program allows you to do six things: first, to inspect the information on an existing item; second, to enter new items; third, to edit data on an existing item; fourth, to record a sales transaction; fifth, to enter information on a purchase transaction; and sixth, to list all items below a set reorder level.

The items in the inventory are stored in a disk file. The number of items that the program can handle is therefore limited to 32,768 parts or by the storage capacity of your disk system. For each item in the file, there are five types of information stored. They are item number, item description, quantity on hand, reorder level, and unit purchase price.

Item numbers for each item are automatically entered by the computer. Each time a new item is added to the inventory list, the computer assigns that item the next available item number. The description field allows you to enter up to 30 characters. For example, if you are entering ribbons for an NEC printer, you might enter **RIBBONS, NEC-3500, 6/BOX** for the description. The next two fields, quantity on hand and reorder level, may contain any integer up to 999999. The final field is price per unit; it may contain any number up to 9999.99 but may not contain a dollar sign. None of the fields that contain numbers may contain a comma.

All screens show both the computer's messages (normal print) and your input (shaded print).

Loading the Inventory Program

In order to run INVENTRY.BAS, place the disk containing MBASIC in drive A and the disk containing INVENTRY.BAS in drive B. Log onto drive B and type

```
A:MBASIC INVENTRY
```

Program Operation

As soon as MBASIC and the program have been loaded, the program automatically starts and presents you with the menu shown in Figure 22-1. Each time the program is run, the number of items in the file is indicated above the menu.

In order to make your selection from the menu, enter the number you wish and press RETURN.

Now let's consider each selection in order.

SELECTION 1—QUERY AN EXISTING ITEM

When you choose selection 1 from the menu, you are first asked to enter the item number. When you enter the item number and press RETURN, the screen displays the following:

```
Enter part number to query: 2

Part number 2     Description: Z-19
Quantity on hand: 5
Reorder level: 3
Price per unit: 696.5

Press <RETURN> to continue...
```

The information stays on the screen until you press RETURN to continue. Pressing RETURN returns you to the menu.

SELECTION 2—ENTER A NEW ITEM

Choosing selection 2 will first display on the screen the next item number to be entered. The word "Description" will be followed by the message **New Item**, and the cursor will appear after the colon to indicate that you should enter a description of this new item. After entering the description, press RETURN. The next question will be

```
There are 8 parts on file.
Choose one of the following functions:
    1 ... Query an existing part
    2 ... Enter a new part
    3 ... Edit an existing part
    4 ... Sales transaction
    5 ... Purchase transaction
    6 ... List parts below reorder level
    7 ... End program/close file
Selection number:
```

Figure 22-1.
Initial menu for INVENTRY.BAS

presented, with the cursor waiting after the colon for your input. The screen with all entries filled in (shaded text) is shown here:

```
Part number: 9   (Push return for no change)
Description: NEW PART                        : Dysan diskettes
Quantity on hand: 0                          : 25
Reorder level: 0                             : 5
Price per unit: 0                            : 5.00

More parts to enter (Y/N)? N
```

Pressing Y clears the screen and allows you to enter information on a new item. Pressing N returns you to the menu.

SELECTION 3—EDIT AN EXISTING ITEM

When you choose selection 3 from the menu, you will again proceed through the questions one by one. You will be shown the current information stored in the computer, and you will be allowed to change this information if you wish. For example:

```
Enter part number to edit: 9
Part number: 9   (Push return for no change)
Description: Dysan diskettes                 :
Quantity on hand: 25                         :
Reorder level: 5                             :
Price per unit: 5.00                         : 6.00

More parts to edit (Y/N)? N
```

If no change to a field is required, press RETURN. This causes the information displayed to be retained and the program to display the next question. In this case, the price per unit was changed from 5.00 to 6.00. When you have answered all of the questions or pressed RETURN instead, you will receive the query **More items to edit**. If you choose Y, you will be asked to enter an item number to edit. If your response is N, you will be returned to the menu.

SELECTION 4—SALES TRANSACTION

Selection 4 centers around an actual sales transaction. On choosing selection 4 from the menu, the first thing you will be asked to enter is the number of the item you wish to sell. The screen will then display the current information on the item. At that point, you will be asked for your second entry, which is the number of units you wish to sell. For example:

```
Enter part number to sell: 9

Part number 9    Description: Dysan diskettes
Quantity on hand: 25
Reorder level: 5
Price per unit: 6.00

Enter number of units to sell: 4
There are now 21 units in stock.

More parts to sell (Y/N)? N
```

On pressing RETURN after your second entry, you will be presented with the number of units now in stock and asked if there are more items that you want to sell. Again, pressing Y will restart the process, and N will return you to the menu.

SELECTION 5 — PURCHASE TRANSACTION

When you choose selection 5 from the menu, you will be asked to enter the part number of the item you wish to purchase. The information stored in the computer will then be presented on the screen, and you will be asked to enter the number of units you wish to purchase. For instance:

```
Enter part number to purchase: 9

Part number 9    Description: Dysan diskettes
Quantity on hand: 21
Reorder level: 5
Price per unit: 6.00
```

```
Enter number of units to purchase: 10
There are now 31 units in stock.

More parts to purchase (Y/N)? N
```

When you enter your response after the question mark and press RETURN, the screen will display the number of units currently in stock. It will also ask if there are more items you wish to purchase. Enter either Y or N.

SELECTION 6 — LIST ITEMS BELOW REORDER LEVEL

Choosing selection 6 from the menu will automatically display on the screen a list of all the items that are at or below the reorder level set in the program. If the stock on hand is less than or equal to this preassigned value, additional items should be reordered. All the information contained in the file on each of these parts is displayed on the screen.

```
Part number 1    Description: OSBORNE
Quantity on hand: 1
Reorder level: 2
Price per unit: 1500
>>--> 1 below reorder level

Part number 7    Description: TELEVIDEO, TERMINAL
Quantity on hand: 2
Reorder level: 2
Price per unit: 675
>>--> At reorder level

 3 parts below reorder level

Press <RETURN> to continue...
```

The arrows in the screen display are intended to draw the operator's attention to items that are at or below the reorder level. Once again you are asked to press RETURN in order to return to the menu and continue with the selections.

SELECTION 7 — END PROGRAM/CLOSE FILE

This final selection from the menu ends the program and closes the files. When all the files are closed, you are returned to Microsoft BASIC. Type **SYSTEM** to get back to CP/M.

Error Messages

Regardless of the precautions you take, it is almost inevitable that the program will at some point encounter an error it cannot handle. In this case, it will transfer control back to MBASIC. If this happens, the next time the program is run, the screen will show the message

```
Files not closed properly
```

If this message appears, choose selection 7, **End program/close file**. When you run the program again, notice the message at the top of the screen that indicates the number of records in the inventory file. If there are fewer records than you expect, you will have to reenter the lost data.

IV.

Appendices

A

Format of Commands, Statements, and Functions

The format notation shown in this appendix is similar to that used in the Microsoft *BASIC-80 Reference Manual.*[1] The MBASIC keywords (statements, commands, and functions) are shown in capital letters and must be entered exactly as shown. Items in lowercase letters enclosed in angle brackets (< >) are to be supplied by the user. For example:

LOAD <filename>[,R]

The LOAD keyword has to be entered exactly as shown. The *filename* is specified by the user, as indicated by the angle brackets. Square brackets are used in the format notation when the material enclosed is optional. In the previous example, the comma and **R** are optional. The **R** must be included if the comma is, since they are both in the square brackets.

A vertical bar (|) indicates a choice for two or more items; in effect, the vertical bar means "or." For example:

RESUME [0 | NEXT | <line number>]

---

[1] *Microsoft BASIC Reference Book* (Bellevue, Wash.: Microsoft, 1979).

This format shows four different uses of the RESUME statement. They are:

RESUME
RESUME 0
RESUME NEXT
RESUME <line number>

The vertical bar means that the RESUME can be followed by 0 *or* NEXT *or* *<line number>*. The square brackets mean that the RESUME statement does not have to be followed by anything.

Curly braces ({ }) indicate that you have an option of two or more items for your entry but that one of the options must be chosen. Each option is separated with the vertical bar (|). For example:

DEF{INT | SNG | DBL | STR} <range(s) of letters>

In this case the curly braces mean that you must specify *DEFINT*, *DEFSNG*, *DEFDBL*, or *DEFSTR*. In contrast to the square brackets, the curly braces mean that you must specify one of the options.

Items followed by ellipses (...) may be repeated any number of times up to the length of line. The maximum line length is 255 characters.

The word "list" inside angle brackets means that items are to be separated by commas. For example, a *<list of variables>* could be **A,B,X$**.

All punctuation, except the square brackets ([ ]), the curly braces ({ }), the vertical bar (|), and ellipses (...), must be entered as shown in the following formats of commands and statements. Of course, if the notation indicates an option of two or more punctuation marks, enter only the appropriate one.

Format of Commands and Statements

AUTO [<line number>[,<increment>]]

CALL <variable name>[(<argument list>)]

CHAIN [MERGE] <filename>[,[<numeric expression>][,ALL]
[,DELETE <range>]]

CLEAR [,[<expression1>] [,<expression2>]]

CLOSE [[#]<file number>[,[#]<file number>...]]

COMMON <list of variables>

CONT

DATA <list of constants>

DEF FN<name>[(<parameter list>)] = <function definition>

DEF USR<integer> = <address>

DEF{INT | SNG | DBL | STR} <range(s) of letters>

DELETE <line number>[-<line number>]

DIM <list of subscripted variables>

EDIT <line number>

END

ERASE <list of array variables>

ERROR <numeric expression>

FIELD [#]<file number>, <field width> AS <string variable>...

FILES [filename]

FOR <variable> = <numeric expression>TO<numeric expression>
[STEP<numeric expression>]

GET [#]<file number>[,<record number>]

GOSUB <line number>

GOTO <line number>

IF <expression> THEN [<statement(s)> | <line number>]
[ELSE {<statement(s)> | <line number>}]

IF <expression> GOTO [<line number>]
[ELSE {<statement(s)> | <line number>}]

INPUT [;][<prompt string>{; | ,}]<variable list>

INPUT #<file number>,<variable list>

KILL <filename>

[LET] <variable> = <expression>

LINE INPUT [;][<prompt string>{; | ,}]<string variable list>

LINE INPUT #<file number>,<string variable list>

{LIST | LLIST} [<line number>[-[<line number>]]]

LOAD <filename>[,R]

LPRINT [USING <format string>;][expr1[, | ;]...]

{LSET | RSET} <string variable> = <string expression>

MERGE <filename>

MID$(<string variable>,<numeric expression>[,<numeric expression>]
= <string expression>

NAME <old filename> AS <new filename>

NEW

NEXT[<list of variables>]

NULL <numeric expression>

ON ERROR GOTO <line number>
ON <expression> {GOTO | GOSUB} <list of line numbers>
OPEN <mode>,[#]<file number>,<filename>,[<record length>]
OPTION BASE {0 | 1}
OUT <port>, <numeric expression>
POKE <address>,<numeric expression>
PRINT [#<file number>,][USING <format string>;][expr1[, | ;]...]
PUT [#]<file number> [,<record number>]
RANDOMIZE [<expression>]
READ <list of variables>
REM <remark>
RENUM [[<new number>][,[<old number>][,<increment>]]]
RESET
RESTORE [<line number>]
RESUME [0 | NEXT | <line number>]
RETURN
RUN [[<line number>]|[<filename>[,R]]]
SAVE <filename> [,A | ,P]
STOP
SWAP <variable>,<variable>
SYSTEM
TRON
TROFF
WAIT <port><numeric expression>[,<numeric expression>]
WEND
WHILE <expression>
WIDTH [LPRINT] <numeric expression>
WRITE [#<file number>,][<list of expressions>]

Format of Functions

In the following function formats, X and Y are numeric expressions; X$ and Y$ are string expressions.

ABS(X)
ASC(X$)
ATN(X)
CDBL(X)
CHR$(X)
CINT(X)
COS(X)
CSNG(X)

CVI(<2-byte string expression>)
CVS(<4-byte string expression>)
CVD(<8-byte string expression>)
EOF(<file number>)
EXP(X)
FIX(X)
FRE({X|X$})
HEX$(X)
INP<port>
INKEY$
INPUT$(X[,[#]Y])
INSTR([X,]X$,Y$)
INT(X)
LEFT$(X$,X)
LEN(X$)
LOC(<file number>)
LOG(X)
LPOS(X)
MID$(X$,X[,Y])
MKI$(<integer expression>)
MKS$(<single-precision expression>)
MKD$(<double-precision expression>)
OCT$(X)
PEEK(X)
POS(X)
RIGHT$(X$,X)
RND[(X)]
SGN(X)
SIN(X)
SPACE$(X)
SPC(X)
SQR(X)
STR$(X)
STRING$(X,{Y | X$})
TAB(X)
TAN(X)
USR<integer>(<variable>)
VAL(X$)
VARPTR({<variable name> |
#<file number>})

B

Error Codes and Messages

This appendix contains the complete list of error codes and messages for MBASIC. A discussion of the most common errors and how you can avoid them is provided in Chapter 13, "Debugging Your Programs."

The first column in Table B-1 lists the two-character codes that are printed by earlier versions of MBASIC. The second column is the error code number used by the ERROR statement and ERR variable (see Chapter 13). The third column contains the error message printed and a brief description of the error.

Table B-1.
Error Codes and Messages

Code	Number	Message
NF	1	**NEXT without FOR** A variable in a NEXT statement does not correspond to any previously executed unmatched FOR statement variable.
SN	2	**Syntax error** A line has been encountered that contains some incorrect sequence of characters (such as an unmatched parenthesis, misspelled command or statement, incorrect punctuation).
RG	3	**RETURN without GOSUB** A RETURN statement has been encountered for which there is no previous unmatched GOSUB statement.
OD	4	**Out of DATA** A READ statement has been executed when there are no DATA statements with unread data remaining in the program.
FC	5	**Illegal function call** A parameter that is out of range was passed to a math or string function. This error may also occur as the result of a negative or unreasonably large subscript, a negative or zero argument with the LOG function, a negative argument to the SQR function, a negative mantissa with a noninteger exponent, a call to a USR function for which the starting address has not yet been given, or an improper argument to MID$, LEFT$, RIGHT$, INP, OUT, WAIT, PEEK, POKE, TAB, SPC, STRING$, SPACE$, INSTR, or ON/GOTO.
OV	6	**Overflow** The result of a calculation is too large to be represented in MBASIC's number format.
OM	7	**Out of memory** A program is too large, has too many FOR loops or GOSUBs, too many variables, or expressions that are too complicated.
UL	8	**Undefined line number** A line reference in a GOTO, GOSUB, IF/THEN/ELSE, or DELETE statement is to a nonexistent line.

Table B-1.
Error Codes and Messages *(continued)*

Code	Number	Message
BS	9	**Subscript out of range** An array element has been referenced either with a subscript that is outside the dimensions of the array or with the wrong number of subscripts.
DD	10	**Duplicate definition** Two DIM statements have been given for the same array, or a DIM statement has been given for an array after the default dimension of 10 was established for that array.
/0	11	**Division by zero** A division by zero has been encountered in an expression, or zero is raised to a negative power. Infinity with the sign of the numerator is supplied as the result of the division, and execution continues.
ID	12	**Illegal direct** A statement that is illegal in direct mode has been entered as a direct mode command.
TM	13	**Type mismatch** A string variable name has been assigned a numeric value or vice versa, or a function that expects a numeric argument has been given a string argument or vice versa.
OS	14	**Out of string space** String variables have exceeded the allocated amount of string space. Use the CLEAR command to allocate more string space or to decrease the size and number of strings.
LS	15	**String too long** An attempt has been made to create a string longer than 255 characters.
ST	16	**String formula too complex** A string expression is too long or too complex. The expression should be broken into smaller expressions.
CN	17	**Can't continue** An attempt has been made to continue a program that was halted due to an error, has been modified during a break in execution, or does not exist.

Table B-1.
Error Codes and Messages *(continued)*

Code	Number	Message
UF	18	**Undefined user function** A USR function has been called before the function definition has been given.
	19	**No RESUME** An error-trapping routine has been entered, but it contains no RESUME statement.
	20	**RESUME without error** A RESUME statement has been encountered before an error-trapping routine has been entered.
	21	**Unprintable error** An error message is not available for the error condition that exists. This is usually caused by an error with an undefined error code.
	22	**Missing operand** An expression contains an operator with no operand following it.
	23	**Line buffer overflow** An attempt has been made to input a line that has more than 255 characters.
	26	**FOR without NEXT** A FOR statement has been encountered without a matching NEXT statement.
	29	**WHILE without WEND** A WHILE statement does not have a matching WEND statement.
	30	**WEND without WHILE** A WEND statement does not have a matching WHILE statement.
	50	**FIELD overflow** A FIELD statement is attempting to allocate more bytes than were specified for the record length of a random file.
	51	**Internal error** An internal malfunction has occurred in MBASIC. Report the conditions under which the message appeared to Microsoft.

Table B-1.
Error Codes and Messages *(continued)*

Code	Number	Message
	52	**Bad file number** A statement or command references a file with a file number that is not open or is out of the range of file numbers specified at initialization.
	53	**File not found** A LOAD, KILL, or OPEN statement has referenced a file that does not exist on the named disk.
	54	**Bad file mode** An attempt has been made to use PUT, GET, or LOF with a sequential file, to LOAD a random file, or to execute an OPEN statement with a file mode other than I, O, or R.
	55	**File already open** An OPEN command for sequential output has been issued for a file that is already open, or a KILL command has been given for a file that is open.
	57	**Disk I/O error** An I/O error has occurred during a disk I/O operation. This is a fatal error; that is, the operating system cannot recover from the error.
	58	**File already exists** The file name specified in a NAME statement is identical to a file name already in use on the disk.
	61	**Disk full** All disk storage space is in use.
	62	**Input past end** An INPUT statement is executed for a null (empty) file or after all the data in the file has been input. To avoid this error, use the EOF function to detect the end of file.
	63	**Bad record number** In a PUT or GET statement, a record number has been given that is either greater than the maximum allowed (32767) or equal to 0.

Table B-1.
Error Codes and Messages *(continued)*

Code	Number	Message
	64	**Bad file name** An illegal form is used for the file name with LOAD, SAVE, KILL, or OPEN (for example, a file name with too many characters).
	66	**Direct statement in file** A direct statement has been encountered in an ASCII-format file by the LOAD command. The LOAD command is terminated.
	67	**Too many files** An attempt has been made to create a new file (using SAVE or OPEN) when all the directory entries for that disk are full.

Source: *BASIC-80 Reference Manual 1979 (Version 5.0).* Bellevue, Wash.: Microsoft, Inc., 1979.

C

ASCII Codes

Table C-1 lists the ASCII codes for characters.

Table C-1.
ASCII Character Codes

DEC	OCTAL	HEX	ASCII	DEC	OCTAL	HEX	ASCII
0	000	00	NUL	17	021	11	DC1
1	001	01	SOH	18	022	12	DC2
2	002	02	STX	19	023	13	DC3
3	003	03	ETX	20	024	14	DC4
4	004	04	EOT	21	025	15	NAK
5	005	05	ENQ	22	026	16	SYN
6	006	06	ACK	23	027	17	ETB
7	007	07	BEL	24	030	18	CAN
8	010	08	BS	25	031	19	EM
9	011	09	HT	26	032	1A	SUB
10	012	0A	LF	27	033	1B	ESC
11	013	0B	VT	28	034	1C	FS
12	014	0C	FF	29	035	1D	GS
13	015	0D	CR	30	036	1E	RS
14	016	0E	SO	31	037	1F	US
15	017	0F	SI	32	040	20	SPACE
16	020	10	DLE	33	041	21	!

Table C-1.
ASCII Character Codes (*continued*)

DEC	OCTAL	HEX	ASCII	DEC	OCTAL	HEX	ASCII
34	042	22	”	76	114	4C	L
35	043	23	#	77	115	4D	M
36	044	24	$	78	116	4E	N
37	045	25	%	79	117	4F	O
38	046	26	&	80	120	50	P
39	047	27	’	81	121	51	Q
40	050	28	(	82	122	52	R
41	051	29	)	83	123	53	S
42	052	2A	*	84	124	54	T
43	053	2B	+	85	125	55	U
44	054	2C	,	86	126	56	V
45	055	2D	—	87	127	57	W
46	056	2E	.	88	130	58	X
47	057	2F	/	89	131	59	Y
48	060	30	0	90	132	5A	Z
49	061	31	1	91	133	5B	[
50	062	32	2	92	134	5C	\
51	063	33	3	93	135	5D	]
52	064	34	4	94	136	5E	^
53	065	35	5	95	137	5F	—
54	066	36	6	96	140	60	‘
55	067	37	7	97	141	61	a
56	070	38	8	98	142	62	b
57	071	39	9	99	143	63	c
58	072	3A	:	100	144	64	d
59	073	3B	;	101	145	65	e
60	074	3C	<	102	146	66	f
61	075	3D	=	103	147	67	g
62	076	3E	>	104	150	68	h
63	077	3F	?	105	151	69	i
64	100	40	@	106	152	6A	j
65	101	41	A	107	153	6B	k
66	102	42	B	108	154	6C	l
67	103	43	C	109	155	6D	m
68	104	44	D	110	156	6E	n
69	105	45	E	111	157	6F	o
70	106	46	F	112	160	70	p
71	107	47	G	113	161	71	q
72	110	48	H	114	162	72	r
73	111	49	I	115	163	73	s
74	112	4A	J	116	164	74	t
75	113	4B	K	117	165	75	u

Table C-1.
ASCII Character Codes (*continued*)

DEC	OCTAL	HEX	ASCII	DEC	OCTAL	HEX	ASCII
118	166	76	v	123	173	7B	{
119	167	77	w	124	174	7C		
120	170	78	x	125	175	7D	}
121	171	79	y	126	176	7E	~
122	172	7A	z	127	177	7F	DEL

D

Answers to the Exercises

Chapter 2

1. A, C, D, E, F, G

2. *a.* String
   b. Numeric
   c. Numeric
   d. String

3. *a.* 26
   b. 27
   c. 15
   d. 4
   e. 32
   f. 27

4.
```
10 LET A = 2
20 LET B = 3
30 LET C = 5
40 X = A + 2*B - C
```

```
50 PRINT X
60 X = (A - B)*C
70 PRINT X
80 X = (B*C)/(A*(A+B))
90 PRINT X
100 X = (A + B)/(C - A)
110 PRINT X
```

5.
```
10 INPUT "A,B,C,D";A,B,C,D
20 SUM = A+B+C+D
30 AVERAGE = SUM/4
40 PRINT "SUM=";SUM
50 PRINT "AVERAGE =": AVERAGE
60 END
```

6.
```
10 INPUT "What temperature would you like converted";F
20 C = (5/9)*(F - 32)
30 PRINT F;"degrees fahrenheit is";C;"degrees celsius."
```

7.
```
10 B = 8:H = 11
20 A = (1/2)*B*H
30 PRINT "Triangle area =";A
40 R = 3
50 A = 3.1416*R^2
60 PRINT "Circle area =";A
70 S = 6
80 A = S^2
90 PRINT "Square area =";A
100 B1 = 8:B2 = 6:H = 4
110 A = (1/2)*(B1 + B2)*H
120 PRINT "Trapezoid area =";A
```

8.
```
10 FIRST$ = "Joe"
20 LAST$ = "Compuwhiz"
30 ADDR1$ = "123 Bit View Drive"
40 ADDR2$ = "Floppyvill. Ca. 98765"
50 PRINT FIRST$;" ";LAST$;"   ";ADDR1$;"   ";ADDR2$
60 PRINT
70 PRINT LAST$;", ";FIRST$
80 PRINT ADDR1$
90 PRINT ADDR2$
```

Chapter 3

1.
```
5  REM Written 3/12/83
10 REM - Triangle
20 B = 8:H = 11
30 A = (1/2)*B*H :       ' Equation for area of triangle
40 PRINT "Triangle area =";A
50 REM - Circle
60 R = 3
70 A = 3.1416*R^2 :      ' Equation for area of circle
80 PRINT "Circle area =";A
90 REM - Square
100 S = 6
110 A = S^2 :            ' Equation for area of square
120 PRINT "Square area =";A
130 REM - Trapezoid
140 B1 = 8:B2 = 6:H = 4
150 A = (1/2)*(B1 + B2)*H :  ' Equation for area of trapezoid
160 PRINT "Trapezoid area =";A
```

2. B (begins with a number) and C (includes a question mark)

3. *a.* `FILES "*.DAT"`
   b. `FILES "??"`
   c. `FILES "??A*"`

4.
```
SAVE "HAPPY"
NEW
LOAD "HAPPY"
RUN
NAME "HAPPY.BAS" AS "STUPID.BAS"
KILL "STUPID.BAS"
SYSTEM
```

Chapter 4

1.
```
10 READ X
20 IF X = -1 THEN END
30 IF X >= 10 AND X <= 20 THEN PRINT X
40 GOTO 10
50 DATA 17, 4, 37, 41, 26, 11, 1, 40, 32, 16, -1
```

2.
```
10 READ COUNT
20 FOR X = 1 TO COUNT
30    READ A
40    SUM = SUM + A
50 NEXT X
60 PRINT "The sum is";SUM
70 PRINT "The average is";SUM/COUNT
80 END
90 DATA 10
100 DATA 16, 28, 83, 47, 32, 7, 19, 81, 57, 93
```

3.
```
10 READ N$
20 IF N$ = "" THEN END
30 PRINT N$
40 GOTO 10
50 DATA "TOM","FRED","GREG","WALT","MARK","SAM","SALLY","MARY","ANN","SUE",""
```

4.
```
10 READ COUNT
20 FOR X = 1 TO COUNT
30    READ N$
40    PRINT N$;" ";
50 NEXT X
60 END
70 DATA 10
80 DATA "TOM","FRED","GREG","WALT","MARK","SAM","SALLY","MARY","ANN","SUE"
```

5.
```
10 REM -                    -=*PAYROLL.C4*=-
20 REM -                    07/21/83
30 REM -
40 INPUT "Number of widgets produced per day (0 to end)? ",WIDGETS
50 IF WIDGETS = 0 THEN END
60 RESTORE
70 READ EMP.RATE
80 IF EMP.RATE=0 THEN 120                'Zero rate signals end of data
90 EMP.EARN=EMP.RATE*8                   'Compute employee earnings
100 TOTAL.WAGES=TOTAL.WAGES+EMP.EARN     'Total employee wages
110 GOTO 70
120 UNIT.COST=TOTAL.WAGES/WIDGETS        'Compute unit cost
130 PRINT "Unit cost = ";UNIT.COST
140 PRINT
150 GOTO 40
160 DATA 4.78,5.01,7.43,0
```

Chapter 5

1. *a.* Renumbers the program, beginning at line 10, incrementing each line number by 15, and starts the new line numbers at 5.
   b. Starts accepting lines, automatically numbering them from line 1000, with each line number 100 greater than the last.
   c. Deletes all lines from the beginning of the program up to (and including) line 70.
   d. Deletes all lines between (and including) 70 and 100.
   e. Starts accepting lines, automatically numbering them from line 3, with each line number 10 greater than the last.
   f. Renumbers the program, beginning at line 90, incrementing each line number by 10, and starts the new line numbers at 100.

2. *a.* **S;H** ESCAPE or press SPACE until the cursor is over the **A** and press **D** five times
   b. **SoDDIum** ESCAPE or press SPACE until the cursor is over the **o** and press **D** three times, then **Ium**
   c. SCI+**D** ESCAPE or **X+D** ESCAPE
   d. **S;IC+**ESCAPE SPACE SPACE SPACE **DD** or **S;DDDD** SPACE **I+A+B** ESCAPE

Chapter 6

1.
```
10 READ A
20 IF A = -1 THEN 50
30 PRINT USING "$$####,.##";A
40 GOTO 10
50 END
60 DATA 7.3845,6752.7,433.789,-1
```

2.
```
10 REM -                    -=*TEMPER.E62*=-
20 REM -                    Fahrenheit to Celsius temperature conversion
30 REM -                    12/05/82
40 REM -
100 PRINT "Temperature conversion"
110 PRINT "Fahrenheit to  Celsius"
120 PRINT "----------     -------"
130 FRMT$="   ###         ###.##"      'This is the format for the table
140 F = 30                         'Start table at 30 degrees F.
150 IF F > 215 THEN 200            'End table at 215 degrees F.
160 C = (5/9)*(F - 32)             'Compute Celsius temperature
170 PRINT USING FRMT$;F;C
180 F = F + 5                      'Print every 5 degrees F.
190 GOTO 150
200 END
```

3.
```
100 PRINT "NAME          AGE   SEX   PHONE NUMBER"
110 PRINT "------------  ---   ---   ------------"
120 FRMT$="\            \  ##    !    \          \"
130 READ NAM$,AGE,SEX$,PHONE$
140 IF NAM$="" THEN 170
150 PRINT USING FRMT$;NAM$;AGE;SEX$;PHONE$
160 GOTO 130
170 END
180 DATA "MIKE",24,"M","413-2807"
190 DATA "LAURA",23,"F","214-5712"
200 DATA "ALICE",28,"F","671-4242"
210 DATA "SAM",26,"M","683-9896"
220 DATA "",0,"",""
```

4.
```
100 READ NAM$,S1,S2,S3,S4
110 IF NAM$ = "" THEN 150
120 AV = (S1+S2+S3+S4)/4
130 IF AV < 70 THEN PRINT USING "Average score for & is ##.#%";NAM$;AV
140 GOTO 100
150 END
160 DATA "MARY",63,51,78,71
170 DATA "DON",83,62,91,51
180 DATA "FRANK",72,77,61,52
190 DATA "BETTY",44,83,71,68
200 DATA "",0,0,0,0
```

5.
```
10 REM -                    -=*C6#5.BAS*=-
20 REM -                    Simple Interest Loan Table
30 REM -                    12/05/82
40 REM -
100 BALANCE = 6000
110 RATE = .145
120 PAYMENT = 250
130 PRINT "Interest table for loan of $6,000, with payment of $250 per month"
```

```
140 PRINT "at 14.5 interest."
150 PRINT "Month    principal   interest  total payment  rem. balance"
160 PRINT "-----  -----------  ---------  -------------  ------------"
170 FRMT$=" ###   $$######,.##  $$###.###      $$###.##   $$######,.##"
180 MONTH = 1                          'Start at month 1
190 TOTAL.INTEREST = 0                 'Accumulated interest payed
200 IF MONTH > 12 THEN 280             'Compute balance for each month
210 PRINCIPAL = BALANCE                'Principal is last month's balance
220 INTEREST = PRINCIPAL*RATE*(1/12)   'Compute interest on princpal
230 TOTAL.INTEREST = TOTAL.INTEREST + INTEREST
240 BALANCE = PRINCIPAL - (PAYMENT + INTEREST)  'Compute new balance
250 PRINT USING FRMT$;MONTH;PRINCIPAL;INTEREST;PAYMENT + INTEREST;BALANCE
260 MONTH = MONTH + 1
270 GOTO 200
280 PRINT
290 PRINT USING "Total interest:  **$####,.##";TOTAL.INTEREST
300 END
```

Chapter 7

1.
```
100 REM - Part (a)
110 FOR X = 1 TO 5
120    FOR Y = 1 TO X
130       PRINT "#";
140    NEXT Y
150    PRINT
160 NEXT X
170 PRINT
200 REM - Part (b)
210 FOR X = 1 TO 5
220    PRINT TAB(6-X);
230    FOR Y = 1 TO X*2 - 1
240       PRINT "*";
250    NEXT Y
260    PRINT
270 NEXT X
280 PRINT
300 REM - Part (c)
310 FOR X = 1 TO 3
320    PRINT TAB(X);"**";TAB(8 - X);"**"
330 NEXT X
340 PRINT TAB(4);"**"
350 FOR X = 3 TO 1 STEP -1
360    PRINT TAB(8 - X);"**"
370 NEXT X
380 PRINT
```

```
400 REM - Part (d)
410 FOR X = 1 TO 7
420    IF X > 4 THEN PRINT TAB(X - 4);"**";
430    PRINT TAB(X);"**";
440    IF X < 4 THEN PRINT TAB(X + 4);"**" ELSE PRINT
450 NEXT X
460 PRINT
500 REM - Part (e)
510 PRINT TAB(5);"*"
520 FOR X = 1 TO 4
530    PRINT TAB(5 - X);
540    FOR Y = 1 TO X
550       PRINT "<";
560    NEXT Y
570    PRINT " ";
580    FOR Y = 1 TO X
590       PRINT ">";
600    NEXT Y
610    PRINT
620 NEXT X
630 FOR X = 1 TO 2
640    PRINT TAB(4);"###"
650 NEXT X
```

2.
```
100 PRINT TAB(4);
110 FOR X = 1 TO 12
120    PRINT USING "  ##";X;
130 NEXT X
140 PRINT
150 PRINT "   +------------------------------------------------"
160 FOR X = 1 TO 12
170    PRINT USING "## !";X;
180    FOR Y = 1 TO 12
190       PRINT USING "### ";X*Y;
200    NEXT Y
210    PRINT
220 NEXT X
```

3.
```
100 INPUT "Press <RETURN> to time integer loop. ";A$
110 PRINT "GO! "
120 FOR I% = 1 TO 10000:NEXT I%
130 PRINT "STOP!"
140 INPUT "Press <RETURN> to time double precision loop. ";A$
150 PRINT "GO!"
160 FOR I! = 1 TO 10000:NEXT I!
170 PRINT "STOP!"
```

4.
```
10 REM -                -=*INTEREST.C6*=-
20 REM -                Simple Interest Table (Double precision)
30 REM -                11/25/82
40 REM -
100 DEFDBL A-Z
110 INPUT "Enter yearly interest rate in percent %",RATE
120 RATE = RATE/100                      'Convert RATE to a decimal
130 INPUT "Enter starting balance $",BALANCE
140 INPUT "Enter number of years to calculate: ",YEAR
150 PRINT
160 PRINT "Month      principal     interest        balance"
170 PRINT "-----  -------------  -----------  -------------"
180 FRMT$=" ###   $$########,.##  $$######.###  $$########,.##"
190 MONTH = 1                            'Start at month 1
200 IF MONTH > 12*YEAR THEN 270          'Compute balance for each month
210 PRINCIPAL = BALANCE                  'Principal is last month's balance
220 INTEREST = PRINCIPAL*RATE*(1/12)     'Compute interest on principal
230 BALANCE = PRINCIPAL + INTEREST       'Compute new balance
240 PRINT USING FRMT$;MONTH;PRINCIPAL;INTEREST;BALANCE
250 MONTH = MONTH + 1
260 GOTO 200
270 PRINT
280 PRINT USING "Ending balance:                    **$########,.##";BALANCE
290 END
```

5. Since **X** is an integer (from line 10), adding .4 to it does not change its value, so it is still equal to 1 each time the FOR/NEXT loop executes.

Chapter 8

1.
```
100 RANDOMIZE
110 PRINT TAB(15);"Random number range"
120 PRINT "0 to 20    10 to 45    -10 to +10    -50 to 0    .34 to 1.83"
130 PRINT "-------    --------    ----------    --------    -----------"
140 FRMT$="  ##          ##          ###           ###         ##.##"
150 FOR I = 1 TO 10
160    R1 = INT(21*RND)
170    R2 = INT(36*RND) + 10
180    R3 = INT(21*RND) - 10
190    R4 = -INT(51*RND)
200    R5 = (INT((183 - 34)*RND) + 34)/100
210    PRINT USING FRMT$;R1;R2;R3;R4;R5
220 NEXT I
```

2.
```
10 REM -                  -=*COSINE.C8*=-
20 REM -                  Print a cosine wave curve
30 REM -                  11/21/82
40 REM -
100 A=20                          'Wave amplitude
110 E=.4                          'Step size
120 FOR X = 1 TO 2*A + 1
130    PRINT "-";                 'Print Y axis
140 NEXT X
150 PRINT " Y axis"
160 YO = A + 1                    'Tab location of X axis
170 FOR X = 0 TO 4*3.14 STEP E
180    Y = YO + FIX(A*COS(X) + .5)        'Compute tab location of point
190    IF Y > YO THEN PRINT TAB(YO);"|";TAB(Y);"*"       'Y is right of X axis
200    IF Y < YO THEN PRINT TAB(Y);"*";TAB(YO);"|"       'Y is left of X axis
210    IF Y = YO THEN PRINT TAB(Y);"*"                   'Y is on X axis
220 NEXT X
230 PRINT TAB(YO - 3);"X axis"
```

3.
```
10 REM -                  -=*C8#3.BAS*=-
20 REM -                  Add to fractions and reduce to lowest terms
30 REM -                  12/05/82
100 DEFINT A-Z                    'Use integers for all variables
110 INPUT "Enter numerator and denominator for 1st fraction: ",N1,D1
120 INPUT "Enter numerator and denominator for 2nd fraction: ",N2,D2
130 IF D1 > D2 THEN LCD = D1 ELSE LCD = D2      'Set LCD to largest of D1,D2
140 WHILE INT(LCD/D1) <> LCD/D1 OR INT(LCD/D2) <> LCD/D2
150    LCD = LCD + 1                         'Find LCD
160 WEND
170 PRINT:PRINT "The lowest common denominator is";LCD
180 '
190 'Add fractions and reduce to lowest terms.
200 'N will be the new numerator and LCD will be the new denominator.
210 '
220 N = N1*(LCD/D1) + N2*(LCD/D2)          'Compute numerator
230 FACTOR = 2
240 WHILE FACTOR < LCD AND FACTOR < N    'Find all factors of N and LCD
250    IF INT(N/FACTOR) = N/FACTOR AND INT(LCD/FACTOR) = LCD/FACTOR THEN 280
260       FACTOR = FACTOR + 1
270    GOTO 290
280       N = N/FACTOR: LCD = LCD/FACTOR         'Reduce fraction
290 WEND
300 PRINT
310 PRINT USING "###      ###      ###";N1,N2,N
320 PRINT       "----  +  ----  =  ----"
330 PRINT USING "###      ###      ###";D1,D2,LCD
```

4. Since we are modeling dice, we want our random numbers to be distributed like real dice. Using **INT(11*RND)+2**

will generate the numbers between 2 and 12 with equal probability; **INT(6*RND)+INT(6*RND)+2** will give the correct distribution.

Chapter 9

1.
```
100 RANDOMIZE
110 FOR WORD=1 TO 10
120    LENGTH=INT(RND*4)+5
130    FOR LETTER=1 TO LENGTH
140       CH=INT(RND*26)+65
150       PRINT CHR$(CH);
160    NEXT LETTER
170    PRINT
180 NEXT WORD
190 END
```

2.
```
100 FOR I = 1 TO 5
110    READ NM$
120    PRINT NM$;
130    COMMA = INSTR(NM$,",")
140    PRINT TAB(25);MID$(NM$,COMMA+2);" ";LEFT$(NM$,COMMA-1)
150 NEXT I
160 END
200 DATA "Smith, Alfred","Jones, Tom","Surges, Mary"
210 DATA "Able, Susan","Waters, Larry"
```

3.
```
10 REM -        CH#9.3
20 REM -        Password entry for a program
30 REM -        1/22/83
40 REM -
50 DATA "ZYXWVU","SAMSMITH","GREG123456",""
60 REM -     *** START ***
100 PRINT "Please enter your password  ";
110 PASSWORD$ = "":CH$ = INPUT$(1)
120 WHILE ASC(CH$) <> 13
130    PASSWORD$ = PASSWORD$ + CH$
140    CH$ = INPUT$(1)
150 WEND
160 PRINT
170 RESTORE              'Set to read first password
180 READ ENTRY$          'Read first password
190 WHILE ENTRY$ <> PASSWORD$ AND ENTRY$ <> ""
200    READ ENTRY$
210 WEND
```

```
220 IF ENTRY$="" THEN PRINT "Invalid password.":GOTO 100
230 PRINT "Password accepted."
240 REM -
250 REM - *** MAIN PROGRAM ***
260 REM -
```

4.
```
10 REM -                    -=*DECODE.C9*=-
20 REM -                    Message decoder
30 REM -                    1/2/83
40 REM -
100 ALPHA$ ="ABCDEFGHIJKLMNOPQRSTUVWXYZ"    'Upper case alphabet
110 CODE$ = "KIEVNHUPOQRAXLTYSZBGWJFCMD"    'One-to-one replacements
120 PRINT:LINE INPUT "Enter a message to decode: ";MESSG$
130 IF LEN(MESSG$) = 0 THEN END
140 DECODE$ = MESSG$                        'Initialize decoded message
150 FOR I=1 TO LEN(MESSG$)
160    INDEX = INSTR(CODE$,MID$(MESSG$,I,1))
170    IF INDEX > 0 THEN MID$(DECODE$,I,1) = MID$(ALPHA$,INDEX,1)
180 NEXT I
190 PRINT "The decoded message is   : ";DECODE$
200 GOTO 120
```

Chapter 10

1.
```
100 RANDOMIZE
110 FOR X=1 TO 10
120    A(X) = INT(RND*100) + 1
130    PRINT A(X);" ";
140 NEXT X
150 PRINT:PRINT
160 LARGEST = A(1): SMALL = A(1)
170 FOR X=2 TO 10
180    IF A(X) > LARGEST THEN LARGEST = A(X)
190    IF A(X) < SMALL THEN SMALL = A(X)
200 NEXT X
210 PRINT "The largest number in the list is";LARGEST
220 PRINT "The smallest number in the list is";SMALL
230 END
```

2.
```
100 RANDOMIZE
110 FOR X=1 TO 10
120    A(X) = INT(RND*100) + 1
130    PRINT A(X);" ";
140 NEXT X
150 PRINT:PRINT
```

```
160 LARGEST = A(1): SMALL = A(1)
170 LX = 1: SX = 1
180 FOR X=2 TO 10
190    IF A(X) > LARGEST THEN LARGEST = A(X):LX = X
200    IF A(X) < SMALL THEN SMALL = A(X):SX = X
210 NEXT X
220 PRINT "The largest number is";LARGEST;"at position";LX;"in the list."
230 PRINT "The smallest number is";SMALL;"at position";SX;"in the list."
240 END
```

3.
```
100 PRINT "List A:"
110 FOR X=1 TO 10
120    READ A(X)
130    PRINT A(X);" ";
140 NEXT X
150 PRINT:PRINT "List B:"
160 FOR Y=1 TO 10
170    READ B(Y)
180    PRINT B(Y);" ";
190 NEXT Y
200 DIM C(20)
210 X=1: Y=1
220 FOR Z=1 TO 20
230    IF Y<=10 THEN B=B(Y) ELSE B=9999
240    IF X<=10 THEN A=A(X) ELSE A=9999
250    IF A<B THEN C(Z)=A(X):X=X+1 ELSE C(Z)=B(Y):Y=Y+1
260 NEXT Z
270 PRINT:PRINT "List C:"
280 FOR Z=1 TO 20
290    PRINT C(Z);" ";
300 NEXT Z
310 END
320 '
330 DATA 7,14,15,19,24,31,38,41,43,49
340 DATA 1,8,13,14,27,29,35,37,40,44
```

4.
```
100 RANDOMIZE
110 LOW=100: HIGH=0
120 FOR X=1 TO 4
130    FOR Y=1 TO 5
140       A(X,Y)=INT(RND*90)+10
150       PRINT A(X,Y);" ";
160       IF A(X,Y)<LOW THEN LOW=A(X,Y)
170       IF A(X,Y)>HIGH THEN HIGH=A(X,Y)
180    NEXT Y
190    PRINT
200 NEXT X
210 PRINT "Largest number in the array is";HIGH
220 PRINT "Smallest number in the array is";LOW
230 END
```

5.
```
100 RANDOMIZE
110 PRINT:PRINT "First array:"
120 FOR X=1 TO 4
130    FOR Y=1 TO 5
140       A(X,Y) = INT(RND*90) + 10
150       PRINT A(X,Y);" ";
180    NEXT Y
190    PRINT
200 NEXT X
210 PRINT:PRINT "Add column 1 to column 5:"
220 FOR X=1 TO 4
230    A(X,5) = A(X,5) + A(X,1)
240 NEXT X
250 FOR X=1 TO 4
260    FOR Y=1 TO 5
270       PRINT A(X,Y);" ";
280    NEXT Y
290    PRINT
300 NEXT X
310 END
```

6.
```
100 RANDOMIZE
110 FOR X=1 TO 6
120    FOR Y=1 TO 8
130       A(X,Y)=INT(RND*101)-50
140       PRINT USING "####";A(X,Y);
150    NEXT Y
160    PRINT
170 NEXT X
180 FOR Y=1 TO 8
190    PRINT " ---";
200 NEXT Y
210 PRINT
220 FOR Y=1 TO 8
230    HIGH=A(1,Y)
240    FOR X=2 TO 6
250       IF HIGH<A(X,Y) THEN HIGH=A(X,Y)
260    NEXT X
270    PRINT USING "####";HIGH;
280 NEXT Y
290 PRINT
300 PRINT
310 PRINT "Number at bottom of each column is largest in that column."
320 END
```

Chapter 11

1.
```
100 PRINT
110 PRINT "Would you like to:"
120 PRINT "       1) Convert meters to feet?"
130 PRINT "       2) Convert liters to gallons?"
140 PRINT "       3) Convert Celsius to Fahrenheit?"
150 PRINT "       4) End?"
160 INPUT "Enter your choice (1-4): ";CHOICE
170 ON CHOICE GOSUB 230,330,430.190
180 GOTO 100
190 END
200 REM
210 REM                    Conversion: meters to feet
220 REM
230 PRINT
240 INPUT "Number of meters to convert to feet (0 to end): ";METERS
250 IF METERS=0 THEN 290
260    FEET=METERS/.3048
270    PRINT METERS:"meter(s) is equal to  ";FEET;"feet.
280    GOTO 230
290 RETURN
300 REM
310 REM                    Conversion: liters to gallons
320 REM
330 PRINT
340 INPUT "Number of liters to convert to gallons (0 to end): ";LITERS
350 IF LITERS = 0 THEN 390
360    GALLONS=LITERS/3.7853
370    PRINT LITERS;"liter(s) is equal to  ";GALLONS;"gallon(s)."
380    GOTO 330
390 RETURN
400 REM
410 REM                    Conversion: fahrenheit to celsius
420 REM
430 PRINT
440 INPUT "Enter Celsius temperature to be converted (0 to end): ";CEL
450 IF CEL=0 THEN 490
460    FAHR=CEL*9/5+32
470    PRINT CEL;"degrees Celsius is equal to ";FAHR;"degrees Fahrenheit.
480    GOTO 430
490 RETURN
```

2.
```
100 DIM A(50)
110 FOR X=1 TO 50
120    A(X)=INT(RND*100)+1
130    PRINT USING "#### ";A(X);
140    IF X/10 = X\10 THEN PRINT
```

```
150 NEXT X
160 PRINT
170 INPUT "Do you want 1) largest or 2) smallest number? ",CHOICE
180 IF CHOICE<>1 AND CHOICE<>2 THEN 170
190 NUMB=A(1)
200 FOR X=2 TO 50
210    ON CHOICE GOSUB 290,340
220    IF COMPARE=1 THEN NUMB=A(X)
230 NEXT X
240 PRINT "The number is";NUMB
250 END
260 '
270 'Compare for largest number
280 '
290 IF A(X)>NUMB THEN COMPARE=1 ELSE COMPARE=0
300 RETURN
310 '
320 'Compare for smallest number
330 '
340 IF A(X)<NUMB THEN COMPARE=1 ELSE COMPARE=0
350 RETURN
```

Chapter 12

1.
```
100 RANDOMIZE
110 DIM WORD$(50),COUNT(26)
120 FOR X=1 TO 50
130    LENGTH = INT(RND*4)+5
140    FOR Y=1 TO LENGTH
150       WORD$(X) = WORD$(X) + CHR$(INT(RND*26) + 65)
160    NEXT Y
170    PRINT USING "\        \";WORD$(X);
180    IF X/7 = X\7 THEN PRINT
190 NEXT X
200 FOR X=1 TO 50
210    CH = ASC(WORD$(X)) - 64
220    COUNT(CH) = COUNT(CH) + 1
230 NEXT X
240 PRINT:PRINT
250 PRINT "Number of words beginning with each letter is as follows:"
260 PRINT
270 FOR X=1 TO 26
280    PRINT USING "!:##   ";CHR$(X+64);COUNT(X);
290    IF X/8 = X\8 THEN PRINT
300 NEXT X
310 END
```

2.
```
100 RANDOMIZE
110 LET NUMB=3
120 FOR X=1 TO NUMB
130    A(X)=INT(RND*100)+50
140 NEXT X
150 WHILE DONE=0
160    DONE=1
170    FOR X=1 TO NUMB+1
180       IF A(X)<A(X+1) THEN SWAP A(X),A(X+1):DONE=0
190    NEXT X
200 WEND
210 FOR X=1 TO NUMB
220    PRINT A(X)
230 NEXT X
240 END
```

3. 7, 10

4.
```
100 DEFINT A-Z
110 OPTION BASE 1
120 SIZE = 100            'This is the array size
130 DIM A(SIZE)
140 RANDOMIZE
150 GOSUB 1000            'Make list
160 GOSUB 1100            'Print list
170 PRINT:INPUT "Number to search for? ",N
180 IF N = 0 THEN END
190 I = 1:GOSUB 1200      'Search list starting at I = 1
200 IF INDEX = 0 THEN PRINT "Not found":GOTO 170
210 WHILE INDEX <> 0
220    PRINT "Number found at";INDEX
230    I = I + 1
240    IF I <= SIZE THEN GOSUB 1200 ELSE INDEX = 0  'Continue searching list
250 WEND
260 GOTO 170
1000 '
1010 'Make an array of random numbers
1020 '
1030 FOR I = 1 TO SIZE
1040    A(I) = INT(RND*100) + 1
1050 NEXT I
1060 RETURN
1070 '
1080 'Print an array of numbers
1090 '
1100 FOR I = 1 TO SIZE
1110    PRINT USING " ###";A(I);
1120    IF I MOD 15 = 0 THEN PRINT
1130 NEXT I
1140 PRINT
1150 RETURN
```

```
1160 '
1170 'Linear search for a number N starting at position I
1180 'Index will be zero if N is not found
1190 '
1200 WHILE I < SIZE AND A(I) <> N
1210    I = I + 1
1220 WEND
1230 IF A(I) = N THEN INDEX = I ELSE INDEX = 0
1240 RETURN
```

Chapter 13

1.
```
100 DEFINT A-Z
110 ON ERROR GOTO 260
120 INPUT "Enter name: ",NM$
130 INPUT "Enter birth date in the form MM/DD/YY: ",BD$
140 FOR I = 1 TO LEN(BD$)
150    IF INSTR("0123456789/",MID$(BD$,I,1)) = 0 THEN ERROR 255
160 NEXT I
170 INPUT "Enter phone number: ",PN$
180 FOR I = 1 TO LEN(PN$)
190    IF INSTR("0123456789-",MID$(PN$,I,1)) = 0 THEN ERROR 254
200 NEXT I
210 PRINT
220 PRINT NM$ : PRINT BD$ : PRINT PN$
230 PRINT
240 GOTO 120
250
260 IF ERR < 254 THEN ON ERROR GOTO 0
270 IF ERR = 254 THEN 300
280    PRINT "Please re-enter birth date."
290 RESUME 130
300    PRINT "Please re-enter phone number."
310 RESUME 170
```

2.
```
10 ON ERROR GOTO 100
20 COUNT = 0
30 READ NM$
40    PRINT NM$
50    COUNT = COUNT + 1
60 GOTO 30
70 PRINT "Printed";COUNT;"names."
80 END
90 '
```

```
100 IF ERR = 4 AND ERL = 30 THEN RESUME 70
110 ON ERROR GOTO 0
120 '
130 DATA "RITA FRYBURGER","SUZAN BLOND","JOE SIMPLE"
140 DATA "EGBERT ZZT","VLADIMIR PUF"
```

Chapter 14

1.

```
10 OPEN "O",#1,"COPY.DAT"
20 PRINT:LINE INPUT "Enter name or <RETURN>: ",NM$
30 IF NM$="" THEN 90
40    LINE INPUT "Address line 1: ",ADDR1$
50    LINE INPUT "Address line 2: ",ADDR2$
60    INPUT "Zip code: ",ZIP$
70    WRITE #1,NM$,ADDR1$,ADDR2$,ZIP$
80    GOTO 20
90 CLOSE #1
```

2.

```
100 COL = 15
110 OPEN "I",#1,"NAMEADDR.SEQ"
120 INPUT "Enter zip code to print: ",UZIP$
130 WHILE NOT EOF(1)
140    INPUT #1,NM$,ADDR1$,ADDR2$,ZIP$
150    IF ZIP$ <> UZIP$ THEN 200
160       PRINT TAB(COL);NM$
170       PRINT TAB(COL);ADDR1$
180       PRINT TAB(COL);ADDR2$;"   ";ZIP$
190       PRINT : PRINT
200 WEND
210 CLOSE
220 END
```

Chapter 15

1.

```
100 OPEN "R",#1,"NAMEADDR.RND",65
110 FIELD #1,2 AS NUMNMS$
120 FIELD #1,20 AS F.NM$,20 AS F.ADDR1$,20 AS F.ADDR2$,5 AS F.ZIP$
130 GET #1,1
140 NUMNMS = CVI(NUMNMS$)
150 PRINT:LINE INPUT "Enter name or <RETURN>: ",NM$
```

```
160 IF NM$="" THEN 270
170    NUMNMS = NUMNMS + 1
180    LINE INPUT "Address line 1: ",ADDR1$
190    LINE INPUT "Address line 2: ",ADDR2$
200    INPUT "Zip code: ",ZIP$
210    LSET F.NM$=NM$
220    LSET F.ADDR1$ = ADDR1$
230    LSET F.ADDR2$ = ADDR2$
240    LSET F.ZIP$ = ZIP$
250    PUT #1,NUMNMS + 1
260    GOTO 150
270 LSET NUMNMS$ = MKI$(NUMNMS)
280 PUT #1,1
290 CLOSE
300 END
```

2.
```
100 COL = 15
110 OPEN "R",#1,"NAMEADDR.RND",65
120 FIELD #1,2 AS NUMNMS$
130 FIELD #1,20 AS NM$,20 AS ADDR1$,20 AS ADDR2$,5 AS ZIP$
140 INPUT "Enter zip code to print: ",UZIP$
150 GET #1,1
160 NUMNMS = CVI(NUMNMS$)
170 FOR I = 1 TO NUMNMS
180    GET #1,I + 1
190    IF ZIP$ <> UZIP$ THEN 240
200       PRINT TAB(COL);NM$
210       PRINT TAB(COL);ADDR1$
220       PRINT TAB(COL);ADDR2$;"   ";ZIP$
230       PRINT : PRINT
240 NEXT I
250 CLOSE
260 END
```

3.
```
100 OPEN "R",#1,"NAMEADDR.RND",65
110 FIELD #1,2 AS NUMNMS$
120 FIELD #1,20 AS F.NM$,20 AS F.ADDR1$,20 AS F.ADDR2$,5 AS F.ZIP$
130 GET #1,1
140 NUMNMS = CVI(NUMNMS$)
150 PRINT
160 PRINT "Choose one of the following:"
170 PRINT "   1 ... Enter names and addresses"
180 PRINT "   2 ... Edit a record"
190 PRINT "   3 ... End/Close files"
200 PRINT
210 INPUT "Enter your selection: ",SEL
220 IF SEL >= 1 AND SEL <= 3 THEN 250
230    PRINT "Invalid selection.  Enter a number from 1 to 3."
240    GOTO 200
250 ON SEL GOSUB 280,470,420
```

```
260 GOTO 150
270 '
280 PRINT:LINE INPUT "Enter name or <RETURN>: ",NM$
290 IF NM$="" THEN 400
300    NUMNMS = NUMNMS + 1
310    LINE INPUT "Address line 1: ",ADDR1$
320    LINE INPUT "Address line 2: ",ADDR2$
330    INPUT "Zip code: ",ZIP$
340    LSET F.NM$=NM$
350    LSET F.ADDR1$ = ADDR1$
360    LSET F.ADDR2$ = ADDR2$
370    LSET F.ZIP$ = ZIP$
380    PUT #1,NUMNMS + 1
390    GOTO 280
400 RETURN
410 '
420 LSET NUMNMS$ = MKI$(NUMNMS)
430 PUT #1,1
440 CLOSE
450 END
460 '
470 PRINT "There are";NUMNMS+1;"records on file."
480 INPUT "Enter record number to edit: ",RECNUM
490 IF RECNUM >= 2 AND RECNUM <= NUMNMS + 1 THEN 520
500    PRINT "Please enter a record number between 2 and";NUMNMS
510    GOTO 470
520 GET 1,RECNUM
530 PRINT "Enter new data or <RETURN> for no change:"
540 PRINT "Name:";TAB(16);F.NM$;TAB(40); : INPUT NM$
550 IF NM$ <> "" THEN LSET F.NM$ = NM$
560 PRINT "Address line 1:";TAB(16);F.ADDR1$;TAB(40); : INPUT ADDR1$
570 IF ADDR1$ <> "" THEN LSET F.ADDR1$ = ADDR1$
580 PRINT "Address line 2:";TAB(16);F.ADDR2$;TAB(40); : INPUT ADDR2$
590 IF ADDR2$ <> "" THEN LSET F.ADDR2$ = ADDR2$
600 PRINT "Zip code:";TAB(16);F.ZIP$;TAB(40): : INPUT ZIP$
610 IF ZIP$ <> "" THEN LSET F.ZIP$ = ZIP$
620 PUT #1,RECNUM
630 RETURN
```

4.
```
1015 ON ERROR GOTO 3000
3000 PRINT "MBASIC error code";ERR;"in line";ERL
3010 IF ERL >= 1180 THEN GOTO 2010      'Close files properly
3020 CLOSE                   'Header record O.K.
3030 END
```

5. If the record length is less than the buffer length, more than one record can fit into the buffer, and accesses to two adjacent records will not cause a disk access.

Chapter 16

1. *a.* 145
   b. 204
   c. 9
   d. 223

2. *a.* &H91 &O221
   b. &HCC &O314
   c. &H09 &O011
   d. &HDF &O337

3. *a.*

X	Y	NOT (X AND Y)
1	1	0
1	0	1
0	1	1
0	0	1

   b.

X	Y	NOT(X) OR NOT(Y)
1	1	0
1	0	1
0	1	1
0	0	1

4.
```
10 DEFINT A-Z
20 INPUT "Enter a binary number from 0 to 11111111: ",B$
30 D = 0
40 FOR I = 1 TO LEN(B$)
50    D = 2*D              'Shift bits left one place
60    IF MID$(B$,I,1) = "1" THEN D = D + 1
70 NEXT I
80 PRINT B$;" binary =";D;"decimal."
```

5.
```
10 DEFINT A-Z
20 PRINT "Size in 'K'    Size in bytes"
30 PRINT "-----------    -------------"
40 FMT$ ="   ##              #####"
50 FOR I = 4 TO 64 STEP 4
60    PRINT USING FMT$;I;I*2^10
70 NEXT I
80 END
```

6. This region is where MBASIC stores the error messages.

7. If the starting address is not a multiple of 16, this puts spaces into the first line so that it lines up with the other lines in the dump.

Chapter 17

1. *a.*
```
10 DEF FNT(P,R,N) = P*(1 + R)^N
```

b.
```
10 DEF FNT(X) = A*X^3 + B*X^2 + C
20 INPUT "Enter coefficients A, B, and C: ",A,B,C
30 INPUT "Enter parameter X: ",X
40 PRINT "t =";FNT(X)
50 END
```

2.
```
10 DEFINT A-Z
20 DEF FNPAD$(N) = RIGHT$(STR$(10000 + N),4)
30 INPUT "Enter a number from 0 to 9999: ",A
40 PRINT FNPAD$(A)
50 END
```

3.
```
100 DEF FNSTOPPRT%=(INSTR(" Xx",INKEY$) > 1)


200 ABORT = 0
210 WHILE NOT ABORT


300     IF FNSTOPPRT% THEN GOSUB 500


400 WEND

500 PRINT : INPUT "Press 'C' to continue or 'Q' to quit: ",A$
510 PRINT
520 ABORT = (A$ = "Q")
530 RETURN
```

4.
```
DEF FNBIT(BYTE,BITNO) = ((BYTE\2^BITNO) AND 1)
```

Index of Programs

Index

Other Osborne/McGraw-Hill Publications